Teaching Modern Foreign Languages in Secondary Schools

The Open University *Flexible*
Postgraduate Certificate of Education

The readers and the companion volumes in the *flexible* PGCE series are: ⸧D

All of these subjects are part of the Open University's initial teacher education course, the *flexible* PGCE, and constitute part of an integrated course designed to develop critical understanding. The set books, reflecting a wide range of perspectives, and discussing the complex issues that surround teaching and learning in the twenty-first century, will appeal to both beginning and experienced teachers, to mentors, tutors, advisers and other teacher educators.

If you would like to receive a *flexible* PGCE prospectus please write to the Course Reservations Centre at The Call Centre, The Open University, Milton Keynes MK7 6ZS. Other information about programmes of professional development in education is available from the same address.

Teaching Modern Foreign Languages in Secondary Schools
A reader

Teaching Modern Foreign Languages in Secondary Schools: A reader introduces and explores a broad range of contemporary issues and key ideas and will provide a useful background for those teaching and training to teach this important subject.

The book is concerned with the bigger picture of modern foreign language education. Divided into sections to help structure reading, it covers:

- The politics and impact of GCSEs and coursework
- Stereotypes, prejudice and tolerance
- Language teaching and citizenship, human rights education, intercultural education
- Communicative grammar teaching
- Supporting boys to achieve in MFL
- The National Literacy Strategy and MFL learning
- Languages research and classroom practice
- Learning styles and gender

The *Teaching in Secondary Schools* series brings together collections of articles by highly experienced educators that focus on the issues surrounding the teaching of National Curriculum subjects. They are invaluable resources for those studying to become teachers, and for newly qualified teachers and more experienced practitioners, particularly those mentoring students and NQTs. The companion volume to this book is *Aspects of Teaching Secondary Modern Foreign Languages: Perspectives on practice*.

Ann Swarbrick was Senior Lecturer in Education at The Open University and had responsibilities for the Open University *flexible* PGCE Modern Foreign Languages course. She is now Language Teaching Advisor at the Centre for Information on Language Teaching and Research (CILT).

Set book for the Open University *flexible* PGCE Modern Foreign Languages courses: French, code EXF880; German, code EXD880; Spanish, code EXB880.

Teaching
Modern Foreign Languages
in Secondary Schools
A reader

Edited by Ann Swarbrick

London and New York

First published 2002
by RoutledgeFalmer
11 New Fetter Lane, London EC4P 4EE

Simultaneously published in the USA and Canada
by RoutledgeFalmer
29 West 35th Street, New York, NY 10001

RoutledgeFalmer is an imprint of the Taylor & Francis Group

© 2002 Compilation, original and editorial matter,
The Open University

Typeset in Goudy by Bookcraft Ltd, Stroud, Gloucestershire
Printed and bound in Great Britain by The Cromwell Press,
Trowbridge, Wiltshire

British Library Cataloguing in Publication Data
A catalogue record for this book is available from the British Library

Library of Congress Cataloging in Publication Data
A catalog record has been requested

ISBN 0–415–26074–4 (hbk)
ISBN 0–415–26075–2 (pbk)

Contents

Illustrations

Figures

Tables

Abbreviations

ABC	Agreement to Broaden the Curriculum
ALL	Association of Language Learning/Australian Language Levels
AQA	Assessment and Qualifications Alliance
AVCE	Advanced Vocational Certificate in Education
BECTA	British Educational Communications and Technology Agency
BTEC	Business and Technology Education Council
CACE	Central Advisory Council, England
CCAC	Qualifications Curriculum and Assessment Authority for Wales
CDA	Critical Discourse Analysis
CGLI	City and Guilds of London Institute
CILT	Centre for Information on Language Teaching and Research
CLT	Communicative Language Teaching
COAG	Council of Australian Governments
CSE	Certificate of Secondary Education
CSG	Curriculum Study Group
DENI	Department of Education Northern Ireland
DES	Department of Education and Science
DfEE	Department for Education and Employment
EFL	English as a Foreign Language
FE	Further Education
FIPLV	*Fédération Internationale des Professeurs de Langues Vivantes*
FLUSS	*Foreign Languages in the Upper Secondary School*, a report by SOEID
GCE	General Certificate of Education
GCSE	General Certificate of Secondary Education
GNVQ	General National Vocational Qualification
GOML	Graded Objectives in Modern Languages
HMI	Her Majesty's Inspectorate
ICT	Information and Communications Technology
LOTE	Languages Other Than English (Australia)
MFL	Modern Foreign Languages
NACELL	National Advisory Centre on Early Language Learning
NALA	National Association of Language Advisors
NC	National Curriculum

NCET	National Council for Educational Technology
NCVQ	National Council for Vocational Qualifications
NFER	National Foundation for Educational Research
NLS	National Literacy Strategy
NVQ	National Vocational Qualification
OCR	Oxford, Cambridge and RSA Examinations
Ofsted	Office for Standards in Education
OMLAC	Oxfordshire Modern Languages Advisory Committee
PHSE	Personal Health and Social Education
QCA	Qualifications and Curriculum Authority
RSA	Royal Society of Arts
SALT	Scottish Association of Language Teachers
SCAA	School Curriculum and Assessment Authority
SCCE	Schools Council for Curriculum and Examinations
SCRE	Scottish Council for Research in Education
SEC	Secondary Examinations Council
SI	Strategy Instruction
SOEID	Scottish Office Education and Industry Department
SSEC	Secondary Schools Examination Council
TEI	Teacher Education Institute
TTA	Teacher Training Agency
VET	Vocational Education and Training

Source

Where a chapter in this book is based on or is a reprint or revision of material previously published elsewhere, details are given below, with grateful acknowledgements to the original publishers.

Chapter 5   This is an edited version of a chapter originally published in Byram, M. and Risager, K. (1999) *Language Teachers, Politics and Cultures*, Multilingual Matters, Clevedon. The book is based on the work of two research teams in England and Denmark. The research focuses upon questionnaires and interviews with teachers in both countries.

Foreword

The nature and form of initial teacher education and training are issues that lie at the heart of the teaching profession. They are inextricably linked to the standing and identity that society attributes to teachers and are seen as being one of the main planks in the push to raise standards in schools and to improve the quality of education in them. The initial teacher education curriculum therefore requires careful definition. How can it best contribute to the development of the range of skills, knowledge and understanding that makes up the complex, multi-faceted, multi-skilled and people-centred process of teaching?

There are, of course, external, government-defined requirements for initial teacher training courses. These specify, amongst other things, the length of time a student spends in school, the subject knowledge requirements beginning teachers are expected to demonstrate or the ICT skills that are needed. These requirements, however, do not in themselves constitute the initial training curriculum. They are only one of the many, if sometimes competing, components that make up the broad spectrum of a teacher's professional knowledge that underpin initial teacher education courses.

Certainly today's teachers need to be highly skilled in literacy, numeracy and ICT, in classroom methods and management. In addition, however, they also need to be well grounded in the critical dialogue of teaching. They need to be encouraged to be creative and innovative and to appreciate that teaching is a complex and problematic activity. This is a view of teaching that is shared with partner schools within the Open University Training Schools Network. As such it has informed the planning and development of the Open University's initial teacher training programme and the *flexible* PGCE.

All of the *flexible* PGCE courses have a series of connected and complementary readers. The *Teaching in Secondary Schools* series pulls together a range of new thinking about teaching and learning in particular subjects. Key debates and differing perspectives are presented, and evidence from research and practice is explored, inviting the reader to question the accepted orthodoxy, suggesting ways of enriching the present curriculum and offering new thoughts on classroom learning. These readers are accompanied by the series *Perspectives on practice*. Here, the focus is on the application of these developments to educational/subject policy and the classroom, and on the illustration of teaching skills, knowledge and understanding in a variety of school contexts. Both series include newly commissioned work.

This series from RoutledgeFalmer, in supporting the Open University's *flexible* PGCE, also includes two key texts that explore the wider educational background. These companion publications, *Teaching, Learning and the Curriculum in Secondary Schools: A reader* and *Aspects of Teaching and Learning in Secondary Schools: Perspectives on practice*, explore a contemporary view of developments in secondary education with the aim of providing analysis and insights for those participating in initial teacher training education courses.

Hilary Bourdillon – Director ITT Strategy
Steven Hutchinson – Director ITT Secondary
The Open University
September 2001

Introduction

This book focuses on many of the varied, rewarding and sometimes challenging aspects of teaching Modern Foreign Languages (MFL). It is written for teachers of MFL at different stages of their career: pre-service, newly-qualified teachers and experienced teachers in secondary schools. The development, understanding and knowledge of teaching MFL are perennial features of every MFL teacher's life. It is a knowledge which is ever changing and which is continually refined in the light of experience in the classroom, the staff room, MFL conferences, interaction with parents and governors and the influence of education policy-makers. All MFL teachers, whether just embarking upon their teaching career or with several years of teaching experience, need to spend some time thinking about the basis of the subject and the principles which inform its pedagogy and learning. The book aims to show what is important about the subject and explores aspects of MFL learning including the nature of communication, motivation, the content of what we teach as well as the implications of that content for the moral, social, academic and linguistic development of pupils.

The book mainly consists of newly-commissioned work, since many of the areas it covers have recently been the subject of some careful re-evaluation and research. The issues debated and discussed here set MFL education in a wide context. Writers have used examples from other European countries and elsewhere to broaden the arguments and to demonstrate that, often, the preoccupations of UK MFL teachers are those of all teachers.

The aim of the book is also to encourage teachers to articulate what they do in their classrooms, to find clear rationales and to develop a strong pedagogical sense. It also attempts to increase teachers' confidence to express ideas about pupils' learning, to take risks and to be creative thinkers. These skills lie at the heart of effective teaching in that they facilitate the engagement of the pupil with a second language and they promote learning.

The book, together with its sister publication *Teaching Secondary Modern Foreign Languages: Perspectives on practice*, has a wide audience. Besides those studying to teach or in the early years of a career, it will be useful to those teachers who support student teachers in school (mentors) in answering the demanding questions they often face. In addition to introducing students to specific language teaching techniques, we need to encourage students to enquire into the merits of various teaching strategies, learning theories, curriculum resources, and the role of schools in a democratic society, so that they do not just accept what is said but they engage with the issues and look for personal solutions based on informed thought. It is important in mentor sessions for students to explore their ideas with an experienced teacher, to explore their own developing thinking. The mentor's role in this instance is to listen and respond to what students say as learners but also to be aware of the pedagogy and methodology we teach in order to be able to demonstrate ideas that are working in the classroom.

The book is structured into four parts. Part 1 begins with a chapter which sets MFL teaching in its historical context and moves on to consider the nature of MFL within the wider context of school and society. This shows that the teaching of MFL is not without its areas of controversy: these include the arguments for and against such issues as early language learning. Often the discussion of these issues has developed into a polarization of position which in turn sets up the expectation that you have to be either for or against a particular argument. In fact the subtleties of teaching and learning are far more nuanced and complex. Eric Hawkins focuses on a specific cause for concern, namely the problem of language learners opting out of MFL at the earliest opportunity. He suggests that the origins of the problem began to manifest themselves fifty years ago with the restructuring of the post-16 curriculum and later the demise of Latin. He suggests some panaceas for our new century. This section also looks at the more recent history of the subject. Barry Jones discusses the legacy of the Graded Objectives movement, the impact of the National Curriculum and the potential of the Nuffield Languages Inquiry. Politics have a profound influence upon what happens in classrooms. Focusing on the controversies around Key Stage 4 assessment and, in particular, coursework, Julie Adams picks up the theme which Hawkins began: unless we look to what the MFL curriculum has to offer pupils at all stages of their learning we are unlikely to staunch the bleeding.

This begs the question, 'What should the languages curriculum include?' In Part 2, we attempt to demonstrate the ways in which teachers can contribute to the cultural and moral development of pupils extending their vision to embrace such concepts as European and global citizenship. To this end we have included an existing chapter by Michael Byram and Karen Risager on European identity. They explore the issues of stereotypes and prejudice in the European context. Furthering the argument for the integration of a study of many aspects of culture, Hugh Starkey argues that language teaching plays a pivotal role in the education of citizens but that this assertion challenges present practice in schools. His chapter argues for the inclusion of human rights education, intercultural studies and citizenship within the MFL curriculum. This section has a strong political dimension. Chris Brumfit has long argued for an integrated language policy for the UK which requires schools to look at language study as a whole rather than compartmentalizing MFL and language as studied in the rest of the curriculum. Here he sets out his ideas for a Language Charter and attempts to set an agenda for the future development of language within the curriculum. On a different tangent Judith Hamilton considers change, its political implications and the impact this has on teachers' careers.

Part 3 includes work which offers new perspectives on perennial concerns for MFL teachers: grammar, the content of lessons, motivation. We look at grammar teaching, what 'communicative' teaching means in this context and the pedagogical points which arise from it. Ann Miller's chapter investigates the North American origins of present practice in grammar teaching and disentangles the muddle which has arisen from different interpretations of the communicative approach. She gives a clear direction for teachers' thinking about where a study of the structure of language resides. Do Coyle discusses the content of the MFL curriculum and sets out arguments for a reconceptualization of the curriculum. Her contention is that the present curriculum short-changes pupils by giving too narrow a focus on the learner as tourist or observer and by not offering enough cognitive challenge. Michael Grenfell looks at the possibilities which open up if pupils learn *how* to learn, discussing the strategies pupils use, or should be encouraged to use, in order to be competent foreign language users. Vee Harris takes up the issue of boys' underachievement, the reasons for this and possible solutions to the problem. This and the Grenfell chapter argue for much more emphasis to be placed on developing pupil autonomy in MFL. All of the chapters thus far have as their focus MFL teaching in the context of the secondary school classroom. The final two chapters of Part 3 take us in a slightly different though related direction. Beate Poole considers the National Literacy Strategy in place in primary schools in England. She assesses the impact this is having and should have on the early years of foreign language learning and teaching. Kim Brown is a teacher educator. She uses her observation notes to analyse some of the positions which student teachers commonly take during their PGCE studies. She offers a rationale for some commonly-seen practice in the languages classroom.

Any discussion of MFL education would be incomplete without considering the place research plays in the development of teaching practice. In Part 4 we focus on four distinct research studies, two of which echo the themes of Part 3, specifically learner motivation and preference. Joanna McPake uses the Foreign Languages in Upper Secondary research project in Scotland as the focus of her discussion while Jeff Lee takes a new look at his and his colleagues' research into the motivation of Year 9 pupils. Both signal the importance of listening to what pupils say about their learning. Amanda Barton continues the theme. In any MFL classroom, pupils will make progress and learn at different rates and in different ways. Her study looks at the effect gender has on learning and at the variety of learning styles employed by boys and girls. A consideration of the ways in which people learn is continued by Salvador Estabanez in his comparative study of Spanish and English readers.

Taken together, all of these separate chapters cannot claim to add up to a complete picture of teaching MFL. They do, however, give some insights into the complexity and challenge of the task. But words and rational arguments about MFL education are pointless unless they affect what goes on in the classroom. My aim is to provide a book which will be a source of inspiration to readers and so also inspire all teachers to encourage innovation and clear thinking in MFL classrooms today.

Ann Swarbrick
December 2001

Part 1

Controversies and disagreements

1 Positioning MFL teaching in schools

Issues and debates

Ann Swarbrick

Introduction

Consider for a moment these three students who, in the past, have completed their PGCE in MFL with the Open University:

- Marc was brought up in Mauritius. His first language was French. When he was ten, his family moved to Britain and he went to school in South London. Despite the fact that his home language was French, his bilingualism was largely ignored at secondary level, though he took GCE French early. He studied Spanish and Mathematics at University during the 1970s and subsequently became a social worker.
- After graduating in French and Spanish from university in the north-east of England where she had been brought up, Jane became a marketing manager. She gave this up to have a family and studied for a part-time MA in child psychology during her eight years at home. She took the PGCE course after her three children had started school, preferring to teach rather than to return to marketing.
- Birgit is a German national married to a major in the British armed forces. They had been posted in various places both in the UK and overseas and during much of this time she had been an undergraduate with the Open University and had become a qualified interpreter. Since her husband was approaching retirement and a more settled life, they bought a house in the south-west of England. They decided the time had come for Birgit to concentrate on her own career. Teaching was something she had always wanted to do.

Each of these students is a well-educated adult, already having a first degree with a high level of proficiency in one or two foreign languages, and in one case a further degree. Throughout their PGCE, they developed their language skills further and demonstrated how they updated their subject specialism. They all had considerable skills and experience of work acquired before they decided to enter teaching. They all had the same goal in following the PGCE course – to become excellent MFL teachers. Yet it is obvious that they are individuals who bring with them their distinct personality, particular skills, interests and values. They initially entered teacher education with views, based on their own experiences, about the nature of MFL, about teaching methods or about the purpose of the MFL curriculum. These earlier experiences acted as a powerful filter, an interpretative framework, through which all the ideas, discussions and activities of their teacher education course passed. As such, what each student brought to their teacher education course was an important dimension to learning to teach.

Research into how people learn to teach has shown the extent and significance of the ideas that students bring with them into teaching, and how these ideas are one of the most important determinants of what they will take from their education course (Grossman 1990, Guillame and Rudney 1993, Zeichner 1993). Research has also shown that these values and beliefs are tenaciously maintained and that many beginning teachers start their career relatively unchanged by their teacher education course. The purpose of this chapter is initially to encourage beginning teachers, new entrants into the profession and experienced teachers to consider what their own beliefs and values are with regard to teaching MFL, and to present the main arguments in the debates about the nature and purpose of MFL in order to challenge the myths and test their beliefs and assumptions. Underpinning this chapter is the acknowledgement that learning to teach MFL also requires being introduced into a particular subject sub-culture and community. It is debate and intervention in teaching MFL which define that community and which are central to the effectiveness of MFL teaching. Participation in the debates and determination of these issues are therefore important for all MFL teachers whatever their stage of development. Discussion and debate with colleagues not only make learning more effective but make professional life more interesting and enable teachers to take more control of what happens in school. Teaching can be an isolating experience – ironic given the number of interactions any teacher has with pupils every day – but teacher/pupil contact is not enough for professional educators; discussion with adults engaged in the same task is essential to maintain interest and excitement. Working closely with colleagues can be a vital stimulus for reflection on how to develop a particular teaching style, or techniques which reflect an individual's own values as a teacher.

The nature of MFL

In arriving at an understanding of the main issues and debates in teaching MFL, a valuable starting point is to consider, briefly in this instance, how the purpose and nature of MFL have changed over the post-war period. Since the introduction of state education in 1870, with the setting up of elementary schools in England and Wales wherever needed, there has been some state support for providing a curriculum which included MFL. For example, the 1871 Elementary Code aimed to widen the curriculum by increasing the list of 'specific' subjects to be included. Languages was one of the subjects to be added to the list, along with, for example, political economy and the natural sciences. These had to be taught according to a graduated scheme of which the Inspector can report that it is well adapted to the capacity of the children and is sufficiently distinct from the ordinary reading-book lesson to justify its description as a specific subject of instruction.

(Elementary Code 1871)

'Specifics' were limited to Standards IV, V and VI and no more than two could be taught at any one time.

Despite this provision for universal language teaching, the reality is that the subject largely remained the preserve of the public and grammar schools. But in the 1960s and 1970s the widespread establishment of comprehensive schools meant for the first time that foreign language study was open to virtually all pupils, at least in the early secondary years.

> This broadening of the 'market' for foreign languages created pressure for change in teaching methods and curricula, to suit the needs of non-traditional groups of learners. Similarly, more active and experiential modes of learning (such as the use of group work) were coming into favour across the curriculum as a whole. These general educational themes again created new expectations and pressures for those concerned more specifically with the teaching and learning of foreign languages.
>
> (Mitchell 1994)

Changes in the nature and purpose of MFL teaching are well illustrated through an analysis of teaching materials. Here are three extracts taken from textbooks for French written at different times. Each illustrates a particular approach to language teaching and is based on an implicit view of the nature of MFL:

1   illustrates the grammar-translation approach (published 1961);
2   illustrates the audio-visual approach (published 1973);
3   illustrates the communicative approach to language teaching (published 1990).

Extract 1

The first extract (p. 6) is from a textbook designed for grammar-school pupils in their third year of learning French.

Each chapter of the book follows a similar pattern: a text followed by listed vocabulary and expressions the reader will encounter in the text, and a series of substitution and drilling exercises. The subject matter of the text is not otherwise exploited. All of the activity around the text dissects the grammatical structures which appear within it. The text itself is written for learners of French; it is not written for a French-speaking audience. The extract here is designed for a lesson in which grammar rules are taught deductively and used for textual analysis. There are plainly right and wrong answers, accuracy is very important and there is a strong emphasis on the written word. In some ways it becomes clear that much of

the language learned from this lesson would be unusable in the world outside the classroom. Practical use of the language is considered as marginally important; the language the learner might use in an encounter with a French speaker is presented in a series of questions in the final section. These, however, have no logic and ask for information which the learner already knows, such as the name and age of the person sitting next to them. The learner is expected to work out different forms and the use of different structures him/herself with reference to the teacher and to the extensive grammar notes at the back of the book. There the rules of grammar are explained in English using grammatical terminology. In many ways this lesson is very challenging for the learner and requires a high degree of autonomy in order to succeed.

Extract 2

The second extract (p. 7) was used widely in the early years of comprehensive schooling. The defining features of this audio-visual course were the reel-to-reel tape and film strips which accompanied it. Again, each lesson follows the same pattern, beginning with a text (this time accompanied by an audio recording) followed by drilling and practice. Pupils are exposed to stock phrases which they repeat until they know them by heart. Questions and answers are repeated in the same way. The aim is accuracy. Selected language structures drive this curriculum; control of grammar is the central element of language learning. As can be seen here, the structures learned are then applied in real-life contexts. Oral/aural work is emphasized. Here the visuals are considered to be an important part of the learning process as is the focus on people, in this case fictional and real. So here it is clear that languages are being learned with the intention of use, certainly more so than in Extract 1.

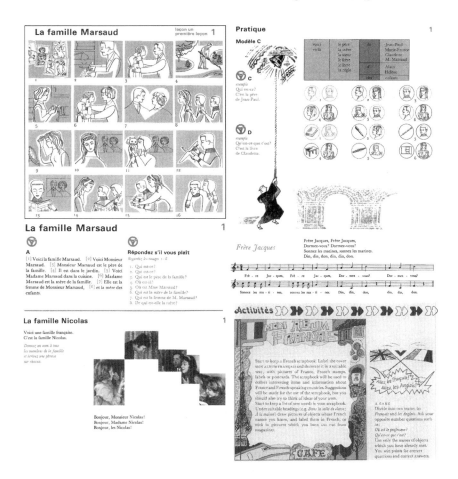

Extract 3

The last extract (p. 8) illustrates some of the guiding principles of the communicative approach. Here the target language is used throughout. Lesson objectives are set for pupils and there are extensive grammar notes with accompanying examples. The book is pupil-centred, often addressing the reader personally; for example, the introduction states, 'you will find a grammar and reference section, which shows you how the French language works and how every part of a sentence gives you important clues about its meaning.' Authentic or pseudo-authentic target language texts are used in place of artificially, structurally controlled exercises. The use of the target language is meaning-oriented; that is, language is not just used to provide practice of a structure, with such activities as role-play becoming important. Pupils are set tasks which allow them to respond personally, for instance making choices and describing photographs for themselves.

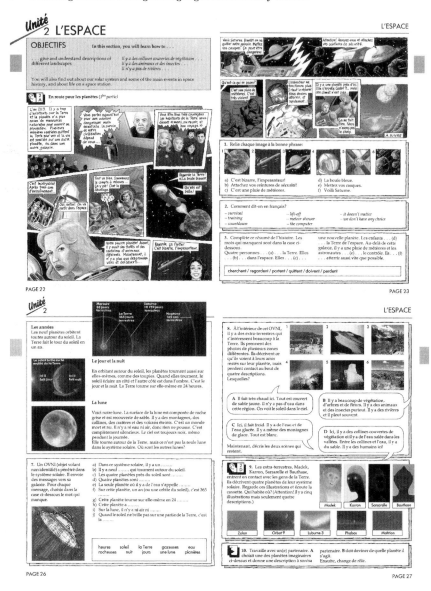

From the different focuses of MFL teaching and learning illustrated in these three extracts, it becomes clear that in teaching MFL the teacher has to bear in mind:

- the audience, the attainment range, age and capabilities of the pupils;
- the purposes of teaching MFL. Is it the acquisition of the written language which will enable the high-attaining pupil to study MFL as any other

'academic' subject and to analyse an accepted canon of literature, or is the main purpose to emphasize language as communication?

- the implicit theory of language learning. Is learning a language best done through the acquisition of its structures through drilling and rote-learning? Or is it located within social interactions requiring verbal communication? Or is a mixture of both required?

As we have seen from these extracts, the function, methodology, pedagogy and purpose of MFL within the state education system have changed significantly over the past fifty years. Whilst there has long been state provision for teaching languages in schools, it is only relatively recently that there has been any statutory definition of what should be taught and to whom. In 1992 the National Curriculum for MFL was introduced, which laid down for the first time what was to be taught. Undoubtedly this had a huge impact on the teaching and learning of MFL.

The impact of the National Curriculum

Though the MFL National Curriculum (NC) did not impose a huge change of direction for many teachers, generally speaking the NC has a relatively turbulent history in England, Wales and Northern Ireland. Though it was a key plank of educational policy in other countries, teachers here had autonomy in their class-rooms until the late eighties. In 1988 a new Education Act entered the statute books and NC working parties were set up to make recommendations in the form of a report (for MFL The Harris Report) to the then Secretary of State for Education and Science, John MacGregor. This group put forward a clear statement about the contribution MFL makes to the curriculum in schools. The National Curriculum Council (NCC) then converted these reports into Consultation Reports which were subsequently converted into Draft Orders and later into legislation. The resultant document, now in its third edition, outlines the expectations of teachers and learners in MFL. It is at one and the same time a programme of study and an assessment tool.

As a tool to make the learning entitlement of children coherent, the NC has had a profound effect on the teaching and learning of MFL. Though it did not set out either methodology or issues of pedagogy, it did give emphasis to the following:

- communicating in the target language;
- development of language skills;
- development of language learning skills and knowledge of language;
- cultural awareness.

In order to ensure coverage of all aspects of the curriculum, teachers in state schools have needed to change their practice in order to accommodate it. This is how one teacher described the impact it had on her teaching as she describes her evolution as a languages teacher:

Over the years my style has developed and changed from when I started to teach. It was very much more structured at the beginning around presenting the new language in terms of a text, exploiting the text, examining the structures and moving on. As regards the actual focus of my teaching it's much more child-centred now. I expect much more of the input of the lesson to come from them. I see myself much more now as the person who gets them to speak German rather than the person who speaks German at them and gets them to understand me. I think the biggest impact that the National Curriculum has had on my teaching is that I am much more aware of individual students. That's made a big difference to my lesson planning and the sort of activities I get them to do.

(Elaine Taylor, Crownhills Community College)

In the name of accountability and clarity, schools have absorbed many changes over the last decade. Many applaud the introduction of the NC. However, given that the year 2000 saw the introduction of the third revised curriculum, small wonder that many teachers feel bruised and exhausted by the demands put upon them. Add to this an unrelenting Ofsted inspection programme and the preoccupations of MFL teachers in the UK begin to become clear.

Having considered some of the background context for MFL practice in schools, let us now turn to current debates.

Controversies and disagreements

There have been many issues of debate over the past twenty years in MFL, our major preoccupations being:

- the place of grammar;
- whether form comes before function or vice versa;
- whether French should lose its dominance as a taught language;
- whether languages should be part of the primary curriculum;
- the place of error correction – assimilating new attitudes and approaches to assessment;
- the use of the target language as the teaching medium;
- whether language can be taught divorced from the culture of the people who speak it;
- the languages which should be taught in schools;
- whether languages should be part of the compulsory curriculum;
- whether and why boys underachieve in languages;
- whether skills development is more important than content;
- the importance of developing pupil autonomy in languages;
- whether ICT has a place in the MFL curriculum and how it can enhance learning.

All of these issues are discussed within this volume. Some, however, have entered the public debate and have been unhelpfully polarized.

This table illustrates just a few of the polarities arising from these issues:

This country needs linguists	English is a global language – learning foreign languages is not a priority
Languages are a vital part of the compulsory curriculum	Languages are among the most unpopular subjects and should be optional
Languages are needed to understand other cultures	Understanding culture is not dependent on knowing the associated languages
The earlier you start languages the better	Early start makes no difference to proficiency
Accuracy is more important than communication	Knowing rules of grammar does not mean you can communicate
ICT will liberate the language learner and transform the nature of the subject	ICT has little to offer MFL teachers and learners

The polarization suggests a simplicity which hides the complexity of the arguments. Let us take these particular issues and discuss some of the main areas of debate arising from them.

Why teach foreign languages in school?

For many years the study of a modern foreign language in the UK has been considered dispensable, the assumption being that the rest of the world speaks English and consequently the British have no need to learn other languages. Such complacency is misplaced. In the preliminary report for the Nuffield Languages Inquiry David Graddol explores the linguistic challenges facing teachers and policy-makers in the twenty-first century. His crystal ball-gazing makes interesting, if not alarming, reading given this commonly-held view of the hegemony of English. He surmises, for instance, that, as 'new Englishes' develop, the native speaker of English will become an irrelevance because:

- global communication will not be based on a single language;
- a greater proportion of the population will need to speak several languages at a high level of proficiency;
- English will be used mainly as a language of wider communication between non-native speakers so that English speakers from the antipodes, North America and Britain will become what he calls 'minority stake holders';
- new Englishes will reflect the mother tongue of the speaker, e.g. Indian or Nigerian English;
- in fifty years time, Arabic, Spanish and Hindi/Urdu will each have roughly the same number of native speakers as English;

- the internet is no longer a monoglot medium. The information available in Spanish, German and Japanese is increasing rapidly and non-English speakers account for an increasing proportion of internet users.

(Graddol 2000)

Indeed the final report of the Inquiry is unequivocal on the position of 'the native speaker' as the only model of competence.

> Native speakers of English may feel that the language belongs to them, but it will be those who speak English as a second or foreign language who will determine its world future … Mobility of employment is in danger of becoming the preserve of people from other countries.
>
> (Nuffield Languages Inquiry 2000)

In surveys of pupils' preferences, MFL is not a popular school subject. One only needs to read the examination statistics and consider the number of pupils who opt out of languages at the first opportunity as they reach the end of compulsory schooling to understand the enormity of the problem. This haemorrhage will, without doubt, affect teacher supply in years to come – no post-16 pupils, so no graduates, so no new teachers. This state of affairs has made the MFL teacher's task onerous in persuading both pupils and headteachers that MFL should have a place in the curriculum. So why is it important for pupils to learn foreign languages?

Vocational reasons

Pupils will need languages for future professional work. This may be the case for a small minority but many languages teachers bear witness to the fact that this utilitarian argument does not draw young people. They cannot visualize themselves as working adults and, realistically, it is unlikely that they will need languages at work unless they specialize at HE level or unless the world of business in this country changes its view of the lack of importance of any language other than English. Even now, since proficiency at native-speaker level is available and preferred by many businesses, the languages graduate is already in a highly competitive market.

Educational reasons

These are the most compelling arguments, in my view, for retaining MFL in the curriculum. They revolve around the foreign language as part of education in its broadest sense and as part of an 'apprenticeship of learning how to learn' (Hawkins 1981). Learning another language can help develop greater confidence and aptitude in the pupils' first language. Foreign languages also can play a crucial part in educating pupils to become citizens of the world.

> Some of the most moving and relevant examples of language learning in practice have been the attempts of the very young and the striving of those with

learning difficulties to communicate in foreign tongues. Through it they have learned about themselves, about the world, about their own language.

(King 1999: 24)

Unless learners see the point in language learning because language study is relevant in its own right and/or because it provides access to knowledge and understanding of value to the learner, then they will continue to opt out of the subject at the earliest opportunity. This may mean teachers creating more opportunities for pupils to study issues in the foreign language which match more closely their intellectual maturity and which stimulate the curiosity of learners.

Moral reasons

Much of the development which has happened as a result of new thinking about the curriculum over the past decade has indeed begun to open up learners' minds to an awareness that other cultures exist and that their attitude to them in some way defines the type of person they are. An awareness of culture will include studying the way of life in other countries, studying its literature and studying those psychological aspects of language and behaviour which define what is and is not acceptable within a culture. In this sense pupils need to confront other cultures if they are to be broadly educated and to understand the arrogance of the monolingual position. The approach teachers take to this issue, the emphasis they place on it, will in some respects define their values and attitudes as citizens of a multicultural, multilingual society. Indeed, if they place emphasis on language only as skill development rather than language as a social and cultural tool for communication, then much that makes learning a language compelling and interesting will be missed:

> Each and every day the foreign languages classroom sets challenges for its learners, requiring them to step outside of Hawkins's 'monolingual prison' and realise that the first language offers only one very narrow window in their perception of the world.
>
> (Holmes 2000)

This view may not be the view of many of the people pupils meet outside the school environment but the role of the MFL teacher is, in part, to confront controversial issues. As Hawkins points out, 'The wise teacher will work with and through the parents the child loves, but the home values are not sacrosanct; the curriculum must respect, but also sometimes challenge, the parochial environment' (Hawkins 1981: 30).

Linguistic reasons

Evidence is coming to light that the explicit teaching of language at word, sentence and text level and the teaching of grammatical terminology within the primary phase help children to be more aware of the structure of language and of language as a communicative code. This can in turn help in developing a knowledge of another language. For instance, Beate Poole in this volume discusses her research on the impact of the National Literacy Strategy on MFL learning. The interviews she conducted with teachers suggest that there is now greater potential for real synergy between the teaching of English and foreign languages. Teachers reported in pupils an increased awareness of language patterns and rules and increased ability to identify regularities and irregularities (Poole, this volume: ch. 13). Instruction in a foreign language can have a direct effect on the development of cognitive processes. The linguistic argument, then, for foreign language learning is strong.

We begin to see here a rationale for teaching languages in schools. Through a study of languages, young people can learn about themselves, about the world, about the power of language as a communication tool, about their own language. They can learn social skills and gain self-confidence through understanding that they are cracking a code which has the potential to open up a new world to them, with horizons far beyond their own village, town or city. They can develop an awareness that others have different perceptions, values, priorities and attitudes. If we consider all of this, then the role of the language teacher stretches far beyond the teaching of lexis or grammar.

Can languages be taught with no reference to culture?

Cultural learning and cultural awareness need to complement the focus on language. Snow and Byram have usefully defined the skills and knowledge appertaining to cultural awareness in terms of four '*savoirs*':

Savoir être
An ability to give up ethnocentric attitudes and ways of seeing other cultures as if they were abnormal deviations from the norms of one's own. This involves changes in attitude and change in perspective, putting oneself in someone else's shoes, however temporarily.

Savoirs
Acquiring knowledge about some aspects of another culture, in particular those values and beliefs which people share and which give them a sense of belonging to a social group, for example a national identity.

Savoir apprendre
An ability to observe, collect data and analyse how people of another culture behave, what values and beliefs they share, how they experience and perceive their world.

Savoir faire
The ability to interact with people of another culture in real time, by drawing upon and integrating the other three *savoirs*.

(Snow and Byram 1997: 10)

Learning about the culture under this definition goes far beyond giving information about lifestyle and festivals, etc. It is about understanding facts about a country but also with consideration of the perspectives taken and attitudes held by different peoples. If teachers accept this wide definition, then language learning and teaching become much richer than considering language as a means of survival on holiday or in commercial transactions. It also gives broader scope for projects which can be undertaken in school visits abroad, such as data collection, interviewing, devising questionnaires, developing observational skills and note-taking. Byram, Morgan *et al.* (1994) consider this in depth with theoretical discussions about the nature of culture-learning, as well as case studies describing ethnography and other approaches to culture and language-learning in the classroom and abroad.

Language competence plainly has a skill component but it goes far beyond that.

> If it were mainly this then teaching languages would be largely a matter of instruction or training. This view of language learning underlies the misguided claim that it is possible simply to teach 'Languages for Special Purposes' or 'Languages for Business', as if there were some functional dimension of language which could be acquired without reference to the culture in which it has its place. All human behaviour has its place within a culture – we cannot learn any forms of behaviour (business etiquette for instance) as if it could be detached from this culture.
>
> (Williams 2000: 12)

Teachers of MFL, then, need to consider the various dimensions of language in order to persuade pupils of their intrinsic value. Pupils themselves need to see the place languages have in their curriculum. Unless we are able to encourage curiosity about other national cultures they will continue to see little point in language learning.

Should languages be taught within the primary curriculum?

In recent years, the issue of primary languages has come to the fore. This has been largely due to a grass-roots movement by parents and teachers in mainly middle-class areas of the country. During the 1990s, French clubs began to appear, particularly in the south-east of England where parents decided that they wanted their primary-aged children to learn a foreign language. These parents accept that learning a language is a 'good thing' even though they do not necessarily speak other languages themselves. Since the primary NC had just been introduced, it was clear that there was no room for additional subjects within the curriculum and, added to this, there was and still is a lack of expertise in primary staff rooms. The problem is less acute where middle schools exist but the issues described below still apply. Thus, with parental pressure and competition between schools mounting, many primary schools introduced after-school language clubs – usually French. The frequency of these clubs increased with the introduction of such commercial ventures as *Le Club Français* which developed a network of teachers and published materials. This piecemeal approach to the introduction of languages at primary level began to cause concerns for such bodies as The National Association of Languages Advisors, who saw many problems arising because of a lack of a coherent approach and strategy. Some LEAs began to provide training and opportunities for schools to introduce languages in a systematic way (Kent and Surrey being just two of many), and the Centre for Information on Language Teaching and Research with the DfEE set up an early language learning initiative to promote and develop the provision and quality of MFL in the primary sector. This included the formation of a National Advisory Centre on Early Language Learning (NACELL) linking these and many other schemes and developing a bank of materials.

The debate about when pupils should begin to have entitlement to MFL education was fuelled further when Tony Blair, the Prime Minister, stated, 'Everyone knows that with languages, the earlier you start the easier they are' (Romanes Lecture, Oxford, December 1999). This indeed reflected the thinking of many of those parents and schools in favour of an early start to language learning but it raises many questions:

- Who will teach languages in primary schools?
- What are the implications for staffing and recruitment?
- What will be the connection between the primary and secondary languages curriculums?
- Who will make the connection?
- Which languages should be taught in primary school?
- Will there be a National Curriculum for primary languages?
- Will there be a need for much more refined and systematic cross-phase liaison?
- What will happen to the rest of the primary curriculum if another subject is added?
- Would language awareness linked to literacy be a better way forward than learning a specific language for a limited amount of time?

All these are issues currently being debated by the MFL teaching community.

One of the problems is that the Prime Minister's 'soundbite', whilst it is resonant of popular myths about languages acquisition, is not supported by definitive research findings. There are as many research studies to argue against starting language learning early (for example, Burstall 1974 and Poole 1991) as there are for it (Larsen-Freeman and Long 1991, Snow and Hoefnagle-Höhle 1978). The argument is not clear-cut. In some research studies, it is shown that primary learners show advantage in some competences such as listening comprehension and pronunciation, but in others, older learners out-perform younger learners in the rate of language acquisition because they have a better knowledge of language patterns, are better at more cognitively-demanding tasks and have better-developed learning strategies and study skills. There are other variables which need to be taken into account as outlined by Sharpe and Driscoll (2000: 79):

The majority of research evidence concerning the comparative rate of acquisition between younger and older learners relates to outcomes as measured by tests, which arguably favour older learners, either because the tests are cognitively too demanding for younger age groups or because the testing techniques are unfamiliar to younger pupils.

The point is not that languages should or should not be taught in primary schools but that a national strategy is essential if it is to succeed, and any such strategy needs to be funded and based on sound research evidence. The arguments for and against and the reasons behind those arguments need to be understood and discussed by teachers and policy-makers before decisions about pupils' futures are made.

The decline of declension

Teachers' attitude to grammar can reflect in some ways their values about languages education and what they think about pupil learning. Peter Morris from Gordano School, Portishead, for instance, sees grammar as a liberating force:

> Well, grammar is an interesting question. It was extremely unfashionable for a while but I think if you teach grammar well, it is a liberator. It allows the students to express ideas beyond set phrases. The challenge really is to reduce it to bite sized chunks so that they can absorb, then build on that.

For him grammar is an issue of equality. He believes that all children have a right to be taught the building blocks of language and that, for low-attaining pupils, a diet of vocabulary-learning and matching pictures to nouns is an insult and an inhibitor to progress.

The question 'Does grammar matter?' may seem odd for anyone educated through grammar-translation – of course it matters. In the grammar-translation method, the way to learn languages was to study grammar and memorize rules and vocabulary through texts.

> Teaching consisted primarily of organising grammar for analysis and application. Reading and writing predominated, and oral skills were seen as very much secondary aims ... Grammar rules were taught deductively and used for textual analysis and comparisons. The accuracy of the resulting translations into and from English were a mark of proficiency and competence in mastering a language ... Accuracy was all.
>
> (Grenfell 1999: 11)

Though many MFL teachers who were trained to teach in the 1960s and 1970s were themselves taught by this method, the vast majority of them have been profoundly influenced by Communicative Language Teaching (CLT) which turned the grammar-translation method on its head. The origins of CLT have their roots in research into how learners learn languages. This approach, a broad school of ideas which took a hold in this country with comprehensivization when languages became a subject offered to most pupils rather than to an elite (see Mitchell 1994, Grenfell (ibid.) and Grenfell (this volume) for a full introduction to the communicative approach), manifests itself in classroom activities which maximize opportunities for learners to use the target language for meaningful purposes, with their attention on the messages they are creating and the task they are completing, rather than on *correctness* of language *form* and language *structure*. Communicating a message effectively became more important than concentrating on the absolute accuracy of the utterance. But certain aspects of grammatical structure are essential if communication is to be effective. There will, for instance, be ineffective communication if someone, unable to construct a past tense, tells another that a meeting is at 3.00 when in fact the meeting was at 3.00 yesterday. So correction of grammatical mistakes plainly does matter but CLT developed a more sophisticated approach to correction. And this is, in my view, where confusion began to arise in teachers' minds. In a bid to get pupils communicating in a foreign language, correction of mistakes in the form of explicitly pointing them out and teaching correct forms, which would inhibit pupils' confidence and flow, took second place and in some classrooms nearly disappeared.

The grammatical mistakes pupils make matter in terms of what they can tell the teacher about the pupils' linguistic development. The reason why is discussed by Keith Morrow:

> Mistakes may matter for two reasons. First, and perhaps surprisingly, they may be direct evidence for what the student knows about the language system. The student of English who says, 'Last night I taked my girlfriend to the cinema' clearly knows that in general the past tense of verbs in English is formed with 'ed.' This will be very important information for the teacher concerned to build upon what the student knows. Second, and less surprisingly, mistakes are equally direct evidence of problems the student is having. Whether he 'knows' that the past tense of this particular verb is irregular and has forgotten it in the heat of the moment, or whether he has never known it at all is a question the teacher may want to address.
>
> (Morrow 1994)

So the reason grammar teaching has become an issue for debate in MFL – in Peter Morris's words it became 'unfashionable' – is because, as CLT has evolved in this country, the explicit teaching of grammar has for many teachers been missed from the equation. Grammar does come into the communicative equation but the ideas associated with it as far as grammar is concerned have often been misinterpreted over a thirty-year period. The process has been not unlike a game of Chinese whispers. In the same way as, in the game, the message whispered down the line becomes muddled and usually results in something hardly approximating to the original, so too some of the central planks of the communicative approach have been eroded from one generation to the next. The message changed from 'grammar matters' to 'grammar doesn't matter'. It is for this reason that, throughout the 1990s, there was confusion within MFL departments about the place of grammar within the largely accepted communicative approach. This was not helped by the near exclusion of the word 'grammar' from the first NC for MFL. Whereas the working party proposals which informed the drafting of the original NC for languages is unequivocal about the importance of grammar –

> Knowledge of structure can (and often should) be consolidated at appropriate places in the process by deliberate learning of their basic features ... Even learners who have thoroughly grasped a structure will need during later work to consolidate their knowledge of it. A well written grammar section can help but a more effective method might be to ask learners at appropriate intervals to summarise their understanding of a structure and give examples of its use.
>
> (DES 1990)

– and devotes ten paragraphs of the report to it, the first edition of the NC watered this down to:

> In learning and using the target language, pupils should have regular opportunities to ... use knowledge about language (linguistic patterns, structures, grammatical features and relationships, and compound words and phrases) to infer meaning and develop their own use of language.
>
> (DES 1991)

However, as Ann Miller points out in this volume, without a grammatical framework to operate within, pupils will be unable to construct language which conveys messages which they themselves want to communicate – the central tenet of CLT.

> they (pupils) may be brought up on a diet of textbooks in which ... a programme is designed according to learners' supposed 'communicative needs', but no attempt is made to provide learners with input that allows them to make generalisations (whether conscious or nor) about rules. They are simply expected to operate with learned by heart routines which have no common structural elements .... If they are constantly asked to produce sentences which they could not construct for themselves, they will achieve little or no autonomy as users of language. They may acquire lexis, but in the absence of grammatical competence, they are obliged, like their peers brought up on decontextualised exercises, to use word-for-word translation from English as a strategy. Indeed, they are in some ways disadvantaged in relation to the first group of learners since, lacking rules, they have no way of learning from their errors and are condemned to repeat them, cast adrift in a sea of approximation.
>
> (Miller, this volume: 154)

If grammar is important, teachers also need to consider how it is to be taught. Interestingly, in a recent European Project (The Iliad Project), a group of teachers interviewed from France, Spain, Austria, Sweden and England were all in sympathy with Sue Simson, a teacher from Turves Green Girls' School, Birmingham:

> I think grammar doesn't make any sense in isolation. You need to put it into a context. So I like to choose a topic that I think is particularly appropriate for any particular element of grammar that I want to teach and set it up initially within a context. Then delve into the rigours of it, work through the patterns, the structures, the exceptions, the rules.

As I discussed in my introduction, there is a propensity for beginning teachers to fall back on their own experience as learners. If grammar was presented to them as rules to be learnt, through drills for instance, in isolation from any communicative situation, then they may feel that this is appropriate for their present classes. This is another area of the grammar debate and one which deserves considerable discussion amongst colleagues. Issues which arise from this are:

- Can grammar be taught in the target language?
- How do teachers differentiate between those structures appropriate for all learners and those for high attainers?
- Is it appropriate to talk about grammar in English and, if so, how does this fit into a lesson taught largely in the target language?
- Is it appropriate to use grammatical terminology and, if so, does there need to be synergy with English colleagues who also teach grammar explicitly?
- Are pupils expected to deduce rules from a series of examples or are they presented with the rules first and then allowed to practise them through a series of activities?

Teachers in any department are unlikely to be unanimous in their answers to these questions but this is one aspect of language debate which will run and run.

New approaches to text using ICT

An exciting prospect and another area of debate for MFL teachers is that the use of ICT in the language classroom is beginning to raise fundamental questions about the way we teach. For instance, accepted consensus in the UK is to introduce new language first and foremost in its spoken form before moving on to the written form. The result has been to push oral proficiency to the fore at the expense of other skills. Since the introduction of the CD-ROM and the internet, we find that language is now often presented in ways which challenge this hierarchy. The new technologies may concurrently require listening, reading, writing and, to a lesser extent, speaking. Pupils come into contact with electronic texts that are presented in different modes – integrating text, images, icons, sound, animation and video sequences. We find that the old divisions of print, audio and video become blurred.

Texts are no longer solely fixed, printed texts with a few illustrations. Electronic texts are not sequential but random, allowing the reader to wander and to choose. These texts are often not permanent. Some websites have a tendency to disappear or change: their strength lies in the fact that they can be continually updated. For teachers, though, this raises issues about how we regard text. We need to learn to be flexible, to adapt quickly to the changing world, to possible technical breakdown and to question the provenance of text.

The importance of engaging in the debate

Teachers sometimes have a disregard for theoretically-based reading. There is a scepticism about intellectual discussion and theoretical thought and yet practice in schools is influenced by these. Why is there so much scepticism about theory in schools? Teachers do theorize but it may be that they lack a technical vocabulary with which they can think about, create and share with each other ideas about teaching and learning (Hargreaves TTA annual lecture 1996). Or they may be unable to apply ideas that they gain through courses or Inset because of lack of time to plan and discuss, because of inappropriate rooming policies, a defined curriculum and rigid exam system.

Nevertheless, we, all of us, need to be aware of the pedagogy and methodology we teach in order to be able to justify why we do what we do. This is particularly true for the growing number of teachers involved in the support of student teachers and newly qualified teachers.

Conclusion

Teachers today are in a world of constant change; there are expectations from outside and inside school. Student teachers and newly-qualified teachers need to be prepared to live on these shifting sands since there is no reason to think that a period of stability and non-intervention is just around the corner. It is important that they learn to develop their voice in the staff room and in their subject associations in order to contribute to the ever-developing definition of language teaching and to our collective understanding of pupils' MFL learning. Without this participation, teaching is in danger of becoming something which is defined by those who do not teach. Where does this leave notions of professionalism?

Further reading

Burstall, C. *et al.* (1974) *Primary French in the Balance,* Windsor: NFER Publishers.
Byram, M. and Morgan, C. *et al.* (1994) *Teaching-and-learning Language-and-culture,* Clevedon: Multilingual Matters.
DES/WO (1990) *Modern Foreign Languages for Ages 11 to 16,* London: HMSO.
—— (1991) *Modern Foreign Languages in the National Curriculum,* London: HMSO.
Elengorn, S. (1961) *Le Pays de Charles. A Third Year French Book,* London: Methuen.

Graddol, D. (1998) 'Will English be enough?', in *Nuffield Languages Inquiry: Where are we going with languages?*, London: Nuffield Foundation.

Grenfell, M. and Harris, V. (1999) *Modern Languages and Learning Strategies in Theory and Practice*, London: Routledge.

Grossman, P. (1990) *The Making of a Teacher: Teacher Knowledge and Teacher Education*, New York: Teachers' College Press.

Guillame and Rudney (1993) 'Student teachers' growth towards independence: an analysis of their changing concerns', *Teaching and Teacher Education* 9(1): 65–80.

Hargreaves, D. (1996) Teacher Training Agency annual lecture.

Hawkins, E. (1981) *Modern Language in the Curriculum*, Cambridge: Cambridge University Press.

Holmes, B. (2000) 'Why teach foreign languages at school?', *Comenius* 19: Autumn, London: Centre for Information on Language Teaching and Research.

King, L. (1999) 'Challenges to multilingualism', in A. Tosi and C. Leung, *Rethinking Language Education. From a Monolingual to a Multilingual Perspective*, London: CILT and Royal Holloway, University of London.

Larsen-Freeman, D. and Long, M.H. (1991) *An Introduction to Second Language Acquisition Research*, London: Longman.

Miller, A., Roselman, L. and Bougard, M.T. *Arc-en-ciel 3 Pupil's Book*, London: Mary Glasgow Publications.

Mitchell, R. (1994) 'The communicative approach to language teaching: an introduction', in A. Swarbrick, *Teaching Modern Languages*, London: Routledge.

Moore, S. and Antrobus, A.L. *Longman Audio-Visual French Stage 1A*, London: Longman.

Morrow, K. (1994) 'Mistakes are the mistake', in A. Swarbrick, *Teaching Modern Languages*, London: Routledge.

Nuffield Languages Inquiry (1998) *Where are We Going with Languages?*, London: Nuffield Foundation.

—— (2000) *Languages: The Next Generation*, London: Nuffield Foundation.

Poole, B. (1999) 'Is younger better? A critical examination of the beliefs about learning a foreign language at primary school', unpublished PhD thesis, Institute of Education, University of London.

Sharpe, K. and Driscoll, P. (2000) 'At what age should foreign language learning begin?', in K. Field, *Issues in Foreign Languages Teaching*, London: Routledge.

Snow, D. and Byram, M. (1997) *Crossing Frontiers. The School Study Visit Abroad*, London: CILT.

Snow, C. and Hoefnagel-Höhle, M. (1978) 'The critical period for language acquisition: evidence from second language acquisition', *Child Development* 49: 1114–28.

Williams, K. (2000) 'Why teach foreign languages in schools? A philosophical response to curriculum policy', Philosophy of Education Society of Great Britain.

Zeichner, K. (1993) 'Traditions of practice in US preservice teacher education programs', *Teaching and Teacher Education* 9(1): 1–13.

2 Drop out from language study at age 16+

A historical perspective

Eric Hawkins

Nine out of ten students stop learning a language at 16.

(Nuffield Foundation Inquiry 2000)

Introduction

A curriculum house with a leaking roof?

When Sir Trevor McDonald, as co-chairman of the Nuffield Foundation two-year inquiry into foreign language teaching, launched the committee's Final Report (Languages: the next generation, June 2000), his first words were to quote the committee's finding: 'Nine out of ten students stop learning a language at 16.'

The drift away from foreign languages at 16 was further confirmed by the publication of the GCE A level results in the following August. They made headlines in the Press. The *Times* announced (17 August 2000): 'STUDENTS SHUN LANGUAGES ... Pupils accused of isolationist attitudes as they abandon learning French, German and Spanish and switch to computer and IT studies.'

The Nuffield Report summed up what 'shunning languages' at age 16 will mean: 'We are on course for the next generation to be disadvantaged, edged out of the employment market both at home and abroad. We are heading towards a minority clinging to monolingualism.'

In practical terms shunning languages at 16 has already led to such a collapse of entries for university degree courses that some universities are closing their language departments. This promises a further drying up of the dwindling supply of graduate linguists from whom our future teachers must be recruited. The 'golden handshakes' of up to £10,000 now on offer to tempt language graduates to train for teaching will be of little effect unless there is a source of graduates to tempt. So the drop out at age 16 threatens the very continuation of language teaching in schools.

The statistics of post-16 drop out had already been set out in the Centre for Information on Language Teaching and Research (CILT) publication *Thirty years of Language Teaching* (Hawkins 1996), which described the foreign language curriculum house as having 'a badly leaking roof'. But it also described the 'house' as having 'insecure foundations'. I believe that there are close links between the leaking roof of our curriculum house and the insecure foundations laid for the house lower down the school. It is a link that may be made clearer by looking into the history of school language study.

Why bother with the history?

There was a time, which some readers may remember, when learning about the history of our discipline formed an essential part of the training of language teachers. In the Cambridge Postgraduate Certificate in Education, for instance, in the 1930s, the history of education had its own three-hour written exam, failure in which meant failure in the whole course. Teaching was entrusted to senior members of the university Faculty of History. The reading list was formidable and, in addition to the weekly seminars, students had to complete a substantial piece of independent research on a chosen historical topic.

Such a requirement may now seem archaic but there is good reason to regret its abandonment. Without a sound grasp of the history of our discipline, there is the danger that teachers will approach each problem they meet as something quite new and so tend to 're-invent the wheel'. There is the even greater danger that administrators, unversed in the history of the discipline for which they have temporary responsibility, may unwittingly destroy what they have not understood. Just such a case, some might allege, was the scrapping, by the Labour Minister, Ellen Wilkinson, in 1949, of the 'group' examination system of School Certificate, which required passes in a broad range of subjects including a foreign language. At the same time, Higher Certificate Subsidiary subjects, which had further encouraged language study by 'non-specialists', were abandoned. Ellen Wilkinson, who had not consulted schools or administrators, surmised, for she had no research to go on, that the change to a much narrower curriculum would somehow benefit less advantaged pupils. This 1949 hatchet work, grasping at a panacea without doing the necessary research, can now be seen as a turning-point in language teaching in the last century and we must return to it.

Avoiding panaceas

History offers many examples of teachers themselves grasping at panaceas. This was brought out by the linguist W.F. Mackey in his widely read *Language Teaching Analysis* (Mackey 1965). In a notable passage, he saw successive generations of language teachers as trudging hopefully along a difficult road, constantly seeking short cuts which all turn out to be dead ends. (Such a dead end was the rush, in the 1960s, to install expensive, mis-named 'language laboratories'.) A recent panacea, flying in the face of research, is the call to 'start at seven' because 'younger is better'. Instead of re-thinking and testing ways to give young learners an adequate linguistic apprenticeship, and with it the 'tools for language learning', the notion is gaining ground that all we need to do is to start at age 7 what is currently done at

11. This is simply a prescription for prolonging early drop out, with no explanation of where the doubling of present numbers of qualified teachers is to come from.[1]

The importance of looking carefully at the historical background of our problems is brought out by L.G. Kelly (1969) in his magisterial *Twenty-five Centuries of Language Teaching*. Kelly reminds us: 'The total corpus of ideas accessible to language teachers has not changed basically in 2,000 years. What have been in constant change are the ways of building methods from them'. Kelly shows how study of the history can throw light on specific 'themes' which still present problems. He cites specifically such 'themes' as the roles of translation, composition and reading, and the teaching of grammar.

H.H. Stern, in his chapter 'Historical Awareness as a First Step' in *Fundamental Concepts of Language Teaching* (Stern 1983: 75ff) usefully compares Mackey's chronological and Kelly's thematic approaches to the history of our subject.

If we are to understand why our 'curriculum roof' leaks so badly and how this may be linked with insecurity of language foundations lower down the school, it will be best to steer clear of hopeful panaceas and learn what we can from the historical background.

Who drops out?

In June 2000, some half a million 16-year-olds took a foreign language in the GCSE examination (341,004 in French, 133,659 in German and 49,973 in Spanish). One might expect these half-million students to see the value of carrying on the language to which they have devoted five years' work, just when it might be put to use exploring the way of life of a foreign people, by reading and travel, comparing it with what they know at home, and thus escaping from the 'monoglot prison'. All these young people will, after all, shortly be seeking employment as citizens of a trading nation whose prosperity depends on its world-wide contacts and understanding of its neighbours' needs and interests. But instead of building on five years' work, nine out of ten of these 16-year-olds, we know, will let their language drop.

Among boys, the decline in numbers carrying on languages has been specially marked. In 1965 some 16,831 boys entered for GCE A level in a foreign language. By the year 2000 this total had fallen to an all-time low of 12,159. (In the same period boys' total subject entries rose from 243,819 to 354,553.) Boys' entries at A level for the commonest school language, French, were 11,221 in 1965, falling to a mere 5,224 in 2000. It is a tragic waste of pupils' effort and of teachers' precious time.

The first thing to observe is that drop out, once past the early stages, is not a new phenomenon. Ten years ago a House of Lords Select Committee felt the need to 'launch a campaign to utter the death knell of the monoglot tradition of English society' (Report of Committee on European Schools and Language Learning 1990). Their Lordships were reacting to a challenging HMI study (*Modern Languages in Comprehensive Schools* HMI 1977). A team of HMI visited 83 schools, a one-in-ten sample of the 831 comprehensive schools which had been established at least since 1971, and had thus had time to accommodate their comprehensive intake. The Report identified a long list of shortcomings, but what caught most attention was the table showing the wasteful drop out at age 14+. The percentages of each age-group studying a foreign language (mainly French) in the 83 schools inspected were:

Age	Percent
11+	89
12+	85
13+	80
14+*	35
15+	33

* the age at which the language commonly became 'optional'

The revelation, in 1977, that some two-thirds of 14-year-olds were dropping their foreign language after only three years, as soon as 'choice' of curriculum was allowed, caused a sensation. Had the 'democratization' of foreign language study in the comprehensive school proved to be an illusion?

The disappointment of this revelation was felt the more acutely because it followed the shock abandonment four years earlier (1974) of the pilot scheme (*French from Eight*). This brave experiment, testing the feasibility of making a start on French at age 8 in primary schools, had been launched by Sir Edward Boyle, paragon of Education Ministers, in 1963 with the powerful support of Dr Farrer Brown, director of the Nuffield Foundation. (For an account of this scheme and of subsequent similar developments cf. Hawkins 1996: 155–77.) The scheme seemed to make an impressive start, arousing widespread enthusiasm among schools and parents and attracting world-wide interest. By 1970 it was estimated that as many as one-third of all primary schools were teaching French. The initial evaluation by National Foundation for Education Research (NFER) in Burstall (1970) gave some grounds for optimism. Four years later, however, the NFER final report (Burstall *et al.* 1974) was negative and signalled the collapse of the scheme, amid much acrimony and controversy.

In the vexed discussion that followed this episode one important aspect of it was strangely overlooked. What was new in the pilot scheme was not really the idea of earlier starting. Though the scheme was a first attempt at a younger start in state primary schools, early starts had long been commonplace in the independent sector. Little clear light was shed on the claim that 'younger is better' because, despite ten years of strenuous effort by central and local government, a trio of problems (teacher supply, the transition of early starters at 11 to secondary school and early drop out from language study once past the 'listen and repeat' stage of the learning, especially by boys) had not begun to be solved when the scheme was aborted.

What was revolutionary in the pilot scheme was that under the scheme any school starting French at age 8 had to undertake to teach the whole of each age-group. No selection of pupils was allowed. At that time (1963) only one pupil in five, at age 11, was offered a foreign language. This was therefore the first time in history that language teaching ceased to be confined to a selected few. How would the four-fifths of each age-group previously excluded from language classes now make out?

Comparison of the two NFER evaluations of the scheme in 1970 and 1974 suggests that for many pupils disenchantment began after the first two years of study. What this points to is that there comes a 'second stage' in the learning which a minority of pupils can take in their stride but for which many pupils are ill-prepared. This was also what the HMI Report of 1977 seemed to show. Why were so many pupils ill-prepared for the later stages of learning? Could there be something missing in their early experience and use of language at home and in the primary school? To the relevance of this question we must return.

Reactions to the HMI Report of 1977

That many pupils could enjoy their languages, if only the right lead were given, was demonstrated by the success of the annual 'Young Linguist of the Year' Festivals. These were organized annually, between 1986 and 1992, by Christine Wilding, following a lead given by CILT and a redoubtable HMI, Betty Parr. A national committee supported by members of the National Association of Language Advisors (NALA) arranged regional heats, followed by a Language Festival Day at Warwick University. At the last of these events, in 1992, before they had to be discontinued for lack of funding, over 8,000 pupils from all over the country converged for the day on Warwick's fine Language Centre. They came together partly to demonstrate their language skills (and be rewarded, the best of them, by prizes of study abroad), but most came simply to share with fellow enthusiasts the sheer enjoyment of exercising their blossoming language skills. (For an account of this movement see Page 1996.)

A partial response from government to the HMI Report of 1977 came with the introduction, in 1988, of a new examination at 16, the GCSE, to replace the existing, more 'academic' GCE O level and the less demanding CSE. The new examination, to be taken by *all* entrants, was intended to offer more accessible incentives for the less able, while still challenging the faster learners. It did have some effect in reducing the early drop out, but staunching the 14+ haemorrhage was only completed by the Education Act of 1988, which made the foreign language a 'foundation' subject, compulsory for *all* pupils up to age 16. This took full effect from 1996 onwards. (Similar legislation was introduced in Scotland in 1989, effective from 1992. cf. Hawkins 1996.)

Sadly, however, as the examination statistics quoted above confirm, the effect of these measures has been merely to postpone the drop out for two years, until age 16, and to increase it from two-thirds of the age-group at 14+ to nine-tenths at 16+. Making the foreign language a 'foundation subject' in 1988 clearly did little to help those pupils who had previously dropped out at 14+. It seemed as if, for lack of some element in their early experience of language, at home and in school, which more fortunate pupils had enjoyed, they saw no point in pursuing a foreign language beyond the early stages. What was needed was some way of encouraging these pupils to be more 'open' to languages and more confident in their attack. This would call for a radically re-thought linguistic apprenticeship in the primary school, opening young minds to linguistic diversity and giving them the 'tools for language learning'. It is just such an approach that Prof. Michel Candelier and his research teams in five European countries are pioneering (*ouverture aux langues* and 'learning how to learn' for pupils aged 8–11) in the exciting European EVLANG project (Candelier 1989). This European research has had little discussion in the UK. It may prove to be very relevant to the problem of early drop out that we are considering.

Early days of the post-16 language curriculum

In order to see how this approach is relevant for our schools, it may be useful to take a closer look at an earlier stage of post-16 language study and examine the factors that have affected curriculum development.

A national examination system for pupils aged 16 and 18 dates from the seminal year 1918, and the 'Fisher' Education Act. This Act was overseen not by a career politician but by an eminent academic historian, H.A.L. Fisher, Fellow of New College Oxford and Vice-Chancellor of Sheffield University, whose classic *History of Europe* (1936) was required reading in sixth forms and universities. Like the other great Education Acts of 1902–4 and 1944, the Fisher Act was a response to a widely-felt need for 're-thinking', as the nation emerged from the horror of a great war. Many of the Act's imaginative proposals, e.g. for a national system of 'continuing education' for all throughout adult life, through 'County Colleges', were never implemented under harsh post-war economic conditions. A new schools examination system, however, was one outcome of re-thinking that did survive.

Before 1918, the school examination system was, frankly, chaotic. The Taunton Commission had, as long ago as 1868, deplored the 'proliferation of examinations' taken in secondary schools. By 1902 the situation had grown worse. To the existing university entrance exams, Civil Service entry, Army and Navy exams, London Matriculation and papers set by the professional bodies, were added the Oxford and Cambridge 'junior' and 'local' exams taken at 14 and 15.

Under the Education Act of 1902, a standing Consultative Committee had been set up and, in 1911, this committee recommended the establishment of an Examinations Council representing the Board of Education, the Local Education Authorities and the university examining bodies. In 1917, the Board of Education took the further step of recognizing the universities as the responsible bodies to conduct a new national schools examination system. Examining Boards were set up, attached to Oxford and Cambridge, London and the northern universities (followed later by others, ten such Boards by 1928) which set papers for the first time in 1918. The pattern that came to be adopted was for a School Certificate (SC) for the majority of candidates, likely to leave school at 16 to enter professional apprenticeships, and the Higher School Certificate (HSC) for those going on to university.

The SC was, from the first, a 'group' examination. For award of the Certificate, passes were required in five subjects, with at least one pass in each of three groups of subjects: the English group, Maths or a Science, and a language other than English. Two of the five passes had to be at 'Credit' level. The 'group' system meant that a pass in a foreign language became obligatory for all pupils staying at school until 16.

In the HSC two kinds of papers were set, Main and Subsidiary. Three Main passes were required for 'Matriculation' (access to university). A Subsidiary pass was worth half a Main pass. At the same time a Secondary Schools Examinations Council (SSEC) was set up with specialist panels for each main subject, representing school and university teachers, chaired by a senior HMI, to advise the President of the Board of Education on the syllabuses in each subject that would be approved.

The Leathes committee report

Meanwhile, in 1915, at the darkest moment of the war, two committees had been set up to report directly to the Prime Minister on the future teaching of Sciences and Modern Subjects. The Modern Languages committee was chaired by Stanley Leathes, CB, an eminent Cambridge historian. For the future development of language teaching in schools between the two world wars, the recommendations of the Leathes committee in 1918 were crucial.

Some of the recommendations of this wide-ranging report (*'Modern Studies'. The Position of Modern Languages in the Educational System of Great Britain*), the only Government inquiry ever conducted into foreign language studies, were far ahead of their time.

In par. 181, for example, the committee drew attention to an existing Board of Education regulation which was little known, and not implemented, allowing teachers to be trained 'by attachment to schools approved by HMI ... The teachers selected to do the training should receive extra allowances and their schools should be frequently inspected'.

Another proposal (par. 187) was that 'however good the proficiency originally possessed by a teacher, it is necessary that he should have opportunities to return from time to time to the foreign country to renew his intimacy and revive his knowledge'.

Par. 188 of the report was, perhaps, the most far-sighted. It proposed that there should be a 'Higher Certificate' for teachers. It might be competed for after five years of teaching and should be a qualification hard to win. 'Real practical skill should be an essential requirement' and there should be evidence, oral and written, of 'further progress in the language'. What the committee had in mind was a Higher Certificate for school teaching *which would carry similar prestige to the doctorate of the researcher and university lecturer.* And this would facilitate 'free circulation between the schools and Universities' as the committee had observed in France (through the *agrégation*).

All these proposals aimed to raise the prestige of school teaching, and keep (and suitably reward) the best teachers in the classroom where their skills were needed instead of compelling so many of the best of them to become administrators.

These proposals had to wait many decades for serious consideration. The most important proposal, for our present discussion, which *was* acted upon, was that

*ALL students in sixth Forms, regardless of their specialism, should keep up, to the age of
18, the study both of a foreign language (at least in the written form) and of English.*

The Leathes committee's recommendations were not mandatory but the new
HSC Examination with its Subsidiary papers for 'non-specialists' greatly encouraged
their implementation. The rule at my own school, Liverpool Institute, in the 1920s
and 1930s, was that all sixth-form scientists had to take, in addition to their Maths,
Physics and Chemistry at Main level, a foreign language and English Literature at
Subsidiary level. Modern language students also took five subjects: History and two
languages at Main level, with Latin and English as 'Subsidiary' subjects. This pattern
was common in the state schools. In the independent 'Public' schools, sixth formers
more commonly took four subjects, two at Main and two at Subsidiary level.

It was this pattern that was abruptly replaced in 1949 by the GCE A level system,
in which candidates commonly took at A level only the three subjects required for
university entrance. (A decade later, an optional 'General Studies' paper was introduced with a foreign language element counting for 10 per cent of the mark.)

The abrupt dropping of the Subsidiary papers, without consultation, caused an
outcry from the schools. These papers had steadily grown in prestige. In some
schools, sixth formers took Subsidiary papers after one year, on their way to the
Main papers, but the pattern at Liverpool described above was more common. In
either case, the Subsidiary papers were clearly encouraging non-specialists not to
drop their language at 16. In the largest Exam Board, the NUJMB, for instance,
the figures for French, the most popular language in 1938, were:

HSC Main French: 1,669
HSC Subsid. French: 2,433

Nationally, total entries for French in 1938 at Main level were 4,752, and for all
languages 5,894. It is not easy to obtain exact national figures for Subsidiary entries
for all languages but, extrapolating from the NUJMB figures for French, we can
calculate that, nationally, Subsidiary entries would have been some 6,500. This gives
a total of some 12,000 sixth formers keeping up a language. Since the total number of
candidates for HSC at that time was not much more than 12,000, it is clear that until
the war came, most sixth formers kept up a language in one form or other *and far
more were non-specialists taking Subsidiary papers, than specialists taking Mains.*

Attempts to broaden the (post-16) curriculum

The history of debate about sixth-form studies for the next fifty years became
largely the story of the failure of attempts to bring back the broader pre-war
programme, which had encouraged 'non-specialist' study of languages post-16+. A
typical proposal was the widely supported 1950s Agreement to Broaden the Curriculum (ABC) scheme. This was a Pact, committing those Heads of schools who
signed it (including the present writer) to support a broader sixth-form programme,
provided that university selectors could be persuaded to accept it. ABC was led by

the Heads of two very different schools, Eton College and Manchester Grammar School, and attracted wide support from both independent and state schools.

The ABC proposal was only one of a succession of attempts to introduce broader post-16 programmes. Every one, however, came up against the objection, from those apparently unaware of how common were five-subject sixth-form programmes pre-war, that the 'gold standard' of A level would be 'diluted' by broadening the sixth-form curriculum.

This was, however, only part of the story of the universities' opposition to broadening post-16 programmes. There was also a growing competition, between universities, to recruit students and a reluctance to put any 'unnecessary hurdles' in the way of candidates applying for places. (For an account of this debate, *Trahison des clercs?*, see Hawkins 1981: 18 *et seq.*)

The universities' reasons for dropping the foreign language requirement for entry were summed up by Cambridge, which, because of its prestige, had been able to hold out longer in the competition for students, but finally gave way in 1979. The *Cambridge Reporter* for that year told the story:

> Cambridge has, from time to time, tried to ensure some breadth of study by candidates for admission even after O level – for example by the Use of English paper and the language paper in the old Scholarship examination. The university gave up such attempts because they tended to discourage applicants from applying to Cambridge. The university concludes that no university in isolation could afford to impose entrance requirements designed to encourage breadth of study in the sixth form ... They would, therefore, have to be imposed by the Department of Education and Science'.

The key phrase is 'because they tended to discourage applicants'. The other universities, less able to compete for recruits, had abandoned the foreign language requirement in 1966, thus seeming to send a signal to candidates (and their advisers at home and in school) that monolingualism was now acceptable in the highest academic circles.

A recent attempt to encourage 'non-specialist' language study was the introduction (in 1988) of 'Advanced Supplementary' (AS) papers. The depressing lack of take-up of these papers can be seen from recent figures:

GCE entries 1999 England and Wales	*A level*	*AS level*
French	8,662	1,984
German	8,916	871
Spanish	5,233	628
Other Modern Languages	4,718	479

It is significant that, when GCE results were published in August 2000, no national newspaper considered the AS figures even worth mentioning.

As these lines are written yet another attempt to 'broaden the curriculum' is launched with 'Curriculum 2000'. This requires Year 12 pupils to study four or five 'half-subjects' for one year. They can then revert to three subjects in the following year. The weakness of this plan is that the foreign language needs to be continued up to age 18 and university entrance, if any significant impact is to be made on rapidly declining recruitment for language degree courses.

What we have seen during the past half-century is the steady collapse of 'non-specialist' language study of the kind that prospered, as we have seen, up to 1949, through the 'group' regulations of School Certificate, requiring a pass in a foreign language, and the practice of many schools regarding Subsidiary subjects in Higher Certificate. The story prompts several questions. Might a firmer national direction of curriculum policy have avoided wasteful drop out at age 16 in languages (and possibly other key subjects)? Where might such direction have come from and why was such direction not exercised until a beginning was made with the Act of 1988?

The role of independent consultative bodies

Before the war, national education policy had been the responsibility of an independent Board of Education (rather like the present Governors of the BBC). The President was appointed by, but not a member of, the Government and he and his committee did not change with changes of governing party. The president from 1924 to 1930 was the scholar (author of *Education at the Crossroads,* 1930) and former diplomat, Lord Eustace Percy, seventh son of the Duke of Northumberland.

The Board was advised by an equally independent Consultative Committee. Its chairman from 1920 to 1934 was Sir Henry Hadow, scholar and musicologist, who was successively Dean of Worcester College, Oxford, Principal of Armstrong College, Newcastle and, from 1919–30, Vice-Chancellor of Sheffield University in succession to H.A.L. Fisher. The six Reports of the Hadow committee, especially *The Education of the Adolescent* (1926) and *The Primary School* (1931), shaped national thinking about education pre-war and led directly to the last 'non-political' Education Act of the century, the 'Butler Act' of 1944. This Act, which introduced the radical new principle of free access to secondary schooling, including free books, travel and school meals, with provision for fees and maintenance at university (subject to a means test), was piloted through the wartime coalition Parliament by its joint authors, the Conservative minister, R.A.B. Butler, and his Labour deputy, Chuter Ede, a former primary school headmaster.

With the Act of 1944, the 'non-party' Board of Education gave way to a Ministry of Education whose Head was a member of the Government and whose policies reflected party political objectives.

It is, perhaps, inevitable that, in a democracy, all decisions about education must, in the end, be political decisions. It is, nevertheless, worth recalling that an independent body, like the old Hadow committee, could sometimes be more radical in its thinking than a political party with elections to win can afford to be. Many young teachers of my age whose apprenticeship was interrupted by service in the war must have kept in their hearts, and brought back to their classrooms afterwards, the challenging statement of intent in Hadow's 1931 Report (the precise wording was owed to R. H. Tawney):

> The primary school is on the way to become what it should be, the common school of the whole population, so excellent and so generally esteemed that all parents will desire their children to attend it ... The root of the matter is, after all, simple. What a wise and good parent would desire for his own children, that a nation must desire for all children.

It was a brave call to arms to hear in 1931, in the midst of the deepest economic depression of the century and from a 'non-party' Board of Education. Sadly, seventy years after Hadow's inspiring call, the divide, in resources and opportunities, between fee-paying 'sheep' and state-school 'goats' grows wider with every passing decade.

The curriculum – a secret garden?

With the passing (in 1944) of the pre-war Board of Education and its independent Consultative Committee, two non-governmental bodies continued to exercise peripheral influence on the curriculum. One was the SSEC already referred to, set up in 1918, and the other a new body created by the Act of 1944, the Central Advisory Council England (CACE) with a separate Council for Wales.

The SSEC had two responsibilities: first to ensure the maintenance of pass/fail standards within each Board from year to year, and second (what proved a much harder task) to ensure parity of standards across the (now eight) examining boards. How much standards differed was demonstrated, in 1967, by the Head of Marlborough College who entered a group of pupils for GCE O level (German) *with two different Boards simultaneously*. The widely different results caused a sensation (for details cf. Hawkins 1970a: 143). The Schools Council, which had taken over from the SSEC in 1964 (see below), reacted by persuading all the Boards to introduce into their French O level tests a common module (a short passage for translation into French) to serve as a 'yardstick' against which to measure each Board's grading scheme. The Boards agreed to this with great reluctance but, after a year's trial, they protested that their examiners could not agree on a common mark scheme and, amid acrimony, discontinued the experiment without putting in its place any other means of ensuring parity of standards.

The only other body advising on the curriculum was CACE. This purely advisory body was appointed for successive three-year periods to report on specific topics, each time under a new chairman. CACE issued several notable reports in the 1950s and 1960s, but for reasons never explained it was disbanded in 1967 and never recalled. Apart from the SSEC's dubious contribution in overseeing examinations, and the reports of CACE which relied solely on their own cogency to achieve any effect in schools, the school curriculum remained a 'secret garden' after the war and the legend grew, endorsed by Heads of schools through their professional bodies, that curriculum planning was solely a matter for the Head and Governors of each school to determine.[2]

In 1962, however, an outstanding Minister, Sir David Eccles, took a first tentative step into the 'secret garden' when he set up, within the Ministry of Education, a Curriculum Study Group (CSG). This move was bitterly opposed by the schools, but the Ministry went further and in 1964 both the Study Group and the SSEC were disbanded and replaced by the new Schools Council for Curriculum and Examinations (SCCE). This body, largely financed by an annual tax levied on all LEAs in proportion to their income from rates, had specialist committees of teachers from school and university, and HMI, for each main curriculum subject. For the next twenty years the Schools Council, though it lacked power to do more than advise on curriculum planning and examining, at least ensured, through a succession of working papers on each subject, that national guidelines for most subjects began to emerge. One of its most influential publications was Working Paper No. 28, issued in 1970, *New Patterns in Sixth Form Modern Language Studies* which was widely discussed and provoked fresh thinking about teaching and examining at the post-16+ level, especially by 'non-specialist' students.

It was not until the Act of 1988, however (with the exception of Sir Edward Boyle's ill-fated pilot scheme *French from Eight*, launched in 1963), that Central Government intervened by legislation in curriculum planning. In 1988 the foreign language became a 'foundation subject' (obligatory for ages 11 to 16 in State Schools). This postponed the 14+ 'drop out' but only, as we have seen, for two years.

The (unplanned) decline of Latin

An example, meanwhile, of how schools could 'drift' into far-reaching, unplanned change in the curriculum was the demise of Latin. It began with the abandonment by Oxford and Cambridge, in the mid-1950s, of Latin as a requirement for entry. At the same time many professions, such as the Law and Pharmacy, followed suit. In consequence Latin began to disappear from school programmes. The decline was slow at first. Entries for Latin (which in 1938 had been 2,589 for HSC Main) had grown by 1965 to 7,901 for GCE A level, incidentally 2,536 more than for German in that year. The sharpest decline coincided with the swing to comprehensive schooling in the 1970s.

Entries for Latin in GCE		1965	1975	1985	1995
O level	Boys	28,500	13,984	9,913	6,776 (GCSE)
	Girls	23,920	15,791	10,015	6,182 (GCSE)
A level	Boys	4,164	1,383	911	762
	Girls	3,737	1,734	1,305	863

The effect of the demise of Latin has been very little discussed. One of the few places where its implications were at least considered was in a brief paragraph (No. 316) of the Report of the Central Advisory Council for Education (CACE 1959).

The Report, under the chairmanship of the economist Sir Geoffrey Crowther, had this to say about the demise of Latin:

> There is very widespread complaint, which we believe to be justified, about the average standards of competence in the use of language among the boys and girls who leave the schools. The greatest efforts should be devoted to improving the standards attained ... The abolition of compulsory Latin by itself would do nothing, and perhaps less than nothing, to achieve this. But the re-examination of the ... requirements of Oxford and Cambridge ... provides an opportunity, which ought to be seized, for re-thinking the whole basis of the teaching of linguistics in schools.

A minority of the committee went further and advocated 'that the Latin require-ment in university entrance should be retained until such time as thought and experiment have clearly shown *that there are other ways of doing what Latin does*'.

One tentative answer to the CACE question: 'What did Latin do?' may be that it made young learners familiar with different ways in which languages can convey meanings.

Linguists distinguish between 'synthetic' languages such as Latin, and 'isolating' languages like English. In synthetic languages grammatical relationships are expressed by inflectional endings. Professor Crystal instances one 'synthetic' feature of Latin (Crystal 1987: 293): 'the ending O in Latin *amo*, "I love", simulta-neously expresses that the form is in the first person singular, present tense, active and indicative'. In English, Crystal explains, there are few such inflections and 'word order changes *are the basis of the grammar*'. The European foreign languages that our young learners meet in the secondary school are all of the 'synthetic' type, like Latin. Young European learners of English, on the other hand, with whom our pupils are often unfairly compared, all *come from* 'synthetic' languages. They face, in English (only, of course, in the early stages), a simpler 'listen and repeat' kind of language task, having few inflections of the verb and no gender agreements etc. to master. This may underlie the apparently superior performance of young Euro-peans learning English.

As the archetypical 'synthetic' language, Latin offered a familiarity with how synthetic languages work. But something else may have been lost with the demise of Latin. Without it, pupils cannot so easily explore how Latin lives on in English, espe-cially in the 'standard' English in which the curriculum is delivered, but which many pupils must meet, almost as a foreign language. (For an interesting introduction to the way Latin lives on in standard English, see *Our Greek and Latin Roots*, Morwood and Warman 1990, in the Cambridge University Press Series *Awareness of Language*.)

As part of the re-thinking of the apprenticeship in language that CACE called for, some revival of the study of Latin may have an interesting role to play.

Two reactions to the CACE (1957) report

The CACE call for re-thinking language in schools did have two immediate outcomes. The first was the decision of the SCCE to commission a programme in 'Linguistics and English Teaching' under the chairmanship of Professor Michael Halliday. The team eventually published an imaginative collection of English language teaching materials for schools under the title 'Language in Use' (Doughty *et al.* 1971). In his introduction to the materials, Halliday referred, for the first time in the UK, to the need for greater 'awareness of language'. (The expression was already current in the USA. cf. I.G. Mattingley's insightful discussion in *Language by Ear and Eye* [Kavanagh and Mattingley 1972]. Halliday argued: 'Each one of us has this ability (to use language) and lives by it but we do not always become aware of it … there should … be some place for language in the working life of the secondary school pupil, and of the student in a college of education'.

The Language in Use materials broke new ground but were sadly neglected by most English teachers. As Professor Chris Brumfit observed: '[teachers of English] are largely untrained in language … little in their training has prepared them to look at language objectively' (Brumfit 1991). An apprenticeship based on literary criticism without training in linguistics scarcely equipped English teachers to understand how children master (or fail to master) language, or to answer the call from CACE to 're-think linguistics in school'.

The second, more positive, reaction came from foreign language teachers. At a conference called by CILT in 1973, bringing together teachers of English and of foreign languages, Halliday's argument for giving language a place in the curriculum was taken further. The proposal was made (cf. Hawkins 1974) that language should become the 'bridging subject', bringing together in fruitful partnership teachers of English and teachers of foreign languages (and of 'community languages') who, at that time, were trained and worked in complete isolation from each other.

This case was further developed (Hawkins 1977, 1981, 1984, 1993 and Donmall 1985) resulting eventually in an international movement (ALA) with its journal, *Language Awareness*. In 2000 the Nuffield Inquiry Report signalled that the case for 'language awareness' in the curriculum had been made by proposing that it should become a 'module' in the 'literacy strategy' of the primary school. 'The content (of the module) would be designed to bridge the gap between English, literacy and foreign languages' (Nuffield 2000: *Recommendation 6.6: 43*).

The relevance of this Nuffield recommendation to the problem of drop out from Foreign Languages is that lack of 'awareness of language' may underlie the learning difficulties met by many pupils when they reach the later stages of foreign language study.

'Democratization' of language study?

The steepest decline in post-16 language studies has generally been seen to date from the universities' dropping of their language requirement for entry in 1966, with its signal that monolingualism was now acceptable in the highest academic quarters. However, the decline also coincided with another factor and it may not be easy to disentangle the two developments.

The second factor was the quickening, from the mid-1960s, of the swing away from selective secondary schooling to comprehensive schools. Because the (selective) grammar schools had been overwhelmingly single-sex schools, this also meant a switch to mixed secondary schooling for most pupils.

In 1965, only an elite of one pupil in five of each age-group, those selected for grammar school, were offered a foreign language. These pupils had been selected largely on a test of their verbal skills which (as research summarized in the Bullock Report (1975) showed) was largely a test of early family background. The four-fifths of each age-group who now came into foreign language classes for the first time were, broadly, those who, having drawn a disadvantaged ticket in the family lottery, lacked a sound grasp of the language in which the school curriculum was delivered and examined, and understood little of how language works.

Many of the boys among them were further disadvantaged by the swing away from single-sex to mixed secondary schooling which meant that, for the first time, boys and girls sat side by side in foreign language classes.

Clare Burstall's 10-year evaluation of the pilot scheme *French from Eight* (Burstall 1970, Burstall *et al.* 1974) had already shown the extent to which girls outperformed boys in French (in fact one commentator suggested that the logical conclusion from the Report was that *French from Eight* should be continued for girls but not for boys!). But Burstall's study also showed that 'both boys and girls did better in single-sex than in mixed schools'.

The coincidence of mixed schooling with post-16 drop out of boys from languages is clear when we compare boys' and girls' A level entries for the three commonest languages in 1965 (date of the famous Crosland Circular 10/65 on comprehensive schools) with entries in 2000. Until 1965 boys' entries for languages grew steadily but then the turn down began.

Entries for A level (girls in brackets)	1965	2000
French	11,221 (14,378)	5,224 (12,997)
German	3,572 (3,535)	2,777 (5,915)
Spanish	1,197 (1,016)	1,719 (3,913)
Total	15,990 (18,929)	9,720 (22,825)

The extent to which boys' drop out at A level reflects performance lower down the school is shown by the percentage of 'good passes' at 16+ scored by girls and boys respectively in the commonest language, French:

Percentage of good passes (A to C) in French		1965	2000
GCE O level	Boys	53.8	
	Girls	62.5	
CSE	Boys	9.9	
	Girls	19.2	
GCSE	Boys		42.5
	Girls		60.1

A boy/girl difference of some nine points in 1965 has now become one of eighteen points. The precise reasons for the difference are, of course, a matter of debate among researchers but a significant factor must be the well-attested 'spurt' in development (including linguistic development) that girls go through several years earlier than boys at puberty. This must equip girls better to engage with the early stages of the secondary curriculum. The boys' corresponding 'spurt' at puberty comes several years later, by which time many choices of curriculum and career have begun to take shape. For an introduction to the issues involved, see the CILT publication *Boys, Girls and Languages in Schools* (Powell 1986).

Girls' linguistic precocity in the secondary school is clearly linked to their earlier physical and emotional maturity. Paediatricians distinguish between 'chronological' and 'developmental' ages of children.

> By developmental age we simply mean the degree to which a child has advanced along the road to full maturity … The commonest measure (of developmental age) is the maturity of the skeleton ('bone age') … At birth the average girl is already some weeks ahead of the average boy in 'bone age' and she gradually comes to be more and more ahead until at puberty *the difference is two years.*
>
> (Tanner 1967)

J.M. Tanner was professor in Child Health and Growth at the University of London Institute of Child Health, and the chief consultant to the Plowden Committee. His account goes on, 'Girls begin puberty on average two years earlier than boys[3] …. Eventually, as the girls' adolescent spurt (in development) is dying away, the boys' begins'.

The tests used for selection for grammar school at 11+ by most LEAs (for instance the Murray House test papers) always carried an instruction to markers 'to add a prescribed percentage to all boys' scores to compensate for their lower marks in the 'verbal reasoning' exam which carried half the total mark'. (Otherwise most grammar school places would have gone disproportionately to girls.) The precocity of girls in English (as well as French) was amply confirmed in all the tests used in Burstall's detailed evaluation of the pilot scheme (see Burstall 1970, 1974). Since confident use of the language in which the curriculum is delivered (and examined) underlies the whole of learning in the secondary school, it is not surprising that girls outperform boys except in subjects such as mathematics which are less dependent on verbal conceptualizing.

That developmental and linguistic maturity are linked is also attested by boys' performance at A level. Their later spurt in 'developmental age', coinciding with later puberty, also coincides with a well-attested late spurt in linguistic performance. In 2000, at A level, 59.1 per cent of boys scored a good pass (A to C) in English, against 59 per cent of girls. In French the percentages of good passes were boys 67.8 per cent and girls 64 per cent. Unfortunately it is during the critical middle school years when girls temporarily outperform boys linguistically, and when boys and girls sit together in language classes for which they are not, on average, equally prepared, that boys drift into the lower streams, with predictable effect on their decisions about future curriculum and career choices.

There must certainly be other contributory reasons why boys lag behind girls across the curriculum in the secondary school. (For discussion of other possible factors, see Barton 2001, this volume.) There seems no doubt, however, that mixed schooling has coincided with boys' drop out from foreign languages, and the need for further research is clearly indicated.

Need for reform of post-16 programmes

Our historical survey has identified, perhaps, some of the factors which currently discourage adolescents, especially boys, from following up their early encounters with foreign languages. The situation is serious enough to call for a radical overhaul of post-16 programmes. Areas where 'action research' is called for would include:

- radical 'broadening' of selection procedures for university;
- experiments with 'reading only' programmes and bi-lingual interaction where each participant uses his/her own language while reading/listening to the foreign language;
- vocationally oriented programmes, e.g. foreign language for sports media, for nurses or secretaries etc.;
- and there must clearly be more equal opportunities for pupils to be 'immersed' in the *spoken* foreign language, regardless of differences in home background, by providing, in each region, well-equipped language teaching centres where pupils can be placed in a simulated foreign environment and where 'intensive' immersion courses can supplement the necessarily 'drip-feed' nature of school programmes.

All of these steps may be useful but we should recall Mackey's advice to beware of grasping at single panaceas. There may be a deeper malaise underlying 'students shunning languages'.

Language learning proceeds in stages

The evidence from the Burstall evaluation of the pilot scheme (Burstall 1974), with early success followed by disenchantment, and the massive drop out at age 14 reported by HMI in 1977, suggests that *mastering a foreign language under school conditions is a staged process*. Most young learners find stage one enjoyable, when they have merely to 'listen to and repeat' undifferentiated chunks of the language. It is the second stage, of adapting the imitated phrases to suit new, unpredictable *contexts and in the written form and especially manipulating the verb*, that poses the problems. Much of the enjoyment and apparent success claimed for 'early start' programmes seems to be based only on observation of young learners in the first stage. What we need to know is why so many pupils are unable to tackle the second stage.

The difference between those adolescents who baulk at the second stage and those who tackle it with confidence can only be due to some difference in their experience of language in the home and in their early years at school. We have been given some clues to what the difference is from work on foreign language aptitude (notably by my colleague Peter Green at York [Green 1975]). His York Aptitude Test, which was a good predictor of success of 11-year-olds, *measured the ease and speed with which pupils could grasp 'meaningful patterns' in language that they had not previously met*. What seems to be needed is more research examining precisely what it is *in early language experience* that builds 'language awareness' and, with it, the capacity, rapidly and surely, to grasp language structure.

Some interesting pointers to ways of giving pupils the 'tools for language learning' are coming out of the EVLANG project presently being conducted in five European universities and directed by Michel Candelier (Candelier 1998). These teams of researchers are devising and testing materials for pupils aged 8–11, designed to 'awaken' young minds to curiosity about linguistic diversity (*ouverture aux langues*) and at the same time arming them with the 'tools for effective language learning'. Candelier and his teams acknowledge that their work follows closely the 'awareness of language' movement in the UK. Recent accounts of this suggest the following components of a revised language apprenticeship in primary school and the early years of secondary:

A *revised language apprenticeship*

1   The first requirement would be close co-operation between teachers of English and of foreign languages (with teachers of, e.g., music, biology, history). Combined working parties in each school would devise and 'team-teach' courses in 'awareness of language', addressing the many questions about language which are currently never part of children's apprenticeship (cf. Hawkins 1984).

2   The 'awareness of language' programme would enrich and support the work at present done in 'literacy' courses. The aim would be, jointly with English teachers, to equip *all* children not only to transact confidently the standard language in which the curriculum of the secondary school is delivered (and examined) but to see the standard form in perspective, and, with some objectivity, to examine

where it came from and how it is changing, how it is learnt, how first language acquisition and second language learning differ, and from this to get some sense of the 'linguistic distance' between English and other languages.

3 A progressive course in 'education of the ear' would aim to make children discriminating listeners to language (see the case argued in MacCarthy 1978).

4 Finally, a serious attempt would be made to arm young learners to overcome the difficulties which upset many of them in tackling the grammar of their foreign language, especially in the written form. The study of how language works is a neglected element in primary teacher training (but one cogently argued for in The Bullock Report *A Language For Life* 1975). The history suggests that a progressive 'awareness of language' apprenticeship in the primary school, giving all learners the 'tools for foreign language learning', and profiting from the lessons of the research in Europe by Michel Candelier and his teams of colleagues (EVLANG Candelier 1998), may, in the long run, be the most constructive way to staunch the adolescent drop out from foreign language classes.

Notes

1 Pendulum Swings and Panaceas: (a) The Nuffield Inquiry Report (p. 40) quotes Tony Blair as authority (!) for the claim: 'Everyone knows that with languages the earlier you start the easier they are'. No other 'authority' is cited in support of this claim which flies in the face of much of the research evidence. The Prime Minister should glance at, for instance, Singleton, D. (1998) *Language Acquisition – The Age Factor*. In a scholarly survey of the field he quotes Cook (1978): 'So far from showing the superiority of children, *most of the hard evidence warrants the opposite conclusion*'. He lists, among other studies which contradict the claim 'younger is better', or express serious doubt, the following: Asubel, D. (1964), Carroll, J.B. (1975), Clark and Clark (1977), Faerch, C. *et al.* (1984), Hatch, E. (1983), Klein, W. (1986), Krashen, S. (1982). (b) For an example of an appealing panacea from the eighteenth century see this notice in the Daily Advertiser, 19 June 1752:

> A Frenchman, a man of learning, is arrived in London from Paris in order to teach the French language ... and the Latin tongue *without exacting any study from his scholars, all study being an obstacle to his method* ... a simple method and one shorter than any which hath been hitherto practised ... enquire at Mr Bezançon's Snuff Shop in Little Earl Street, the Black Boy by the Seven Dials. (quoted in Hawkins 1981)

2 More recent research than Tanner (1967) may suggest that initial hormonal triggers of puberty may actually be detected earlier in boys but the early triggers do not seem to promote a spurt in boys' 'bone age' growth in step with that of girls. Girls' marked earlier spurt in this respect, noted by Tanner, is well attested.

3 Secret garden of the curriculum: The Act of 1944 confirmed a 'daily act of worship' and weekly periods of Religious Education as *obligatory* items in the curriculum of all state primary and secondary schools. Until 1988 this remained the only government intervention in the 'secret garden' of the curriculum (save for Sir Edward Boyle's ill-fated pilot scheme, *French from Eight* 1963–74). The English grammar school was, in this respect, a mirror image of the French lycée, where, in a curriculum largely prescribed centrally, religious teaching was (is) *forbidden by law*. My conclusion is that the introduction of the foreign language earlier could only be justified if it were part of a radical re-think of the whole linguistic preparation that children receive for the language challenges of the secondary curriculum. Unless all learners, and especially boys, are given the tools for foreign language learning at KS2, an early start is likely to lead only to early drop out when the linguistic going gets hard, a pattern with which history has made us familiar.

Further reading

Asubel, D. (1964) 'Adults versus children in second language learning', *Modern Language Journal* 48: 420–24.

Brumfit, C.J. (1991) 'Language awareness in teacher education', in C. James and P. Garrett (eds) *Language Awareness in the Classroom*, London: Heinemann.

Bullock, A. (1975) *A Language for Life*, Report of Committee of Inquiry appointed by the Secretary of State for Education and Science (Margaret Thatcher), London: HMSO.

Burstall, C. (1970) *French in the Primary School, Attitudes and Achievement*, London: NFER.

Burstall, C. *et al.* (1974) *Primary French in the Balance*, London: NFER.

CACE (Central Advisory Council England) (1959) Chair: Sir Geoffrey Crowther, *15 to 18*, London: HMSO.

Candelier, M. (1998) 'L'éveil aux langues à l'école primaire – le programme européen EVLANG, in J. Billiez (dir.) *De la Didactique des Langues au Plurilinguisme. Hommage à Louise Dabène*, pp. 299–308, Grenoble: CDL-Lidilem.

Carroll, J.B. (1975) *The Teaching of French as a Foreign Language in Eight Countries*, New York: Wiley.

Clark, H. and Clark, E. (1977) *Psychology and Language: An Introduction to Psycholinguistics*, New York: Harcourt Brace Jovanovich.

Cook, V. (1978) 'Second language learning: a psycholinguistic perspective', *Language Teaching and Linguistics: Abstracts* 11(2): 73–89. Reprinted in Kinsella (ed.) (1982) *Surveys 1*, Cambridge: Cambridge University Press.

Crosland, A. (1965) Ministry Circular 10/65. *Requesting LEAs to Submit Plans for the Reorganisation of Secondary Education*, London: HMSO.

Crystal, D. (1987) *The Cambridge Encyclopedia of Language*, Cambridge: Cambridge University Press.

Donmall, B.G. (ed.) (1985) *Language Awareness*, NCLE Papers and Reports 6, London: CILT.

Doughty, P.J. *et al.* (1971) *Language in Use*, London: E Arnold.

Faerch, C. *et al.* (1984) *Learner Language and Language Learning*, Clevedon, Avon: Multilingual Matters.

Green, P.S. (1975) *The Language Laboratory in School – Performance and Prediction: The York Study*, Edinburgh: Oliver & Boyd.

Hadow, (Sir) W.H. (1926) Chair: Report of Consultative Committee. Board of Education: *The Education of the Adolescent* and (1931) *The Primary School*, London: HMSO.

Hatch, E. (1983) *Psycholinguistics: A Second Language Perspective*, Rowley MA: Newbury House.

Hawkins, E.W. (1970) 'The A level Syllabus', in C.V. Russell, *Post O-level studies in Modern Languages*, Pergamon Press.

—— (1974) 'Case for a new subject; the study of language', in G. Perren (ed.) *The Space Between*, Reports and papers 10, London: CILT.

—— (1977) 'A possible way forward. Appendix D', in P.H. Hoy (ed.) *The Early Teaching of Modern Languages*, Nuffield Foundation.

—— (1981) (revised edn 1987) *Modern Languages in the Curriculum*, Cambridge: Cambridge University Press.

—— (1984) (revised edn 1987) *Awareness of Language – An Introduction*, Cambridge: Cambridge University Press.

—— (1993) 'Language awareness', in R. Asher and J. Simpson (eds) *The Encyclopedia of Language and Linguistics*, 4: 33–8 , Oxford: Pergamon.

—— (ed.) (1996) *30 Years of Language Teaching*, London: CILT.

HMI (Her Majesty's Inspectorate) (1977) *Matters for Discussion 3. Modern Languages in Comprehensive Schools*, London: HMSO.

Kelly, L.G. (1969) *25 Centuries of Language Teaching*, Rowley MA: Newbury House.

Klein, W. (1986) *Second Language Acquisition*, Cambridge: Cambridge University Press.

Krashen, S. (1982) 'Accounting for child-adult differences in second language rate and attainment', in S. Krashen, R. Scarcella and M. Long (eds) *Child-Adult Differences in Second language Acquisition*, Rowley MA: Newbury House.

Leathes, S. (1918) (Chair) Report of Committee to Prime Minister, '*Modern Studies*'. *The Position of Modern Languages in the Educational System of Great Britain*, HMSO (Cd. 9036).

House of Lords (1990) *Report of Committee on European Schools and Language Learning*, London: HMSO.

MacCarthy, P. (1978) *The Teaching of Pronunciation*, Cambridge: Cambridge University Press.

Mackey, W.F. (1965) *Language Teaching Analysis*, London: Longman.

Mattingley, I.G. (1972) 'Language awareness', in J.F. Kavanagh and I.G. Mattingley *Language by Ear and Eye*, Cambridge MA: MIT Press.

Morwood, J. and Warman, M. (1990) *Our Greek and Latin Roots*, Awareness of Language Series, Cambridge: Cambridge University Press.

Nuffield Languages Inquiry (2000) *Languages and the Next Generation*, Final Report, London: The Nuffield Foundation.

Page, B. (1996) 'The Association for Language Learning (ALL)', in E.W. Hawkins (ed.) *30 Years of Language Teaching*, London: CILT.

Singleton, D. (1998) *Language Acquisition – The Age Factor*, Clivedon, Philadelphia: Multilingual Matters Ltd.

Stern, H.H. (1983) *Fundamental Concepts of Language Teaching*, Oxford: Oxford University Press.

Tanner, J.M. (1967) Contribution to opening chapter, 'Children, their growth and development' in Vol. 1, CACE (1967) idem.

Taunton, (Baron) H.L. (Chair) (1864–8) Schools Inquiry Commission on schools not included in Newcastle Report on elementary education (1861) and Clarendon Report on public schools (1864).

3   Modern Languages
Thirty years of change

Barry Jones

Introduction

In the 1970s the teaching of Modern Languages seemed to be causing Her Majesty's Inspectorate (HMI) concern. Whereas the majority of subjects in secondary schools were taught to all children no matter what their ability, only a proportion of the school population learnt a foreign language. According to an HMI report published in 1977, many comprehensive schools in a survey of eighty-three secondary schools 'restricted the modern language to perhaps 60–80 per cent of the pupils' (DES 1977: 4). The report adds:

> By the fourth secondary year (age 14–15 years), a modern language was optional for the majority of pupils: in all types of school visited during the survey, only slightly more than a third of the pupils in this age group were still engaged in such studies.
>
> (ibid: 8)

Much language learning, if the inspectors are to be believed, was also characterized by some or all of the following features: under-performance in all four language skills; the setting of impossible or pointless tasks for average (and in particular less able) pupils and their abandonment of modern language learning at the first opportunity; excessive use of English and an inability to produce other than inadequate or largely unusable statements in the modern language; inefficient reading skills; and writing limited mainly to mechanical reproduction which was often extremely inaccurate (DES 1977: 8).

Such was the opinion of HMI. A teacher writing in the *Audio-Visual Language Journal* in 1978 described a number of other problems too. He analysed the situation from both his and the pupils' points of view. He wrote:

> I have been in a comprehensive school for over thirteen years, and each year I have taught CSE (Certificate of Secondary Education) classes. It has been very hard work, demanding an inordinate amount of preparation and a great expenditure of energy in an attempt to motivate the apathetic core that exists in every CSE class. But the examinations are always a bitter disappointment

and a derisory return for those children who have shown interest and worked well: a grade higher than 4 is rare, even though the candidates always include children who have the potential for a 1 or 2.

(Richards 1978: 171)

From these two perspectives, pupil motivation and the examinations' system seem to be at least two causes for concern, especially in the teaching of foreign languages to children of moderate ability. The CSE, first introduced in 1965, and the GCE O level (General Certificate of Education Ordinary level) examinations, in existence long before, seemed inappropriate and needed revision.

It was in this context of producing an examination better suited to the needs of learners of all abilities, and of motivating all children aged from 11 to 16, especially those of average and below average ability, that the General Certificate of Secondary Education (GCSE) and Graded Objectives in Modern Languages (GOML) were developed. A combination of the new, joint 16+ examination and the GOML movement was seen by many people as realistic ways of assessing and motivating the whole ability range of pupils in secondary schools.

Graded Objectives in Modern Languages

The Graded Objectives movement achieved its momentum in the late 1970s, early 1980s. It was prompted largely by a feeling among teachers that, in the context of the proposed new 16+ examination, the majority of their pupils could not be expected to sustain their interest and motivation for five years without some formal indications of successful learning.

> The principle of a five year course which must be completed before a public examination could be taken [was considered unacceptable]. The first principle of the graded objectives scheme was therefore that the traditional five year course to CSE/O level should be broken up into a set of shorter-term objectives, each one leading to the next and each one building on its predecessor.
>
> (Harding, Page and Rowell 1980: 3–4)

The second principle of the Graded Objectives movement was that learners should be given worthwhile and realistic tasks to do which were:

- achievable by all abilities of learners;
- known to teachers and learners by being detailed and defined in advance of the tests (hitherto not a feature of CSE or O level where test syllabuses did not exist);
- not related to any particular age of learner;
- specified in a defined syllabus.

A Graded Objectives syllabus (based on the work of Harding 1974: 163–4) was characterized by division into:

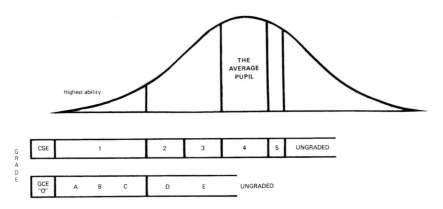

THE CSE EXAMINATION IS DESIGNED TO GRADE 60% OF THE ABILITY RANGE IN EACH SUBJECT

Figure 3.1   A comparison of grades obtained in CSE and O level examinations

- receptive (listening and reading) skills and productive (speaking and writing) skills;
- a list of the topic areas within each skill in which competence would be assessed, e.g. speaking – personal conversation (name, age, address; family, etc.).

By setting objectives which could be completed and assessed every six weeks, or on a weekly basis, or even during a single lesson, teachers found that their classes became keen to achieve the defined goals. Success was rewarded and documented. Progress was rapid. Tasks were short, defined in advance, and appeared very relevant to the learners who were frequently cast in the role of visitor to the foreign country. Certificates were awarded for different levels of achievement and most specified in detail the language competencies which had been successfully demonstrated by the learners. Figure 3.2 shows an example from Cambridgeshire (1982).

Because some GOML syllabuses listed the learning objectives, the language needed to fulfil them and the topics to be covered, teachers and learners had a clear idea of what was to be achieved both linguistically and thematically. The four language skills of listening, reading, speaking and writing were mostly assessed separately and pupils had the possibility of achieving success according to their particular language strengths. Level 1, in most schemes, did not include assessment of writing skills, and limited reading to notices, signs and very short texts, so tended to give even the weaker linguists a chance to prove that they were capable of communicating effectively at an elementary level in a limited but listed range of situations.

Much of the pioneering work of the 1970s was influential in the formulation of the National Curriculum for modern foreign languages.

**HOMERTON COLLEGE
CAMBRIDGE**

**CAMBRIDGESHIRE
COUNTY COUNCIL**

This is to certify that . . . .

of . . . . *School*

has successfully completed a range of tasks in

FRENCH at LEVEL ONE
(Details of the skills and topic areas are listed overleaf.)

Alison E. Shrubsole.
. . . .
Principal, Homerton College

. . . .
Chief Education Officer

Date of award: . . . .

. . . .
Head Teacher

CAMBRIDGESHIRE GRADED OBJECTIVES IN MODERN LANGUAGES

FRENCH   LEVEL ONE

The holder of this Certificate has shown the ability, at a simple level, to cope successfully with the listening and speaking needed to:-

— *make personal contact with a French speaker*

— *talk about themselves, their house and home, free time and interests*

— *ask for similar information in return*

— *ask the way and understand directions*

— *go shopping*

— *order snacks and drinks*

— *express some personal needs*

— *enquire about and express some feelings and to recognise signs related to the above topics.*

Figure 3.2 Level One Certificate from Cambridgeshire (1982); front and back

The GCSE

At the same time as the Graded Objectives movement was establishing itself, the production of a new 16+ examination was being initiated. This new examination was to be an amalgamation of the CSE and GCE O level.

In order that the new syllabuses and examinations should reflect the views of all those involved, including teachers, the first years of the 1980s saw extensive consultation exercises in every subject area. A document published by the Department of Education and Science and the Welsh Office (DES/WO 1983), *Foreign Languages in the School Curriculum: A consultative paper*, was circulated widely to schools, universities, local education authorities, examination groups, professional associations and other interested organizations.

Subject groups were set up by the new Secondary Examinations Council (SEC) to write national criteria for each subject in the school curriculum. The document *GCSE. The National Criteria: French* (DES/WO 1985) was published in the same year as a national guide to the GCSE was commissioned. Referring to the national criteria, the guide, designed specifically for teachers, states:

> The national criteria represent a consensus between the teaching profession, the Examination Boards and Groups, the users of examination results, the Secondary Examinations Council and the Government. The criteria are framed in such a way as to allow considerable freedom to Examining Groups and teachers to develop different syllabuses and schemes of assessment. They are also framed to ensure that the criteria themselves can develop and that curriculum innovation is not stifled.
>
> (Jones 1986: 5)

What then were the main features of a school course which conformed to the national criteria for French? After pilot joint GCE O level and CSE examinations had been trialled in 1987, the first flurry of (Secondary Examinations Council approved) GCSE syllabuses and examinations gave some indication of the changes which had been made. These included content of syllabuses and courses defined in terms of:

1   Role: interviewee, narrator, etc.
2   Settings:

- town and country
- home
- school
- work
- places of entertainment
- places of public transport
- private transport
- at the *Syndicat d'Initiative*
- shops, markets and supermarkets

- cafés and restaurants
- hotels, youth hostels, campsites, holiday homes
- dentist's or doctor's surgery, chemist
- garage and petrol station
- bank and *bureau de change*
- lost property office and police station

3   Topics:

for Basic level

- personal identification
- house and home
- geographical surroundings
- school
- free time and entertainment
- travel
- holidays
- meeting people
- shopping
- food and drink
- weather and seasons
- accommodation

for Higher level

- work and future
- emergencies
- services
- lost property

Within each of these there were precise, specified tasks. In the topic 'weather and seasons', for example, candidates should be able to:

- describe current weather conditions;
- understand people talking about the weather and simple written weather forecasts;
- make comments about the weather in casual conversation;
- talk about the climate of their own country;
- understand simple predictions about weather conditions.

(from Midland Examining Group syllabus 1988)

Each syllabus also contained:

- complete vocabulary lists with words marked for receptive or productive competence;
- lists of structures and grammatical features which were to be taught;

- specimen papers in the four skill areas of listening, speaking, reading and writing;
- assessment procedures and criteria.

The GCSE was thus born.

The National Curriculum for Modern Foreign Languages

In 1988 the GCSE was in its first year. Teachers were beginning to understand how to organize their teaching in terms of specified topics and settings, defined lists of language and divisions into Basic and Higher levels. Coursebooks and collections of audio cassettes had begun to provide 'authentic' materials, and 'authentic' tasks were being devised around them. Most teachers spent time during their summer holidays or during a trip with children collecting 'realia' in the form of tickets, programmes, pamphlets, timetables – all, in the words of the national criteria for French, to 'meet the requirement that material presented to candidates should be carefully selected authentic French' (DES/WO 1985: 3) and, for Basic reading,

> that candidates should be expected, within a limited range of clearly defined topic areas, to demonstrate understanding of public notices and signs (e.g. menus, timetables, advertisements) and the ability to extract relevant specific information from such texts as simple brochures, guides, letters and forms of imaginative writing considered to be within the experience of, and reflecting the interests of, sixteen-year-olds of average ability.
>
> (ibid: 3)

For Higher level reading the criteria state: 'To the range of types of text (listed under Basic reading) will be added magazines and newspapers likely to be read by a sixteen-year-old' (ibid: 3).

Another reform in all schools, both primary and secondary, was, however, just about to bring about even greater changes than those experienced when GCSE came into being. In 1988 Parliament passed the Education Reform Act. This provided for

> the establishment of a National Curriculum comprising core and other foundation subjects, to be taught to all pupils of compulsory school age in maintained schools, for each of which there are to be appropriate attainment targets, programmes of study and assessment arrangements. [The Act defines attainment targets as] the knowledge, skills and understanding which pupils of different abilities and maturities are expected to have by the end of each Key Stage [and programmes of study as] the matters, skills and processes which are required to be taught to pupils of different abilities and maturities during each Key Stage'.
>
> (DES/WO 1990: 1)

The four consecutive Key Stages cover the years of compulsory schooling from 5 to 16, Key Stage 1 being for 5- to 7-year-old children, Key Stage 2 for ages 7 to 11, Key Stage 3 for ages 11 to 14 and Key Stage 4 for ages 14 to 16.

A National Curriculum MFL working group was established in August 1989. This group published its report in July 1990. The report sought to

> represent the [working group's] unanimous view as to how the ambitious goal of making at least one modern foreign language available to virtually every secondary school pupil – and more than one to as many as possible – might be achieved.
>
> (DES/WO 1990: vii)

After a period of wide consultation – the NCC received 562 responses to the working group's final report – a Draft Order and then the Order in its final form were published (DES/WO November 1991), the latter coming into force on 1 August 1992.

To understand what was made statutory, it is perhaps helpful to look at the sections within the Order. These were:

The four Attainment Targets (ATs)

- Listening AT1
- Speaking AT2
- Reading AT3
- Writing AT4

and their associated levels and statements of attainment.

Table 3.1 The development of pupils' ability to communicate in speech

Level	Statements of Attainment	Examples
	Pupils should be able to:	
1	(a) respond very briefly to what is seen or heard	Say 'yes', 'no'; give name and age; name objects and familiar items in pictures
	(b) imitate with approximate pronunciation and intonation	Repeat simple questions, new words and phrases, greetings, numbers 1–10, rhymes, songs, tongue-twisters
2	(a) produce short simple responses to what is seen or heard	Give a simple description of people, places, objects (e.g. colour, size)
	(b) give and find out simple information	Ask and answer simple questions (e.g. about themselves and their families)
		(continued)

Level	Statements of Attainment	Examples
2 (cont.)		
	(c) ask for help with comprehension	Ask for help in relation to the task (e.g. 'I don't understand'; use stock phrases to ask 'What does — mean?', 'What's the (FL) for —?'
3	(a) initiate and respond with intelligible pronunciation using memorized language	Take part in a brief prepared 'first-meeting' conversation with someone of the same age met on holiday
	(b) adapt memorized words and phrases	Vary statements about the opening and closing times of different institutions (e.g. bank/post office … opens/closes at … 10.00/11.00)
	(c) express feelings, likes and dislikes in simple terms	Give short reactions (e.g. 'it's good', 'it's boring', 'I agree'; 'so do I', 'I like/dislike —'
4	(a) initiate and respond in conversation or role-play on familiar topics using appropriate forms of personal address	Ask and answer questions (e.g. about leisure activities or food preferences) using a questionnaire with other pupils and adults
	(b) give a short presentation or prompted talk on everyday activities, interests or future plans	Speak for a short time, using notes or a prepared speech on hobbies, life at home or intended career
	(c) offer simple explanations in response to the question 'Why?'	Give simple reasons for liking/disliking different types of TV programme or school subjects

Source: Department of Education and Science and the Welsh Office (1991) *Modern Foreign Languages in the National Curriculum*, London: HMSO

The Programme of Study

Part I

The headings here gave indications of what was required, namely learning and using the target language. Teachers and learners were therefore expected to use the foreign language in class in all years. This was, perhaps, the aspect of the NC statutory requirements which was considered to be one of the greatest challenges and which led to numerous in-service sessions and a number of publications on the topic.

- developing language learning skills and awareness of language, including the understanding of grammatical features and relationships;
- developing cultural awareness;
- developing the ability to work with others;
- developing the ability to learn independently.

Part II

Here teachers, and their schemes of work, had to ensure that pupils 'explore seven Areas of Experience over the period of each Key Stage'. The Areas of Experience were:

- Area A: everyday activities;
- Area B: personal and social life;
- Area C: the world around us;
- Area D: the world of education, training and work;
- Area E: the world of communications;
- Area F: the international world;
- Area G: the world of imagination and creativity.

(DES/WO 1991: 27)

In order to help teachers meet these statutory requirements, the NCC published non-statutory guidance in the form of a pack of teaching ideas which focused particularly but not exclusively on:

- the Attainment Targets;
- the Programmes of Study;
- using the target language;
- progression and its implementation;
- differentiation and its implementation;
- information technology;
- planning the curriculum;
- managing the curriculum;
- cross-curricular issues.

(NCC 1992)

These and other related issues and practices were discussed, trialled and evaluated by teachers in their departments and in in-service training sessions. Many teachers had three posters supplied by the National Curriculum Council (1992) on the walls of their classroom or department room so that they could remind themselves of:

- examples of Information Technology-related tasks;
- Attainment Targets and Statements of Attainment (which described what pupils should be able to do at each of the ten levels in Listening, Speaking, Reading and Writing);
- Programme of Study Part 1 (learning and using the Target Language) and Part II (Areas of Experience).

Schemes of work were written by school MFL departments so that specific reference was made both to the Programmes of Study and to the expected level(s) of attainment to be reached by pupils in Key Stage 3 (KS3), assessed for the first time in the summer of 1995, and then in KS4 with new GCSE examinations in summer, 1997.

Evidence of pupils' work for KS3 assessment was kept in abundance by teachers uncertain of what and how much would be required for a fair assessment of their pupils' attainment levels at the age of 14. They were also aware that Ofsted inspectors would need to see this evidence during a school inspection, and that parents and school governors had a right to be shown it, if they so requested. Keeping careful records, as well as, at times, pupils' actual work, became essential. Frequently schools would have elaborate systems in place for recording, sometimes week by week, what individual pupils had done in the four Attainment Targets of Listening (AT1), Speaking (AT2), Reading (AT3) and Writing (AT4).

Themes of conferences just before and for a few years after 1 August 1992, when the National Curriculum came into force, are revealing of teachers' concerns and needs. A conference organized by CILT in July 1994 had sessions entitled:

1   The National Curriculum in MFL: what we envisaged (by a member of the NC working party)
2   The NC observed – issues emerging (by an HMI)
3   Differentiation
4   Fun with grammar for all abilities
5   A creative approach to GCSE
6   Activities to extend more able learners
7   Motivating the less able pupil
8   Making assessment manageable
9   Progression: what does it mean in practice?

It is clear from these titles that amongst teachers' concerns at this time were:

- how well they (and their schemes of work) were meeting the requirements of the National Curriculum and to what extent their classroom and school practice reality mirrored what the authors of the Working Party had intended (1);
- how what they were doing in school conformed to the requirements of Ofsted (2);
- how to teach in such a way that they were able to meet the needs of pupils of differing abilities (3, 6 and 7);
- what place grammar was to have in their Modern Language teaching and how to make the teaching of grammar appealing to all learners (4);
- how to include within an essentially transactional and topic-based GCSE syllabus imaginative and creative activities (5 and perhaps 6 and 7);
- how to motivate and challenge both more able and less able pupils, as well as ensure progression, over the five-year course; this was a particular problem with GCSE which had a topic-based syllabus and appeared to require teachers to revisit and revise topics already tackled in earlier years in the two years' run-up to the GCSE examinations at 16 (6, 7 and 9);

- how to assess pupils' attainment – already outlined above – in such a way that disproportionate amounts of time were not spent on keeping evidence and records of pupils' work (8).

An HMI speaker, quoting inspection evidence gathered in 1992 and 1993 from 160 secondary schools, listed amongst others the following gains as a result of the 1991 National Curriculum requirements:

- all pupils were studying a MFL in KS3;
- diversification of languages (German or Spanish) in KS3 had risen from 5 per cent of schools in 1984 to 40 per cent of schools in 1994;
- attainment in Listening and Speaking (AT1 and AT2) had improved;
- simple, accurate written accounts were being produced (AT4);
- teaching was well planned, varied and often included multi-skill activities;
- the use of the target language in class by teachers had 'dramatically increased'.

However, the 'challenges' which were identified emphasized a need for:

- pupil-pupil language use to be extended and developed;
- more extensive reading; this was reported as still limited to coursebooks and/or short texts;
- greater discussion of ideas, and pupils to take the initiative in speaking;
- more activities which would encourage independent work.

Another CILT conference held in November 1994, entitled *Taking the National Curriculum into Key Stage 4*, had as its session titles:

- Differentiation
- Pupil use of the target language
- Reading and creative writing
- Pupil autonomy

thus echoing the concerns already outlined. Response to the NC was generally positive with teachers creatively and imaginatively interpreting its requirements, yet at the same time identifying aspects of their practice for which they needed help and guidance.

Consultation on the 1991 NC took place in Autumn 1993, as a result of which changes were made. As claimed in a pamphlet from the School Curriculum and Assessment Authority (SCAA) in 1994 this was 'in order to make Part I more user-friendly and to slim Part II'.

The main points of change may be summarized as:

- teachers had fewer specified criteria (reduced from 76 points to 39) to take into account when planning schemes of work;

- the four Attainment Targets were slightly renamed: Listening and Responding (AT1), Speaking (AT2), Reading and Responding (AT3) and Writing (AT4);
- linguistic and cultural understanding was linked;
- the section on *how* pupils should be taught was removed;
- the Area of Experience – Area G – relating to The World of Imagination and Creativity was removed. In essence it reappeared in a new Part I which stated that 'pupils should be given opportunities to explore imaginative and creative activities';
- examples for classroom practice – in the opinion of some teachers the element which gave the National Curriculum some meaning in terms of what to do in their lessons – were removed.

The simplified version, *Modern Foreign Languages in the National Curriculum,* was published in January 1995 (DFE/WO 1995). Teachers set about rewriting their schemes of work so that these reflected the revised Programmes of Study and Attainment Level descriptions, a task which took considerable time given the detailed changes in the document. Coursebook writers and publishers published amendments to the ways in which their new wave of coursebooks reflected the revised NC requirements and levels.

The SCAA, chaired by Sir Ron Dearing, published a detailed, 90-page guide to teachers to help them with assessment, entitled *Consistency in Teacher Assessment: Exemplification of Standards* (1996). Since this included examples of pupils' written work as well as an audio cassette of spoken tasks in French, German, Spanish and Urdu, it gave teachers, for the first time in the era of national curriculums, clear, concrete guidance on how to assess their learners.

In 1997, SCAA published a further, 63-page guide, this time 'to help teachers integrate the Programme of Study of the National Curriculum into their scheme of work' (op. cit.: 3). Its particular focus was on 'the skills and understanding that should be developed through the target language'. Its format was very practical with photocopiable pages and numerous examples explaining and exemplifying how to plan for and monitor progression. It also suggested tasks for pupils at all levels of attainment, and made links across the curriculum.

A new GCSE

New GCSE examination syllabuses were in operation from 1995 with the first examinations in 1997 (Short Courses) and 1998 (Full Courses). Teachers found a number of significant features, all of which had to be taken into account when preparing Year 10 and 11 classes.

1   The context for assessment was based on the five Areas of Experience in the National Curriculum and was divided into twelve topic areas. An example from one of the examination boards (London Examinations 1997) was as follows:

- Life at home
- Food and Drink
- Health and Fitness
- School
- Myself, Family and Friends
- Free Time and Social Activities
- Home Town and Local Area
- The Environment and Society
- Further Education and Work
- Language and Communication in the Workplace
- Travel at Home and Abroad
- World Events and Issues

Teachers had, therefore, to ensure coverage of all these twelve topics in both their teaching and their revision.

2   Candidates could use a bilingual dictionary in certain circumstances: not in the listening test but during the preparation period prior to the spoken test; in the reading test and in the writing test. Although some examination boards gave helpful suggestions as to when using a dictionary could help a candidate, teachers realized that the use of a dictionary was a skill which needed careful teaching and practice. In many schools this was started from the first year of secondary school in Year 7.

3   In the oral tests, topics were mapped against the five Areas of Experience. At Foundation and Higher Tier (new names for Basic and Higher Level) tests were in the form of role-plays and general conversation; at Foundation 'candidates aiming at grades D and C [were required] to refer to past, present and future events and to express personal opinions'; at Higher 'to produce longer sequences of speech using a variety of vocabulary, structures and time references in order to express ideas and justify points of view' (London Examinations 1997).

Teachers frequently needed therefore to conduct mock oral examinations in order to cover the syllabus, practise these particular forms of oral testing, ensure the candidates' use of all the appropriate tenses and, in particular, encourage their pupils to express ideas and justify their points of view. Unless these aspects were carefully rehearsed, even competent candidates could be penalized if, for example, they were not given an opportunity by their teacher examiner during the oral test to demonstrate competent use of present, future and past tenses, or to express and *justify* their opinions.

4   Coursework was an option. This involved a new kind of planning and counselling as it was a new activity for both teachers and pupils.

5   Rubrics in the examination were given either by means of pictures or in the target language. The use of English on the examination papers was limited to 10 per cent.

Teachers had therefore to train their learners to understand the target language rubrics and to know how to interpret the icons, some of which were non-topic-specific and some specific to particular topics (for example weather).

Teachers who were responsible for teaching and monitoring classes in school from 1991 to 1997 would, in six years, have had to:

- change their teaching for Years 7 to 11 very radically to meet the requirements of the 1991 NC;
- write schemes of work and devise assessment procedures for use in school post-1991, then revise them extensively after 1995;
- prepare for the new GCSE examinations and change particularly the focus of their work in Years 10 and 11.

These years represented for many teachers a period when little remained static and most aspects of their professional lives were subject to change and were under scrutiny at the same time. Their professional practice was reported on extensively in individual schools' Ofsted inspection reports – Ofsted secondary school inspections started in the 1993–4 academic year – and in other publications such as *MFL Inspected: Reflections on Inspection Findings 1996–97* (Dobson 1998).

Information and Communications Technology (ICT)

In the 1991 National Curriculum, there was a statement that 'all pupils should have opportunities in both Key Stages to develop information technology capability through the programmes of study' (op. cit.: 21). In the 1995 version, this statement was repeated with minor alteration (op. cit.: 1).

Since this time considerable initiatives have focused on helping teachers in all subjects to understand what this might mean in practice. The helpful work of and publications from the National Council for Educational Technology (NCET), renamed the British Educational Communications and Technology Agency (BECTA) (website address http://www.becta.org.uk), have exemplified and continue to illustrate a range of ICT possibilities to be used in the teaching and learning of modern languages.

In 1999 the Teacher Training Agency (TTA) outlined a programme of training to 'equip teachers with the necessary knowledge, skills and understanding to make sound decisions *about when, when not and how to use ICT effectively in teaching particular subjects*' (their emphasis) (TTA 1999: 1). The question being asked is how the use of ICT can *enhance* modern language learning. Guidance and exemplification in the form of recent publications (see, for example, those from CILT) are beginning to show that it can, although some uses of ICT may not be very effective. The TTA cites the government's education strategy and the £230m made available between 1999 and 2002 to support teachers. (op. cit.: 1). There is no doubt that, given sound principles, convincing illustration and a range of examples of imaginative classroom practice, modern languages teachers, like their colleagues in other subjects, will see how to make the most of this powerful resource.

Advanced level

Information sheet 10 published by CILT in December, 1995 is entitled *Guide to the new GCE A- and AS level examinations* (CILT 1995 *New* is in emphasis). In 1995 teachers who taught in 11–18 schools were changing their post-16 practice as well as when teaching Years 7–11. In September 1995, they began to prepare their sixth form, or Year 12 students, for the new AS level examinations in June 1996, and then A level in June 1997.

The AS course was to 'occupy half the study time of an A level course, have the breadth but not the depth of an A level, require learning to the same standard, and provide the core for an A level' (op. cit.) The emphasis in the syllabus was on knowledge of contemporary society and linguistic competence. The examinations were seen as a 'continuum from GCSE and involved an increased use of the target language both by the teacher and by the students'. Of all the changes, that which affected teachers most was that literary and non-literary topics were to be taught and questions answered in the target language. As a subsequent CILT information sheet stated, not unsurprisingly,

> there is some evidence that, when dealing with current affairs and cultural/ sociological/economic topics, students may tend towards extensive *descriptions* rather than *analysis* and reasoned *argument*. We cannot assume that our post-16 students will have acquired the ability to treat a topic *discursively* – whether in a foreign language or, indeed, in their own.
>
> (CILT 1996)

The same CILT publication admitted that the 'present AS level has not succeeded in encouraging students to pursue a broader range of studies' (ibid.) This was a finding in Sir Ron Dearing's Review of Qualifications for 16- to 19-year-olds which appeared in March 1996. A level and AS level syllabuses were again under review.

It was not, however, until 1999 that new AS and A level subject criteria for modern languages were published (QCA 1999). These provided a framework within which the examining boards created their new syllabuses, called, in a changed terminology, 'Specifications'. These came into operation for courses starting in September 2000. Teachers of post-16 students are, at the time of writing, having to organize their Programme of Work to accommodate:

- six modules or units, three to be taken in Year 12 leading to Advanced Subsidiary (AS) level, and three in Year 13 leading to A level (known as A2);
- a coursework option;
- resit possibilities: one resit is allowed per unit.

The more significant changes for a post-16 MFL teacher might be:

- in writing and in speech the students' ability to develop an argument and sustain and justify a point of view is at a premium;

- there is an increased emphasis on grammatical accuracy in all four skill areas;
- themes selected for study (for example as part of the oral component) must all relate to the target language country; this has implications for resources;
- there appears to be an intensive (and short) period to prepare students in Year 12 for the oral component in the AS examinations (September–May);
- no external examiners will be provided, so teachers will have to conduct the oral examinations themselves (statement issued by at least one of the examination boards November 2000);
- students will need to develop a range of study skills because it is clear that there is insufficient time during the post-16 course for the teacher to provide all the materials needed, as well as to assess individual needs, monitor progress and provide detailed feedback. Independent learning skills will be required and, for many students, these may need to be developed and taught explicitly.

Conclusion

Historical descriptions may serve several purposes. Understanding the past often helps explain the present and determine the future. It may also have lessons, both positive and negative, from which we can benefit. Knowing how established practices have developed may help teachers in school and teachers-in-training understand the professional beliefs and performance of others. Topic-based syllabuses, for example, can, in part, be traced back to the Graded Objectives movement where teachers adopted

> a communicative view of language ... to make the linguistic content of a course more relevant to learners' needs [and to] provide the teacher with alternative ways of organising this content into teaching units (e.g. lessons or series of lessons).
>
> (Littlewood 1981: 76)

Readers may wish to go back to the principles which underpinned modern language teaching or to re-evaluate existing methodology. They may wish to compare present practice with the relative optimism of the 1980s, or, as is most likely, to be eclectic in their teaching and evaluate, take and use what they think may work well from other times and other contexts.

Readers may wish to explore the different swings of the pedagogical pendulum that have taken place over thirty years. These have moved from a grammar–translation method to a communicative approach, which, in its practice, sometimes showed a certain reluctance to teach grammar explicitly; then, as is in evidence in the latest version of the National Curriculum (QCA 1999), to a requirement to adopt more overt grammar teaching whilst still retaining an implied context-based syllabus organization. These years show clearly the tensions between what Canale and Swain defined, in 1980, as grammar-based, communication-based and situational approaches (Canale and Swain 1980: 2).

The thirty years also illustrate how, in the first ten to fifteen years of our period, the teachers' voice was clearly audible in many significant developments: in CSE and GCSE Mode III examinations, teachers wrote their own 16+ syllabuses and examination papers; during the Graded Objectives movement many schools in the UK had their own regional syllabuses, tests and certificates mostly devised by teachers for teachers. Gradually, however, government agencies began to control these initiatives and to determine what should be taught, when and to whom. Extensive consultation, especially with the introduction of the first NC, did take place, but this has been less apparent and increasingly less thorough with subsequent versions. School inspection has, of course, always taken place but, since 1993, many new inspectors have been appointed by Ofsted. Clear and detailed criteria for inspectors have been formulated without consultation and inspections have become more rigorous and more frequent. Teachers have become accountable for most of what they do and decreasingly in control of what they teach, how it is taught and how it is assessed.

This chapter has not attempted to outline the theories, where discernible or explicit, behind the changes which have been described. This has been done elsewhere (Pachler 2000). It has, however, attempted a detailed description of perhaps what has affected, in increasingly significant and direct ways the majority of teachers in their day-to-day professional practice.

Postscript – the Nuffield Inquiry and the Council of Europe

In 1998 an independent inquiry, funded by the Nuffield Foundation, was set up to consider the following questions and to make recommendations:

- What capability in languages will the UK need in the next twenty years if it is to fulfil its economic, strategic, social and cultural aims and responsibilities, and the aspirations of its citizens?
- To what extent do present policies and arrangements meet these needs?
- What strategic planning and initiatives will be required in the light of the present position?

(Nuffield Languages Inquiry 1998: 4–5)

Its findings in summary form were:

- English is not enough.
- People are looking for leadership to improve the nation's capability in languages.
- Young people from the UK are at a disadvantage in the recruitment market.
- The UK needs competence in many languages, not just French, but the education system is not geared up to achieve this.
- Government has no coherent approach to languages.
- In spite of parental demand, there is still no UK-wide agenda for children to start languages early.
- Secondary school pupils lack motivation and direction.

- Nine out of ten children stop learning languages at 16.
- University departments are closing, leaving the sector in deep crisis.
- Adults are keen to learn languages, but are badly served by an impoverished system.
- The UK desperately needs more language teachers.

The Inquiry's main proposals were:

- Designate languages a key skill.
- Drive forward a national policy.
- Appoint a languages' supremo.
- Raise the profile of languages.
- Give young children a flying start.
- Improve arrangements in secondary schools.
- Make languages a specified component of the 16–19 curriculum.
- Reform the organization and funding of languages in higher education.
- Develop the huge potential of language learning in adult life.
- Break out of the vicious circle of inadequate teacher supply.
- Establish a national standards framework for describing and accrediting language competence.
- Co-ordinate initiatives linking technology and languages.

(Nuffield Languages Inquiry 2000)

In 2001 the Council of Europe published a Common European Framework for Languages: Learning, Teaching, Assessment (English version: Cambridge University Press; French version: Didier). This unique document is the culmination of work begun in 1971 with the collaboration of many members of the modern languages teaching profession across Europe and beyond. It has been written with two main aims:

1   To encourage practitioners of all kinds in the language field, including language learners themselves, to reflect on such questions as:

- what do we actually do when we speak (or write) to each other?
- what enables us to act in this way?
- how much of this do we need to learn when we try to use a new language?
- how do we set our objectives and mark our progress along the path from total ignorance to effective mastery?
- how does language learning take place?
- what can we do to help ourselves and other people to learn a language better?

2   To make it easier for practitioners to tell each other and their clientèle what they wish to help learners achieve, and how they attempt to do so.

(Council of Europe 2001)

There is to be a Guide (Trim 2001, forthcoming) which highlights questions of relevance to teachers and teacher trainers, designed to promote a principled analysis of our practice as teachers and learners irrespective of the country in which we operate. The same Framework, and related chapters in the Guide, are also addressed to curriculum planners and those responsible for examinations and assessment. Perhaps if we in the UK were to take note of the substantial research and expertise which the Framework document represents then there could be a coherent national policy linked to related assessment procedures, describing and accrediting language competence, and providing coherence and direction in teaching, learning and assessment. Some of the recommendations of the Nuffield Inquiry could then be realized. It is for teachers and all others engaged in modern language teaching and learning to make our voices heard. Nuffield has produced the recommendations and the Council of Europe the Framework; it is for us to produce the action.

Further reading

Canale, M. and Swain, M. (1980) 'Theoretical bases of communicative approaches to second language teaching and testing', in *Applied Linguistics* 1(1), Spring 1980.

Centre for Information on Language Teaching and Research (1995) *Information Sheet 10 Guide to the new GCE A- and AS level examinations*, CILT.

—— (1996) *Information plus 2 Information and issues for teaching GCE A- and AS level examinations*, CILT.

Council of Europe (2001) A *Common European Framework for Languages: Learning, Teaching, Assessment*, Cambridge: Cambridge University Press (English); Didier (French).

Dearing, R. (1996) *Review of Qualifications for 16–19 Year Olds*, SCAA Publications, (March).

Department for Education – Welsh Office (1995) *Modern Foreign Languages in the National Curriculum*, London: HMSO.

Department of Education and Science (1977) *Modern Languages in Comprehensive Schools* (HMI series: *Matters for discussion 3*), London: HMSO.

Department of Education and Science – Welsh Office (1983) *Foreign Languages in the School Curriculum: A Consultative Paper*, London: DES/WO.

—— (1985) *General Certificate of Secondary Education. The National Criteria: French*, London: DES/WO.

—— (1990) *Modern Foreign Languages for Ages 11 to 16*, London: DES/WO.

—— (1991) *Modern Foreign Languages in the National Curriculum*, London: HMSO.

Dobson, A. (1998) *MFL Inspected: Reflections on Inspection Findings 1996/97* CILT.

Field, K. (2000) 'The changing place of Modern Foreign Languages in the curriculum', in K. Field (ed.) *Issues in Modern Foreign Languages Teaching*, London: RoutledgeFalmer.

Harding, A. (1974) 'Defined syllabuses in modern languages', *Audio-Visual Language Journal* 12(3).

Harding, A., Page, B. and Rowell, S. (eds) (1980) *Graded Objectives in Modern Languages*, London: CILT.

Jones, B. (1986) *GCSE French: A Guide for Teachers*, Secondary Examinations Council in collaboration with the Open University, Open University Press.

Littlewood, W. (1981) *Communicative Language Teaching,* Cambridge: Cambridge University Press.

London Examinations, Edexcel Foundation (1997) *GCSE Syllabus MFL Full London Examinations,* London: Edexcel Foundation.

Midland Examining Group (1988) *French Defined Content and Specimen Papers for General Certificate of Secondary Education,* Midland Examining Group.

National Curriculum Council (1992) *Modern Foreign Languages Non-Statutory Guidance,* National Curriculum Council.

Nuffield Languages' Inquiry (1998) *Where are we Going with Languages?* Nuffield Foundation.

—— (2000) *Languages: The Next Generation,* Nuffield Foundation.

Pachler, N., (2000) 'Re-examining communicative language teaching', in K. Field (ed.) *Issues in Modern Foreign Languages Teaching,* London: RoutledgeFalmer.

Richards, D. (1978) 'CSE examinations in Modern Languages: a plea for realism', *Audio-Visual Language Journal* 16(3).

School Curriculum and Assessment Authority (1994) *Commentary on the Revised Proposals for MFL,* pamphlet from School Curriculum and Assessment Authority.

—— (1996) *Consistency in Teacher Assessment: Exemplification of Standards Key Stage 3,* School Curriculum and Assessment Authority.

—— (1997) *Modern Foreign Languages in the National Curriculum Managing the Programme of Study Part 1: Learning and Using the Target Language,* School Curriculum and Assessment Authority.

Teacher Training Agency (1999) *The Use of Information and Communications Technology in Subject Teaching: Identification of Training Needs Secondary Modern Foreign Languages,* Teacher Training Agency.

Trim, J. (ed.) (2001) *A Guide to the Common European Framework for Languages: Learning, Teaching, Assessment* Cambridge: Cambridge University Press (English); Didier (French).

QCA (1999) *June GCE Advanced Subsidiary (AS) and Advanced (A) Level Specifications: Subject Criteria for Modern Foreign Languages,* QCA.

—— (1999) *The National Curriculum for England Modern Foreign Languages,* DfEE/QCA.

4 If you can't beat them ...

The politics and impact of the GCSE and coursework

Julie Adams

> All public forms of assessment attract criticism. Given what is at stake, it would be odd if they did not.
>
> (NATE 1980: 1)

The GCSE, first examined in 1988, was intended to provide a scheme of assessment for examination of the whole ability range at 16+, and this is reflected in its name, amalgamated from the GCE and CSE exams it superseded. The GCE O level was academically abstract, norm-referenced, negatively marked, and tested only the top 20 per cent of the ability range. While the CSE was usually a more viable option for the next 40 per cent of the ability range, it never achieved the currency value of the O level with employers and parents. The GCSE inherited some of the credibility problems of the CSE along with its name, so that barely an exam season goes by without widespread discussion of the GCSE in the media. This chapter therefore examines first the political background to the GCSE and its assessment by coursework. The rest of the chapter then examines the consequences of using coursework as a means of assessment in MFL. This includes looking at the evidence in favour of assessment by coursework, and its particular impact on MFL. It also looks at the way in which writing in Key Stage 4 has changed because of the possibility of assessing it by coursework.

The politics of the GCSE

Although not without its shortcomings, the GCSE in modern languages and other subjects was largely welcomed by teachers who saw it as a fairer and more intrinsically worthwhile mode of assessment. Indeed, in 1989, Ted Wragg described the improvements brought about by the GCSE to the then Prime Minister Margaret Thatcher who is reported to have said: 'Oh good, I'm so glad to hear it and I do so agree with you' (Wragg 1995: 31). In retrospect, the decision of a Conservative government to introduce the egalitarian and innovative GCSE seems surprising – all the more so when set against their later 'back-to-basics' movement. It is not uncommon for writers to use strong language such as 'radical' and 'major development' to describe the introduction of the GCSE, even where they are not being critical (Pimm and Selinger 1995: 48). The political right was almost unanimous in its criticism of the GCSE, and yet it was a right-wing government who had introduced this exam. The (right-wing) Hillgate group explains away this anomaly by saying that 'little trust can be placed on [sic] the GCSE examination – devised as it was by the very educational establishment against which the Government has now been compelled to take legislative measures' (Hillgate 1987: 19). Ball describes how hostility to the GCSE arises from its perceived role in the decline of the education system and therefore ultimately its part in Britain's recession (Ball 1990: 53 and 25). Both he and Gipps describe how the GCSE is seen as lowering the standards at 16+ even though more pupils are taking more examinations than ever before and are achieving higher grades:

> The ... problem seems to be that more pupils are gaining GCSEs than was the case in the old days of O level and CSE. (This of course, was one of the intentions of GCSE.) This has been interpreted as meaning that standards must be falling.
>
> (Gipps 1993: 35)

However, the findings of a SCAA/Ofsted study confirm that there is equivalence of standards across subjects between the GCSE and its O level equivalent from 1975 to 1995 (*TES* 6 December 1996a/b). Despite this it has become an annual ritual, described by the *TES* as 'seasonal silliness' (*TES* 22 August 1997) and by Wragg as 'the Great Annual Educational Paradox' (Wragg 1995: 55), to claim that standards at 16+ have fallen, and programmes such as Channel 4's *Dispatches* even make allegations of exam-rigging (*TES* 13 June 1997).

The politics of coursework

The introduction of the GCSE also saw the inclusion of coursework as a regular feature of 16+ assessment, although it had already been a feature of some CSE syllabuses. If the GCSE itself has attracted criticism, then assessment by coursework, described by Scott as one of its 'four key elements' (Scott 1989: 9), has been even more contentious. Ball describes 'the exposition of polarities' where educational initiatives are divided into the 'sacred' and 'profane', with both GCSEs and coursework belonging to the 'profane' (Ball 1990: 45). What is perhaps surprising is the level of excitement that the use of coursework as an assessment tool creates, such as The *Times* branding GCSE coursework a 'cheat's charter' (The *Times* 26 October 1996). Coursework was re-evaluated in the 1996 Dearing Review of the KS4 curriculum, when the maximum amounts of coursework were restricted in favour of terminal examinations. Whilst many in education have become used to interference from above in the curriculum (Watkins 1993: 81), it still seems surprising that the then Prime Minister John Major should have involved himself directly in the minutiae of school-based assessment. Watkins believes that Major's intervention to limit the amounts of coursework showed 'no understanding why coursework is so important and pedagogically, particularly for girls. He has ignored the importance of the motivation it provides for pupils throughout their two-year course' (Watkins 1993: 81). Gipps feels strongly that cutting the amount of coursework had little to do with pedagogical considerations and was more about political objectives:

> All in all, this looks like regression flying in the face of 'expert' opinion, that now derided commodity. What lies behind it is the belief from the right, particularly the Centre for Policy Studies, that the only appropriate form for high status examinations is the one we have had in the past in that 'golden age' we all remember when education served us so well – the terminal unseen examination.
>
> (Gipps 1993: 34)

Moreover an interview that Ball conducted with former Secretary of State for Education, Sir Keith Joseph, suggests that coursework was an unintentional innovation:

> I invented the GCSE, I invented the differentiation. I said I'd only agree to unify the two examinations provided we established differentiation, and now I find that unconsciously I have allowed teacher assessment, to a greater extent than I assumed.
>
> (Ball 1990: 174)

This might partially explain the later about-turn of the Conservative government on coursework. Quicke explains how the use of coursework has fuelled the arguments of those claiming a drop in standards since the introduction of the GCSE:

> it is alleged not only that the content [of the GCSE] is easier but also that methods of assessment have favoured girls. Thus, for example, the 'hardworking but not too bright' girl does better because coursework now counts for more.
>
> (Quicke 1998: 229)

This implies that any serious consideration of the GCSE is not really complete without a discussion of the role that assessment by coursework plays in teaching, learning and testing in the KS4 curriculum.

In defence of coursework

It is not difficult to find supporting evidence for coursework as a means of assessment: Gipps (1993: 33), Palmer (1970), City and Guilds (1984) and Burke (*TES* 26 September 1986) all point to the fact that 'assessment motivation' is spread over a longer period rather than just before the terminal examinations, thus avoiding 'the intense psychological pressure created by examinations' (Palmer 1970: 57). SEC feels that this 'can offer a fairer treatment to the hard-working pupil whose attainment never receives proper credit in formal examinations because of the anxiety they bring about' (SEC 1985: 4).

But what evidence is there that coursework is a desirable form of assessment? There are occasional calls to end the system of matriculation at 16+ (Bird and Dennison 1987: vii, *TES* 4 July 1997a) and the 'expensive and bureaucratic' GCSE (*TES* 4 July 1997b). These views would seem to argue for a greater prominence to be given to forms of 'hidden assessment' such as coursework, which assess work that the pupils would have been doing anyway. Some of the suspicion directed towards coursework could be a reflection of the view that disembedded learning has more value than situated cognition (Lave 1988). And yet, those qualities that coursework is said to promote, such as meeting deadlines, organizing one's own work, research skills and so on, are the very qualities sought by potential employers. Ball says that 'the introduction of the GCSE, with its emphasis on coursework and project work, received a unanimous vote of support from those speaking for industry' (Ball 1990: 107). He goes on to say: 'process assessments [among others] ... enable a greater range of the students' behaviours to be made public and to be made subject to assessment' (Ball 1990: 127).

One advantage of continuous assessment is that it can reward 'the process of a learner's learning' (Page and Hewett 1983: 24 and Palmer 1970: 57), rather than just the end-product. This reflects the view that periodic assessment permits '"assessment motivation" [to be] spread evenly throughout the course and not relegated to the last few months or weeks' (Palmer 1970: 58). If, as Parr says, good practice in assessment usually involves 'gathering evidence over time and making judgements about it based on clear criteria' (Parr 1997: 2), then continuous or periodic assessment allows the teacher to collect a 'better quality' of evidence. This is reflected in the National Curriculum which demands a 'rounded judgement' based on the pupil's performance 'across a range of contexts' (SCAA 1996: 2). Unfortunately, continuous assessment is frequently misunderstood (Thorogood 1992: 18 and Page and Hewett 1987: 24) and instead becomes 'continual testing, which has obvious disadvantages' (CILT 1970: 70–1).

There is a wide consensus that coursework creates fairer assessment as it offers wider coverage than terminal examinations:

- it avoids arbitrary sampling (Palmer 1970: 57);
- [coursework] requires coverage of a wider part of the syllabus rather than 'topic-spotting' for an exam (Gipps 1993: 33);
- some skills and knowledge, especially those related to processes and methods of work, cannot be appropriately assessed in a terminal examination .... Coursework assessment is ideally suited to the setting of real-life tasks and problems (City and Guilds 1984: 4, 7);
- coursework may increase the reliability of the assessment by providing wider evidence of the candidate's achievement demonstrated on different occasions in samples of work which more fully represent the range of assessable abilities (SEC 1985: 5).

Conversely both Palmer (1970: 58) and Horton consider that coursework can adversely affect the achievement as 'a significant percentage of the final grade could be awarded at an early stage, misrepresenting ability at the termination of the course' (Horton 1987: 48). This may not be a problem in GCSE MFL as all boards permit the submission of the best pieces of coursework from any point in the GCSE course.

There is also widespread concern over the reliability and integrity of coursework assessment; the introduction of the GCSE roughly coincided with greater account-ability in education via the public mechanisms of examination league tables, publication of inspection findings and 'naming and shaming'. Therefore it could be argued that, if teachers are involved in the assessment of their own pupils, there might be a tendency to err on the side of generosity. Palmer thinks 'malpractice (copying and plagiarism) is easier to get away with' in coursework and therefore necessitates some form of control such as a *viva* (Palmer 1970: 58). Continuous assessment has earned the reputation of being 'necessarily subjective' whilst examinations are seen as 'potentially more reliable especially with "objective" methods' (Palmer 1970: 56–9). This, however, does not take account of the fact that all decisions on performance are ultimately subjective, whether that decision is taken by a teacher carrying out continuous assessment, an external examiner, or even an Ofsted inspector.

The impact of GCSE and coursework on MFL

Despite claims that the GCSE, for the first time, provided suitable assessment for the whole ability range at age 16, it still contained a great deal of differentiation. This seems little more than the 'sheep and goats' divide that used to happen in the pre-GCSE patterns of examining, and Roberts states: 'Underneath the rhetoric of equality lurks a two-tier system reminiscent of the old GCE/CSE divide' (Roberts 1992: 24). For example, the GCSE 'Short Course' supposedly diversifies provision via an exam which is supposed to be half the amount (i.e. content), not half the level of difficulty. Unfortunately the short course has often been inappropriately targeted at the less able, rather than used as an opportunity for curriculum enrichment (by allowing pupils to study two languages in less curriculum time). Both the 'Full' GCSE and the 'Short Course' contain tiered papers in each examined skill. The tiers use different question types with more straightforward assessment methods in the foundation tier, such as simple recognition of language, whereas the higher tier contains more complex questions such as drawing of inferences and more target language questioning. Even in assessment by coursework, there is differentiation by both task and outcome.

In the British educational context, foreign languages have long been seen as a 'difficult' subject and it has not been uncommon for pupils to achieve a lower grade in languages than they do for other subjects (Bird and Dennison 1987: 10, DfEE 1996: 4). Clark says that pupils questioned in her research 'singled out [MFL] as an area of difficulty', and 36 per cent of pupils ranked MFL their most difficult subject, while 62 per cent placed it in their top three (out of ten) for difficulty (Clark 1998b:

32). Pachler and Field (1997: 142) believe that in the past much of the blame for this lay with the examination system:

> the emphasis on formal grammatical accuracy characterising GCE 'O' level and CSE examination syllabi has been said to have contributed to a lack of pupils' success in MFL and a lack of popularity of the subject amongst pupils at secondary school.
>
> (Pachler and Field 1997: 142)

Similarly, Littlewood reports that the then Secretary of State for Education reacted 'with "yawning despair" (her own words) ... [and] went on: "The present ... syllabuses are almost calculated to put the average child off language learning altogether"' (Littlewood 1989: 6).

The GCSE in modern languages – based on a communicative, topic-based approach to learning *authentic* language – was a radical departure from the old O level (although some CSE syllabuses had similar features). Although success in the GCSE still depended on much rote-learning, now it was at least contextualized. Like both the CSE and Graded Objectives in Modern Languages (GOML), the GCSE is positively marked. It had long been part of staff room lore that, to learn how the O level worked, you had to become an examiner. The advent of the GCSE meant that there were no longer any secrets about the way in which marks were awarded: exemplification materials and mark schemes were readily available, and boards held training meetings for teachers. Moreover, boards published syllabuses which contained not just details of the scheme of the assessment, but detailed lists of the vocabulary, notions and functions to be tested at each level in each topic area.

Clark (1998a: 1) believes the GCSE has had a 'significant impact' on the teaching of modern languages, but whilst there has been a steady rise in the numbers of pupils studying a language to 16 and succeeding in the GCSE, 'the achievements of girls far outstrip the boys'. As already mentioned, there is a widespread belief that coursework has played a major part in boosting girls' achievements at GCSE and A level:

> It has been suggested that boys would have been just fine if there had been no introduction of GCSE examinations or a National Curriculum in the mid to late 1980s. ... But changing both the curriculum and assessment methods tipped the balance unfairly in the direction of the girls.
>
> (Pickering 1997: 79)

It follows then, that as coursework becomes a more prominent feature of MFL assessment, it might be reasonable to assume that girls will be even further advantaged in their MFL studies. However, Elwood and Comber strongly refute this:

> There is a widespread perception that girls' success in the GCSE can be solely accounted for by their success in the coursework elements of examinations. Further investigations into this issue at GCSE showed this not to be the case ....

The same questions regarding gender, coursework, and performance have been asked in relation to the A level ... What seems to be evident from the data ... is that coursework contributes less to the overall grade for females than it does for males. Females perform slightly better at coursework than males, but it is the examination papers that contribute most to their overall performances.

(Elwood and Comber 1995, quoted in Pickering 1997: 80)

The questions raised by assessment by coursework range even further than gendered achievement. The cumulative nature of language acquisition raises questions about the suitability of continuous assessment for MFLs, in addition to those of reliability, flexibility and arbitrary sampling faced by all subjects. In the GCSE MFL, terminal examinations and continuous assessment are usually offered with complete parity, although they may in fact measure very different things. This is reflected in Page and Hewett's view of GOML; they believe that changing the *method* of assessment had an impact on the *content* of the assessment:

> possibly for the first time, the wider educational – one might say moral – implications of a system like this are set down as quite conscious goals which learners are encouraged to pursue: not only 'coping with problems', 'organising the tasks', 'using pair strategies', but also 'being polite', 'working co-operatively', and 'presenting material neatly'. In this way the planners of the scheme show again that they see pupils not only as language learners but as whole individuals, and language learning as having an effect on their development as individuals.
>
> (Page and Hewett 1987: 37)

This is reflected more recently in the AQA GCSE syllabus from 1996 which included in its list of aims: 'encourage positive attitudes to foreign language learning and to speakers of foreign languages and a positive approach to other cultures and civilisations' (AQA 1999: 3). It also states that some of these 'cannot readily be translated into measurable objectives' (AQA 1999: 2). It can be argued that the conditions for writing under coursework are more conducive to the investigation of cultural aspects of the language (Adams 1998: 4 and 19).

The shift towards communicative competence in MFL teaching demanded assessment more geared towards performance, i.e. the learner's ability to communicate. However, teaching pupils to perform well in such communicative tasks often occurred at the expense of grammatical and structural development. Kalantzis *et al.* propose that a true measure of communicative competence in the active skills is not just a measure of the overall performance, but also the strategies and skills used in the process of performing that task (Kalantzis *et al.* 1990: 206). It is worth considering whether holistic competence in MFLs can be reduced to separate skills, although the experience of the O level, GCSE, GOML and CSE would seem to dictate that the key skill in examination success is memory and rote-learning, whether that is applied to lexis or grammatical constructions. This leads to the question of whether coursework is a good test of holistic and communicative competence.

The current conception of GCSE coursework would appear to be based less on *continuous* assessment and more on *periodic* assessment of writing (though this does not mean to imply that either form of assessment has more validity than the other) (Adams 1998: 3). Page and Hewett point out that 'performance of the task at any given moment does not guarantee that the learner could still perform the task at a later date'. They go on to remind us that 'this is, of course, true of all assessment, even of the most traditional sort' (Page and Hewett 1987: 29). If the purpose of MFL assessment is to 'assess whether a learner can perform a particular task using language' (Page and Hewett 1987: 24), it should make little difference whether the candidate is assessed now or later. The main difference here becomes one of memory. However, performance in examination conditions is still seen as being the 'gold standard' of linguistic performance, as one GCSE Chief Examiner quoted here implies: 'The purist in me dictates that any linguist worth their salt could write under exam conditions' (Adams 1998: 3).

Coursework assessment in MFL

In the early years of the GCSE teachers of some subjects could conduct up to 100 per cent of their assessment by coursework, and '100 per cent coursework' was a popular choice for GCSE English Language and Literature, for example. MFL teachers became accustomed to pupils using coursework deadlines in other subjects to excuse their lack of MFL homework, and for this reason alone many welcomed the introduction of coursework into MFL as it helped to establish their subject on an equal footing with others: 'If you can't beat them, join them!' However, MFL was excluded from the introduction of coursework in the 1980s, and continued to be assessed by 100 per cent terminal examination. This meant that success in MFL examinations continued to be very reliant on formulaic rote-learning and retentive memory.

As early as 1970, the Schools Council (Working Paper 28: 24) recommended a new pattern of language study in the sixth form in that students should present a module of coursework, possibly based on a well-planned study visit to the country or an area of cultural comparison, and many teachers chose to use continuous assessment under CSE Mode III (Palmer 1970: 59), and the GOML scheme. Despite this prior experience, the first significant appearance of MFL coursework in public examinations was not until 1992 when the new SEG Modular GCSE allowed for continuous assessment of work that pupils were carrying out in the class. This was reflected by a module of coursework in some of the A level sylla-buses of the mid-1990s. So it is not clear why the Dearing review of 1996 suddenly included coursework for MFL, after having excluded it for ten years, at a time when all other subjects were having their total proportions of coursework reduced. One possible interpretation of this is that the introduction of innovative assessment methods into MFL coincided with the weakening of its position in the KS4 curric-ulum, i.e. (cynically) MFL is not really an important subject, so it does not really matter how you assess it.

The 1996 restrictions on the amount of coursework also applied to MFL, where the submission of a maximum of 30 per cent of coursework in place of terminal examinations was to be permitted. Given that GCSE MFL is organized around four skills which each account for 25 per cent of the result, a figure of 30 per cent does not fit easily. SEG decided to retain its modular GCSE, albeit in a modified form, which incorporated the maximum permitted 30 per cent coursework assessment and the compulsory requirement of 50 per cent by terminal examination. The other GCSE boards decided to offer coursework in writing as an alternative to the writing paper in the terminal examination. The London board/Edexcel also offered the choice of speaking or writing to be offered for the coursework element, but this option is available in only three languages, and is not widely taken up. Although it is possible to advance many of the same arguments for assessment of speaking by coursework as are used here for writing, there still seems to be no easy solution to the management of multiple cassettes of pupil performance from across the GCSE course. Coursework is now a familiar feature of A level syllabuses, so assessment by coursework in KS4 can only help to prepare pupils effectively for later study.

The results of those cohorts being assessed by coursework do seem to show clear improvement: in research carried out with MFL teachers in London in 2000, without exception they believed that coursework had had a beneficial effect on their GCSE results 'even the first time they tried it' (Adams 2000: 5). This kind of improvement can be accounted for by pedagogic features, and the London teachers all pointed out that the greater freedom offered by coursework assessment helped them to improve many aspects of their practice as well as improved results. Perhaps surprisingly, interviewees said that doing written coursework had helped to improve pupils' oral work (Adams 2000: 18).

However, Horton (1987) and Palmer point out how 'the demands [of coursework] on the teacher are much greater' (Palmer 1970: 58) and could lead to overload: 'From the outset, however, a major concern must be to ensure that coursework is integrated into the curriculum and does not become a sudden and unwelcome burden on pupils and their teachers' (SEC 1985: 8). The teachers in the London research had all willingly taken on assessment by coursework and were keen to continue with it. This is an important point as teachers choose whether or not to do GCSE coursework in the first place, they choose the exam board, they select the tasks (even in those syllabuses where the exam boards provide a bank of tasks), they decide which pupils are entered for GCSE and they assess their own pupils' writing. So at a time when teachers and their unions are boycotting certain administrative tasks, they willingly choose to take up the extra workload of assessment by coursework. Buckby provides a further clue from the GOML years as to why teachers should be willing to do this:

> The practice of setting short-term, realistic targets, with each unit of work rewarded by a certificate not only proved very motivating for pupils, but also engaged the enthusiasm and professional commitment of their teachers, who felt empowered by the [GOML] scheme.
>
> (Buckby 1981: 45)

Although MFL teachers were not doing coursework in the early years of the GCSE, many were assessing the oral component of the GCSE terminal examination, therefore allocating 25 per cent of the total marks, so the principles of the kind of assessment required in coursework were not new to them.

Beyond the baguette – the impact of coursework on MFL writing

> Virtually all other schemes rejected writing as a skill to be taught and assessed in the earlier levels because it did not seem to be a sufficiently communicative objective. The writing of pen-friend letters, for example, was assumed to be appropriate for later levels only. Even where schemes have set up Mode 3 CSE or O level equivalents, writing has frequently still been omitted because of the difficulty of finding suitable communicative tasks. The new GCSE requires a test in writing for the higher grades and there the tasks almost always consist of writing letters or postcards or leaving short written messages. The range of activities is fairly limited.
>
> (Page and Hewett 1987: 26)

Swarbrick borrows the term a 'retreat from print' to describe the recent history of writing in MFL (Swarbrick 1994: 142, 127). Previously writing dominated the O level as it was used in a variety of language performances such as translation, dictation, composition and comprehension questions. Indeed, until the advent of the 'alternative O levels', it was not uncommon for O levels to have no oral/aural element at all. Conversely, in the GOML schemes writing was often omitted completely (OMLAC 1981: 74). Similarly the level of attainment in writing at CSE level was so low that it was questioned whether it was worth doing at all (Dyson 1970: 27). The pattern of the weakening of the importance of writing continued with the introduction of the GCSE. Taking a paper in writing was compulsory only for grades C and above, a factor which M'Caw found detrimental:

> An examination which denigrates or neglects the importance of writing in the target language and comprehending how this language works may be well-intentioned, and may succeed in making things easier for the G,F,E, or even D candidates. But it is extremely unkind, and indeed unfair, to those pupils who expect a Grade C or higher, for they will be at a disadvantage later on at A level, when they find themselves with only the very basic writing skills.
>
> (M'Caw 1987: 86)

Writing was re-introduced as a compulsory element of the post-Dearing GCSE which may also provide clues for the belated decision to include coursework in the GCSE MFL – if writing was to be compulsory for all pupils, then alternative modes of assessment might need to be offered. Watkins provides a clue to the potential impact of assessing MFL writing via coursework rather than terminal examination and says that in other subjects there is evidence of 'the skills such as drafting and writing an extended essay which can be tested in no other way' (Watkins 1993: 81). Clark argues that much of the writing in the MFL classroom might be 'alienating for boys' with its choice of letter writing/penfriend scenarios which are 'more likely to appeal to girls and the ways in which they have been socialised' (Clark 1998a: 31). To counter this she suggests 'the inclusion of alternative writing tasks which might be 'more motivating for boys'. The use of coursework for the assessment of writing at GCSE allows for the inclusion of a far wider set of topics and tasks than is possible with the comparatively limited repertoire of the terminal examination' (Adams 1998: 4, 19). Early research evidence points to increased motivation and improved standards in MFL writing assessed by coursework (Adams 1998, CILT Motivation conference and Adams 2000). Writing under coursework conditions (rather than in terminal examinations) allows for the inclusion of tasks which no longer have to 'fulfil the criterion of authenticity' (Lee and Dickson 1989: 70). Lee and Dickson go on to say:

> If we look further, though, than the context of letters … or variations on the theme of correspondence … we can find other activities which not only provide pupils with opportunities to learn and practise a range of skills (writing and other skills) but which also have a separate, inherent purpose.
>
> (Lee and Dickson 1989: 70)

Conclusion

It is unlikely that coursework and the GCSE will ever be entirely free of accusations of 'profane' practice, such as claims that an English teacher wrote her own pupils' coursework (The *Guardian* 11 July 2000). Hopefully, empirical research will continue to strengthen the evidence of coursework's role as a positive element in teaching and learning. In the London research, the teachers contrasted the weaknesses of their practice when preparing candidates for the terminal exam in writing (rote-learning of hypothetical penfriend letters) with the wider range of approaches they were able to adopt under assessment by coursework. If we are to retain the interest of Year 9 pupils and motivate them to succeed in KS4, then we should heed Fried-Booth's advice and take advantage of the greater range of activities that assessment by coursework offers:

> Great advances can be made by the beginner, but at intermediate level the student often reaches a 'plateau', from which there is little incentive to move on. It is at this crucial point in learning – the intermediate level – that project work can offer the much-needed incentive.
>
> (Fried-Booth 1986: 8)

References

Adams, J. (1998) *On Course for GCSE Coursework*, London: CILT.

—— (1998) 'Motivation in Writing', paper given at CILT Motivation conference, 6 March 1998, London.

—— (2000) 'Raising Standards in MFL writing through GCSE coursework', in *Raising Standards in Modern Languages* 8, Studies in Modern Languages Education, April 2000.

AQA (1999) *GCSE Syllabus for 2001 and 2002 Modern Languages*, Manchester: Assessment and Qualifications Alliance.

Ball, S. (1990) *Politics and Policy Making in Education: Explorations in Policy Sociology*, London: Routledge.

Bird, E. and Dennison, M. (1987) *Teaching GCSE Modern Languages*, London: Hodder & Stoughton.

Buckby, M. (1981) *Graded Objectives and Tests for Modern Languages: An Evaluation*, London: Schools Council.

Chitty, C. and Simon, B. (eds) (1993) *Education Answers Back: Critical Responses to Government Policy*, London: Lawrence and Wishart.

CILT Reports and Papers 4 (1970) 'Examining Modern Languages', abridged proceedings of a conference held at State House, 19/20 March 1970, London: CILT.

City and Guilds (1984) *Coursework Assessment*, London: City and Guilds of London Institute.

Clark, A. (1998a) *Gender on the Agenda*, London: CILT.

—— (1998b) 'Resistant boys and modern languages', in Clark and Millard (1998a), op. cit.

Clark, A. and Millard, E. (eds) (1998) *Gender in the Secondary Curriculum: Balancing the Books*.

de Jong and Stevenson (1990) *Individualizing the Assessment of Language Abilities*, Clevedon: Multilingual Matters.

DfEE (1996) *Statistical Bulletin*, London: HMSO.

Dyson, A. (1970) 'CSE Mode III examinations in modern languages', in CILT Reports and Papers, no. 4, op. cit.

Elwood, J. and Comber, C. (1995) 'Gender differences in A level examinations: the reinforcement of stereotypes quoted', in Pickering (1997), op. cit.

Fried-Booth, D. (1986) *Project Work*, Oxford: OUP.

Gipps, C. (1993) 'Policy-making and the use and misuse of evidence', in Chitty and Simon (1993), op. cit.

The *Guardian* (11 July 2000) 'Fiddling the figures to get the right result'.

The Hillgate Group (1987) *The Reform of British Education*, London: Hillgate Group.

Horton, T. (1987) *GCSE: Examining the New System*, London: Harper & Row.

Kalantzis, M., Slade, D. and Cope, B. (1990) 'Minority languages and mainstream culture: problems of equity and assessment', in de Jong and Stevenson (1990), op. cit.

Lave, J. (1988) *Cognition in Practice: Mind, Mathematics and Culture in Everyday Life*, Cambridge: CUP.

Lee, B. and Dickson, P. (1989) *Assessment in Action: A Guide for Language Teachers*, Slough: NFER.

Littlewood, W. (ed.) (1989) *Developing Modern Language Skills for GCSE*, Walton-on-Thames: Thomas Nelson.

M'Caw, G. (1987) 'Modern languages', in J. North (ed.) (1987) *The GCSE: An Examination*, London: Claridge Press.

National Association of Teachers of English (NATE) (1980) *Coursework in English: Principles and Assessment*, NATE Examinations Booklet no. 3.

Oxfordshire Modern Languages Advisory Committee (OMLAC) (1981) *New Objectives in Modern Language Teaching*, London: Hodder & Stoughton.

Pachler, N. and Field, K. (eds) (1997) *Learning to Teach Modern Languages in the Secondary School*, London: Routledge.

Page, B. and Hewett, D. (1987) *Languages Step by Step: Graded Objectives in the UK*, London: CILT.

Palmer, B. (1970) 'The use and efficacy of continuous assessment', in CILT Reports and Papers 4 (1970), op. cit.

Parr, H. (1997) *Assessment and Planning in the MFL Department*, London: CILT.

Pickering, J. (1997) *Raising Boys' Achievement*, Stafford: Network Educational Press Ltd.

Pimm, D. and Selinger, M. (1995) 'The commodification of teaching: teacher education in England', in F. Wideen and P. Grimmett (1995), op. cit.

Quicke, J. (1998) 'Gender and underachievement: democratic educational reform through discourse evaluation' in A. Clark and E. Millard (1998a), op. cit.

Roberts, A. (1992) *Modern Languages in the National Curriculum: The Harris Report in Perspective* (Occasional Paper no. 1), London: University of London Institute of Education.

SCAA (1996) *Consistency in Teacher Assessment, Exemplifications of Standards in Modern Foreign Languages: Key Stage 3*, London: SCAA.

Schools Council (1970) *New Patterns in Sixth Form Modern Language Studies* (Working Paper no.28), London: Evans Brothers/Methuen Educational Limited.

Scott, D. (1989) *The GCSE: An Annotated Bibliography and an Introductory Essay*, Warwick: University of Warwick.

Secondary Examinations Council (SEC) (1985) *Coursework Assessment in GCSE*, London: SEC.

Swarbrick, A. (ed.) (1994) *Teaching Modern Languages*, London: RoutledgeFalmer.

Times Educational Supplement (TES) (26 September 1986) 'Putting teachers back in charge'.

—— (6 December 1996a) 'Have standards stood the test of time?'.

—— (6 December 1996b) 'Report on exam defies pessimists'.

—— (13 June 1997) 'TV exam-rigging claim ruled unfair'.

—— (4 July 1997a) 'A GCSE in thinking aloud'.

—— (4 July 1997b) 'Trade in for a new model'.

—— (22 August 1997) 'Seasonal silliness'.

Thorogood, J. (1992) *Continuous Assessment and Recording*, London: CILT.

The *Times* (26 October 1996) 'Pupils view GCSE coursework as a cheat's charter'.

Watkins, P. (1993) 'The National Curriculum – an agenda for the nineties', in Chitty and Simon (1993), op. cit.

Wideen, F. and Grimmett, P. (eds) (1995) *Changing Times in Teacher Education: Restructuring or Reconceptualization*, London: Falmer.

Wragg, E. (1995) *The Ted Wragg Guide to Education*, Oxford: Butterworth–Heinemann.

Part 2
MFL, schools and society

5   Stereotypes, prejudice and tolerance

Michael Byram and Karen Risager

The language teaching profession often has an ambivalent attitude to the affective dimension of language learning. Although much lip-service is paid to the promotion of 'tolerance', textbooks on language learning tend to concentrate on what is known about the cognitive acquisition of a language system. Although statements of aims for language teaching by ministries of education and the like sometimes refer to the promotion of positive attitudes – this is the case in England though not in Denmark – it is left to the individual teacher to make something of this and chance occurrence of anecdote or chance expression of stereotypes are frequently the only basis for any steering of or influence on learners' affective development.

Yet the notions of European integration and of European identity, however undefined they may be, obviously pre-suppose some affective change in future European citizens, young or old. Integration does not necessarily mean uncontested harmony nor conflict-free tolerance, but it does pose a challenge to all educationists, and language teachers in particular, to address prejudice towards others, whether they are of another country, another race, another gender, another social class, another religion, or whatever the basis of their otherness.

The education and training of language teachers seldom address these issues and most have to work out their position and their methods for themselves. English and Danish language teachers tend to differ in their views on how 'positive' or 'realistic' an image of the target-language country they should promote. In interviews we were able to ask them, on the other hand, how they respond to negative images, particularly in the form of stereotypes.

We also have seen how some teachers stress the importance of the general educational effect of language learning and the need to make links with other subjects in the curriculum and with young people's experience of all kinds of otherness in their lives beyond the classroom. In discussing specifically the question of attitudes, one Danish teacher expressed this general educational dimension by comparing foreign language teaching with first language teaching:

> I see my task in language teaching more and more similar to teaching Danish, which is a learning about our reality. And we do that in English too. And that has changed from, if I look back ten or fifteen years, when it was as if English was like a box for itself. It isn't like that any more. I simply wouldn't think I was

doing things properly, if I didn't include the foundation, or the feelings about what is happening [around us].

(DK 114, f, 40, En)

Therefore in this chapter we shall focus on what teachers said in interviews about their handling of stereotypes and related attitudinal or affective issues, how systematically they include this in their work, what methods they use and what learning effects they hope for.

National stereotypes and the process of European integration

Previously we gave an account of teachers' attitudes to the process of European integration and the European dimension in education. Here we shall focus in particular on how teachers view the development in Europe with respect to pupils' possible development of tolerance towards other European countries.

Some of the Danish teachers have a relatively optimistic view of this in so far as they say that prejudices and stereotypes are above all directed at immigrants and refugees in Denmark, not people from other European countries.

[Question: There are those who say that European integration means that tolerance among European peoples grows. What do you think about this?] Yes, you could well think that … When they criticise someone, then as we all know it is mostly refugees and foreign workers. It's not the European Union.

(DK 48, f, 50, Ge, En and Fr)

It is perhaps worth noting here that such a statement pre-supposes that the populations in European countries, or the European Union, are culturally homogeneous, i.e. not multicultural in themselves and include various groups of ethnic minorities.

Another Danish teacher thinks that the pupils do have prejudices but that these are on a humorous level and don't need to be taken seriously:

[Question: What about attitudes to the other Europeans?] But there's nothing negative there. Well, we have these prejudices, – statements from time to time, you do it yourself a little, when you want to make a joke at others' expense. But otherwise.

(DK, 520, m, Ge, En, and Fr)

One English teacher says much the same: 'I tend to find that most of the time the majority of pupils don't really believe them anyway. I think they are intelligent to realise it's just a standing joke really, you know' (UK 88, m, 20, Fr and Ge). Whereas one Danish teacher thinks she has never heard her pupils express prejudice: 'I have never heard anyone say that the French are like this, or the Swedes are like that, the Germans are like that. I never really have' (DK 622, f, 50, En).

However, there are also pessimistic views of the situation in Europe:

[Question: Some people think that the process of European integration will mean greater tolerance towards other European nations. Can you see any sign of that?] No. No, I don't think I really can. I think at the moment rather the opposite. There is a tendency to become embattled. They build walls around themselves. That's perhaps what Europe wants to do too, to embattle itself with respect to Japan or the USA or other powers.

(DK 169, m, 30, En)

This English teacher answers the question with reference to the reunification of the two Germanies:

I don't see why one leads from the other really. The Berlin Wall is an example of that really. It is easier to hold your principles in the abstract, isn't it. It is actually when the realities of integration come about that there are irritating details about your neighbour that begin to be right up your nose, aren't there.

(UK 168, f, 30, Fr and Ge)

One Danish teacher is very critical about apparent tolerant attitudes:

No, I think it's rubbish. As long as we as Danes cannot get to grips with what is a proper tolerance with respect to the Greenlanders, it's utopic to talk about tolerance in these contexts. It's a rather fictional concept. I wouldn't mind talking about it when we've taken Spaniards, Italians and whatever else, and put them in various families. It's only when you get near together that things really hold up or show what they're made of. It's not so difficult to be tolerant towards a Spaniard or an Italian as long as they are down there where they are. But then it's still just a paper attitude.

(DK 178, m, 30, Ge and Fr)

This teacher expresses an attitude we found again and again among both Danish and English teachers: the conviction that tolerance can be attained above all or exclusively through personal contact with people from other countries or cultures.

There are differences in national stereotypes between pupils in England and Denmark, differences which have something to do with the two countries' relationships with their respective neighbouring countries. In England it is the [negative] stereotypes about the French which dominate, presumably because Britain and France have been in relationships of conflict for several centuries. Furthermore, French is the traditional and often the only foreign language, which often means that it is seen as the foreign language *par excellence*. Consider how an English teacher tells how if he says he is a language teacher, then he usually gets the reaction: 'Oh I was no good at French at school!' (UK 88, m, 20, Fr and Ge).

English pupils' stereotypes of the French are described here in all brevity: 'They all think the French stink of garlic and wear stripy t-shirts. I mean they still think that' (UK 83, f, 20, Fr, Ge and Sp). This is often the image found in other research (Byram *et al.* 1991; Dark *et al.* 1997).

In Denmark it is the [negative] stereotypes about the Germans which dominate, which has to be seen against the background of the fatal Danish defeat by the Prussians and the Austrians in 1864, the Second World War and Denmark's dependent position with respect to big brother Germany. Some Danish stereotypes of Germans are described here: 'They have some stereotypes: Germans wear yellow rubber boots and raincoats, and such things. They have quite a lot of stereotypes of Germans, precisely because we live so close to Marielyst' (DK 39, 20, En, Ge and Fr). One teacher talks about German, English and French in Denmark:

> In my school it has been very necessary to break down prejudices. Because especially in German we meet prejudices that the Germans are like this or that, and so when we deal with German culture, German every day life and a little with German newspapers, then we see that the Germans really have the same problems, and that they also have many opinions the same. In English it is not quite so important, because English is very popular and the English are of course very interesting people, since they produce so much for youth culture, so we don't have the same problems. And with respect to French we have to deal with the idea that French is refined, and so we talk a little about what French has influenced us in, and of course what the language can be used for when we get a bit nearer to the culture.
>
> (DK 292, f, 60, En, Ge and Fr)

However, the teachers do not just talk about national stereotypes. They also mention social and gender stereotypes from time to time:

> I find that the kids are more tuned in to, certainly, gender stereotypes than they used to be in the past. They often say 'Well, that's sexist', and often it isn't but, you know, something they like to bring up … Race is a different matter. I find a fair bit of racism here. Usually fairly covert. They don't go out of the way with it but you come across it. And when it comes up, I usually attack the person coming up with it and challenge his views. You usually find it's what his dad says.
>
> (UK 130, m, 30, Fr and Ge)

A systematic approach?

In an earlier investigation of the teaching of languages and cultures, we found that the effect of language teaching on young people's perceptions of and attitudes towards other peoples and cultures was negligible (Byram *et al.* 1991). We attributed this lack of success in what teachers themselves often claim as a principal purpose, to the powerful countervailing influence of the media and other factors outside school and, significantly, to the lack of a systematic, planned approach to the cultural dimension in teaching.

It was not surprising to find a similar situation still prevalent in the accounts given by some teachers, whether in England or Denmark:

If I've heard them talk about other people with some nickname, then I try to talk to them, about why they do it. Usually they have some strange explanation about it's because they have heard others say it, or it's something they've got from home. So I try to talk to them and sometimes to find a text which throws light on the subject.

(DK 49, f, 30, En and Ge)

There is no doubt that many teachers recognize the importance of the contribution language teaching could and should make to the development of appropriate attitudes:

I really do think it is a cultural responsibility. And that it is a very important cultural responsibility. Among the really basic human characteristics, it's not obvious that it was so important to be tolerant. I don't know. But it is in our society. If we can't be tolerant towards one another, I think we will end by killing each other, and that's also why we are Christians, I think. But all religions have the same element no doubt.

(DK 639, f, 40, Fr)

The notion that the foreign language teacher can contribute to this specifically by comparison with other societies is proposed by one teacher, although there might be many people who would wonder about the belief that England should be offered as a model:

[Question: The racism and prejudices which are expressed, are they particularly directed towards those who are called, in the debate, refugees or immigrants, or is it also a question of differences between European countries?] No, it is exclusively about refugees and immigrants among young people, I think. [Question: Do you think that language teaching also ought to have the responsibility of dealing with the topic of racism, even if it is about quite different countries than England, Germany and France?] Yes, very much so, because if you take England, there are many different peoples, and they have gradually become integrated into England, and you can use that as a good model for us here. And I do so.

(DK 87, f, 40, Ge and Fr)

The English teachers, probably because of their preoccupation with the National Curriculum and assessment, tended to argue that there ought to be assessment of the cultural dimension. This would then assure a more systematic approach:

My own personal opinion is that the cultural is more important than the linguistic. But having said that there's no point trying to tell people about the way other people live if those people weren't actually able to go and settle into that sort of life style and communicate. So you can't really have one without the other. That's what I feel. And at the end of the day, language is really, even within schools, there's that ultimate end, an exam to pass.

(UK 88, m, 20, Fr and Ge)

Another teacher proposes an examination which would complement the linguistic. She appears to favour an exam which would focus on knowledge acquired, although other aspects of cultural competence could be assessed too (Byram *et al.* 1994):

> But I would like to see a non-language specific section of the GCSE exam. I mean, going back to the old European Studies, Background Studies. I'd love to see that. I think that would complement what they're having to do now.
>
> (UK 107, f, 30, Fr and Ge)

Another teacher shares this view and argues that even if the curriculum includes a cultural dimension, it will be ignored unless it is assessed:

> I don't think it's ever going to get any better, despite the good things that were said about cultural awareness in the National Curriculum. I think that at the end of the day, parents expect their kids to get As, Bs, Cs or whatever and employers and everybody else do. And unfortunately that means that the cultural dimension tends to ... It can be a handy excuse to push the cultural dimension to one side.
>
> (UK 130, m, 30, Fr, Ge and Sp)

Methods and techniques

Since there is little systematic planning in teachers' handling of the affective and attitudinal dimension, we ought perhaps to speak less of a methodology, which would imply a rationale, than of a number of techniques. These are nonetheless interesting because they are little documented.

Because of the emotive potential of discussions of stereotypes and prejudice, some teachers readily admit that they do not stick to the foreign language as a medium, despite the pressures to do so:

> I do think there is a great danger these days we're going to go overboard with the target language to the detriment of the culture, which needs to be brought in as well. I've just been around in teaching for so long I've seen these new ideas come, get thrown out, and only through time will we discover that. But it's a question of balance really. I just wonder whether we're just tipping the scales, certainly at the lower level, a little bit too much linguistically.
>
> (UK 199, f, 40, Fr)

Danish teachers have the advantage that they teach other subjects and may deal with emotive issues there. They too feel a pressure to use the foreign language where possible, but if necessary some will switch to Danish:

> So we do it as much as possible in English, since that's where they have the most vocabulary [as opposed to other foreign languages]. If the question [of stereotypes] comes up in an English lesson, we try to say in English, what each of us thinks about the topic. But sometimes it becomes so complicated, and so I think it is after all important that they should be able to state their opinions. And it has to be discussed, and so we say it in Danish. I think that is appropriate, because an English lesson is something more than just language learning. I think we should deal with what pupils think, it's important to discuss, and so we do it in Danish. So it doesn't matter if it's an English lesson.
>
> (DK 323, f, 50, En, Ge and Fr)

Others nonetheless stick to the foreign language and therefore have to accept the limits of what can be discussed. This is clearly an issue which individuals decide for themselves but which the profession needs to debate as a matter of urgency and importance.

One widely-held view is that the development of knowledge about others will lead to tolerance: 'I have to believe that the more one knows about other people and other cultures, the more understanding one gets, the more tolerant one becomes. I think you have to believe that' (DK 395, m, 40, En).

This has to be approached with some caution, however, as Morgan (1993) has shown. There is no necessary link between levels of knowledge and tolerant attitudes. The tone of this teacher's statement probably reflects the views of many others and their wish to believe that what they can teach, that is, the knowledge they have, will have the desired effects. It suggests that there really is a need for more teacher training in the cultural dimension, as we have said. Others, however, reveal that they use discussion techniques, and these are more likely to lead to opportunities for pupils to express their opinions and attitudes and perhaps to modification of them as much by their peers as by their teachers.

Apart from class discussion, the techniques described by teachers include the use of video satellite television (see also Sorani and Tamponi 1997). These and other telematic innovations clearly have the potential to offer learners a more direct experience of otherness in the classroom. Another option is to ensure that 'stereotypes' is a topic introduced into the syllabus of another subject such as 'Personal and Social Education' or, as described by one teacher, is part of a special cross-curricular programme: 'We had two days across the school, cross-curricular themes, and we in the languages department chose to do a module based on stereotypes' (UK 69, m, 40, Fr and Ge).

We have also seen in earlier sections that Danish teachers described how they seized the opportunity of talking with pupils about prejudice offered by the presence of other children in the classroom. Clearly this has to be handled very sensitively and one Danish teacher said he avoided all reference to stereotypes and prejudice because it would be dangerous in the presence of foreign children in the classroom.

One technique which several teachers mentioned is what could be called 'holding up a mirror':

> Occasionally, you'll get a kid who will come up with 'frog' or 'croak', or whatever and I'll say 'OK, roast beef' and they say 'What?' and you then go into this stereotype that they [the French] have of the English. And they're saying 'That's rubbish, because we don't all eat roast beef', and I say the French don't all eat frogs' legs. You know, attack it in a fairly light-hearted way.
>
> (UK 130, m, 30, Fr, Ge and Sp)

In discussing this same technique one of the Danish teachers makes the link with a more general function of language teaching we have found elsewhere too: the power of others' views of us to make us re-consider our perceptions of ourselves:

> Yes, what being a Dane is, being an Englishman, a typical Englishman, all those generalised statements. I do indeed deal with that. And we have some very interesting things about how foreigners see us Danes. What we stand for. Because it's not something you go around thinking about. We just think it's the normal thing, and we see everything from our little world here. But when you look at Denmark on the map and see that it's such a little speck, and in general read and hear about other cultures' ways of seeing us, then it can be very interesting.
>
> (DK 318, f, 50, En, Ge and Fr)

One of the English teachers even takes this a step further by using a well-known book written about the English by a foreigner, Mikes's *How To Be An Alien*, as a means of deliberately taking an outsider perspective on what young people often believe is 'natural' and is indeed 'second nature' to them.

It is evident from our interviews that some teachers have developed a range of techniques and chosen particular kinds of texts which challenge learners' stereotypes and prejudices about others but also their assumptions about themselves. It is clearly an aspect of language teaching which requires sensitivity:

> And I think many of our texts are so wide-ranging that there are lots of good things in them about all sorts of things. And the pupils are not afraid of talking about all kinds of things, if they just have something where it's mentioned. They shouldn't just be drawing on themselves. There are many things in their own experience but they don't always dare use it.
>
> (DK 411, f, 30, Fr and En)

Learning a foreign language, as this teacher suggests, provides that Archimedean point from which they can move their own world.

This is not to say that all teachers hold these views and use these techniques.

Some have not thought about these issues before, or have thought that they are not part of their responsibility. Others deliberately avoid them because they are so sensitive and emotive. However, when language teachers accept the responsibility of introducing young people to otherness, not only in the classroom but also in visits to other countries, they cannot avoid the issues of stereotyping and prejudice.

Visits and exchanges

As we have seen, teachers typically believe that tolerance can only be developed if pupils have personal contacts with people abroad, live with them, work with them and so on. This is in fact a very serious criticism of traditional language teaching. What is its point if it is not able to contribute to increased tolerance in Europe, or at least an increase in understanding and the ability to relate meaningfully to other cultures?

The inadequacies of the classroom as an effective location for the changing of attitudes were argued by one of the English teachers:

> I think people will always be, will always have scorn for Europeans until they've actually been there, well, met any Europeans really. I mean, even from bad experiences – I don't think many pupils have been on trips and come across naturally bad individuals and that's clouded their vision about that country. I think most of them have come back with, certainly, positive attitudes about the people who live in the country, definitely. As I would say, after a foreign trip but not before.
>
> (UK 88, m, 20, Fr and Ge)

This rather extreme view, which also refers implicitly to the insularity of English people and its effect on language teaching, would certainly not be shared by all. Nonetheless it does raise the question of how effective classroom teaching can be in terms of attitude development, when there is little understanding or methodology on which to draw. We suggested in the previous section that those teachers who trust in the effect simply of the acquisition of knowledge are not supported by the literature.

That the effect of an experiential learning can be significant, would, however, probably be acknowledged by most teachers. It can challenge the assumptions of the privileged and liberal:

> Whatever one thinks about our little Denmark, we are very privileged. And the young people then discover – as I have at least, to a high degree – may also discover that Denmark is a country which is far ahead in many respects, but they also discover, when they then come back with the things they have observed, they discover sometimes, by questioning things, whether the liberal direction is the proper one, or whether there are in fact gender differences, for example.
>
> (DK 646, m, 30, En, Ge and Fr)

The responsibility of providing opportunities for real contacts with people of a different country and culture is one of the factors which makes language teaching different. It is also a resource issue, as one of the Danish teachers points out: '[Tolerance] only comes, I think, when people try to live together. So that's why I think that exchanges are good, if we could use some resources on them' (DK 165, f, 50, Ge).

Yet this is an issue which is only just beginning to be taken seriously in the professional literature as it becomes clear that we need a 'pédagogie des échanges' (Alix and Bertrand 1994; Mitteregger 1997; Byram 1997b; Snow and Byram 1997).

However, it is not always necessary to make visits and exchanges abroad in order to meet people from other cultures and some teachers also point out that the encounter can also take place in pupils' own daily life, irrespective of where they live:

> On the west coast you can hear German being spoken throughout the summer, or foreign languages as a whole, but mainly German. That has to have an influence on their attitudes, that they meet these people. It creates some contacts. I've seen various combined marriages.
>
> (DK 520, m, 50, Ge, En and Fr)

But another points out that the prejudices do not necessarily disappear:

> Yes, we also have it with the Germans. It can't be avoided here, where we have so many Germans. We are the district which has the largest number of tourists in Denmark, even if we think of Copenhagen. So we have more tourists, and we have a lot of Germans here, and that rubs off. The children have prejudices about the Germans, I think ... but they can't live without them, because they have their summer jobs.
>
> (DK 87, f, 40, En, Ge and Fr)

Furthermore there are possibilities in so far as the class itself is multicultural:

> Culturally speaking, I think it means an awful lot that they are involved closely with it in their daily lives. That there are friends in the class with different cultural and religious backgrounds, and we have a wide spectrum of foreign-speaking pupils.
>
> (DK 261, m, 40, En, Fr and Ge)

And there is one precise example mentioned in the context of teaching French:

> I had one girl last year who wore an Islamic scarf on her head, and there was great fuss about it in France, in schools, and it was very political, really very political, and I drew on her in that case.
>
> (UK 2, f, 40, Fr and Sp)

Gender and other social factors

Gender is a relatively well-known factor in socio-linguistics and in language teaching, with respect to both mother tongue and foreign language (Tannen 1990; Powell 1986; Bayley and Ronish 1992), but so far it has only been investigated in connection with the more specifically linguistic, especially linguistic interaction and attitudes towards the language use of the two genders. Börsch (1982, 1987) is an exception who has investigated male and female university students' motivation in the choice of language studies, and who discusses students' attitudes to language itself and their attitudes to residence in the foreign country.

Our study indicates that gender is an important factor in the cultural dimension of language learning if for no other reason than teachers' expectations of pupils. Many of the teachers we interviewed had views on the gender difference which were very firm. However, we lack empirical evidence for whether their views have any foundation in reality, especially with respect to pupils' attitudes to other European nationalities.

One Danish teacher, for example, summarizes several aspects of a possible difference in gender which also introduces some developmental psychological factors – and the age dimension is of course also a possible relevant factor:

> I think girls are more outgoing than boys. It's they who express more interest in travelling and experiencing, than boys do. Boys are much more goal-orientated with respect to what they should be educated for. I think boys are much more security-seeking than girls ... When we talk about the older pupils, those who have gone beyond puberty, then the girls are more tolerant. And girls are also more in languages than boys.
>
> (DK 125, f, 30, En, Ge and Fr)

Another teacher also talks about differences in interests in subjects: 'I think boys are more interested in the social science areas and history, and girls are maybe a little more interested in sitting and doing grammatical sentences and analysis – but it could be coincidence', and later in the same interview, she says:

> I showed them something I took off television, a natural history programme from Schleswig-Holstein and so I said, 'And now you should write down five things you think are interesting here and then from that I will make eight groups'. And that's when the boys wrote: Ditmarsken, war and history, and none of the girls did. One of the boys also wrote Bismarck. The girls wrote down nude-bathing, nature and castles.
>
> (DK 165, f, 50, Ge)

Our study also shows that there are certain differences between female and male teachers with respect to what view they wish to give of foreign societies and cultures. In the questionnaire, English and Danish teachers were asked to express their agreement or disagreement with the following two statements:

- It is the task of the teacher to present a positive image of the foreign culture and society. [Question 55]
- It is the task of the teacher always to present a realistic and sometimes negative image of the foreign culture and society. [Question 63]

In Denmark the majority disagreed with the first statement and an overwhelming majority (90%) agreed with the second. However, if we consider the distribution between men and women teachers, there is a significant difference. It was mainly women who agreed with the first statement and mainly men who agreed with the second. Women language teachers in Denmark are apparently more inclined to wish to give a positive picture. In England too, a very large majority disagreed with the first statement (91%) and six out of ten agreed with the second although one out of five were undecided. When women were compared with men the difference in numbers disagreeing with the statement was very small and there were in fact as many who were undecided. This suggests some difference between Denmark and England but further investigation would be needed to clarify the significance.

There were two other statements in the questionnaire which were interesting in this context:

- Personal contact with people from relevant countries (exchanges, penfriends, etc.) creates tolerance towards countries and their inhabitants. [Question 64]
- Knowledge about culture and society creates tolerance towards the countries and their inhabitants. [Question 65]

A large majority of Danish teachers agreed with the first statement (95%), and here there was no significant difference between men and women. The rate of agreement with the second was also high (92%), but this time there was a significant difference and men believe less in this view than women do. In England, a majority of teachers agreed with the first statement but less than in Denmark (81%) and a similar number (84%) agreed with the second. For Question 64, there was no difference between men and women, as in Denmark. With respect to Question 65, again the difference in numbers disagreeing was so small as to be insignificant, which appears to contrast with the tendency in Denmark, and again there were more undecided than disagreeing.

Although the statistical data reveal at best some indications worth further investigation, it seems that there is a potential pedagogical problem. Are women/girls a little more idealistic in intercultural contexts than men/boys? And if this is the case, how shall we handle this? In any case, our results indicate that there is an important issue here for the cultural dimension in language teaching. There is perhaps also an important pedagogical question: Is it necessary to use different methods with each sex? Is there an argument for periods of single-sex teaching? Or is it, on the contrary, important to always have mixed groups? Do the typical topics in lessons appeal more to girls than boys? It is at least possible to devise a form of language teaching which includes boys' interests, as for example is the experience with the development of language teaching in technical schools in English for Specific Purposes (for example, Jakobsen Pedersen 1993).

Some teachers think that the issue of gender is linked with that of social background. For example, the following quotation makes a very clear statement about causal relationships between these two factors:

> If we are talking about gender, it's my firm belief that girls are much more inclined to be outward-looking. It can also be linked with the fact that I am a woman too and they perhaps identify with me. But it also quite clearly something to do with social status. I think in fact that those girls who come from a middle-class home really are the most motivated, and are the most mobile. Those from upper-class homes are very often so spoilt, and they have some poor experiences. I also have some of course from unemployed families, and they are also keen to take part in the lessons, I think. And some of them are surprisingly positive, because you could easily imagine that if you are carrying some rather less positive things in your 'baggage', you would not have much interest left over to see beyond your own situation.
>
> (DK 283, f, 40, En and Fr)

The English teachers also tend to link social class with opportunities to travel:

> I suppose it could be that those students who come from families where they are more likely to have travelled, that those students feel a greater commitment towards language learning. Those students are going to be more proficient in their own language – which obviously has a great deal of bearing on it – and maybe those students again with the greater self-assurance can envisage themselves actually travelling abroad and being more independent.
>
> (UK 168, f, 30, Fr and Ge)

Many teachers also think that they can see differences in pupils' degree of tolerance in this respect, even if they themselves warn against generalizations. Some English teachers mentioned the traditional elite image of foreign language learning which meant that the relatively socially advantaged pupils chose to study languages. However, with the introduction of the National Curriculum, this principle is no longer applicable for the first foreign language, although it is still relevant for the second. Some Danish teachers also mention the topic, not in connection with German or English, but with French.

Here too there is a potential pedagogical problem. Does pupils' social background have significance for the cultural content and methods of language teaching and if so, how? Is it, for example, important to ensure that those pupils whose families cannot afford to travel abroad at least join a school trip or exchange? Is it important that the class is involved in a trip abroad? What about the relationships and co-operation with parents? Can we influence their attitudes to otherness? How important is the inclusion of anti-racist pedagogy and the teaching of human rights and democracy in foreign language teaching?[1] And what is the significance of teachers' own social background?

Clearly there are many questions here which are connected with pupils' and teachers' different pre-conditions, expectations and interests, questions which it is important to investigate by pedagogical development and research.

Note

1   For an approach to anti-racist and human rights education based on work in the cultural dimension but intended for all teachers, see Byram and Zarate (1995).

Further Reading

Alix, C. and Bertrand, G. (eds) (1994) *Pour une Pédagogie des Échanges (Le français dans le Monde: Numéro Spécial)*, Paris: EDICEF.

Bayley, S.N. and Ronish, D.Y. (1992) 'Gender, modern languages and the curriculum in Victorian England', *History of Education* 21(4): 363–82.

Börsch, S. (1982) *Fremdsprachenstudium – Frauenstudium*, Tübingen-Staffenberg.

—— (ed.) (1987) *Die Rolle der Psychologie in der Sprachlehrforschung*, Tübingen: Gunter Narr.

Byram, M. (1991) '"Background studies" in English foreign language teaching: lost opportunities in the comprehensive school debate', in D. Buttjes and M. Byram (eds) *Mediating Languages and Cultures*, Clevedon: Multilingual Matters.

Byram, M. (ed.) (1997b) *Face to Face. Learning Language and Culture through Visits and Exchanges*, London: Centre for Information on Language Teaching.

Byram, M., Morgan, C. *et al.* (1994) *Teaching-and-Learning Language-and-Culture*, Clevedon: Multilingual Matters.

Dark, S., Digard, M., Nicholas, R., Simpson, A., Smith, P. and Byram, M. (1997) 'The study visit and cultural learning', in M. Byram (ed.) *Face to Face. Learning Language and Culture through Visits and Exchanges*, London: Centre for Information on Language Teaching.

Jakobsen, K.S. and Pedersen, M.S. (1993) *Sproget på arbejde. Om undervisning I teknisk fremmedsprog*, Copenhagen: Erhvervsskolernes Forlag.

Mitteregger, S. (1997) 'Training language teachers in the pedagogy of exchanges – towards the development of socio-cultural competence', in M. Byram and G. Zarate (eds) *The Sociocultural and Intercultural Dimension of Language Learning and Teaching*, Strasbourg: Council of Europe.

Morgan, C. (1993) 'Attitude change and foreign language culture learning', *Language Teaching* 26(2): 63–75.

Powell, R. (1986) *Boys, Girls and Languages in School*, London: Centre for Information on Language Teaching and Research.

Snow, D. and Byram, M. (1997) *Crossing Frontiers. The School Study Visit Abroad*, London: Centre for Information on Language Teaching and Research.

Sorani, D. and Tamponi, A.R. (1997) 'Satellite TV: a flexible learning environment to promote cultural awareness', in M. Byram and G. Zarate (eds) *The Sociocultural and Intercultural Dimension of Language Learning and Teaching*, Strasbourg: Council of Europe.

Tannen, D. (1990) *You Just Don't Understand: Women and Men in Conversation*, New York: William Morrow.

6 Language teaching, citizenship, human rights and intercultural education

Hugh Starkey

> Through the study of foreign languages, pupils understand and appreciate different countries, cultures, people and communities – and as they do so, begin to think of themselves as citizens of the world as well as of the United Kingdom.
>
> (DfEE/QCA 1999a: 14)

Introduction

In this chapter I argue that, as the statement above from the National Curriculum for England indicates, language learning has a pre-eminent role in the education of citizens. Such an assertion challenges practices, reinforced by the Programmes of Study for the National Curriculum and GCSE examinations, that limit language learning to an instrumental process for consumers rather than citizens.

By acknowledging language learning as part of education for democratic citizenship, we assert ambitious aims for our work as language teachers. That is not to say that such aims are unrealistic for schools. I shall argue that certain conceptions of language teaching, far from opening horizons and stretching pupils, constrain them in all too familiar places (particularly classrooms and homes) where their ascribed role is to be subordinate to teachers and parents. Just at the time when, as adolescents, they are striving towards independence, adulthood and citizenship, the experience of language learning constantly reminds them of their status as pupils and children. It is hardly surprising that this often creates resistances. Those who, in the early 1980s, created what they perceived as relevant and realistic Programmes of Study for languages, may have misjudged. A more challenging programme, in tune with the rest of the curriculum, may provide the motivation that is so essential for successful learning of languages.

For the Council of Europe, language learning is a key component of education for democratic citizenship; a participative process developed in various contexts which, *inter alia*:

- equips men and women to play an active part in public life and to shape in a responsible way their own destiny and that of their society;

- aims to instil a culture of human rights;
- prepares people to live in a multicultural society and to deal with difference knowledgeably, sensibly, tolerantly and morally;
- strengthens social cohesion, mutual understanding and solidarity.

(Council of Europe 1999)

If we think of language learning as contributing substantially to this 'participative process', we need to ask questions about the content, the teaching strategies and the overall context in which we teach. It follows that we should be concerned to ensure meaningful integration with the curriculum as a whole and Citizenship and Personal Health and Social Education (PHSE) in particular. Such curriculum integration is promoted in the documentation of the National Curriculum and of the examination boards.

The aims of education for democratic citizenship, above, broadly correspond to those for citizenship in the National Curriculum for England:

> Citizenship gives pupils the knowledge, skills and understanding to play an effective role in society at local, national and international levels. It helps them to become informed, thoughtful and responsible citizens who are aware of their duties and rights. It promotes their spiritual, moral, social and cultural development, making them more self-confident and responsible both in and beyond the classroom. It encourages pupils to play a helpful part in the life of their schools, neighbourhoods, communities and the wider world. It also teaches them about our economy and democratic institutions and values; encourages respect for different national, religious and ethnic identities; and develops pupils' ability to reflect on issues and take part in discussions.

(QCA 2000: 4)

The aims have in common a particular emphasis on values: active engagement in public life; a culture of human rights; intercultural skills for living in a multicultural society; a commitment to social cohesion and solidarity. Central to education for citizenship is a knowledge and understanding of human rights.

A culture of human rights means living and working in a climate where respect for human dignity and equality of rights are basic minimum standards. Human rights are accepted by all the governments and major religions in the world as universal standards, even if some governments fail to live up to their own rhetoric. Human rights are therefore the basis of a system of values that is independent of any particular culture, be it ideological, religious or national. A knowledge and understanding of these internationally validated, non-ideological, secular standards is therefore a particularly important asset for language teachers, whose professional role requires them to mediate between languages and cultures (Buttjes and Byram 1990).

What are human rights?

Human rights are set out in internationally recognized texts and provide a legal, ethical and moral framework for the regulation of relationships between states, between people and between states and people. Although human rights have antecedents in the eighteenth century, notably the French Declaration of the Rights of Man and the Citizen of 1789, international, as opposed to national, statements of human rights are a mid-twentieth century, post-war phenomenon.

The United Nations was established in 1945 to support international efforts to achieve justice, peace and freedom in the world through the promotion and protection of human rights. This new international standard was set up in opposition to the values promoted by the explicitly racist nationalist regimes of the 1930s and early 1940s, whose leaders had used discrimination, repression, war and genocide as instruments of policy. The basis for the new post-war world order is the fundamental belief in human beings as being equally endowed with inherent dignity.

Human rights were adopted as the underlying principle of international law with the drafting of the *Charter of the United Nations* in 1945. They were first comprehensively defined in the *Universal Declaration of Human Rights* adopted by the General Assembly of the United Nations in 1948 (Johnson and Symonides 1998). René Cassin, who helped draft the *Universal Declaration of Human Rights*, categorized the rights as:

- personal rights such as: equality before the law and equal entitlement to rights; right to life, liberty and security of person; freedom from slavery, torture, arbitrary arrest; right of fair public trial and presumption of innocence;
- rights in relationships between people, such as: right to privacy; freedom of movement; right to nationality; right to marry, have children, own property;
- public freedoms and political rights including: freedom of thought, conscience and religion; right to freedom of opinion and expression; right of peaceful assembly; right to elect a government;
- economic, social and cultural rights including: right to work, rest and leisure; adequate standard of living for health; education; participation in cultural life.

He also noted that the final three articles of the Universal Declaration emphasize the rights to a social order, at all levels up to global, where human rights can flourish. In particular, the final article outlaws actions and activities intended to destroy rights and freedoms (Osler and Starkey 1996).

In 1953 member states of the Council of Europe signed the *European Convention of Human Rights and Fundamental Freedoms* which gives legal force to those rights and freedoms contained in it and provides a court to which individuals may take their cases. All individuals living in Europe are protected in this way, not just citizens of member states. Both the Council of Europe and the European Union are intergovernmental organizations founded explicitly on human rights principles.

The *European Convention* is also the basis in Britain of the *Human Rights Act*

(2000). With this act, the rights guaranteed by the Convention have to be acknowledged in any legal proceedings in Britain including any future legislation (Klug 2000). The Act also requires all public authorities to exercise their powers in a way that respects human rights. Working in the public sphere, teachers need an understanding of what this means in the educational context.

The *United Nations Convention on the Rights of the Child* (1989), which has been adopted by virtually every country in the world, is a further indication of the universal acceptance of legal obligations to respect human rights. The rights in this convention are the entitlement of all young people under the age of eighteen. They guarantee a right to the provision of shelter and essential services, including education; protection from harm and exploitation; and participation appropriate to age and maturity in decisions that concern them (Verhellen 1997, 2000).

Universal acceptance that human rights standards apply to all children and adults throughout the world was confirmed in the Vienna Declaration of June 1993. Representatives of states accounting for 99 per cent of the world's people reaffirmed their commitment to the *Universal Declaration of Human Rights* as the means to freedom, justice and peace in the world (UNHCR 1994). Thus, human rights attach to all human beings equally, irrespective of origin, status, culture or language.

Democracy and citizenship depend on an acceptance by governments and individuals of human rights. Democracy depends on individuals having freedom of conscience, freedom of movement, the right to peaceful assembly and media constrained only by the need to protect the rights and freedoms of others. Non-democratic regimes are characterized by the use of censorship, restrictions on freedom of movement and assembly and for discriminatory legislation. Citizenship describes the relationship of individuals to communities and to governments where human rights are agreed standards.

Human rights and language teaching: aims and values

International human rights instruments include commitments to education and definitions of goals. Article 26 of the *Universal Declaration of Human Rights* states that: 'Education shall be directed to ... the strengthening of respect for human rights and fundamental freedoms. It shall promote understanding and tolerance amongst all nations, racial or religious groups'. *The Convention on the Rights of the Child* includes a commitment to provide education directed to 'the development of respect for human rights'. Language teaching is a vehicle for transmitting such knowledge and understanding of human rights and a policy instrument for promoting intercultural understanding in a spirit of human rights (Osler and Starkey 2000a; Starkey 1996, 1997, 1999, 2000).

Language learning, by definition, is an intercultural experience. Comparisons will inevitably be made, by teachers, learners, and in course materials, between behaviours, practices and institutions in the cultures of the learners and the target culture. In a multi-ethnic community such as in Britain, there will be, within any given language learning group, learners with experience of and feelings of identity with a wide variety of cultures. 'Through foreign language education, learners have the opportunity to engage with people with other values, meanings and behaviours, potentially but not necessarily in a pluralist mode ... for a multicultural society' (Byram and Guilherme 2000: 71). Without a frame of reference, comparisons between cultures, both within the learning group and between the learners and the target culture, may be the occasion for stereotypes, racist or sexist comments or jokes and derogatory remarks. These contradict the spirit of human rights, which is to be respectful of others. Stereotyping also negates the aims of education in general and of language learning in particular. A knowledge and understanding of human rights equip teachers and learners to engage with other cultures on the basis of equality of dignity.

The National Curriculum (NC) for England is prefaced by a statement of values and purposes, which applies to all aspects of the curriculum including, of course, modern foreign languages. The statement sets out the need for 'a broad set of common values and purposes that underpin the school curriculum and the work of schools'. It starts to define these 'common values' as follows:

> Foremost is a belief in education, at home and at school, as a route to the spiritual, moral, social, cultural, physical and mental development, and thus the well-being, of the individual. Education is also a route to equality of opportunity for all, a healthy and just democracy, a productive economy, and sustainable development. Education should reflect the enduring values that contribute to these ends. These include valuing ourselves, our families and other relationships, the wider groups to which we belong, the diversity in our society and the environment in which we live. Education should also reaffirm our commitment to the virtues of truth, justice, honesty, trust and a sense of duty.
>
> (DfEE/QCA 1999a)

This statement emphasizes that education is a means both to individual development, and to an improved democracy and a stable world. These priorities are in line with policy positions taken by the Council of Europe, the European Union and UNESCO. Their fulfilment depends on citizens, including young people, having an understanding of their own human rights, and a commitment to the equal entitlement of all other human beings to enjoy these rights. Such a commitment entails responsibilities, a sense of reciprocity and solidarity (Osler and Starkey 2001).

The NC statement of values and purposes spells out common values in the language of human rights. Further, it encourages schools to use a statement of values, developed by the National Forum for Values in Education and the Community, which declares, under the heading 'Society': 'We value truth, freedom, justice, human rights, the rule of law and collective effort for the common good.' This explicit endorsement of human rights as core values underpinning the curriculum is echoed in the Citizenship Programmes of Study, where the key concepts, identified by the Advisory Group on Citizenship (QCA 1998) and included in the Initial Guidance for Schools are listed as:

- democracy and autocracy;
- co-operation and conflict;
- equality and diversity;
- fairness, justice, the rule of law;
- rules, the law and human rights;
- freedom and order;
- individual and community;
- power and authority;
- rights and responsibilities.

(QCA 2000: 20)

These concepts, to be acquired by all those studying the curriculum, are of particular value to those studying and teaching languages and cultures. We can observe the importance attached to democracy, equality, and freedom and to human rights, which is emphasized by the repetition of 'rights and responsibilities'.

The Initial Guidance on Citizenship also states that planning for the implementation of Citizenship should include a whole-school approach (QCA 2000: 10). Amongst other things this means that each curriculum subject has a potentially important role to play. The contribution of Modern Foreign Languages (MFL) is exemplified, rather perfunctorily in the Initial Guidance and in more detail in the syllabuses for GCSE produced by the examination boards. I will argue that these suggestions underestimate the potential of language learning to contribute to this area.

Citizenship and language teaching at Key Stages 3 and 4: low expectations

How is the synergy of Citizenship and MFL to be achieved within the prescribed Programmes of Study? At first sight there should be limitless scope, since the NC 2000 has dispensed with contexts for the languages taught. If teachers can choose any content, then why not subjects associated with Citizenship and issues of freedom, equality, inclusion and human rights (DfEE/QCA 1999a,b)?

In practice, the content is largely determined by the commercially produced textbooks and course materials available within schools. These may be based on earlier versions of the NC, which themselves were heavily influenced by earlier curriculum development initiatives such as Graded Objectives in Modern Languages (GOML). The GOML movement, dating from the mid-1970s, attempted to make the study of a language in school a relevant experience for learners. Those involved therefore tried to imagine concrete situations in which young people might wish to communicate in a second language. The rationale is described by one pioneer of this movement:

> Young school learners would probably make a first visit (abroad) with a school party where their most pressing needs would be taken care of. They would want to buy postcards, a present to take home, an ice cream and a coke and use

some polite expressions to people they met. Later they might go on an exchange where they would need to converse with the family, exchange some personal information, express likes/dislikes and preferences and possibly use services such as a bank and a telephone. Later again they might go independently with their parents and act as interpreters for the rest of the family.

(Page 1996: 100)

Although the chosen scenarios give the learner a role as actor in an intercultural setting, the prominent purpose imagined for the visit is tourism, with the learner largely in the role of consumer rather than citizen. Moreover, in spite of hypothesizing different contexts for communication, including the role of interpreter, there is no suggestion that students will take with them any curiosity or any social, historical, economic or political awareness.

The list of topics to be studied for GCSE when it was introduced in 1988, is revealing of this confined communicative universe: personal identification; house and home; geographical surroundings; school; free time and entertainment; travel; holidays; meeting people; shopping; food and drink; weather and seasons; accommodation (Jones 1994: 25).

In fact, although the Programmes of Study for Key Stages 3 and 4 have been freed of specific content, the influence of textbooks and examinations results in learners remaining stuck in the role of tourist/consumer for the five years of their secondary schooling: 'Perhaps the biggest problem (and the main cause of boredom) is that those topics are visited and revisited year after year adding on a little more vocabulary each time' (Callaghan 1998: 6). This vision of the language learner as child within the family, pupil within the school and consumer within society has persisted, so that the speaking test in GCSE French will be based on:

- home life;
- school life;
- self, family and friends;
- free time;
- your local area;
- careers, work, work experience;
- holidays.

(OCR 2000a)

This list is restrictive and, indeed, conservative in that it provides no encouragement to learners to look outside their own personal sphere. Even interest in the target culture can only be evoked in the context of holidays. It is perhaps not surprising that language teachers have recently tended to see themselves as developing skills rather than cultural knowledge (Byram and Risager 1999).

There are, as we shall see, ways of remedying this and teaching Citizenship through this selection of topics. However, reference to the public sphere has to be consciously introduced in spite of rather than because of the topics.

The descriptions of contexts within which communication is deemed to take place appear at first sight to be more ambitious:

> Candidates will be required to show knowledge of the following contexts which are based on the NC Orders for Modern Foreign Languages:
>
> 1   Everyday activities
> 2   Personal and social life
> 3   The world around us
> 4   The world of work
> 5   The international world
>
> (OCR 2000a)

However, in the first NC, there were seven areas and study included the world of communications, the world of imagination and creativity, the world of education and training (alongside work) (Jones 1994: 27).

The trimming of these areas of experience occurred with the first revision of the NC (DfE 1995). From this time the potentially interesting and ambitious Programme of Study that could be derived from 'work', 'international world', 'communications' and 'imagination and creativity' was re-defined in terms that reduced expectations and removed any vestige of intellectual challenge. The infantilizing GOML perspective was reinforced, as teachers and learners were expected to concentrate on the language of the classroom, home life and school, food, health and fitness, self, family and personal relationships, free time and social activities, holidays and special occasions. Contexts 4 and 5 above were relegated to being studied 'in addition'.

One consequence is that the learning of languages may lack broad appeal. Callaghan (1998) points out that the majority of subtopics in the GCSE syllabus appeal to girls rather than boys, though several are equally disliked by both sexes. For example, she found that House and Home was enjoyed by girls, who liked to describe room furnishings in detail. The boys tended merely to list items of electrical equipment. Family and Daily Routine includes descriptions of household tasks. However, girls are much more likely to have experience of these tasks than boys. She concludes:

> Children are taught to speak a language as if they lived in a moral vacuum and that the only interactions they are likely to have are with shopkeepers ....This sanitised version of life makes French particularly unpalatable to boys who, on the whole, prefer realism and facts.

She suggests that, if the teaching was re-structured to include a debate on the gendering of household tasks, this could include both groups more equally and promote some awareness of equality issues.

Language teaching and citizenship: taking opportunities

It is possible to teach a Personal Health and Social Education programme in the target language and still cover the restricted GCSE list of topics, as some coursebooks have demonstrated (e.g. Miller *et al.* 1990). Questions of healthy eating, of lifestyle, future plans, and life projects can be taught in the language studied and include a comparative cultural dimension.

The Edexcel draft specification for GCSE for 2001 chooses a slightly broader range of topics, namely:

- At Home and Abroad
- Education, Training and Employment
- Health and Fitness
- House, home and daily routine
- Media, entertainment and youth culture
- Social activities

(Edexcel 2000)

Although the subtopics suggest that the emphasis on tourism and on personal interests and information prevails, nonetheless, the second and third headings correspond with the PHSE programme and the fifth has 'current affairs, social and environmental issues' as its final subtopic. This suggests a need for what the Citizenship guidelines refer to as 'political literacy'. The inclusion of such a potentially interesting approach could well be motivating for learners who otherwise are faced with topics well below the interest level of those encountered elsewhere in the curriculum.

Whereas in other curriculum areas, learners are expected to exercise critical judgement and explore issues, this is rarely the case for the domestic, consumer and tourist agenda that constitutes so much of language learning. However, the same topics addressed critically and problematized can contribute to Citizenship:

> Conversations are likely to be very different, if, under the heading of travel, the role-play is ... immigration officer and black tourist. (This) ... might offer some insights into immigration policy and an opportunity for raising some very open-ended questions. Food and drink are potentially interesting and controversial issues. Questions of health, of power, of advertising, of hunger and starvation in the world, hence of justice, are all areas of enquiry in this topic. Finding one's way around town may lead to all sorts of discoveries that tourist boards and even governments would not wish to be revealed. Why are there people ... sleeping under bridges or in cramped hostels? Daily routine invites questions about life-style and its impact on the environment.
>
> (Starkey 1990)

The example of the role-play given above was intended to shift perceptions rather than be an example to be followed in a teaching situation. Role-play is a very useful technique in language teaching, as in PHSE and education for citizenship. It is a technique that requires attention to warm-up, ensuring participants feel comfortable with the task and taking care when going into role and when coming out of role. Moreover, particular care is required if learners are to take on roles which involve them in racist or sexist discourse, as the feelings of both players and audience risk running out of control. The introduction of role-play is a good opportunity for language teachers to collaborate with their colleagues teaching drama (Ur 1982; Wessels 1987).

A move away from closed and true/false questions in reading and listening comprehension, to open-ended questions where opinions are genuinely sought and discussed, can invigorate language classes. The communication gap can also be the opinion gap. Examination boards do recognize the possibilities for languages to address Citizenship. For instance, OCR suggests:

> This specification provides opportunities to contribute to the teaching of the Key Stage 4 Citizenship programme of study in the following areas:
>
> - 1g – the importance of a free press, and the media's role in society, including the internet, in providing information and affecting opinion;
> - 1i – the United Kingdom's relations in Europe, including the European Union;
> - 1j – the wider issues and challenges of global interdependence and responsibility, including sustainable development and Local Agenda 21;
> - 2a – research a topical political, spiritual, moral, social or cultural issue, problem, or event by analysing information from different sources, including ICT-based sources, showing an awareness of the use and abuse of statistics;
> - 2b – express, justify and defend orally and in writing a personal opinion about such issues, problems or events;
> - 2c – contribute to group and exploratory class discussion, and take part in formal debates;
> - 3a – use imagination to consider other people's experiences and be able to think about, express and critically evaluate views that are not their own.

There does, however, seem to be an ambivalence about these suggestions. The Board seems to suggest that such a programme is too ambitious: 'It is recognised that the limited level of mastery of a modern foreign language at GCSE will affect candidates' performance of all the above activities.' It could well be that language teaching has got itself into a vicious circle of low expectation and low achievement. By adjusting the interest level, whilst retaining a careful grading of the language, a more stimulating learning environment may be created.

Citizenship and languages at AS and A levels

The programme for AS level remains remarkably similar to that for GCSE, namely:

> Media (newspapers, magazines, TV and radio); Advertising (the role and influence of advertising); The arts (aspects of cultural life, e.g. film, theatre; the arts as part of leisure time); Daily life (patterns of daily life; daily routine; school); Food and drink; Sport and pastimes; Travel, transport and holidays (tourism as a modern phenomenon; friction between tourists and local inhabitants; holidays and foreign travel; tourism and the environment); Human interest news items.
>
> (OCR 2000b)

The main opportunities for developing political literacy through this programme are likely to be in respect of the ownership and influence of the media, cultural policy and the major questions raised around tourism which is, at this level, problematized.

At A level the syllabus is awash with thorny political issues, including:

1   Social issues:

- urban and rural life; housing problems; social exclusion; employment and unemployment; leisure activities; immigration and qualification for residence; the role of women; equality of opportunity for minority groups; religion and belief; patterns of churchgoing; religious minorities.

2   The environment:

- the individual in his/her surroundings; effect of the environment on individuals; personal and individual ways of contributing to environmental awareness.
- pollution: global warming; acid rain; air, water pollution; noise; destruction of rain forests; damage to animal world; solutions and cost implications.
- conservation: saving endangered species and landscapes.

3   Law and order:

- the role of the police; patterns of crime; public protests and demonstrations; juvenile delinquency.

4   Politics:

- including consideration of far right parties.

> (OCR 2000b)

The study of such issues provides opportunities for developing two of the three main aspects of Citizenship as defined in the NC, namely 'social and moral responsibility' and 'political literacy'. However, the study of texts about political issues does not, of itself, lead to political literacy. Other skills need to be developed simultaneously. A Council of Europe Recommendation on 'teaching and learning about human rights in schools' suggests that these are:

> skills associated with written and oral expression, including the ability to listen and discuss and to defend one's opinions; skills involving judgement such as … the identification of bias, prejudice, stereotypes and discrimination; social skills, in particular recognising and accepting differences.
> (Council of Europe 1985; Osler and Starkey 1996: 181–3)

Adopting a human rights approach to language teaching provides a sound framework within which controversial issues can be examined. Debate is conducted showing respect for persons, particularly other interlocutors, as the essential dignity of human beings is acknowledged. Disparaging remarks about individuals or groups who are not present is also inappropriate behaviour and therefore unacceptable. On the other hand, if respect for human rights is regarded as a standard, judgements can be made about the words or actions of individuals, governments or cultural groups. In this way uncritical cultural rela-tivism can be avoided.

This perspective needs to be made explicit to the learners from the start and one way of addressing this is the study of human rights instruments in the target language. Such a study enables students to link the various topics they cover to wider issues of human rights and is likely to prove interesting and popular (Starkey 1996: 108).

Simultaneously procedural ground rules need to be established and adopted for discussion and debate in class. Whether the context is pair work, group work or whole-class discussions, agreements such as the following apply:

- Participants are expected to listen to each other and take turns.
- Where a discussion is chaired, the authority of the chair is respected.
- Even heated debates must be conducted in polite language.
- Discriminatory remarks, particularly racist, sexist and homophobic discourse and expressions, are totally unacceptable at any time.
- Participants show respect when commenting on and describing people portrayed in visuals or texts.
- All involved have the responsibility to challenge stereotypes.
- A respectful tone is required at all times.

It goes without saying that teachers are party to these agreements and will not use sarcasm, irony and disparaging judgements.

The A level syllabus includes the study of far right political parties in France and Germany and terrorist organizations in Spain (OCR 2000b). In a democratic society it must be assumed that this has been chosen in order to demonstrate the unacceptability of the discourses and actions of such movements. An understanding of human rights as the basis for democracy is essential background for such study. This is particularly important when preparing an essay topic such as one proposed by an examination board in its specimen material, namely: 'Explain the success of the National Front amongst some sections of the French population' (OCR 2000b). Without reference to human rights, such a topic invites the rehearsal and indeed the justification of racist policies.

Developing intercultural skills through language learning

How are teachers to help their students to study authentic texts critically? Material in textbooks or, indeed, from examination boards may contain stereotypes of ethnic minorities, for example. One answer lies in the development of skills of critical discourse analysis and critical cultural awareness.

Critical discourse analysis (CDA) 'is a type of discourse analytical research that primarily studies the way social power abuse, dominance and inequality are enacted, reproduced and resisted by text and talk in the social and political context' (van Dijk 1997). CDA can provide a set of guidelines for interrogating an authentic text, so that students engage with the content critically at the same time as they attempt to understand other more superficial aspects of the text. For instance, learners may confront texts of a possibly xenophobic nature to explore the discourse mechanisms of racism.

As an example, students of Spanish studied newspaper articles on the theme of immigration. They were asked to examine closely the texts, looking for certain discourse features such as the following:

- Sources, perspectives, arguments.
  Are they institutional? From the majority group? Do minority perspectives find expression? Are the sources of evidence made explicit?
- Vocabulary, connotations, names.
  Different words for 'immigrants'. Different descriptors.
- Implications and presuppositions,
  e.g. 'the best antidote against immigration is …' implies that immigration is a social illness against which society has to fight.
- Extrapolation of statistics,
  e.g. 'By 2010 there will be … .'
- Active and passive constructions,
  e.g. 'Thirty-two immigrants deported to Africa' – no mention of who was responsible.
- Rhetorical expressions.
  Metaphors and similes: 'Fortress Europe'; 'an avalanche of immigrants'.
- Us versus them.
  Our democracy, our jobs, their religion, their culture.

Having made this critical analysis of the linguistic and stylistic features of the press coverage of immigration, students felt confident to discuss the issue and to make comparisons with coverage in their own national and local press. They then wrote an account of their findings and their feelings about them (Prieto Ramos 1999).

Another useful approach is provided by Cultural Studies, which is an academic discipline with its roots in Britain in the 1950s and 1960s but acknowledging the intellectual contribution of French academics such as Barthes, Bourdieu and Foucault (Storey 1996). It can be focused on cultural forms found within particular national communities, such as French Cultural Studies (Forbes and Kelly 1995). In essence culture is conceptualized as 'neither aesthetic nor humanist in emphasis, but political' (Fiske 1987).

The introduction to a textbook on British Cultural Studies produced in Romania describes the expectations of the authors for the learner:

> This book is less concerned about making you learn information by heart than with encouraging you to *process* the information contained here. For example, in the class on Scotland you are asked to *compare* what a Scottish person says about Scotland and what a compilation from reference books says about Scotland. You do not have to learn one or the other, but you do have to learn the process of comparison. The same process of comparison of different kinds of information takes place in many classes. In others, you are asked to *apply* concepts such as 'gender' or 'nation as imagined community' in your analyses of society. In short, what we want is to provide you with the skills to *argue* ... not learn by heart.
>
> (Chichirdan *et al.* 1998: 10)

Sources of information used in this approach are authentic texts, including audio recordings and a variety of written documents and visuals such as maps, photographs, diagrams and cartoons. The activities involve understanding, discussing and writing in the target language. The approach to the materials is always critical. There is every reason for applying such principles to all topics studied in the target language. It is a question of challenging the reader by bringing together texts and visuals which present contrasting views. It is also a question of applying key concepts, such as those in the Citizenship curriculum above, to the reading and discussion of the texts.

Both the CDA and the Cultural Studies approaches help to develop what Byram (1997) characterizes as critical cultural awareness. This is an ability to evaluate critically and on the basis of explicit criteria such as human rights, perspectives, practices and products in one's own and other cultures and countries. This involves the ability to:

- Identify and interpret explicit or implicit values in documents and events in one's own and other cultures, using a range of analytical approaches to place a document or event in context and be aware of the ideological dimension.
- Make an evaluative analysis of the documents and events by reference to an explicit perspective and criteria such as human rights, liberal democracy, religion, political ideology.

- Interact and mediate in intercultural exchanges, being aware of potential conflict between one's own and other ideological positions and attempting to find common criteria. Where this is not possible, to negotiate agreement on places of conflict and acceptance of difference.

I am arguing that the development of such awareness should start at the outset of language learning and be continually reinforced throughout the stages of learning. This has wider implications for schools (Osler and Starkey 2000b, c).

Conclusion

Motivation is all-important in language learning and, indeed, in language teaching. Learner motivation can be increased by engaging curiosity, confronting alternative perspectives and broadening horizons. Teacher motivation is increased when the learners achieve results and are themselves motivated. It is also increased when teachers feel that they are contributing something significant to the learners' experience. This is more likely to occur when there is a learning partnership which critically examines evidence, facts and sources, asks real and significant questions and collectively attempts to draw conclusions.

There is a further significant task for language teachers, namely promoting commitment to democracy and sustainable development based on an understanding of human rights. Motivation and progress are likely to follow when teachers and learners have a common commitment to developing language skills and simultaneously developing the skills of citizenship.

Further reading

Buttjes, D. and Byram, M. (eds) (1990) *Mediating Languages and Cultures*, Clevedon: Multilingual Matters.

Byram, M. (1997) *Teaching and Assessing Intercultural Communicative Competence*, Clevedon: Multilingual Matters.

Byram, M. and Guilherme, M. (2000) 'Human rights, cultures and language teaching', in A.Osler (ed.) *Citizenship and Democracy in Schools: Diversity, Identity, Equality*, Stoke-on-Trent: Trentham Books, 63–78.

Byram, M. and Risager, K. (1999) *Language Teachers, Politics and Culture*, Clevedon: Multilingual Matters.

Callaghan, M. (1998) 'An investigation into the causes of boys' underachievement in French', *Language Learning Journal* 17: 2–7.

Chichirdan, A. *et al.* (1998) *Crossing Cultures. British Cultural Studies for Twelfth Grade Romanian Students*, Bucharest: The British Council.

Council of Europe (1985) *Recommendation (R(85)7) of the Committee of Ministers on Teaching and Learning about Human Rights in Schools*, Strasbourg: Council of Europe.

—— (1999) *Declaration of the Committee of Ministers of the CdCC and Programme of Education for Democratic Citizenship* (CM(99)76).

Department for Education (1995) *Modern Foreign Languages in the National Curriculum*, London: HMSO.

Department for Education and Employment/QCA (1999a) *The National Curriculum for England*, London: DfEE/QCA.

DfEE/QCA (1999b) *Citizenship Key Stages 3–4. The National Curriculum for England*, London: DfEE/QCA.

—— (1999c) *Modern Foreign Languages. The National Curriculum for England*, London: DfEE/QCA.

Edexcel (2000) *Draft Specification Edexcel GCSE in Modern Foreign Languages French (1226) First examination 2003.*

Fiske, J. (1987) 'British cultural studies and television', in R. Allen (ed.) *Channels of Discourse: Television and Contemporary Criticism*, Chapel Hill, NC: University of North Carolina Press.

Forbes, J. and Kelly, M. (1995) *French Cultural Studies*, Oxford: OUP.

Johnson, M. Glen and Symonides, J. (1998) *The Universal Declaration of Human Rights: A History of its Creation and Implementation, 1948–98*, Paris: UNESCO.

Jones, B. (1994) 'Modern languages: twenty years of change', in A. Swarbrick (ed.) *Teaching Modern Languages*, London: Routledge, 18–32.

Klug, F. (2000) *Values for a Godless Age: The Story of the UK's New Bill of Rights*, Harmondsworth: Penguin.

Miller, A., Roselman, L. and Bougard, M. (1990) *Arc-en-ciel 3*, London: Mary Glasgow Publications.

Osler, A. and Starkey, H. (1996) *Teacher Education and Human Rights*, London: Fulton.

—— (2000a) 'Intercultural education and foreign language learning: issues of racism, identity and modernity', *Race, Ethnicity and Education*, Vol 3.2: 231–45.

—— (2000b) 'Citizenship, human rights and cultural diversity', in A.Osler (ed.) *Citizenship and Democracy in Schools: Diversity, Identity, Equality*, Stoke-on-Trent: Trentham Books: 13–18.

—— (2000c) 'Human rights, responsibilities and school self-evaluation', in A. Osler (ed.) *Citizenship and Democracy in Schools: Diversity, Identity, Equality*, Stoke-on-Trent: Trentham Books: 91–112.

—— (2001) 'Human rights, responsibilities and values in education', in D. Lawton, J. Cairns and R. Gardner, *World Year Book 2001: Values and Culture in Education*, London.

Oxford, Cambridge and RSA Examinations (2000a) *OCR GCSEs in French, German, Spanish and Gujerati.*

—— (2000b) *OCR Advanced Subsidiary GCE in French, German, Spanish; OCR Advanced GCE in French, German, Spanish.*

Page, B. (1996) 'Graded objectives in modern languages (GOML)', in E. Hawkins (ed.) *30 Years of Language Teaching*, London: CILT, 99–105.

Prieto Ramos, F. (1999) 'Teaching against prejudice: the critical examination of press articles on immigration in the language class', paper presented at the International Colloquium Xenophilia/Xenophobia and Propagation of Languages, Saint-Cloud, Paris 15–18 December 1999.

Qualifications and Curriculum Authority (1998) *Education for Citizenship and the Teaching of Democracy in Schools*, final report of the Advisory Group on Citizenship (the Crick Report), London: QCA/98/245.

—— (2000) *Citizenship at Key Stages 3 and 4. Initial guidance for schools*, London: QCA.

Starkey, H. (1990) 'World studies and foreign language teaching: converging approaches in textbook writing', in D. Buttjes and M. Byram (eds) *Mediating Languages and Cultures*, Clevedon: Multilingual Matters, 209–27.

——— (1996) 'Intercultural education through foreign language learning: a human rights approach', in A. Osler, H. Rathenow and H. Starkey (eds)*Teaching for Citizenship in Europe*, Stoke: Trentham, 103–16.

——— (1997) 'Foreign language learning and citizenship: issues for lifelong learning', in I. Davies and A. Sobisch (eds) *Developing European Citizens*, Sheffield: Sheffield Hallam University Press, 187–208.

——— (1999) 'Foreign language teaching to adults: implicit and explicit political education', *Oxford Review of Education*, 25(1) and (2): 155–70.

——— (2000) 'Human rights', in M. Byram (ed.) *Encyclopedia of Language Teaching and Learning*, London: Routledge.

Storey, J. (ed.) (1996) *What is Cultural Studies? A Reader*, London: Arnold.

UNHCR (United Nations High Commissioner for Refugees) (1994) *Human Rights: The New Consensus*, London: Regency Press.

Ur, P. (1982) *Discussions that Work*, Cambridge: CUP.

Van Dijk, T. (1997) (ed.) *Discourse as Social Interaction*, London: Sage.

Verhellen, E. (1997) *Convention on the Rights of the Child*, Leuven: Garant.

——— (2000) 'Children's rights and education', in A.Osler (ed.) *Citizenship and Democracy in Schools: Diversity, Identity, Equality*, Stoke-on-Trent: Trentham Books.

Wessels, C. (1987) *Drama*, Oxford: OUP.

7 The role of Modern Languages within a language in education policy

Christopher Brumfit

Background

The changes seen in the 1988 Education Reform Act were the most substantial in British education since it was first established as a major state concern in 1870. They included for the first time a National Curriculum for all learners, and – among many other results that were not necessarily expected by the government – this effectively established a language policy in British education by laying down which languages should be taught, and by intervening directly in the methodology of teaching languages, including first, second and foreign languages within the National Curriculum and subsequent legislation.

Linguistic issues in general had been addressed seriously in the 1970s, most notably in the Bullock Report (1975) on the teaching of English, while foreign languages had seen Modern Languages in the Comprehensive School in 1977 followed under the new Conservative government by Foreign Languages in the School Curriculum: a consultative paper in 1983. Also relevant to language teaching was the last of the major reports, by a working group set up before the Thatcher government was elected, Education for All (also known as the Swann Report) on the education of ethnic minorities and published in 1985. This raises a large number of language teaching concerns, picking up some of the issues briefly addressed in the Bullock Report, relating to bilingual learners.

For foreign languages alone, major policy documents were published at regular intervals following the Education Act of 1988; at the same time general changes to curriculum and assessment practices affected modern languages along with all other subjects. Nonetheless, by laying down so precisely details of curriculum and assessment that had previously been left to local initiative, the government found itself providing answers to questions that it may not have intended to ask.

Any language policy for a country like Britain has to establish a clear position in relation to three main issues. First, how does it relate to the dominant position of English in the country and in the world in general? Second, how does it relate to the other languages active outside schools in the country? Third, what role does it see for foreign languages? Government thinking in the early language proposals (up to about 1992) could be distinguished by three main principles on these issues, none of which was the result of explicit argument in the supporting documents, but which could be clearly seen when the final documentation appeared (see Brumfit 1995: 2 for fuller discussion).

In relation to the first issue, there was little evidence that the role of English in the world should change our approaches to the teaching of modern foreign languages. However, it was certainly assumed that 'language development' in practice meant 'English development'. The effect of this assumption was to marginalize those bilingual learners who brought insights to school from languages other than English (except in Welsh, as we shall see below), and also to lose an opportunity to relate learning foreign languages to the advanced language development of learners' first languages. Both the curriculum for English, and the Kingman Report on teaching English language which preceded it in 1988, assumed that the whole business of language development was tied to development of English. We could call this 'English linguicism'.

How this came about can be seen partly in the developing policy on the second issue. This picked up from comments in the Swann Report (1985), which claimed that establishing community/heritage languages (those brought from home by bilingual learners who live in the UK) in schools may lead to negative social consequences, by ghettoizing ethnic minorities. Thus, it was suggested, such languages should only appear as single academic subjects at secondary level. Although the 1985 Report made it clear that all language groups wanted support for their heritage languages in schools, its conclusion was that the communities themselves privately, not the State through schooling, should take responsibility for this. The Report's discussion is preceded by a summary of the advantages of bilingual schooling, arising from studies of successful bilingual teaching and learning in many other countries. Improvement could be expected to confidence, motivation, cognitive development and linguistic skills, as well as symbolically to community status. This order of priority is strikingly different from the list of 'advantages of bilingualism' listed in the Welsh Office consultative document on the curriculum for teaching Welsh (WO 1989: 6). This, unlike the Swann Report, highlights social and cultural advantages at the beginning of its list, including nationhood and territoriality, and our responsibility for language maintenance and tradition. A clear distinction is made here between an 'indigenous' minority language, and those of minorities who have no traditional territory, and the claim is reinforced by the commitment to teach Welsh to everyone at school in Wales, whether they want to learn it or not – and also for no-one living outside Wales, as the curriculum for England indicates. (It should be noted that the so-called 'National' Curriculum legally referred only to England and Wales, so the issue of Gaelic was subject to separate legislation for Scotland, which had, like Northern Ireland, separate but similar legislation.) The effect of this position is that education in England and Wales operates a territorial bilingual policy, but has no position on bilingualism in other languages as an individual asset. In fact other languages were put together with foreign languages for curriculum purposes. So the principle is 'territorial bilingualism'.

The DES report on Modern Foreign Languages of November 1991 offered an indication of the response to our third issue. The relevant part of the statutary instrument (39) says:

> Schools must offer one or more of the official languages of the EC (Danish, Dutch, French, German, Modern Greek, Italian, Portugese, Spanish). Schools may in addition offer one or more of the non-EC languages listed (Arabic, Bengali, Gujerati, Hindi, Japanese, Mandarin or Cantonese Chinese, Modern Hebrew, Panjabi, Russian, Turkish, Urdu). Pupils choosing to do one of the non-EC languages do not have to study one of the official languages of the EC as well. But the non-EC language will not count as the foundation subject unless the school offers all pupils concerned the possibility of studying an official language of the EC to meet the National Curriculum requirements.

The rationale thus seems to be that in school learners should have the option of learning languages with a political and territorial base in the European Community. If they reject this, they may learn some officially specified languages which either have territory outside UK but few speakers inside (e.g. Japanese), or which have communities inside (e.g. Bengali). However, some large UK language groups (Polish, Irish, or Welsh outside Wales) are not offered such an option.

The attitude to these languages is further clarified when it becomes apparent that (apart from the extra provision for learning Chinese and Japanese characters) all these languages are to be taught in schools to beginners as if they are modern foreign languages. This could be called 'scholingualism', perhaps – the treatment of all languages in the community (apart from Welsh) as scholarly or academic languages.

In fact the implications of this statement were ignored in practice (foreign languages taught in schools are overwhelmingly French, with some Spanish, German and other languages). Even the position of heritage languages could to some extent be fudged by what could be argued to be minor amendments to assessment procedures. At the same time, much of the post-1997 Labour Government's National Literacy Strategy reinforces the centrality of English to general language development, even while advice to teachers is beginning to encourage appreciation of what bilingual learners bring to the classroom. But although they have sometimes been ignored in detail, in so far as there are general principles, they still appear to be these three:

1   general language development takes place through English;
2   multilingualism is territorially based;
3   all other language work is foreign language learning for beginners.

These three principles result in something of a muddle. The first is made difficult because many teachers have learners in their classrooms who develop their linguistic abilities through languages other than English, and who regularly cross and mix languages. The second is simply sociolinguistically untrue (for example, Ethnologue, the American-based survey of languages in the world, lists twenty-seven non-indigenous languages with substantial populations in UK, plus a number of others with smaller numbers; see also the discussion of Alladina and Edwards 1991, under Principle 3 below). In relation to the third, conventional foreign language teachers could only benefit from the naturalness of language use that heritage language speakers bring, so that this should be exploited whenever possible, not ignored. And further, they cannot avoid their learners' all too frequent awareness of the power of English as an international medium of communication. In practice, fewer learners achieve high competence in foreign languages in English speaking countries such as UK and Ireland than anywhere else in Europe. This is unlikely to be a result of anything that teachers, or even learners, do so much as a general, semi-conscious national awareness that foreigners' English is increasingly likely to be better than English-speakers' other languages. However undesirable this is, we cannot ignore that the success of the teaching of English as a Foreign Language (in the context of the American-dominant global economy) is having effects on the motivation of English-speakers to learn foreign languages. In such an environment, foreign language teaching needs to be able to adjust its goals – perhaps, for example, to concentrate on language learning as a means of understanding the multicultural, multilingual world in which we shall necessarily live during the lifetimes of our learners. Whatever adjustments are made, a rigid separation of pragmatic needs for foreign language communication, and allegedly limited cultural needs for bilinguals, will be inappropriate for the foreseeable future. Finally, in addition to this, language work in Classics also has something to contribute to many schools' activities, and is increasingly being used for enhancing a cultural awareness of the past. That too should fit into a policy.

Against this background it has been difficult for teachers and teacher trainers to maintain a principled position. This is partly because of the sheer speed of change, and partly because anyone with any relevant expertise was bound up in the administration of the changes themselves, and either too busy, or else perceived by a government suspicious of the teaching professionals, to have too much of a vested interest for their criticisms to be taken seriously.

But it is nonetheless possible to produce a principled position which is compatible with current National Curriculum legislation, and – since the structure of the curriculum is in a state of permanent review and revision – such a position is very important if revisions are not to be simply the prey of fashion or the latest whim of the civil servants or politicians who have the power. The more centralized the system, the more important well-argued principles become.

Key principles

In the following section, I shall try to present key principles that could underlie the teaching and learning of language within British education. These have been developed over the years through the work of the Centre for Language in Education at the University of Southampton, and are based partly on interpretation of international research on processes of language learning and teaching, and partly on work in Britain, including consultation and redrafting suggestions from language teachers in many places. In Southampton, studies of learners and teachers of English mother tongue, foreign languages, ethnic minority languages, as well as investigations of teachers in training, support the general position outlined below, as does work from many other teachers and scholars elsewhere in the country.

Principle 1: a policy for language, not policies for languages

Learners do not experience separate languages as totally independent activities, except in so far as school administration forces them to. They joke across and with languages, they play with words from other languages, and (as much sociolinguistic research demonstrates) wherever languages are in contact they mix and influence each other. Consequently, language provision in schools cannot helpfully be broken down into completely disconnected compartments. In practice, learners develop an ever-extending linguistic repertoire through interaction with their social environment. The problem for foreign language teachers in schools, separated as they are by National Curriculum and departmental structures, is to tap foreign languages into this inevitable and integrated process. Schools can assist and guide language development, and can help it to be more effective than it would be unassisted, but in the national language the process continues with or without schools. Moving from the intimate language of the home to the more public discourses of the school, or from the improvisation of speech to the more controlled environment of reading and writing, are not permanent shifts where one mode is left behind and another adopted. We move to and fro all the time, in and out of different styles and different dialects and – to varying degrees – across different languages. In contemporary Britain (as the analysis of one evening's viewing on a single television channel makes abundantly clear) stylistic, dialectal and linguistic variation is an unavoidable fact of our environment, and as language users we all participate in creating that environment. So because language is so central to processes of learning and processes of socialization, and because we live in such a rich and potentially fluid environment, thinking about one part of the language curriculum in isolation from other parts makes very little sense. Drawing the separate parts together is sensible because of the ways we learn languages, because of the ways we use them, and because of the nature of our linguistic environment. For foreign language teachers, too, Europe is increasingly becoming a more mixed language environment, and learning to operate across languages (including those not chosen at school) is going to be a more and more important skill.

Principle 2: recognize the fact of English dominance in world communication

In the UK, any coherent language policy for foreign languages must start with the central fact of the British situation: that English is the main language and that, because of the dominance of the US, it is the language of world economic power. The majority of fluent English users in the world are now non-native speakers. This is true of no other language, and because this is true, teaching foreign languages in the UK poses problems that are not found in more multilingual countries, or in those where the economic pull of English as a foreign language provides strong motivation to learn. A language policy for Britain must recognize the implications of this fact, and at the same time be sensitive to the negative effects it may have. These vary from the effects on individuals, such as complacency about the need to learn other languages, to institutions that risk arrogance leading to racism and xenophobia in their approach to non-native-speaking groups. But even more important than these, because less obvious and more subtly damaging, is the implicit assumption than monolingualism is the norm, which can imperceptibly shift into an assumption that not just monolingualism but monodialectalism is the norm, especially for 'educated' people. This view is damaging, and not just because it causes its adherents to be insensitive to the wide variation of linguistic styles that make up anybody's dialect (including that of highly educated speakers). Users need language to conceal as well as to reveal, and it is the interplay between language as a private identity-making process and language as an encounter of public transaction and communication that makes it dynamic and flexible. To start with the current fact of the linguistic hegemony of English is realistic; to rely on it for a curriculum is to misunderstand the nature of language and of communication. Once again, if we examine the European context, we find a greater and greater concern with English as an international language, owned as much by the many highly competent non-native speakers as by native speakers. In this new multilingual environment, foreign language teachers have to help British learners to relocate themselves culturally, as well as cope linguistically. (Note, however, that accepting the current position does not mean accepting that there may be no major change: see Crystal 1997, Graddol 1997, McArthur 1998, Brumfit 2001 for further discussion of some of these issues.)

Principle 3: recognize bilingual learners

In addition, any language policy which is to command widespread acceptance by the monolingual majority must simultaneously be responsive to the complexities of the British linguistic context for bilingual learners. The most notable achievement of the new National Curriculum is that it is an entitlement for all learners, not just a way of creaming off the clever to further learning. A language policy must therefore be just to all learners, and at the same time accept the needs of typical learners. Although there are no reliable figures on bilingual speakers in Britain, Alladina and Edwards (1991) report on thirty-two separate and active speech communities within UK, and the 1987 ILEA reported 172 languages active in London schools. A survey in the Southampton area showed that more than seventy minority language maintenance classes had been active in the 1990s, and twenty-six different new languages could be learnt from scratch in adult education classes. If the policy is to be an entitlement policy, it must not differentiate between English and other languages as the starting point at birth, although of course any curriculum has to distinguish certain end points as more important than others.

Recognition of all languages active within Britain is a necessary precondition for starting the process of language learning. But effective use of the language(s) of work, public life and government is an essential end point for participation in democratic processes, so English (and in some areas other languages) is necessary as a minimum condition for adult life.

Principle 4: recognize the basic functions of language

Language can be said to perform three main roles. It has a pragmatic function as a means of getting things done in the world ('Open up!'). It has a learning and conceptualizing function as a means of understanding the world, of making sense of ideas and evidence ('Now how do I make sense of this …?'). And it has an archive function as a means of storing understandings from the past ('The rules of chess', or even a shopping list). Different languages will provide bases for different kinds of experience. Some (and particularly the major languages of national and international communication, including English) will provide a basis for action in the world as well as for learning and conceptualizing. Some (and particularly mother tongues in the early years) will be crucial at particular stages as the major means by which learning takes place. Some (particularly classical languages and those with strong literary, religious and scientific traditions) will have a major role to play in reinforcing understanding of heritage – a result of the archive function. All may have some role to play in relation to each function, but how these roles operate for particular speech communities at particular times will vary.

Principle 5: acknowledge the role of language in maintaining and establishing group identities

In addition, language use will be closely bound up with individuals' and groups' identities, and in so far as those are contested because of particular social or political frameworks, language may become a symbol of independence or subservience, and language issues a central issue in debates about power and cultural autonomy. Thus the privileged status of Welsh in British education, compared with, say, Punjabi or Cantonese, is largely a product of assumptions about the political role and social coherence of Wales (see discussion in the introduction to Alladina and Edwards 1991).

Principle 6: recognize resource implications in relation to local conditions

Principles that cannot be realized for lack of money, teacher supply or other resources are worth nothing. This should be a statement of what can be done as far as resources permit, and should recognize that local conditions vary because the home and school linguistic profile varies from place to place.

LANGUAGE CHARTER FOR BRITAIN

It is the policy of _____

(insert name of departments, institution, or other authority)

to enable all learners, to the maximum extent possible within available legislation and resources

1   to develop their own mother tongue or dialect to as confident and effective a use as they wish to operate;

2   to develop competence in a range of styles of English for educational, work-based, social and public-life purposes;

3   to develop their knowledge of how language operates in a multilingual society (ideally including basic experience of languages other than their own that are significant either in education, e.g. classical languages or the local community, e.g. heritage languages);

4   to develop as extensive as possible a competence in at least one foreign language, tailored to the anticipated cultural and practical needs of the next generation.

It is our belief that the development of these four strands in combination will contribute to an effective language curriculum for Britain in the twenty-first century more than emphasis on any one of them separately at the expense of the others.

Signed   _____

Date   _____

The Language Charter for Britain

What, then, do such principles imply for all learners in schools? If we assume that a specification of entitlement is what is required, what could that look like? I have tried to encapsulate a proposal for an agreed agenda in the form of a charter for all language learners. This charter offers an agenda to define what – subject as always to resource limitations – we should be trying to provide as an entitlement (see Brumfit 1986 for the first outline of the charter idea, and Brumfit 1995 for a development of the ideas in relation to National Curriculum provision, but this version has been modified from the versions given there in the light of discussions with teachers and others). Note that in other countries similar categories can apply, but the languages used in each section will of course differ. For foreign languages to thrive in schools, they should be systematically linked to provision under all three of these headings. Why?

Very briefly, they should be linked to (1) because there is convincing research evidence that people learn second languages well when they are confident language users, and they develop that initial confidence through their mother tongues. Further, as their repertoire extends, the standard language, the languages of literacy, and eventually foreign languages, have the potential to grow out of that confident language use. At the same time institutions cannot give an open commitment to all potential first languages, and nor can or should they compel users to operate with languages that they may or may not wish to use. A welcoming of diversity and an encouragement of effective use may be all that can be offered in some institutions; in others, with large numbers of speakers of the same language, bilingual teachers and bilingual work in class may be possible and, in such places, modern language departments would have a responsibility to work in liaison with such teachers.

They should be linked to (2) because English is the dominant language of education and public life, so competence in foreign languages should accept and relate to the competences that are required in English. Further, translation, interpreting, mixed English/FL activity, cross-referring to activities taking place in English – all these will help to overcome the distance between English and foreign languages that is so distinctive a feature of UK culture. The link between grammar and descriptive work in English and that required in foreign language learning needs to be made clear also.

They should be linked to (3) because unless all learners understand what it is to be part of a multilingual country in a multilingual continent, in a multilingual world, the point of FL learning will be lost. And knowledge about language helps effective language learning.

The definition of (4) is of course the prime task of foreign language teachers.

Implications of the Language Charter for the curriculum

Language is a vehicle for a wide range of activities and, as we have argued above, is closely bound up with personal development, concept formation and identity. Simultaneously, it is tied in to public and private communication processes. The language curriculum must therefore reflect a range of activities with different purposes.

Drawing upon our discussion of the functions of language, we can define them broadly for the Charter as follows, with the operational consequences following:

Function	Operational consequence
Developmental and concept-creating	Helping learners to become confident users for purposes of their own choosing, to become creative and imaginative, to be willing to think about and reflect on their own language practices.
Understanding heritage	Making sense of past achievement and traditions with language.
Functional	Enabling learners to operate with the conventions demanded by society.

Most language work should incorporate aspects of all three of these.

Furthermore, enabling this to happen requires the curriculum to draw upon institutionalized language practices: within language work specifically, literature, drama, and media understanding may be significant elements; within other subject areas, understanding the genres of scientific or historical writing (for example) becomes important. Implementation of the Language Charter requires integration of all these activities, though the ways in which this will happen will vary at different levels of education, and with different language groupings.

The Charter proposal is based on views of social justice. It is entirely compatible with National Curriculum orders, but it provides a coherence and a focus on learners' entitlement which is more specific than offered there.

It could also be translated into any level of education, for it can be adapted to pre-school, community, further and higher education as well as mainstream schooling and provides a rationale for language teacher education.

Specifying its implications with greater delicacy for particular groups is a task primarily for practitioners. As an illustration, some implications for foreign language learners in schools and in universities are spelt out below (see Mitchell and Brumfit 1997 for a consideration of the implications for bilingual learners).

Implications for the Foreign Language curriculum in schools

From the Charter's first requirement:

a   a recognition by foreign language teachers that second language use is not a replacement of, but an extension of, mother tongue activity, and that this should affect the pedagogical strategies adopted;

b   a willingness by teachers to acknowledge the bi- and multilingual skills brought by learners with mother tongues other than English, and to incorporate this awareness into pedagogy wherever appropriate.

From the Charter's second requirement:

a   systematic curriculum links between work in foreign languages and in English classes, either by liaison where appropriate on multilingual activities/tasks crossing subject boundaries, or by exploiting and following development in the English curriculum by related activities of a simpler kind in the foreign language class.

From the Charter's third requirement:

a   systematic use of cross-reference between the multilingual/multidialectal characteristics of the target language world communities, and those of the English-speaking world (and, where appropriate, of other language groups);

b   constant recognition of the target language as a code used in specific social contexts, with learning related to all the functions of language identified in earlier discussion.

From the Charter's fourth requirement:

a   consistent pressure to ensure that the foreign language curriculum is genuinely made accessible in appropriate ways to all learners;
b   a willingness to reassess, on a regular basis, the role of foreign languages in the overall package provided by the Charter, particularly in view of the changing role of English in the world and the anticipated needs of English-speaking learners.

Thus the implications for foreign language school-teaching operate mainly at the level of pedagogy.

Finally, since there should be a close relationship between what schools do and what university offers (partly because schools are dependent on universities for the supply and knowledge-base of teachers of foreign languages, and partly because universities must develop their curriculums for learners who have been through the school system), let us consider what the Charter implies for higher education.

Implications for foreign languages at university

For learners in higher education this charter would need to build on what had happened in school through the GCSE, GNVQ and A level routes. But there are still key themes for higher education to consider which arise directly out of what students will bring from their experience of language in the community and their experience of language teaching and learning in schools.

From the Charter's first and second requirements

In relation to personal growth and public competence, the university's prime role will be ensuring fluency and confidence in the target language and associated specialist cultural needs. But the extent to which this can derive from their understanding of their other languages (and cultures) of effective use (whether English or minority languages) will be a matter for methodological discussion. In so far as good practice in teaching is followed, building on the linguistic understanding that students bring is essential. So universities will have to provide more than simply effective use of the target language. What is clear in addition, though, is that personal needs and motivations apply in consideration of what cultural institutions are deserving of study, what learning procedures are adopted, what literary works are chosen, and what theoretical orientations are adopted – for all of these interact with the personal preferences and concerns of students. In contrast, the external factors – the pragmatic or social needs – will be determined more by decisions about the appropriate language(s) of government and power, the styles used by social or professional groups that students may be expected to join, and by the needs of the professions they may be expecting to enter, whether language teaching, interpreting, translation, journalism, business, or simply informed understanding of target cultures. Thus universities differ from schools, not just in the age and level of competence (sometimes) of learners, but in the extent to which learners may be increasingly developing clearly defined goals about target subcultures they wish either to join, or at least to monitor.

From the Charter's third requirement

On top of these there is a concern about the role of conscious knowledge about language (and culture) in enabling students to improve their learning capacity and to cope with their roles as participants in cross-cultural encounters. Understanding sociological and psychological aspects of language learning and use will be valuable to many students, but both in this area and in cultural studies there are three different approaches which can be taken. All of these have their place, but they support different aspects of cultural/linguistic awareness. A descriptive approach takes the nature of the language or culture as a given, and provides meta-awareness of a set of features which are not problematized, but which reflect a consensus view of the object of study. A reflexive approach asks students to locate themselves within the culture and emphasizes the inter-relationship of personal responses and external stimuli. A 'critical' approach tries to unpack the hidden meanings in the language or culture to enable students to detect unanticipated biases and distortions. It is clear that the reflexive and critical approaches may have a symbiotic relationship with each other; but it is equally the case that any selection of items for a cultural or linguistic curriculum must make claims about the representative nature of these for the objectives of the curriculum. A degree of descriptive typicality is necessary for any selection of items if a curriculum is to have credibility, and this logically precedes decisions about personal response or the unpacking of unforeseen meanings. So it is difficult to avoid an involvement with all three approaches.

Finally, in relation to the third requirement, the question should be raised about the role of foreign language departments in asking students to encounter alien experiences, and to cope with them. Should there be some contact with so-called 'exotic' languages (that is, those with quite different linguistic structure from English or French)? Should cultural surprise be deliberately cultivated within the curriculum? Should the intensive and successful rapid language learning experience that used to be part of the Language Centre's work at the University of York be more widespread? How much positive experience of destabilization should there be?

From the Charter's fourth requirement

Of course universities will have their role pre-defined by student choices of language, course options and course combinations. Some (though diminishing numbers in recent years) may be opting beyond the Charter for competence in more than one foreign language, and the university's general role will be to go beyond the minimum requirements of the Charter to specialist areas, in ways which have been outlined in the previous discussion.

Thus, in a well-organized world, schools should be able to provide universities with learners who are:

- confident and fluent in their use of first language/variety of English, if they wish to be;
- competent and accurate in standard English;
- aware of the nature of language and how it operates socially;
- possessors of basic competence in at least one foreign language.

The National Curriculum could in principle deliver these; even in so far as it does not, the responsibility to build on what is actually provided by A level and typical entry levels cannot be avoided. The task of universities has to be first to build on these foundations, and to work to make the foundations more realistic (if necessary through such proposals as the 'Language Charter', or through proposing better alternatives). The second task is to ensure that the issues discussed in this paper are taken seriously within higher education as well as within the school system. The result of this will be that issues of coherence, which are increasingly important in a view of language work within the humanities, will begin to be resolved. Links, therefore, between the experience of students who share specific foreign languages with other foreign languages, with English or with classics, can draw upon a common specification of what linguistic understanding may be available through schooling, and therefore what may be shared in development within higher education. Criteria can be developed for shared contributions to a unified student experience across history, area studies, philosophy, and even business or engineering, and links between BAs in modern languages and PGCEs for teaching can be made more systematic.

Further specifications, for higher education generally outside foreign language departments, or for FE provision, using the basic school provision as the starting point, would also help to establish a firm basis for language development within national educational policy. The advantage of this proposal over the present National Curriculum is that this centres on the learning process and the individual entitlement within it. From the individual language of home develops both the advanced literacy and the publicly required confident use of English on the one hand and, eventually, the foreign language provision, on the other. Everyone is entitled to develop the linguistic resources they bring to education, while the national requirement for capacity to participate in British democratic life, and in the multilingual world of which Britain is a part, is still central.

Given the problems of foreign language learning arising from the strength of English, such a view of policy seems worth addressing. If it does nothing else, it attempts to establish an agenda which is more coherent than that currently provided by the National Curriculum or by the diverse practices of schools and universities. Whether it provides a means of overcoming our inherited weakness in foreign language learning, only time can tell. But if this vision of future possibilities is too difficult to realize, it should at least challenge others to produce a better one. For without some generally agreed vision, we shall be ill-equipped for a world in which other countries are developing their own with great vigour.

Further reading

Alladina, S. and Edwards, V. (1991) *Multilingualism in the British Isles* (2 vols), Harlow: Longman.

Brumfit, C.J. (1989) 'Towards a language policy for multilingual secondary schools', in J. Geach (ed.) *Coherence in Diversity*, London: CILT (originally a lecture given in 1986).

—— (ed.) (1995) *Language Education in the National Curriculum*, Oxford: Blackwell.

—— (2001) *Individual Freedom in Language Teaching*, Oxford: Oxford University Press.

Crystal, D. (1997) *English as a Global Language*, Cambridge: Cambridge University Press.

DES (Department for Education and Science) (1975) *A Language for Life* ('Bullock Report') London: HMSO.

—— (1977) *Modern Languages in Comprehensive Schools*, London: HMSO.

—— (1983) *Foreign Languages in the School Curriculum: A Consultative Paper*, London: HMSO.

—— (1985) *Education for All: The Report on the Committee of Inquiry into the Education of Children from Ethnic Minority Groups*, ('Swann Report') London: HMSO.

DES/WO (1991) *Modern Foreign Languages in the National Curriculum*, London: HMSO.

Ethnologue (1996) www.sil.org/ethnologue/

Graddol, D. (1997) *The Future of English?* London: The British Council.

McArthur, T. (1998) *The English Languages*, Cambridge: Cambridge University Press.

Mitchell, R.F. and Brumfit, C.J. (1997) 'The National Curriculum experience of bilingual learners', *Educational Review* 49(2): 159–80.

WO (Welsh Office) (1989) *Welsh for Ages 5–16*, Cardiff: The Welsh Office.

8   Change

Looking beyond Europe

Judith Hamilton

This chapter is about change, because, if you are a trainee teacher, unquestionably you are going to have to deal with it. I present my own view of change seen from a perspective of ten years outside the UK in places as diverse as New Zealand, Tanzania, South East Asia, the South Pacific, the USA and Australia. Here I will deal mainly with countries in which English is their first language, but it seems important to mention that other experiences working on language and education policies in very poor countries influence my thinking.

My belief is that you should start seriously to plan your career from the moment you start your training. Your career is your responsibility and you cannot rely on local authority advisers to steer you in the right direction. While teacher training is traditionally concerned with the technical aspects of teaching, in this rapidly changing world it pays to keep in touch with movements outside the profession and indeed outside the country. A recent experience looking at the language needs of the business community has underlined for me the importance of keeping an eye on the big picture.

Historically, with a background in European languages, predominantly French, and an experience of overseas residence or travel formed mainly, if not exclusively, in Europe, UK language providers look to Europe when they think of changes they would like to see. My sense is that Europe presents an inadequate model for change in the UK. I would also contend that it is inappropriate for language teachers to present a purely European model of the languages they are teaching. To deal with the first point: our decision-makers are as much if not more influenced by movements in English-speaking countries as by those in Europe, certainly as far as economic policies are concerned. Indeed, while for years providers have been pointing to the very favourable conditions given to the teaching of English in countries like Finland, Sweden, Holland and Germany, and making arguments for similar provision for languages here, those who control the budget look to the States, Australia and New Zealand. In these countries it is increasingly the case that less is expected of the state, and more of the individual.

As regards my second point about the presentation of a mainly European model, we tend to teach French, and to a lesser extent Spanish and Portuguese, with reference mainly to the country of origin. This is to ignore a vast area of rich experiences from many other countries, as well as some serious global issues. Learners, as future world citizens, would benefit if they were encouraged to view these issues through a non-European lens, with other perspectives, via other media and in another language. Current affairs, social issues and historical events often look quite different from a Latin American or African perspective.

All new teachers change things, one way or another, and some actually set out to change things. Whether you are proactive or reactive, it is infinitely preferable to be prepared. First you have to understand the system, and what is possible within it, and if necessary, you have to work out how to get around it! Just as no-one can teach you a language against your will – ask minority groups in countries where a national language is foisted on them by a majority – no-one can 'understand' a system on your behalf. This is something you have to do for yourself. It makes sense to work on this, because you are likely to be spending some time within this system. Getting a false or partial understanding may not only be costly in career terms, it can make you seriously unhappy.

Perhaps one of the most disappointing discoveries we make when we start teaching is that, in fact, most schools are themselves not learning institutions; that is, the entity itself, unlike successful modern companies, is not geared up to learn – and, of course, to learn is to change. Schools, and groups of people who work in them, mostly dislike change, resist it and at best barely tolerate it. Interestingly, institutions appear to display less antipathy to change when it comes to technological/scientific or pseudo-scientific innovation. This is because such change is socially neutral, and therefore legitimized by our habit of seeing technology as 'progress'. Changes which alter the balance of power and/or social relations, however, tend to threaten the existing social fabric, and the status of individuals.

I have written elsewhere[1] about factors which influence the ability to change things within a school, based on my own experience as Principal Teacher of Modern Languages (Head of Department). I used the model devised by Michael Porter to analyse the competitive advantage of nations.[2] Porter says that there is a need for a number of conditions to be right in order for change to take place: factor conditions, demand conditions, firm strategy and rivalry, related and supporting industries/developments, chance and government.

- Factor conditions are the resources available – human and material. They would include, for instance, teachers' qualifications, their level of commitment, their age, as well as resources and funding.
- Demand conditions are the extent to which the 'market' wants the product. In different areas of the UK, parents, employers, and the local public are likely to have different opinions as to the value of language competence. Demand conditions from a sophisticated clientele tend to produce a high-quality product. This may account for the fact that it seems somewhat easier to motivate middle-class pupils in the leafy suburbs of southern England than in other less favoured parts of our country. Demand conditions probably also account for the unequal geographical spread of French in primary schools.
- Firm strategy, structure and rivalry conditions have to do with the goals, the social norms and management of the institution, some of which can act as

determinants of the success or failure of innovation. Rivalry could mean what the school down the road is doing to attract the brightest pupils. Whether it should have a place within a state education system is a healthy topic for debate.

- Related and supporting industries refer to those structures and circumstances in the environment which might be said to offer support to particular innovation, such as a friendly teacher training establishment or enthusiastic export business in the area.

- Chance is sometimes on the side of the innovators, and many a business has been glad of a lucky break. It can work for departments too, particularly if they enter their pupils' work for competitions or make bids for funding.

In this chapter I am going to limit myself for lack of space to factors related to government, whose influence on teachers' careers I think I have underestimated in the past.

Example 1: ideology and isolation in New Zealand

Contrary to what governments and education ministers like to have us believe, they are rarely a source of original thinking. Governments, or more often their officials, frequently get their ideas from economics and its hybrid offspring, management theory. The influence of educational economists is rarely mentioned in the education debate in the UK, but it should not be underestimated. Everyone wants an 'efficient and effective' education service, school, department or whatever these days. Listen for that phrase. It is a key to a certain way of viewing the world. It may help you in your career to learn to use it, but I believe it may in the long term help you more if you understand some of the history behind its use. I first saw signs of what was to come in the UK when I visited New Zealand in the early 1990s and first encountered public choice theory, otherwise known as 'managerialism', in action. This is a brief account of the 'reforms' which took place there at that time. You will see many things which resonate with our own experiences here; no secret, it was their model we copied and to some extent continue to copy. Meanwhile in New Zealand the new government is trying to undo some of the harm.

In 1987 New Zealand engaged in a major political experiment, driven by an ideology of rigid adherence to market principles. 'Outputs', 'rates of return', 'rationalization', became the order of the day. Economists and businessmen were recruited to lead the changes; under the guise of 'increased local control' and 'greater parental choice', the public was sold the notion of an education system over which they, the consumers, would have a more direct say. What in fact occurred was an increased central control with, at the same time, the delegation, some say dereliction, by government of their responsibility for the actual running of the service, a positive encouragement to inequality of provision, and the ensuing demoralization and de-skilling of the teaching force.

By passing the buck for implementation of the new policies to schools and their governing bodies, to outside agencies and consultants, government virtually abnegated all responsibility for the education service. With this separation of policy from implementation, the Ministry was able to wash its hands of any defects within the system. The teachers carried the can.

New Zealand is important because of the amount of cross-fertilization of ideas and policies between government officials there and here from the very outset of the reforms. Downsizing and outsourcing meant the virtual end of subject advisers and all of this led to the increased isolation of individual teachers and school departments. Lack of professional help and guidance contributed both to the sense of isolation of teachers, and to the attrition rates which then led to teacher shortages. By the middle of 1993 teacher trainers were suffering staff cuts of around 10 per cent. Funds for secondary trainees were effectively reduced by 24 per cent. To quote one colleague: 'It's everyone for himself at the moment – there is no-one who cares about how we feel and we now have no-one to turn to for professional help and guidance.'

The loss of institutional memory, the loss of the notion of public service in education, and the loss of expertise earned from a long apprenticeship mean that the agenda to which many individuals started to work became one more of self-seeking than of public service. This fits perfectly with public choice theory, the main thrust of which is that disinterested behaviour does not exist.

When any institution is destabilized, it is not only people that disappear: traditions of service built up over years, links forged with other institutions, attitudes to work, the willingness to undertake tasks for the general good, team spirit, the appreciation of experience, so that individual one-off performance is not viewed as the sole criterion for advancement, all these go too. Worse, once gone, an institution is gone for ever; it cannot be remade in the way that 'targets', 'outputs', 'policy', etc. can be remade to suit the trend of the moment.

It has to be said that a new government in New Zealand may be changing some of the above. However, the effects remain. It is now the case that some 20,000 New Zealanders are emigrating each year to Australia, many of whom are graduates who seek to avoid the repayment of loans for their university courses which they were forced to take out by the previous administration and which they can see no way of repaying in the present economic climate.

Issues and implications

The New Zealand experience highlights both the effects of economic and public management policy on teachers, and the isolation of individual professionals. It also demonstrates the need for teachers to prepare themselves for changes in their circumstances and the increasing importance of career planning and direction. Language teachers in the UK, like their counterparts in New Zealand, are part of an ageing profession, with an insufficient number of people joining and remaining in the service. This means that for you the school may not be the prime source of new ideas. Rather, you may find your colleagues expecting you to provide these for them.

One source of ideas, and something which has enhanced my own career, is contact with our professional associations: the Association for Language Learning, (ALL) and the Scottish Association for Language Teachers (SALT). Attending conferences and local meetings gives the much-needed contact with teachers from all over the country, and newsletters and journals keep you up to date. The role of associations is also to provide a voice for the profession. Associations can change things. The national language teachers' association in Portugal managed to lower class sizes for languages by using arguments from documentation provided by the Fédération Internationale des Professeurs de Langues Vivantes (FIPLV), 'a global network of support for language professionals' to which both UK associations are affiliated. Being a member of an association gives you access to a world of educational expertise beyond the confines of these shores.

For those who seriously plan a career, there is a need to demonstrate a seriousness about professional development. It is all too easy to become isolated and stale. Teachers rarely, if ever, read books about teaching. Discussions about pedagogy, unless within formal meetings such as one-off 'Inset' days, virtually cease once teachers hit the classroom, both because they don't have the time, and because institutions are themselves not innovative. It is people who innovate. To potential innovators I would suggest consideration of the influence of the conditions I mentioned earlier with reference to the Porter model. This lets you analyse the circumstances within which a department, or indeed an individual teacher, operates. If you make use of favourable factor conditions, demand conditions or related and supportive developments to bring about changes, you are more likely to succeed than if you rush in like a bull at a gate. Detailing successful examples from elsewhere and demonstrating experiences beyond the walls of one's own school can also help make a case for change, which is why it makes sense to explore the local scene and enlist the support of those who can make their voices count.

Teachers who keep on learning keep developing and have more rewarding careers. One opportunity which a career in teaching offers is free, or relatively low-cost, access to acquiring new skills. Our best companies expect their employees to work constantly on self-improvement, often at their own expense. Nowadays you are expected to hit the ground running – and keep running! It is not merely a question of keeping up to date, but of constantly adding to one's set of skills as a matter of course. Learning about management theory, for instance, makes a great deal of sense, if only because these days this is a 'language' you need to speak in order to get things done.

Example 2: fast-tracking in the USA – recruitment and training

In New Zealand, the drive towards an 'efficient and effective' service led managers to define tasks, set targets, and then look for people who could 'do the job'. 'Getting the job done' has become the main concern of administrators in most countries, rich or poor. It does not matter to them whether the people they hire to 'do the job' have a long-term interest in or commitment to the institution or to the system as a whole. To some it little matters to what extent these people hold traditional qualifications. 'Fast-track entry', partnered by on-the-job training is viewed by educational economists as a highly cost-effective way of addressing teacher shortages. Some also consider it to be a better way of teacher training.

In the US, 'getting the job done' has become for some States and school districts no longer a matter of choice. The *New York Times* of 24 August 2000 reports how acute teacher shortages and demands for higher standards have led, in a country where educational options like vouchers and charter schools are already accepted, to a new model of teacher pre-service training which calls into question the notion of standards, who shall set them, and indeed whether teacher training institutions are necessary at all.

The premise is that existing programmes in Schools of Education produce graduates of low quality. Too much time is spent on pedagogy, and not enough on subject knowledge. This kind of teacher training, it is said, is all very well for the elementary school system, but it fails to meet the needs of older learners. Note in this context that leading educational economists from the World Bank, and other shapers of governmental opinion about education in rich as well as in poor countries, see the provision of textbooks as far more cost-effective than any form of teacher training.

In the US, individual states have created their own programmes to produce teachers in as short a time as three months. The new approaches are said to stem as much from a concern with quality as with quantity – there is a need to attract good people into classrooms, and many of these are put off by the perceived poor quality of teacher education schools. 'Teach for America', a non-profit organization, has in the last ten years been concerned with putting fresh graduates into schools after a short time of training during the summer. Criticisms have not been slow in coming, particularly from professors of education.

Fast-tracking looks set to be an issue for language teachers here in the near future. The *Times Educational Supplement* of 3 November 2000 suggests that a new scheme is already under discussion with some teacher training institutions.[3]

Issues and implications

Given the existing shortfall in teacher recruitment, the debate as to what matters most – content area expertise or pedagogy – is likely to be of increasing relevance to the language teaching profession in the UK, whether or not the expansion in provision, recommended by the Nuffield Report, comes to pass.[4] The recommended extension of compulsory language learning at both ends of the educational experience may please providers in the short term. However, moves to expand language teaching into primary schools raise questions about qualifications and training. I, for one, cannot see how you can expand language provision and balance the budget without a much more flexible approach to qualifications. And then comes the additional factor of standards.

Although we cannot predict the future, we can nevertheless perceive trends and directions. However it is to be achieved, it seems likely that demand for languages will increase, along with the requirement for more language teaching and probably more varied means of delivery. Strategic management of any increased provision is, moreover, likely to be devolved to people who by and large are unaware of how language teachers think, and uncaring as to what they would wish. The challenge for the profession, it seems to me, is to articulate a realistic way forward before someone else does.

Those who might wish to impose 'reforms' on us are likely to present us with questions such as the following:

- Is there a real need for pre-service training for all would-be language teachers? Could top graduates and native speakers not be 'fast-tracked'?
- Does sixth-form teaching really require the same level of methodological competence as other teaching? Could we not make savings and exemptions here?
- If on-the-job training is more cost-effective, should resources not be diverted to it from existing models?
- The shortage of teachers means some colleges are reluctant to refuse entrance to all but the most obviously unsuitable candidates. This leads to problems within schools which then have to 'weed out' the unsatisfactory ones. Would not the interests of the profession be better served if experienced teachers were the gatekeepers of standards from the beginning and took a leading role in selection and training?
- How do you balance a high ability in language use against an ability in pedagogy?

There are of course plenty of people who speak the languages which we might want to see taught in our schools. Indeed, even if you exclude native speakers, it is likely that a higher level of expertise in use of other languages exists outside the teaching profession than within it. This is a new concept for the British, and one which was not the case some years ago, when many of the best language graduates went into teaching. It was not at all unusual to have in a languages department, as I did when I first started teaching in a large Scottish comprehensive school, a PhD and a majority of Honours over Ordinary graduates.

In fact, this school offered a model of a languages department which would fit in well with present recommendations to diversify more in the languages we teach in schools. There were almost equal numbers of French, German and Spanish learners, and most teachers had university degrees in more than one language – and some picked up competence in a third from covering colleagues' classes, took examinations in the language and sometimes taught parts of classes or modular courses in it. This is a practice which, later in my career, when I was running my second department, was much discouraged by Her Majesty's Inspectorate, who demanded university qualifications in all subjects taught, including short-course modules in Italian taken 'for fun' by sixth-form pupils with a teacher holding the equivalent of an A level. At the time I started to wonder whether these demands for 'high standards' were not in fact a straitjacket. Ought the powers that be not in fact encourage such practice? Can we really go on with a situation in which over 93 per cent of school pupils are learning French?

Most teachers and school management teams are in favour of diversification. Its role is seen as central to any national languages strategy. Yet the problem is that it is almost totally incompatible with the demand-driven spread of French, and bedevilled with problems of ensuring continuity of learning from primary to secondary. In the case of which languages to teach, and who should decide this, there are also lessons to be learnt from what has taken place in Australia – see below.

One final word on fast-tracking. Given the defects of my own college training, I was extremely fortunate to be employed in what was generally reckoned to be 'a good stable'. We did not call it 'mentoring', but that is in fact what I received. Debates about methodology raged within my first department. From these we young teachers learnt a great deal, not only about language and linguistics, and how to analyse error, but also how to put our own case – an excellent preparation for job interviews. Mentoring is of course one way of preparing new teachers and it has the valuable spin-off that the mentors themselves increase their own knowledge and skills. Peer-mentoring is a way of keeping on one's toes, and this is indeed something you can do for yourself, if you have agreeable (and argumentative) colleagues such as I had.

Example 3: policy and providers' expectations in Australia[5]

Australia leads the English-speaking world in reforming national attitudes to language learning. In the last twenty-five years there have been sixteen reports prepared for state governments on the need to increase the number of Australians learning language. Languages have been seen as part of a much larger whole, involving and embracing notions of citizenship and what it means to be Australian. Transforming attitudes to languages other than English in Australian society has been accompanied by ambitions to transform attitudes to speakers of these languages.

In the 1980s, in the face of a disastrous drop in numbers taking a language (almost always French), Australia started to edge its way towards a national policy for languages. The history and outcomes of this process have some important lessons for those dreaming that one day our government will solve all our problems through injections of large amounts of funding.

The Australian Language Levels (ALL) Guidelines were developed in the late seventies in South Australia by teams of teachers, teacher trainers and advisers, with imported expertise from as far away as Scotland. They produced a generic framework for the teaching, learning and assessment of some thirty Languages Other Than English (referred to in Australia by its acronym 'LOTE') in primary and secondary schools. At this time both Australia and the UK were engaged in a process of curriculum renewal whose intellectual roots lay in the field of Applied Linguistics. Applied linguists, mostly with a background in EFL, brought communicative methodology to the front of the language reform agenda world-wide. The work of the same key individuals has dominated subsequent developments in language teaching and learning, although the methodology they described has often been misunderstood and misapplied. In the UK what emerged was known as 'the GOML movement' (Graded Objectives in Modern Languages), and the history of GOML provides an interesting contrast to what happened in Australia.[6]

Whereas UK regional schemes were concerned mainly, though not exclusively, with European languages taught within the school system, the ALL project reached out beyond the school community, and linguistic diversity was at the heart of curriculum renewal. The languages of indigenous and immigrant populations had their own syllabuses and levels, drawn up by practitioners, aided by various experts from inside and outside Australia. From the ALL project emerged a series of papers highlighting the need for a National Language Policy.

Throughout the eighties and nineties a considerable amount of interchange in terms of both personnel and ideas took place between Australia and the UK, not only in the field of languages, but also in the field of economics. The latter was important for what was to come: remember, this was the high period for market forces. Yet a completely different trend was to be seen within the profession. Soon language professionals in Australia were to find themselves at odds with those whom they had earlier made their allies. In terms of language education, providers believed they had found an answer to the problems of motivation, methodology, materials, examinations and syllabus design. As they saw it, the answer lay in responsible ownership of the process by both teachers and learners. As economists saw it, only the effective and efficient delivery of a marketable product came to matter. A marketable product is of course incompatible with the process-based approach of those who were experimenting with a truly 'communicative methodology' which went beyond that which many textbooks had sold to the teaching profession.

A great deal of what happened subsequently can best be understood in relation to the impact of public choice theory and managerialism, which led in New Zealand, Australia and eventually here in the UK to the now familiar processes of rationalization, privatization and down-sizing which affect practically every aspect of life, and which have undoubtedly changed national mindsets. The same thinking in the education sector has produced an emphasis on measurement, accountability, league tables, target-setting and performance indicators. What has to be remembered about public choice theory is that disinterested behaviour does not exist. You motivate employees by the application of rewards and threats. There is no such thing as a vocation. Teachers who spend extra hours on all sorts of crazy activities do this because they believe they will be rewarded in some way – if only perhaps in another life!

Policy initiatives at national commonwealth level date from the release of the National Policy on Languages (otherwise known under its author's name as the 'Lo Bianco Report'). This report was influenced, but not totally dominated by, economic data relating to Australia's developing trading relationships in southeast Asia. Lo Bianco, who is both a linguist and an economist, believes that the linking of export figures to languages studied was crucial to the implementation of the subsequent policy. It was this which 'sold' the report to Australia's politicians. What happened subsequently has undoubted pointers for us in the UK.

At the time of the Lo Bianco Report, which was eventually adopted in 1987, the economic export-oriented argument was part of a much wider whole. The Report itself reflected understandings about the relationship between language learning and the development of citizenship and interpersonal skills, its relationship to learning within the curriculum in general, and the need to celebrate and foster heritage and indigenous languages. Its concern for equity, for instance, extended to the inclusion of sign language for deaf citizens. A very positive outcome from the Report was the resourcing and funding of tertiary institutions which played an important role as centres of information and development. My own impression is that around this time the Australian public started to talk about languages, not only because parents and grandparents could hear children trying out at home what they had learnt in the classroom, but also because politicians were keen to run with an issue which they could link to increasing prosperity.

An increased emphasis on economic rationalism was accompanied by an awareness of serious problems relating to literacy throughout Australian society. In the 1990s news that up to 10 per cent of the population were not functionally literate shocked the country. The strategic importance of language and literacy skills to Australia's national development and the well-being of all Australians was seized on by politicians, and in 1991 *The National Policy on Languages* became *Australia's Language: The Australian Language and Literacy Policy*. In 1991 came mention of targets. *The Year 2000: the Commonwealth White Paper on National Language and Literary Policy* stated that 'the proportion of Year 12 students studying a language other than English should be increased to 25 per cent nationally by the year 2000'.

In 1993 a survey by AGB McNair of the attitudes to Asian languages among Australian businesses involved in East Asia-related trading reported that 45 per cent of middle-sized businesses foresaw a future need for Asian languages, in contrast to which fewer than 4 per cent of Year 12 students were actually studying an Asian language. This survey was quickly followed (1994) by the Council of Australian Governments (COAG) Report – *Asian Languages and Australia's Economic Future* which recommends that Japanese, Chinese (Mandarin), Indonesian and Korean should be supported in preference to other languages.

COAG acknowledges that it takes over three times as long to achieve even basic proficiency in Japanese or Chinese as it does in European languages. It sees this as an argument for an early introduction to these languages. It does not address the opportunity costs involved, particularly when the basic skills of literacy (and now numeracy) also require attention. The text recommends Chinese (Mandarin) as one of its four key languages, but fails to recommend the maintenance of the language among Chinese speakers.

The picture today varies from state to state. However, to quote Angela Scarino, Head of the School of International Studies at the University of Adelaide, a 'nonsensical form of target-setting dominates policy-making, which is highly influenced by the formulations within the COAG Report'. While the present take-up rate for languages has increased in some states to around 15 per cent, it is nowhere near the 25 per cent target recommended in the 1991 Commonwealth White Paper and the COAG Report. Angela Scarino believes that the current case rests on the premise that languages are not academically rigorous: they are merely a skill, and have no place in a university.

Issues and implications

Potentially worrying is the fact that funding for non-COAG languages is increasingly hard to find. A similar approach to the oversupply of French in the UK would have considerable employment implications for teachers trained only to teach French. One reading of submissions to the Nuffield Inquiry is that while there is an increasing demand for languages, the present 'product' falls far short of what consumers require.

A particular problem for teachers of French is that the poor performance of pupils in languages in UK schools generally, and the low demand evidenced by a vastly decreased uptake at senior level, are often blamed on the – to my mind somewhat simplistic – perception that French is 'difficult', and not popular with boys. I tend to distrust such perceptions. Whatever you think about the problems related to teaching French rather than another language, there is surely all the more reason to equip yourself with skills beyond those limited to your subject, and to ensure that broader educational objectives are tangible outcomes of what takes place in your classroom.

For me it seems that there is a need in the UK to know much more about demand: to determine the state of demand; to learn how to stimulate demand; and how best to meet it. I also believe that there is a need for teachers to equip their pupils with transferable skills. If we argue that oversupply in French is not a problem, because learning French gives us easy access to other languages, we should be able to justify that claim by learning other languages ourselves, and letting our pupils find out how they can do this too. If we have taught French effectively, and our pupils have really 'learnt how to learn', then they ought to be able to do something with a passage in Italian, given a dictionary and a bit of time.

Jo Lo Bianco sees an important role for language educators as that of educating the purchaser. He sees it as our job collectively as a profession to turn the public into a sophisticated purchaser of language products, and to ensure that these products have more than a short shelf-life. As Porter tells us, a sophisticated market tends to co-exist alongside a wide range and high quality of product. On the other hand, the loss of faith and confidence attached to failure to learn a language can be extended to the whole school and education system. Language learning, therefore, has to be understood by both providers and public as a cumulative process, which can be interactive and humanizing in ways not applicable to some other forms of knowledge. Language learning demands of learners an investment of themselves, and this can be a negative or a positive experience, depending on the understanding and skill of the teacher. At its best, the language classroom should make manifest values of tolerance, and demonstrate real and sustained sensitivity to other cultures. This is not something which a book or technology can do. It is totally dependent on the knowledge and skill of individual teachers.

Notes

1   Hamilton, J. (1996) *Inspiring Innovations in Modern Language Teaching*, Cleveland: Multilingual Matters.
2   Porter, M.E. (1990) *The Competitive Advantage of Nations*, London: Macmillan.
3   See www.fasttrackteaching.gov.uk and www.tes.co.uk for more details.
4   See www.nuffieldfoundation.org
5   This section has been adapted from a report commissioned by the Nuffield Languages Inquiry.
6   Page, B. and Hewett, D. (1987) *Languages Step by Step*, CILT.

Part 3
Developing strategy

9   Communicative grammar teaching

Ann Miller

Grammar. The word is redolent of tedium and grind, the dreary rules and restrictions which shackle the brightly coloured bird of communication and prevent it from soaring freely. Or so my students tell me. 'I like communicating' (or 'I'm good at communicating') but 'I hate (or 'I'm no good at') grammar.' On the other hand, many of them have a perverse desire to experience the pain of grammar at its most excruciating: they do not feel that they are 'doing grammar' unless the rules are abstracted from any plausible real-life context. Neither of these two positions is tenable: unless 'communication' is reduced to the low-level performance skill of asking for a cup of coffee, it is obvious that it cannot be achieved without grammatical competence. Conversely, the teaching of grammar through decontextualized exemplar sentences divorced from any real-life setting is not only pointless but also counter-productive.

Knowing the rules

The value for language learners of 'knowing the rules' depends both on what is meant by 'knowing' and on what is meant by 'rules'. The debate over the value of explicit knowledge of grammatical rules as against the implicit knowledge which is manifested through competence goes back to the work of Chomsky. Chomsky's conception of competence was, however, limited to syntactic competence; a wider definition of competence was first put forward by Dell Hymes, who introduced the term 'communicative competence' in 1972, in acknowledgement of the fact that successful language learners need skills which go beyond a grasp of the syntactic system. Without an understanding of the conventions which regulate exchanges between speakers and writers, grammar rules alone will not enable learners to communicate. 'Communicative competence' is characterized by a Council of Europe document produced in 1996 as involving three components: linguistic competence, sociolinguistic competence and pragmatic competence. These same three components, sometimes differently named, occur in the work of various theorists, but in some cases a further category, discourse competence, is included. (See Canale and Swain 1980, Moirand 1982.) Boundaries between the terms and definitions tend to vary, but the components may be broadly characterized as follows:

- Linguistic competence: this may be taken as synonymous with syntactic competence, although some writers include rule systems at other levels, such as phonological rules.
- Discourse competence: this would include the ability to deal with both *cohesion* (the devices through which a spoken or written text hangs together, such as the pronoun system which allows for referring back and forwards, or the use of general terms to substitute for particular terms previously mentioned, as in 'I hate Sundays', 'So *do* I'), and *coherence* (relationships operating over longer sequences which determine, for example, that an invitation should be followed by refusal or acceptance).
- Sociolinguistic competence: this would include the ability to deal with different registers of language.
- Pragmatic competence: this would include an ability to deal with interpersonal language, including the use of indirect rather than direct language where appropriate.

It also includes the ability to encode and decode speech acts; it is clear that whilst in English a suggestion may be made using the future tense ('Shall we go?') the present would be used in French in the same context (*On y va?*).

Hymes's original article and the subsequent elaboration of his argument by other theorists have major implications for language teaching, the most important of which is the relationship between syntactic competence and the other components of 'communicative competence': in other words, the broadening out of the notion of 'rules', 'codes' or 'conventions' of which users of a language need to be in command. This question will be discussed further on in this chapter. We will return first to Chomsky, however, whose insight about the nature of 'knowing' rules had a profound effect in changing the way in which teachers saw the purposes and priorities of language teaching.

Explicit knowledge or competence?

As long ago as the 1950s, Chomsky provided a model of the child as active learner of its own language, able to produce sentences which it had never heard but which it had generated on the basis of its developing syntactic competence (Chomsky 1957). Chomsky cited as evidence the over-generalization of rules which occurs in the language of small children: 'I breaked it', 'you runned'. Chomsky was always concerned to emphasize that his work had no relevance to the work of foreign language teachers, but by spelling out what is obvious – that explicit knowledge of the rules of a language is in no way a precondition for speaking it fluently – he effectively torpedoed the intellectual foundations of a conception of language learning which valued the learning of rules for their own sake. This is a view which still casts a long shadow over language teaching; for those of us who were brought up on didactic methods (statement of rule followed by exercises embodying rule), there may be a certain nostalgia about the certitudes that we feel that those rules gave us. It is, then, all the more important for us to remember that those methods were designed with the primary aim of achieving just that: a knowledge of rules. Chomsky's work helps us to see that if there is a relationship between knowing rules and speaking a language, it is in fact the latter which would seem to be the precondition for the former. He emphasizes that adults do not teach grammatical rules to the children in their care: when and if these rules are learned they make sense to the child on the basis of what s/he already knows through use of the language.

The logic of Chomsky's position for the work of language teachers would not necessarily imply that explicit teaching of grammar should be banned, but rather that it should support the other objectives in a language teaching programme; it cannot be an objective in its own right. In the 1980s the work of Stephen Krashen, who, unlike Chomsky, did address the issue of language teaching, offered a far more radical view, and so widespread was the influence of Krashen's work that it might be said to have turned grammar teaching into a transgressive activity. Krashen formalized the distinction between explicit rule learning, which he describes as 'learning', and the unconscious building up of a model of the language, which he describes as 'acquisition'.

It is important to emphasize that Krashen's own experience as a language teacher was in an English as a second, not a foreign, language context, and the research which engendered his theories was not based on the language development of subjects who were in a foreign language learning situation. The impetus for the research came, in fact, from work done on mother tongue acquisition. In 1973 Roger Brown had published an influential study of the order of acqustion of a number of grammatical morphemes (such as markers of plurality, past tense, etc.) by children learning English as a first language. He demonstrated that although the morphemes were acquired at a different rate by the three children whose language development he monitored, they were acquired in much the same order. Following on from Brown, a number of studies were carried out in the 1970s into the order of morpheme development in the language of second language learners (Larsen-Freeman 1976, Dulay, Burt and Krashen 1982). These studies measured the order in which certain morphemes were acquired. The individuals investigated were resident in the US and were necessarily interacting in English on a daily basis. They included children and adults, some of whom had received classroom instruction as well as day-to-day contact with the language. The findings of the researchers were remarkably consistent: the order of acquisition of morphemes in the second language tended to be similar, no matter what the first language background of the learner, although it was not the same as the order that had been observed in the case of the first language learners. Perhaps more interestingly, the researchers discovered that most of the errors made by the L2 learners could not be attributed to interference from their first language and that, moreover, they were of the same type (over-generalization of rules, for example) as errors made by L1 learners.

These research findings provided the justification for an approach to language teaching which took as its central tenet the notion that the acquisition of the second language followed a 'natural sequence': learners were innately programmed to acquire morphemes in a certain order, which would be affected neither by teaching (or 'instruction') nor by correction of errors. The role of the teacher was the provision of comprehensible input, or, as Krashen put it, 'i + 1': the teacher must expose the learner to language just one step beyond his/her current level of competence in order to allow his/her processing mechanisms to go to work. In Krashen's view, if learners were communicating messages, then they must be learning (Krashen 1981). The great value of Krashen's work was to emphasize that teaching does not necessarily lead to learning: not all of the foreign language 'input' that the learner receives will be in a form which the learner can process and thus turn into 'intake'. Krashen also insisted that conscious control of language struc-ture, explicit rule learning, had only a secondary role to play, that of 'monitoring' output and enabling the learner to self-correct. Formal learning could only ever be a back-up mechanism; the aim of the teacher should be to encourage acquisition, by the provision of meaningful language. Krashen is clear that there is a role for the teacher: just as those who look after children learning their first language or those who come into contact with foreign speakers of a language are able to simplify their own language to make it comprehensible (by the use, respectively, of 'caretaker talk' and 'foreigner talk'), so the teacher must expose the learner to a simplified version of the target language. 'Teacher talk' is delivered more slowly than native speaker talk, it has a reduced lexicon, utterances are shorter and complex sentences are fewer. It does not, however, imply the presentation of language in an order predetermined by a syllabus based on grammatical progression; this is likely to 'undershoot' or 'overshoot' the learner's requirement for input at the optimal 'i + 1' level. By 'rough tuning' of the input, Krashen maintains, there is more chance that it will be sufficiently, but not too far, beyond the learner's current stage.

The very widespread dissemination of Krashen's views led to the orthodoxy which held sway for much of the 1980s, according to which both error correction and grammar teaching were banished (or, more accurately, forced underground; many teachers went on doing both, but felt guilty about it). There are, however, major difficulties with the application of Krashen's theories to the situation of learners in a foreign language classroom. These theories were largely based on research into the language development of students who, like Krashen's own students, were living in a country where the target language was spoken and were thereby exposed to much interaction in informal situations. They were necessarily receiving input in context-rich settings which considerably supplemented what-ever input was provided by their teacher. It is obvious that the situation of the second language learner is radically different from that of the foreign language learner, who receives virtually all of his/her language input within the classroom. Foreign language learners simply do not receive enough exposure to the target language to make meaningful generalizations about rules (whether consciously or unconsciously); teachers cannot afford to rely on random input. Their job is not only to simplify input; they must also ensure that structures recur at more than a random rate.

Krashen himself has little to say about the work of teachers in a foreign language teaching situation. When he does venture onto this terrain, however, the example that he offers is so bizarre that it suggests that he can only conceive of 'grammar' as being divorced from a context of use. We will return to the question of explicit rule-teaching, but a consideration of Krashen's example of a fragment of a grammar lesson will lead us, first, back to a discussion of what is meant by 'rules'.

Rules for the construction of a syntactic system, or rules for communication?

The sequence quoted by Krashen is taken from a French class for adults which he himself attended in Los Angeles (Krashen 1981).

Teacher: Fait-il beau aujourd'hui?
Student: Non, il ne fait pas beau maintenant.
Teacher: Irez-vous cependant à la plage pendant le weekend?
Student: Oui, j'irai cependant à la plage pendant le weekend.
Teacher: Irez-vous à la plage bien qu'il ne fasse pas beau?
Student: Oui, j'irai à la plage bien qu'il ne ….

Krashen describes this sequence as an example of the 'Pucciani-Hamel' approach. The method is, apparently, 'inductive, that is, students are led to induce, or guess, the rules'. Krashen goes on to explain that 'in a typical lesson, the teacher asks what are hopefully meaningful, interesting questions of members of the class in hopes of preparing a context for the target structure'. The above conversation is cited as having the purpose of teaching the conjunction *bien que* and 'the fact that its presence requires the following verb to be in the subjunctive mood'. Krashen explains his scepticism about the 'apparent' success of the method: he diplomatically describes the teacher as 'excellent', but suggests that although the explicit goal of the class was learning and conscious control of structure, it is likely that the real reason for the success of the class was the fact that it was conducted entirely in French. The teacher's explanations of grammatical structure, together with her classroom management talk and occasional anecdotes, were conducted in a simplified code which provided optimal, albeit incidental, input for acquisition. (A further reason for its success would seem to lie in the fact that, by his own admission, the students were all 'highly intelligent, highly motivated and mature'. Most had had considerable prior experience of learning French.)

Krashen does not, then, acknowledge that there is any distinction to be made between the second language and foreign language learning situations. The alternatives are equally stark: randomly selected (but appropriately simplified) input which will allow for acquisition, or exercises designed to teach grammar, whether inductively or deductively, which can at best make some contribution to the learner's ability to 'monitor' his/her output. It is, surely, hardly surprising that Krashen stresses the pointlessness of grammar teaching when the only example of it that he offers makes it clear that he equates the teaching of grammar with the attempt to induce learners to construct an abstract model of the language (the written language, moreover) which bears no relationship to any context of use.

Krashen does, briefly and tantalizingly, suggest that 'communicative' exercises would be of more value than grammar exercises, even though he still feels that the scatter-gun effect of informal use of simplified language is more likely to provide material at the i + 1 level. He specifies that the goal of such exercises would be the gaining of 'acquired or subconscious knowledge' rather than the 'formal and conscious' knowledge aimed at by grammatical exercises.[1] In fact, the major criterion for deciding that an exercise is 'communicative' must surely rest on whether or not the language being practised is appropriate to the context (real or simulated) in which the utterances occur. The fact that the exercise that Krashen quotes is intended to promote 'formal and conscious knowledge' seems considerably less problematic than the fact that the exemplar sentences are completely inappropriate to the (somewhat minimal) context with which they are associated. Although Krashen says that the exercise is intended to prepare a 'context' for the target structure, it would seem that the notion of 'context' here seems to be limited to that of creating a structural slot in the sentence to allow for the use of *bien que*. It does not involve the setting up of a plausible real-life setting within which grammatical choices would relate to features of the situation such as interpersonal relations and intended communicative outcomes encoded through speech acts. The exercise will not encourage the development of the components of 'communicative competence' referred to earlier in this chapter.

Sociolinguistic competence

- The language used in the example is wholly inappropriate for a spoken language exchange, where inverted question forms would not be used.
- The structure *bien que* followed by the subjunctive has a low frequency of occurrence in spoken language, so that it becomes particularly incongruous when associated with vocabulary relating to trips to the beach.

Discourse competence

- The exchange as a whole also breaks discourse rules by requiring the respondent to repeat sections of the questions; in an authentic exchange this is inconceivable: *à la plage* would be replaced by the pronoun *y*.
- Discourse competence also requires the language user to participate in exchanges where speech acts are sequenced in a coherent way. The question of sequencing speech acts does not arise in connection with Krashen's exercise, since none of the sentences actually corresponds to a speech act.

Pragmatic competence

It is impossible to interpret the exchange as a real-life speech act, or sequence of speech acts.

- The first question asks the respondent for information that must already be known to both speakers: it is immediately recognizable as belonging to that curious set of utterances which occur only in foreign language drills.
- The next question offers itself as an enquiry about the interlocutor's plans for the weekend, in itself a plausible speech act (although often in fact a pretext for a different, underlying, speech act which is not directly expressed: 'If you are going to the beach, can I come with you?'). It is simply not possible, however, that such an enquiry would be formulated in the future tense. The quaint syntax would have to be reformulated to turn the exemplar sentence into a possible utterance: *Vous allez à la plage ce weekend?*
- The third question of the sequence is so oddly phrased and implausible that it is difficult to suggest a speech act with which it could be associated (other than that of 'practise a grammatical rule'). If one speaker wished to find out how determined his/her interlocutor was about going to the beach no matter what the weather, s/he would not use *bien que* but rather some formulation such as: *Et même s'il ne fait pas beau, vous y irez quand même?*.

The absurdity of the sequence quoted by Krashen lends a rather baroque and obscure tone to the discussion of the link between the teaching of syntax patterns and the teaching of communicative competence. But it should be clear from Krashen's negative example that a set of exemplar sentences cannot just be strung together or marshalled into a sequence such as 'enquire about someone's intentions'. If the grammatical structures are inappropriate for the realization of that particular speech act, then the utterances will be incorrect and would be rejected as such by a native speaker. The job of the teacher, as well as that of offering appropriately simplified input, is to associate grammatical structures closely with speech acts and with interpersonal relations, and to ensure that discourse rules are not broken or that written language grammar is offered as acceptable in the spoken language.

Krashen's teacher, apparently, aimed to teach the structure *bien que* and to emphasize that it is followed by the subjunctive. She might have begun, not by choosing a disembodied sentence to exemplify the structure, but by running through a few instances of the use of *bien que* in her head, out of which a scenario and a few *dramatis personae* might have arisen. If she was determined to use spoken rather than written language, she would have had to presuppose a degree of formality in the setting, which would be apparent in the register of the language in which the structure was embedded. The type of speech acts which are suggested by the use of *bien que* seem to relate either to:

- expressing a contradiction or paradox, or to
- making concessions to an opponent's argument but continuing to take up an opposing stance.

To practise the use of *bien que* to express a contradiction, one might imagine a context in which, for example, a careers officer complains to a headteacher about the unreasonable demands made by students. The formality of the relationship between participants in the conversation would naturalize the use of *bien que*.

Eric: Bien que ce jeune homme ne sache pas nager, il veut devenir plongeur sous-marin.
Julie: Bien qu'elle ne comprenne pas un mot d'anglais, elle veut être interprète.
Fabien: Bien qu'il ait peur des araignées, il veut être explorateur.

Students can then continue the list, and may be helped by being supplied with a few careers and some vocabulary.

To practise making concessions using *bien que*, students can be presented with the structure in the context of a formal (perhaps broadcast) debate on subject matter which justifies the formal register implied by *bien que*.

La plage est surpeuplée au mois d'août: il y a trop de touristes.
Bien qu'ils soient nombreux en haute saison, cela ne dure qu'une courte période.
Cet envahissement de la côte augmente la pollution.
Bien qu'il y ait un accroissement des nuisances, nos systèmes de traitement assument cette variation saisonnière.

After a few more examples, students are given pairs of sentences in which they are asked to supply the second speaker's response. They can be offered as much prompting, in terms of suggested nouns and verbs, as the teacher feels they need.

La qualité de vie des habitants se dégrade: le bruit est insupportable.
Bien que ... (un peu de bruit; contribuer à l'économie locale).

The relationship between structure and speech act

It is obviously not the case that there is a one-to-one correlation between the speech act and grammatical structure, and some theorists have suggested that this is a problem for syllabus design. This viewpoint was expressed in a lecture given at the Centre International d'Etudes Pédagogiques at Sèvres in 1998, by the distinguished writer on language teaching methodology, Francis Debuyser. His handout bore the heading 'Non-correspondence between speech acts and constructions' and went on to affirm: 'This is the principal difficulty for the maintaining of a grammatical progression. Several different grammatical constructions can correspond to one speech act and, conversely, a single grammatical form can correspond to different speech acts.'[2]

Debuyser gave the example of the different grammatical forms which can be used to realize the speech act *dire de faire*, including some which realize it with a considerable degree of indirection:

- a verbless utterance: *La porte!*;
- an imperative: *Faites cela!*;

- the present indicative: *Vous faites cela*;
- the future indicative: *Vous ferez cela*;
- the immediate future: *Vous allez faire cela*;
- the infinitive: *Fermer la porte* (on a sign);
- interrogatives with modal verbs, often in the conditional tense: *Pourriez-vous faire cela? Voudriez vous faire cela?*
- constructions using performative verbs: *Je vous prie/ordonne/demande de faire cela*;
- indirect speech acts, such as *Il fait froid* implicitly expressing *Fermez la fenêtre*.

Debuyser then gave the converse example of the different speech acts which can be realized by the imperative, including:

- orders: *Circulez!*;
- requests: *Passe-moi le sel*;
- advice: *Prenez des vacances*;
- instructions: *Ajoutez cent grammes de beurre*;
- prayers: *Donnez-nous notre pain chaque jour*;
- pleas: *Ne me quitte pas!*;
- invitations: *Asseyez-vous, Reprenez un peu de gâteau*.

His premise was that 'a progression founded on pragmatic objectives is incompatible with a grammatical progression'.

We can counter this difficulty firstly by enlisting none other than Krashen. Whatever the pitfalls for the foreign language teacher of relying on random input, we can agree with Krashen that there seems to be no compelling reason why grammatical structures should be introduced in any particular predetermined order, although Krashen's own proviso that input should be simplified does exclude certain structures at the early stages. We might then go on to call into question Debuyser's assumption that there needs to be a *progression* of pragmatic objectives; it is difficult to see what justification there would be for claiming that any one speech act should be taught before any other. (There is no obvious reason, for example, to follow the progression that tends to be followed by mother tongue learners, where the linguistic resources enabling the child to demand that basic needs should be satisfied tend to develop early, along with the language of making and maintaining social contact.)

Freed from the necessity of trying to map one predetermined order onto another, the teacher can steer a path between them, guided, I would suggest, by the following principles:

1   Students cannot learn (or 'acquire') a grammatical structure unless they are exposed to multiple examples of it.
2   Each of those examples must occur in the context of a plausible speech act. Knowledge of rules in isolation from any context of use will promote the use of anglicisms since the only links that students will be able to create between abstract syntactic system and speech act will be the ones that operate in their own language.

3   Students must understand how grammatical choices can correspond to the expression of social and interpersonal relationships. The most obvious example of this is the choice between familar and polite forms, but these correspondences operate across much wider areas of the language.

If we return to Debuyser's example of the imperative as our structure to be taught, principle (1) would determine that they be exposed to as many examples of it as possible in the confines of available time, and principle (2) that these examples should embody real-life speech acts, although there is no reason to bring in every single speech act that could be associated with the structure. Orders and instructions might be a good initial choice since these occur frequently in the classroom and can allow of a behavioural response which makes learning more memorable: *Fermez vos livres, Ouvrez vos cahiers, Tracez une ligne, Ecrivez votre nom, Ecrivez la date, Posez vos crayons*, etc. Students can take a turn at giving orders, but they must do so in the role of the teacher, since students need to understand the interpersonal issues which are at stake here, in accordance with principle (3). These can be raised explicitly by giving students a set of sentences which they are told are grammatically correct, and asking them to judge which ones would actually be acceptable in terms of the codes of interpersonal behaviour. For example:

Professeur à élève:	Taisez-vous.
Elève à professeur:	Ouvrez la fenêtre.
Parent à enfant:	Ne parle pas la bouche pleine.
Employé à employeur:	Donnez-moi une augmentation de salaire.
Client à vendeur:	Donnez-moi une baguette.

Students would be led to the conclusion that in some of the cases an alternative to the imperative would have to be found. Cultural issues are obviously involved here, since the final example on this list, whilst acceptable in French (especially if followed by *s'il vous plaît*), is only marginally so in English. Students would be enabled to realize, in fact, that in French the imperative may be used for the speech act 'request' as well as 'order' or 'instruct'. In English a request of this type would more commonly involve the use of a modal auxiliary ('Could you …?', 'Would you …?').

Given that further practice of the structure will simulate a situation outside the classroom, it is important that the roles involved are clearly delineated. A degree of exaggeration and dramatization may be helpful: a tyrannical or capricious employer is giving orders to an underling, or simply to a robot: *Préparez le dîner, Lavez la voiture, Allumez la télévision, Nettoyez la maison, Promenez le chien*, etc. This activity can give rise to miming games and, again, there will be a progression from comprehension to production as a student takes on the role of employer.

The importance of relating examples both to speech acts and to social relationships is not always understood, and this can result in the production of exemplar sentences which would be unlikely to occur as real-life utterances. A trainee teacher on a recent course designed an exercise in which students were asked to transform

Spanish sentences containing second-person verbs into sentences containing imperatives. The list of sentences contained items such as:

- Tu cantas
- Tu lavas la ropa
- Tu bailas
- Tu planchas

Students were expected to turn these into *¡Canta! ¡Lava la ropa! ¡Baila! ¡Anda!*

No context was offered to justify the utterance of either the original or the transformed set. The trainee teacher had been told to 'provide a context' for an activity intended to teach the imperative, but had understood 'context' rather as Krashen seems to, as indicating a structural slot in an exemplar sentence. In fact, with some modification of the verbs selected, the original sentences could be related to a speech act, that of instructing someone as to their duties (the familiar form would be acceptable in Spanish in this context). The transformation activity could then be used to show how the choice of a different structure implies a change in the interpersonal relationship, thereby complying not only with principle (2) but also with principle (3). Unless we assume that the person is being employed as an entertainer as well as a domestic servant, we will need to confine ourselves to verbs which would be likely to occur in that context, and so drop *cantar* and *bailar* and supplement the list with a few more verbs in the semantic field of domestic work: *fregar los platos, pelar las patatas*, for example. The transformation to the imperative would then correspond to a transformation of the situation: instead of merely listing duties, the employer is demanding, in a rather peremptory manner, that they be carried out instantly.

The second-person present tense structure could, of course, correspond to a different speech act: a complaint to someone about his/her annoying habits, for example, if *cantar* and *bailar* were retained, along with other verbs denoting activities likely to cause irritation. Here a transformation into negative imperative sentences would provide a very plausible set of requests to stop the behaviour, perhaps delivered to a close acquaintance with some exasperation.

If we want our students to be effective interpersonal and intercultural operators as well as effective manipulators of grammatical structures, then we need to make sure that they are alert to the way in which these two levels are related; this is why principle (3) is important. Debuyser's list of different ways of realizing the speech act, *dire de faire*, offers striking evidence as to how immediately one can assign a particular type of interpersonal relationship and setting to each different structure; the examples of modalized structures using the conditional tense quite obviously imply a degree of politeness absent from the imperative. There is, therefore, every reason why students should be aware that there is more than one way of realizing the same speech act. Clearly one would not simply call a unit of work *dire de faire* and expose students to Debuyser's complete list of structures; such a procedure would in any case be unlikely to comply with principle (1). The imperative is a relatively simple structure and may be covered at an early stage. This is also the case, for instance, of the infinitive. Both structures may be used to realize the speech act *dire de faire* but they are by no means interchangeable in terms of the way in which they are used. As Debuyser suggests, the infinitive tends to occur in the context of written notices. These presuppose an impersonal, institutionalized authority, and are particularly associated with negative commands. It would be appropriate, therefore, in a unit of work on orders and instructions, that students should be involved in the comprehension and subsequent creation of signs and notices expressing commands and prohibitions of various kinds through the use of the infinitive: *Ne pas toucher au rétroprojecteur, Ne pas jeter de papiers par terre, Ne pas parler anglais dans cette salle, Ranger les tables après le cours, Ne pas coller de chewing gum sous les tables, etc.*

At a later stage of their course, students will revisit 'order and instructions' when they deal with more complex structures such as the conditional tense and the use of modal verbs. They will now be in a position to appreciate the gradations in politeness implied, for example, by the choice of *Pouvez-vous me chercher un verre d'eau?* as opposed to *Pourriez-vous me chercher un verre d'eau?* and can be invited to contrast these with *Cherchez-moi un verre d'eau.* These distinctions can be worked on quite explicitly through activities in which students are asked to choose the structure that would correspond to different sets of circumstances. Role-plays can sometimes take the form of deliberately demonstrating how to offend one's hosts, one's guests or one's employer by the use of inappropriate structures. (The Basil Fawlty style of hotel management offers scope for activities of this type.)

For Debuyser, a particular difficulty arises out of the fact that many speech acts are realized indirectly: *Vous avez une voiture?* has the surface features of a request for information, but so unlikely is it that an interlocutor would understand it as such that a simple affirmative answer would verge on the unacceptable. *Oui – je peux vous déposer quelque part?* would in most cases be the expected response. Given that indirection is a key aspect of interpersonal skills, it would seem important for students to be aware of the devices that the language has for operating in this area. In fact, somewhat paradoxically, this sophisticated skill is often associated with relatively simple constative language, or straightforward information questions, since the purpose of indirection is to avoid committing oneself to a high-risk speech act by disguising one's utterance as something more innocuous, like the giving or requesting of information. Rather than inviting you to the cinema, I will simply remark on the fact that a certain film is showing, or ask if you have seen it. Rather than asking you to go for a drink, I will casually say that I am thirsty, or ask if you are. It is therefore possible, for example, that at the stage when students are working on the use of the conditional tense for invitations (*Vous aimeriez …? Cela vous plairait de …?*), they should consider how the same invitations could be issued indirectly. They will find that they already have the linguistic resources to achieve this. Similarly, in the case of requests made using the conditional tense (*Vous pourriez …? Cela vous dérangerait de …?*), comparisons can be made with the efficacy of a more indirect approach. (How might you ask your parents for a loan?)

How explicit should grammatical explanations be?

If we return to the example of the imperative, it is clear that it would be quite impossible within the confines of a school timetable to give students enough exposure to all forms of the imperative for them to 'acquire' competence in using the structure. The features which enable generalizations to be made are in any case not always present in the surface structure of utterances: *faites* and *dites*, for instance, lack the ending which distinguishes the plural or formal imperative form in other verbs. Second language learners may hear enough examples of *faites* and *dites* in the same kind of contexts in which they are hearing *allez* and *écoutez* to work out for themselves that there is some equivalence between these items in spite of their formal difference, but foreign language learners need more guidance. This is true to an even greater extent in the case of the singular imperative forms: learners simply could not establish for themselves a pattern on the basis of examples such as *prends, écoute, fais, finis* and *viens*. Students need help in order to be able to look at these items not as individual and inexplicably disparate terms but as part of an overall system of verb conjugations in which a pattern emerges, and in which exceptions are flagged as such. Once learners are in control of the verb conjugation system and of ways of denoting the members of the set, through the use of terms such as 'person' and 'singular' or 'plural', they will be able to integrate into it items which there is not time to practise thoroughly. Most often, they will be dealing with more than one system: some of the verbs used regularly in the imperative form in a classroom context are reflexive (*Asseyez-vous*), and others are habitually used with an object pronoun (*Ecoutez-moi*). If students are to move beyond learned-by-heart knowledge of a small number of often-used phrases, and be able to construct their own utterances, they need to be aware of these intersecting patterns. Teachers are not forced to teach all the patterns at once, however; they should feel free to pre-select input to eliminate examples which are likely to be confusing.

The stage of the teaching sequence at which the rule should be introduced is a matter for the teacher's judgement, but we always need to beware of assuming that because we have explained a rule, albeit with the help of lines and columns and differently coloured OHP pens, it has become operational for students; we cannot wire our diagrams directly into students' brains. If students experience language in action, through receptive exposure and concentrated practice, they will be in a position to formulate the rule inductively, with some guidance. If the language to which they are exposed has a clearly delineated context, they will be in a position to relate the syntactical abstraction to the way that it is used in the foreign language, which may or may not resemble the way in which it is used in English. Infinitives are not used in English, for instance, to give instructions. It is at the stage when they have encountered the relevant language in use that learners can benefit from a visual representation of the system, or systems, to which it belongs; this is when the coloured OHP pens can most usefully come into play.

The confusion between 'communication' and the learning of routines

Students who claim to be 'good at communication' but to have an aversion to grammar tend, sadly, to mean that they can get their meaning across by having heavy recourse to an anglicized sentence structure. This may work as an emergency communication strategy with the ever-stoical 'sympathetic native speaker', but it has no future (as I wearily tell them) as a language learning strategy. (Neither does it bear any resemblance to the error pattern observed in second language learners by the researchers whose work is referred to earlier in the chapter.) The reliance on anglicism characterizes students who have come from two quite different routes.

They may have been exposed to a didactic approach where grammatical rules were taught as abstractions, and so have no way of mapping grammar onto speech act and interpersonal context other than by falling back on English conventions.

Alternatively, they may have been brought up on a diet of textbooks in which, in misplaced application of Krashen's theories, a programme is designed according to learners' supposed 'communicative needs', but no attempt is made to provide learners with input that allows them to make generalizations (whether conscious or not) about rules. They are simply expected to operate with learned-by-heart routines which have no common structural elements. For example, in one of the early units of the Year 7 textbook which has been a market leader in recent years, pupils are exposed to: *Mon père m'a offert des baskets et ma grand-mère une cassette vidéo; J'ai reçu un jogging et un pull; Mon père m'a acheté un walkman; Je me suis acheté un walkman* (Briggs, Goodman-Stephens and Rogers 1992). It is hard to see how any processing mechanisms that learners possess could go to work on exemplar sentences which are at once complex and syntactically disparate, and which could scarcely be classified as 'comprehensible input' for students at such an early stage of their course; these sentences would clearly be far beyond Krashen's magic i + 1 stage of competence.[3] Language development in any individual is of course uneven: all children have as part of their repertoire some routines, groups of words which they use as if they were single items, or holophrases ('don't want to', for example). Foreign language learners will also need some routines: they will need to say, for example, *Je n'ai pas de stylo* before they have learned negative constructions. But if they are constantly asked to produce sentences which they could not construct for themselves, they will achieve little or no autonomy as users of the language. They may acquire lexis, but in the absence of grammatical competence, they are obliged, like their peers brought up on decontextualized exercises, to use word-for-word translation from English as a strategy. Indeed, they are in some ways disadvantaged in relation to the first group of learners since, lacking rules, they have no way of learning from their errors and are condemned to repeat them, cast adrift in a sea of approximation.

Conclusion

This chapter has sought to argue that the application of Krashen's theories to the foreign language classroom has been both inappropriate and damaging. It has also argued, though, that there is no contradiction between the mastery of grammar and the ability to communicate; on the contrary, these are mutually-dependent and reinforcing skills. Students need to be helped to formulate the rules which underpin their use of structures, but they need also to understand how structural choices relate to real-life language use, where speaking involves both doing and interacting.

Notes

1 The classroom activities suggested in Krashen and Terrell 1983 suggest a number of engaging activities for the ESL classroom, categorized by topic areas. There is no aim of building in structural patterns.
2 This is a translation of Debuyser's original handout, which was in French.
3 It is, in fact, the structural disparity of the input offered on this course that makes comprehension so difficult. A useful comparison may be made with Jenkins and Jones 1992, in which structural regularities are built into the language to which students are exposed for the purpose of carrying out communicative tasks.

Further reading

Briggs, L., Goodman-Stephens, B. and Rogers, P. (1992) *Route Nationale*, Stage 1, York, Nelson.
Brown, R. (1973) *A First Language*, Cambridge, Massachussetts: Harvard University Press.
Canale, M. and Swain, M. (1980) 'Theoretical bases of communicative approaches to second language teaching and testing', *Applied Linguistics* 1, 1–47.
Chomsky, N. (1957) *Syntactic Structures*, The Hague: Mouton.
Council of Europe (1996) *Cadre européen de référence*, Strasbourg: Council of Europe.
Dulay, H., Burt, M. and Krashen, S. (1982) *Language Two*, New York: Oxford University Press.
Hymes, D. (1972) 'On communicative competence', in J.B. Pride and J. Holmes (eds) *Sociolinguistics*, Harmondsworth: Penguin.
Jenkins, J. and Jones, B. *Spirale*, Sevenoaks: Hodder & Stoughton.
Krashen, S. (1981) *Second Language Acquisition and Second Language Learning*, Oxford: Pergamon Press.
—— (1982) *Principles and Practice in Second Language Acquisition*, Oxford: Pergamon Press.
Krashen S. and Terrell, T. (1983) *The Natural Approach: Language Acquisition in the Classroom*, Oxford/San Francisco: Pergamon Press/Alemany.
Larsen-Freeman, D. (1976) 'An explanation for the morpheme acquisition order of second language learners', in *Language Learning* 26, 125–34.
Moirand, S. (1982) *Enseigner à communiquer en langue étrangère*, Paris: Hachette.

10 Towards a reconceptualization of the MFL curriculum

Do Coyle

> If you always do what you've always done, you'll always get what you've always got. If what you are doing is not working, do something else.
>
> (O'Connor and Seymour 1990)

Introduction

This chapter sets out to challenge modern foreign language (MFL) teaching and learning in our schools in the early years of the twenty-first century by suggesting that currently the needs of the next generation are not being substantially met. This chapter also sets out to challenge the reader by claiming that, unless there is a significant reconceptualization of the modern languages curriculum in our schools, then MFL learning may well be in the balance – to revert to an 'option' reserved for an elite group of so-called linguists or to reinvent itself as a genuine entitlement for all learners embedded in a repertoire of flexible life skills.

Britain is not monolingual. English is not 'owned' by the British. Yet despite the changing face of the British nation, there is a general disregard for languages other than English, matched by a deep-seated and misguided belief of supremacy in the linguistic stakes. What are the implications of the fact that in the very near future there will be more speakers of English as a foreign, second or alternative language than those who speak it as mother tongue? How do we attach a sense of urgency to the fact that plurilingualism rather than monolingualism is the 'norm' in the twenty-first century?

In England, there is no national policy promoting 'other' languages, yet the polyglot reality of the British people is evident – in our communities, in our services and industries and especially in our schools. For one-third of school children in London alone, English is not the home language. In fact, according to the latest census, thirty-nine languages other than English are spoken as first languages – Bengali, Punjabi, Gujarati, Turkish and Mandarin being amongst the most widespread. Whilst acknowledging that 'in a world of alliances and partnerships we need to understand where others are coming from ... the ability to communicate across cultures ... is a key skill' (Nuffield Language Inquiry 2000), nonetheless an independent inquiry into the nation's language capability reporting in 2000 – the Nuffield Inquiry – concluded that whilst foreign language competence is crucially important, 'at the moment we are doing badly; and we must do better'. Doing better, however, does not lead us to quick-fix solutions. Rooted in societal insecurities, 'we persist in believing that our national identity is in danger of being swallowed up in some European amalgam'. From a historical perspective, 'We in these islands grow up more suspicious of and defensive towards people and things foreign further than most: the *hooligans anglais* phenomenon and much of the so-called debate on Europe bear regular witness' (Jones 2000).

The optimism prevalent in MFL teaching and learning in the late eighties and early nineties was short-lived, to be replaced by a growing sense of disillusionment witnessed by learners who voted with their 'disaffected feet'. At the start of that decade there was an emphasis on the effective implementation of the first National Curriculum foregrounding target language use and explicit grammar teaching. Building on communicative principles tried and tested during the eighties' Graded Objectives movement, demonstrating the 'irresistibility of the idea whose time had come' (Page 1996) and a 'Languages for All' policy resulting in a steady rise in MFL national examination entries at 16+, it seemed as though the scene was set for a fruitful period of foreign language learning in Britain's secondary schools.

And yet in the following decade, teachers are once again fighting to maintain compulsory language learning to age 16, the number of students studying a foreign language to age 18 has dramatically fallen, university language departments are threatened with closure and the shortage of language teachers has reached crisis level. A case of *plus ça change?* Revisions to the National Curriculum have not succeeded in fostering cohorts of motivated learners who perceive language learning opportunities as providing them with skills essential to their future working lives – in fact nine out of ten students stop studying a foreign language after the compulsory five-year period. The message was and is clear: Britain's linguistic capability lags behind that of its closest neighbours. The 1995 European White paper's recommendation for all citizens to have proficiency in *three* European languages sits uneasily with national realities and is quite simply unattainable in the current learning climate.

At the macro level it is easy to identify national factors and deep-rooted attitudes which might militate against a perceived necessity for foreign languages in the secondary curriculum – commonly referred to as an 'island mentality' promulgated by English speakers in a world dominated (it is said) by the English language. Yet these do not account for the survival of Britain's heritage languages (such as Welsh or Gaelic), the polyglot nature of inner city schools and the nonsensical claim that the British are poor language learners.

However, at the micro level, the legacy of a widely-accepted yet narrow interpretation of the so-called 'communicative approach' common to most language learning classrooms, with its prescribed syllabus topics based on 'formulaic' transactional language, inadvertently promoted a reactive rather than interactive role for learners. The resulting 'dead bodies, talking heads' syndrome (Legutke and Thomas 1991) is symbolized by demotivated, linguistically-disempowered adolescents who are discouraged from 'taking control', impeded by a pedagogy which 'closes down' spontaneous interaction. Legutke and Thomas go on to describe in harsh terms a typical language classroom as 'a largely ego-impoverished and teacher-centred one-way street, in which display questions still dominate, concerns for accuracy by far out-number fluency attempts, and where communication is hard to find' (1991: 6).

Learners in these contexts do not have a voice. Efforts targeting teacher 'comprehensible input' (Krashen 1983) are not matched by learner 'comprehensible output' (Swain 1985). Classroom discourse is typified by univocal teacher control where the Initiate–Respond–Feedback sequence (Sinclair and Coulthard 1975; van Lier 1996) is the most common form of teacher–learner 'script':

Teacher: La tornade a tué combien de personnes?
Student: Trois.
Teacher: Très bien!

The paradox is clear: at the time of an identified need for improved national language capability, young people are 'opting out' of language learning – linguistic currency is acknowledged and valued by only a few. So where do we go from here?

> Capability in other languages – a much broader range than hitherto and in greater depth – is crucially important for a flourishing UK. The scale of what needs to be done has become ever more striking as our work has gone on. At the moment, by any reliable measure we are doing badly. We talk about communication but don't always communicate. Educational provision is fragmented, achievement poorly measured, continuity not very evident. In the language of our time, there is a lack of joined-up thinking.
>
> (Chairman of Nuffield Inquiry, Sir Trevor MacDonald 2000)

In the absence of a coherent national approach, the Nuffield Language Inquiry (2000) thus signalled the need for 'joined-up thinking' in terms of developing a Language Strategy. As a contribution to this process, I should like to consider both the content and classroom context of language learning and respond to two recommendations: to raise the profile of languages and to explore how the teaching and learning of modern foreign languages may be developed in the next few years in our secondary schools.

The (dis)content of language learning

Much has been written in the past few years criticizing the content of foreign language syllabuses (Coyle 1999a, 1999b, 2000a). As was noted in the introduction to this chapter, the pragmatic appeal of predictable scenarios for future foreign language use has given way to an overemphasis on topics, transactional 'scripts' and tedious role-plays. I would claim that this approach just does not work for the majority of learners. Whilst language practice and production are essential to the language learning process, opportunities for *using* language both to communicate and to learn have tended to be restricted either to those who have already acquired linguistic skills – i.e. more advanced or able students – or others who have had 'privileged' experiences involving, for example, European curriculum projects or exchange visits abroad. Whilst the initial 1990 MFL National Curriculum identified general topics to be covered in Programme of Study Part II, the revised MFL Curriculum (1999) simply states:

> During key stages 3 and 4, pupils should be taught the knowledge, skills and understanding through (i) working in a variety of contexts, including everyday activities, personal and social life, the world around us, the world of work and the international world.
>
> (MFL National Curriculum 1999: 17)

Moreover, 'the knowledge, skills and understanding' referred to are based on twenty-two discrete elements which focus principally on language skills (10) and language learning skills (5). Knowledge and understanding relates to areas of applying grammar (3) and cultural awareness (4). In my view, the essentially skills-based yet 'content-free' nature of the National Curriculum liberates teachers to go way beyond the traditional thematic approach. The *Breadth of Study* section positively encourages this in prescriptive statements requiring the development of the foreign language through:

- using the target language creatively and imaginatively;
- listening, reading or viewing for personal interest as well as for information;
- using the target language for real purposes;
- producing and responding to different types of spoken and written language;
- using a range of resources, including ICT, for accessing and communicating information.

It seems then that the National Curriculum is not a *constraining* factor in what goes on inside the MFL classroom – it is open to wide and varied interpretation and encourages teachers and learners to respond accordingly by prescribing language development in general terms of knowledge and understanding of the target language, language learning skills and learning strategies as well as cultural awareness. Why then do learners perceive modern language study as boring and anodyne?

According to Norman (1998) it is rather the textbook and examination syllabus which currently dictate the content of the MFL teaching curriculum and its speed of delivery. Many text books are in fact based on grammatical progression built around a series of topics – myself and my family, leisure time, school, daily routines and so on. At best, such topics allow the students to make cultural comparisons between their own lives and those of others. At worst, they are rooted in a sterile context generating cognitively undemanding material, whilst the medium of expression becomes progressively complex.

> As long as the content of communication is narrowly defined in terms of topics, which in most cases is repetitive, at least by comparison with the mother-tongue curriculum in the primary school, and contains little in terms of cognitive challenge and 'new' knowledge, then it will be difficult to break out of the current language learning mould.
>
> (Coyle 1999a: 158)

This dilemma leads me to pose a fundamental question: what *is* the content of MFL lessons? Does learning how to talk about one's day in school in a foreign language constitute content? In the latter case the content is 'known' – only the communication code has changed. Or is the 'real' content to do with the underlying grammatical system of the target language which enables students to talk about what is often already known? Even if the latter case is justifiable, it does not address the application of the language within a communicative context. Recently when a Year 6 primary school student was asked what she thought she most wanted to learn to say in French once her MFL studies started at secondary school, she replied, in disbelief that I should have even asked such a question, with: 'Why, anything I say in my own language of course!' As Genesee (2001) points out: we learn our first language not in order to learn it. Surely this should also be the case for the second or third, not withstanding additional intellectual or literary gains from such an undertaking?

Making connections

A useful starting point for reflecting on these issues may be to consider how modern foreign language learning relates to the whole curriculum. An early draft of the 1990 National Curriculum took what retrospectively appears to be a 'radical' stance in explicitly promoting cross-curricular linking. 'The full potential of the National Curriculum will only be realized if curricular planning involves the overlap of skills and content across the different subjects' (DES 1990). Furthermore, this document proposed three models for widening the MFL curriculum. These are as follows:

1   *redefining curricular boundaries* through work developed within modern languages courses, such as a Year 8 MFL project on a region in Spain, based on email links with a partner school.
2   *crossing curricular boundaries* through co-operation between modern languages and other departments, such as a joint Year 10 Geography and MFL field studies visit to Normandy with different elements to be submitted as coursework for both GCSE subjects.
3   *breaking curricular boundaries* through teaching other subjects mainly or entirely in the foreign language for a specific period of time. This might range from, say, team-teaching in German a three-week 'module' on diet including a comparison of diets between Britain and Namibia to a two-year GCSE Geography course taught in French.

The three models may have a different focus but all are underpinned by a common principle – to encourage the development of communication, cognitive and metacognitive skills, whilst exploring different ways of using language. Despite such a flexible framework, only a minority of schools took up the challenge. Instead, the 1990 version of the National Curriculum omitted explicit references to cross-curricular links, leaving more innovative curriculum-planning to the pioneers.

In terms of 'curricular connectivity', the revised MFL Curriculum (1999) falls short in its explicit linking with other subject areas, in my view bordering on tokenism and an absence of 'joined-up thinking'. Only ICT and English are identified as subjects relating to MFL. It is interesting to note that ICT, like modern foreign languages, is divided in terms of 'knowledge about' or skills in 'how to use' ICT and the content of its application – an email contains a message, a pie chart contains data, video conferencing provides a mean to communicate, yet all of these are tools which do not in themselves determine the content of the communication. Whilst the English curriculum can draw on 'literature' in the broadest sense to provide some content, the revised NC (1999) chooses to highlight only two common elements shared by MFL and English: understanding different grammar systems and their interrelationships and redrafting (writing) skills. Of course knowledge and the application of a grammar system do include, to an extent, elements of 'content', and constitute an area which I feel deserves more attention in terms of developing literacy; I shall return to this point subsequently. I would, however, argue that linking the MFL curriculum with other subject areas such as Geography, History or Science allows content to be shared between different subjects and potential learning outcomes to be strengthened. It foregrounds the message that learning is challenging, not just 'fun'! Extending an individual's world knowledge through the foreign language adds a sense of purposefulness and value which is not evident from describing a recent holiday using at least three grammatical tenses. Most importantly, it enables the foreign language to be used for the purpose of communicating *and* the purpose of learning. For example: 'pupils should be taught how and why historical events, people, situations and changes have been interpreted in different ways and how to evaluate these interpretations' (History National Curriculum: 20). Developing an understanding of historical enquiry can also involve 'considering experiences and perspectives of people in [other] countries and communities' (MFL National Curriculum 4d).

The following transcript from a Year 9 Geography lesson, using French as the medium for instruction, illustrates this point. The students (S1, 2, and 7) are discussing equatorial rainforests. The teacher (T) is encouraging the students to focus on the meaning of their answers and to think about the height of the trees – notice it is not always the teacher who asks the questions (… denotes interruption):

T: Quelle hauteur ont les arbres? Les arbres ont de quelle hauteur?
S2:   Quarante mètres …
S7:   … des arbres? [in disbelief, then laughs in disagreement]

T: Quarantes mètres? C'est beaucoup … quarante mètres. Tu mesures combien, euh? Qui est le plus grand de la classe? B, tu es le plus grand?

S2:   Euh, ah oui, euh, je ne sais pas en mètres, mais, mais euh …

T: … Six pieds?

S2:   Cinq pieds huit, et vous?

T: Cinq-huit? Cinq pieds huit? Bon, moi je mesure un mètre quatre vingt-dix.

S1:   Oui, mais qu'est-ce que ça en pieds?

T: Je ne sais pas, c'est? …

S1:   … Hein, Monsieur, êtes-vous [et] plus grand que toi? …

T: … Un mètre quatre vingt-dix …

S1:   … Non, elle est six quatre …

T: Deux mètres environ … quarante mètres les arbres, vingt fois plus grands que toi??? …

S2:   Mais oui!

(Coyle 1999b)

Whilst adopting a holistic view of the school teaching curriculum remains an ideal, there is evidence of a sea-change as more and more schools, especially those with Language College status, are exploring more integrated models of foreign language learning in attempts to motivate students and create a language promoting ethos. One such case reported in the Nuffield Inquiry involves: '[Mixed ability classes of] 11 year olds at Hasland Hall School, an 11–16 comprehensive school in Chesterfield, study Geography, ICT, History and Personal and Social Education through the medium of French' (Nuffield Languages Inquiry 2000: 46). In many schools, however, the battle to 'raise standards', gain promotion within the league tables or change D grades to C grades at GCSE means that subjects vie for curriculum time, and competition between subject departments does not easily favour collaborative planning and delivery. More radical solutions require a risky leap of faith! And yet:

> Good opportunities are being wasted. … Measures to improve pupils' enjoyment and interest in language learning could be taken but overwhelmingly are not. Bilingual teaching – where subjects such as History or Geography are taught in the foreign language – remains a rarity, and no accreditation is available for such courses.
>
> (Nuffield Languages Inquiry 2000: 46)

Languages across the curriculum

Whilst Curriculum 2000 is in essence an 'inclusive curriculum', a curriculum which attempts to respond to the needs of all students by providing differentiated learning opportunities, it is perhaps ironic that where the document cautiously promotes cross-curricular work of a *suitably challenging nature* i.e. developing content shared between different subjects, it lies somewhat exclusively in the camp of high achievers.

For pupils whose attainments significantly exceed the expected level of attainment within one or more subjects during a key stage, teachers need to plan suitably challenging work. As well as drawing on materials from later key stages at higher levels of study, teachers may plan further differentiation by extending the breadth and depth of study within individual subjects or by planning work which draws on the content of different subjects.

(DfEE 1999: 21)

The rather more controversial view that using a foreign language to learn about and understand elements of other subjects is an achievable objective for all students whatever their ability is substantiated by interesting evidence from the Hasland Hall case cited above: 'It was found that lower ability children who had followed the bilingual programme performed better in English than those who had not. Boys seemed to do especially well' (Nuffield Languages Inquiry 2000). This example suggests that increasing student awareness of how languages work, including the mother tongue, encourages transfer of learning between L1 and L2. It also suggests that broader links between literacy levels in L1 and L2 may be beneficial; for example, enabling students to access and learn through using longer and more varied texts would at least provide alternatives to the decontextualized small chunks of contrived written language so often the diet of the textbook, especially in the early stages. Besides, 'connecting' literacy between languages also builds on the Bullock Report's view (1975): *all* teachers are teachers of language. Perhaps it is an opportune time to revisit and redefine the 'language across the curriculum' to include and promote *languages* across the curriculum.

A language is a system which relates what is being talked about (content) and the means used to talk about it (expressions). Linguistic content is inseparable from linguistic expressions. In subject matter learning we overlook the role of language as a medium of learning. In language learning we overlook the fact that content is being communicated.

(Mohan 1986)

Such thinking could integrate literacy and communications across the curriculum to include strategies for using and developing languages and ICT in a coherent and differentiated way. It would potentially afford students a wider variety of opportunities to use the foreign language to learn, to think, to create and to understand as well as to communicate.

Thinking – the fifth language skill

The drive to make language learning 'fun' is widespread yet in my view misguided. Of course teachers want their students to enjoy their learning but the notion that 'fun' will motivate students to engage long-term with language learning does not address the underlying complex problems, one of which is that the cognitive level of MFL tasks is often inextricably linked to the linguistic level of the learners.

> Research has shown that cognitively undemanding work, such as copying or repetition, especially when there is little or no context to support it, does not enhance language learning ... by actively involving pupils in intellectually demanding work, the teacher is creating a genuine need for learners to acquire the appropriate language.
>
> (Smith and Paterson 1998: 1)

There is no denying that the cognitive skills involved in processing language input and output are indeed complex and demanding: working out structural rules, understanding the norms of use and appropriateness or sequencing utterances which are meaningful and can be understood. In addition, developing a repertoire of communicative strategies, building up a vocabulary, memorizing chunks of language and learning to use an alternative linguistic code with its own particular set of rules are themselves cognitively challenging. Whilst this can be turned to advantage through adopting alternative approaches to the learning of grammar, through inductive teaching for example, such practice is not widespread. Unless grammar teaching and learning are contextualized through meaningful language use and learners begin to take ownership of the language, then grammar *per se* remains a conceptually difficult irrelevance. There is well-documented evidence to support the claim that under these circumstances students find language learning 'hard'.

The Ashfield case study (Coyle 1996), however, reported that during a Year 8 Science module taught through the medium of French, students needed to compare and describe different planets. This required meaningful exploration of adjectival usage, including the comparative and superlative forms. The students not only grasped the underlying grammatical concepts (e.g. by describing the relative positions and properties of Jupiter, Mars, Sun and Earth) but used them appropriately and spontaneously in different contexts. In the Science lessons, meaning was always the focus of teaching, learning experiences and tasks. The linguistic demands were pragmatic: students needed to communicate with the teacher, one another, or texts, in order to access or apply content. In so doing, the cognitive demand of the task required students to call upon their existing knowledge, concepts, skills and strategies. This strengthened the connections between the elements of language being practised or learned, concept development and previous knowledge. According to Met (1998: 3), strengthening and making connections amongst concepts and knowledge increases learning and retention. These then can be classed as quality learning contexts.

More recently the shift in pedagogical emphasis from teaching to learning has not only brought with it a focus on the role of social interaction in the classroom, but also on thinking skills, problem-solving and learning styles. This has led to increased interest in teaching initiatives such as CASE (Cognitive Acceleration through Science Education), CAME (Cognitive Acceleration through Mathematics Education) and the Thinking Through Geography Programme. What all these approaches share is an explicit emphasis on developing learners' problem-solving skills. More recently, the notion of accelerated learning is giving way to the concept of *curriculum enrichment*. As early as 1993, Nisbet claimed that 'before the century is out, no curriculum will be regarded as acceptable unless it can be shown to make a contribution to the teaching of thinking'. So what contribution can and does the MFL curriculum make to developing learner thinking?

MFL materials are usually designed to develop the learners' knowledge, skills and understanding of the linguistic system, not for the learning and understanding of 'new' knowledge and concepts, or as a means to process and evaluate information. I propose that widening the content base of language classrooms by integrating the teaching and learning of new and alternative concepts linked or 'borrowed' from other disciplines allows teachers to focus attention on developing and using skills such as analysing, synthesizing or predicting. Based on 'reasoning-gap' rather than 'information-gap' which according to Prabhu (1987) 'brings about a more sustained preoccupation with meaning', the following transcript taken from a different Year 9 MFL class plots four students' target language use during a problem-solving activity. The students (F1, 2, 5 and 8), unaided by the teacher, have been given some clues and have to allocate residents' names to appropriate houses. The language used here is unscripted and 'natural'. The students were so engrossed in task completion that they seemed unaware of the language used.

F5:	Je pense que ça [pointing to house] c'est Claude
F1:	Oui, à mon avis …
F2:	Agnès, c'est quoi?
F1:	Agnès? La maison de Agnès a un[e] porte blanche
F8:	C'est pas ça et pas ça [to self]
F1:	C'est comme … tu tu …
F2:	… et Bernard eum peut-être … non, il n'y a pas un de porte entre deux fenêtres chez Bernard
F8:	Ah … so, ça c'est Claude [in low voice]
F2:	La maison entre deux
F1:	Ah, c'est de Bernard … C'est la maison de Bernard …
F2:	Oui
F5:	La maison de Bernard …
F8:	Alors … alors Claude, c'est …
F1:	Alors Claude c'est ça
F2:	Ça … Parce que …
F5:	La maison de er … Claude est
F2:	Claude … au dessus de la … regarde il y a un, deux, trois … et alors
F8:	Oui voilà – on a fini

(Coyle 1999b)

Whilst the language used may be unremarkable from a linguistic perspective, it is in fact the language of thinking – spontaneous, learner-driven, focused and integral to successful task completion involving suggesting, hypothesizing, reasoning and so on. Baker (1996), using Skutnabb-Kangas' earlier work, argues as follows:

> The four basic language abilities are commonly regarded as speaking, listening, reading and writing. However, there are times when a person is not speaking, listening, reading or writing but is still using language … the language for *thinking* may be a fifth area of language competence.
>
> (Baker 1996: 7)

Building on Baker's suggestion, it might be a useful point of reflection to consider how the 'fifth' skill might be integrated as an element in the MFL prescribed Programme of Study of the NC with associated attainment descriptors. MFL departments may wish to audit the cognitive and linguistic demands they make on their learners by plotting a cognitively demanding–undemanding axis against a linguistically demanding–undemanding axis.

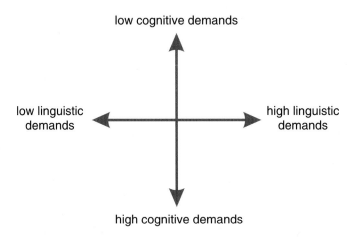

Typical classroom tasks for particular classes can be placed in the resulting quadrants. Resulting discussions may well focus on what constitutes cognitively demanding tasks, and the pedagogic purpose, if any, of cognitively and linguistically undemanding activity. Perhaps one of our greatest challenges is nurturing our learners through a challenging yet linguistically accessible diet.

In 1999, McGuiness published *From Thinking Skills to Thinking Classrooms*. This report, as well as giving a comprehensive review of current theories and practice in developing student thinking skills, also provided a range of taxonomies and approaches. McGuiness reached the conclusion that for thinking skills to be effectively developed they must be embedded in the wider curriculum – another call on curricular connectivity.

> It became increasingly clear that developing children's thinking goes far beyond an understanding of how children learn. Issues to do with curricular design, availability of curricular materials, the nature of pedagogy, teachers beliefs about learning and teaching as well as their professional development come to the fore. Perhaps it is not surprising that the emphasis has shifted from

thinking as a skill to concepts such as thinking curriculum, thinking class-rooms and schools for thought.

(McGuiness 1999)

Related to the thinking curriculum is the concept of teaching for understanding, advocated by Gardner *et al.* (1999). He argues for raising learner understanding rather than skill levels in the drive to raise standards. In his view, students do not use their skills to illuminate their understanding or to motivate them to further their learning independently. Teaching for understanding, Gardner maintains, is about teaching for 'uncoverage' of the curriculum rather than for 'coverage'.

> Certainly the greatest enemy of understanding is coverage – the compulsion to touch on everything in the textbook or the syllabus just because it is there, rather than taking the time to present materials from multiple perspectives, allowing students to approach the materials in ways that are congenial to them but that ultimately challenge them, and assessing understandings in as direct and flexible a manner as possible.
>
> (Gardner and Boix-Mansilla 1999: 82)

Whilst Gardner's work is critiqued as lacking analytical underpinning (Banks, Leach and Moon 1999), nonetheless it once again serves to challenge the current *modus operandi* in our schools and makes way for alternative 'learning routes', accommodating constructs such as multiple intelligences or different learning styles. In the case of Swanwick Hall School in Derbyshire (Thomas 2000), focusing on three major preferred learning styles (visual, auditory and kinaesthetic) as a basis for MFL teaching has brought with it an increase from 32 per cent to 71 per cent in A–C grades at GCSE in the space of three years. Here students are invited to speculate, memorize and work things out for themselves whilst the language is firmly rooted in context and the seeds of progression are sown. The head of department, Peter Rodgers, also underlines the importance of unpredictability in the language learning context.

> It is surprising how quickly they develop the technique of making it up as they go along. They never know what they will turn over next and the element of unpredictability increases motivation. It also extends their vocabulary as it makes them say things they wouldn't come out with otherwise.
>
> (Rodgers, in Thomas 2000)

Contexts for talk

Many of the issues raised in exploring the current MFL learning context focus pedagogic attention on a learning curriculum rather than a teaching curriculum. They emphasize the importance of preparing learners to think and discover for themselves and in so doing learn how to deal with and accept unpredictability and uncertainty. Dealing with uncertainty in the MFL classroom demands preparing students not only cognitively but also linguistically. Teaching learners how to 'talk' in the foreign language rather than just 'speak' involves an ideological leap from a rigidly-structured framework for developing grammatically ever more complex spoken language to a classroom context where student interaction, chat, banter and play with language (including joking) are not only the norm but are facilitated from the first MFL lesson.

> As foreign language instructors we need to view our classroom as the social organisation that it is and we need to participate in dialogic activity with learners so that they may achieve cognitive and linguistic self-regulation in ways that are socioculturally acceptable. In short, our task is to enable learners to find their voice, their speaking personality, their speaking consciousness.
>
> (Holquist and Emerson 1981: 434)

However, learner 'talk' doesn't just happen. Enabling learners to 'find their voice' requires flexible yet rigorous planning, scaffolding and development and a fundamental redefinition of MFL classroom discourse. According to van Lier (1996), 'all in all if we were to put quality in one word, it would have something to do with participability' (1996: 47). So what kind of pedagogic practice encourages and facilitates participability?

According to Leith (2000), 'free speech is the key to confidence in the target language'. Leading the TALK project, a national professional development initiative aiming at spontaneity in the MFL classroom, Leith reports that with

> subtle changes to how they interact with pupils, additional planning strategies and raised analytical awareness, most teachers can get conversation and creative sentence-building going very quickly ... Talking for real also requires learners to think deeply about how language fits together, with obvious benefits for all four language skills. Talkers generally have a richer pool of language and grammatical understanding on which to draw. Most noticeably, boys become more motivated when they speak and bring their own humour and personalities to their language learning.
>
> (Leith 2000: 12)

In this transcript, two students (G5 and G1) are trying to solve a computer printout problem with their Geography projects. (T) is their teacher. These students are not 'exceptional' linguists; they are simply operating under the accepted and agreed norms of their classroom, where French is the means of communication.

G5:   Tu peux faire en blanche et noire et après avec les couleurs. Qu'est-ce que tu peux faire? ... et je ...

G5:   ... Il faut que tu changes ...

G1:   ... Mais pourquoi?

G5:   Il faut que tu changes parce que c'est pas bien fait – regarde – c'est comme ça – il faut changer, oui?

G1:   D'accord, je sauf [I'll save it] ... allez demande à Monsieur Y, Monsieur Y [shouting out], est-ce que moi et F5 on peut aller à l'information technique pour faire quelque chose sur Ghana?

T: Oui, je peux téléphoner à R qui peut venir ici ...

G1:   ... Non, non, parce que nous voudrez aussi le laser jet

T: Ah bon – vingt minutes ...

G1:   ... D'accord ... couleurs ou pas en couleurs?

G5:   Pas en couleurs parce que la dernière fois j'ai essayé – c'était pas bon. Et imprimez la carte mais en noir parce c'est pas nécessaire pour les couleurs. Après on va changer, écris sur l'ordinateur ...

G1:   ... Les choses que j'ai fait je peux faire aujourd'hui pour la semaine prochaine. ... non, aujourd'hui est pour la semaine prochaine – je fais en français, on traduit en français.

(Coyle 1999b)

This is talking. This is thinking. This is communicating. This is participability.

Therefore if social interaction in the thinking and talking classroom is pivotal to learning, then as practitioners we need to know more about how it works and under what circumstances students are encouraged to spontaneously use and effectively learn though the target language, regardless of their ability. In my view this adds up to working towards a better understanding of classroom interaction and resulting discourse between teacher and learners and between learners and learners. It implies deepening our awareness of the balance between regulation or control and unpredictability or uncertainty – clearly both are needed in order to scaffold as well as ultimately liberate the learner to use *free speech* previously referred to. We know, for example that over-regulation, be it by the teacher, textbook, syllabus or curriculum, in effect closes down learner thinking and significantly reduces participability. It calls for extending the repertoire of classroom tasks which facilitate collaborative learning, problem-solving and task-based activities. It also exposes the need for modern languages teachers to learn from and share practice with colleagues working in other disciplines – pedagogical issues such as comparing how the Science teacher, Geography, History and Foreign Language teachers organize role-plays and simulations remain unarticulated and unconnected.

Connecting, linking and 'joined-up thinking'

My aim in writing this chapter has been to provoke thinking and reflection leading towards a reconceptualization of language teaching and learning. It has not been my intention to diminish the importance of foreign language learning nor to leave unacknowledged some of the excellent practice witnessed in MFL classrooms, but rather to elevate it to a position where:

- learning a foreign language is considered a key skill;
- language skills are not only *developed* in language lessons but are *used* in different ways across different areas of the school curriculum;

- language learning is valued within the curriculum for its contribution to developing cognitive, metacognitive, communicative and life skills.

Are we entering a period where a more rational and strategic approach to language learning will be adopted? Certainly the Nuffield Language Inquiry has set a national agenda for reform, offering a range of options, solutions and recommendations including amongst others *Recommendation 7.8*: Offer incentives for schools which create bilingual sections:

> Financial incentives should be made available for schools to introduce bilingual sections, in which a major part of the curriculum would be taught through the medium of a new language. Bilingual sections could be initiated independently or as part of a 'contract' with a primary school making similar provision. Schools would provide classes in each year group, with children remaining in a bilingual class as they move up the school. Entry to bilingual classes where at least half the timetable would be taught through the medium of another language would be through parental choice. There should be arrangements also for public examinations at age 16 in bilingual form for selected disciplines.
>
> (Nuffield 2000: 49)

Whilst some may perceive these moves as radical, a rapid growth in European provision for content and language integrated learning (CLIL), matched by a global urgency to use plurilingual skills, serve to reinforce the fact that Britain must respond to national and international pressure to deliver a coherent language strategy, building on both successful innovation and messages of discontent. Examples of curriculum development, classroom research, scientific research, collaborative initiatives and theoretical constructs all call for a reappraisal of what goes on in our classrooms as 'normal' practice. If we are to achieve what Leat calls 'productive synergy', if we are to halt the de-professionalization of language teachers denied 'elaborate conceptual thinking', if we are to listen to the learners and help them find their voice, then the key players in the language field have to connect. Above all a pedagogy which forefronts constructs such as message, enrichment, strategic discourse, participability and thinking can begin to respond honestly and professionally to this lamentable comment from a Year 11 male student: 'It has taken me five years to learn how to talk about nothing'.

In the words of Bruner (1999), making those connections, working towards joined-up thinking and reconceptualizing what constitutes effective practice in the language classroom from the teaching curriculum to the learning and thinking curriculum, demands professional confidence, pedagogic assertiveness and an unassuming openness to evaluation and negotiation by all those involved. After all: 'A choice of pedagogy inevitably communicates a conception of the learning process and the learner. Pedagogy is never innocent. It is a medium which carries its own message' (Bruner 1999: 17).

Further reading

Baker, C. (1996) *Foundations of Bilingual Education*, Clevedon: Multilingual Matters.

Banks, F., Leach, J. and Moon, B. (1999) 'New understandings of teachers' pedagogic knowledge', in J. Leach and B. Moon (eds) *Learners & Pedagogy*, Paul Chapman Publishing/Open University Press.

Bruner, J. (1999) 'Folk pedagogies', in J. Leach and B. Moon (eds), *Learners & Pedagogy*, Paul Chapman Publishing/Open University Press.

Bullock, R. (1975) *The Bullock Report*, London: HMSO.

Commission of the European Communities (1995) White Paper, *Teaching and Learning – Towards the Learning Society*, Objective IV, Council of Europe, Brussels, DGV.

Coyle, D. (1999a) *Francophonie*, March issue, Association for Language Learning.

—— (1999b) 'Breaking the rules of the game: adolescent voices speak out', unpublished thesis, University of Nottingham.

—— (2000a)'Meeting the challenge – the 3Cs curriculum', in S. Green (ed.) *New Perspectives on Teaching and Learning Modern Languages*, ch. 9, Multilingual Matters.

—— (2000b) 'Raising the profile and prestige of Modern Foreign Languages in the whole school curriculum', in K. Field (ed.) *Issues in Modern Foreign Languages Teaching*, ch. 17, RoutledgeFalmer.

Coyle, D. and Leith, J. (1996) 'Content-oriented language learning', *Comenius News 7*, CILT.

DES/WO (1990) *Modern Foreign Language Group Initial Advice*, London: HMSO.

DfEE (1999) *The National Curriculum for England and Wales, Modern Foreign Languages* (Curriculum 2000).

Gardner, H. and Boix-Mansilla, V. (1999) 'Teaching for understanding in the disciplines – and beyond', in J. Leach and B. Moon (eds) *Learners & Pedagogy*, Milton Keynes: Open University Press.

Genesee, F. (2001) 'Remarks', *Plurilingual Hubs in the New Millennium conference*, The Polytechnic University, Hong Kong.

Holquist, M. and Emerson, C. (1981) 'Glossary', in M.M. Bahktin, *The Dialogic Imagination: Four Essays*, Austin: University of Texas Press.

Jones, S. (2000) 'Enthusiastic pursuit' in *TES, Curriculum Special: Modern Languages*, Autumn 2000.

Krashen, S.D. (1983) *Second Language Acquisition and Second Language Learning*, NY: Pergamon Press.

Leat, D. (1998) *Thinking Through Geography*, Cambridge: Chris Kington Publishing.

Leith, J. (2000) 'The chattering classes', in *TES, Curriculum Special: Modern Languages*, Autumn 2000, pp.11, 12.

Legutke, M. and Thomas, H.F. (1991) *Process and Experience in the Languages Classroom*, London: Addison Wesley Longman.

McGuiness, C. (1999) *From Thinking Skills to Thinking Classrooms: A Review and Evaluation of Approaches for Developing Pupils' Thinking*, Research Report 115, DfEE, London: HMSO.

Met, M. (1998) 'Curriculum decision-making in content-based language teaching', in C. Cenoz and F. Genesee (eds) *Beyond Bilingualism: Multilingualism and Multilingual Education*, Multilingual Matters.

Mohan, B. (1986) *Language and Content*, Reading, MA: Addison-Wesley.

Nisbet, J. (1993) 'The thinking curriculum', *Educational Psychology*, 13: 281–90.

Norman, N. (1998) 'Prescription and autonomy in modern language curricula and materials in Great Britain and Germany', *Language Learning Journal*, 17: 48–56.

Nuffield Languages Inquiry (1998) Moys, A. (ed.) *Where Are We Going With Languages?* London: Nuffield Foundation.

—— (2000) *Languages: The Next Generation*, London: Nuffield Foundation.

O'Connor, J. and Seymour, J. (1990) *Introducing Neuro-Linguistic Programming*, Mandala Press.

Page, B. (1996) 'Graded objectives in ML (GOML)', in E. Hawkins (ed.) *30 Years of Language Teaching*, London: CILT.

Prabhu (1987) *Second Language* Pedagogy, Oxford: Oxford University Press.

Rodgers, P. quoted in A. Thomas 'A mix of chance and challenge', in *TES Curriculum Special: Modern Languages*, Autumn 2000.

Sinclair, J. and Coulthard, M. (1975) *Towards an Analysis of Discourse*, Oxford: Oxford University Press.

Skutnabb-Kangas, T. (1988) in T. Skutnabb-Kangas and J. Cumins, (eds), *Minority Education: From Shame to Struggle*, Clevedon: Multilingual Matters.

Smith, J. and Paterson, F. (1998) *Positively Bilingual: Classroom Strategies to Promote the Achievement of Bilingual Learners*, Nottingham: Nottingham Education Authority.

Swain, M. (1985) 'Communicative competence: some roles of comprehensible input and output in its development', in S.M. Gass and C.G. Madden (eds) *Input in Second Language Acquisition*, Massachussetts: Newbury House.

Van Lier, L. (1996) *Interaction in the Language Curriculum: Awareness, Autonomy & Authenticity*, NY: Longman Group Ltd.

11 Developing learning strategies
Strategy use in the teaching and learning of MFL

Michael Grenfell

Take a moment to consider the question: what is language? This is not a trivial exercise designed simply to perplex. Rather, I want to suggest that the way we think about language largely determines the way we set about trying to teach and learn it. This chapter is about different models of language and what might result in terms of classroom pedagogy. In particular, it deals with a way of conceptualizing language which may have something radical to suggest about how we approach the job of teaching it. This way of thinking about language involves the strategies learners use to become competent, and what the teacher might do to develop them. It draws on work from applied linguistics and what we know about language learning processes (see McDonough 1999). It links with principles of practice which might guide our actions in the classroom. Firstly, however, I want to offer one response to my opening question.

Thinking about language

It is in the nature of human beings wishing to know more about something to observe it closely. Let us use the analogy of the motor car. From a distance we can see what it does. We might even be inside one or using it ourselves to get us to where we want to go. However, if we go beyond this natural acceptance of its use, we get down to describing its various systems and component parts. The traditional approach to language has followed more or less the same pattern. Classically, language *is* its grammar and vocabulary, and there is no end of dictionaries, lexicons, and reference grammars cataloguing the nuts and bolts of what makes language tick.

Drafting linguistic details in this way is a useful means to know a language. However, a theoretical leap is then made: if we have a good description of a language, and we can learn this description, then we have learnt the language. Teaching language like this means imparting the description through explanation and exercises to help memorization.

This approach reflects how languages have been taught and learnt over the centuries since classical times (see Richards and Rodgers 1986 for a summary of various approaches to language teaching, their backgrounds, theoretical bases and practice). Certainly, what is known as the grammar–translation method predominated in language teaching for much of the last century. Here, progress in language was seen as the understanding and application of increasingly complex grammar rules and acquiring an ever-expanding bank of vocabulary (the recent National Literacy Strategy in Britain is at least in part based on a similar model of progression: sentence level grammar and key vocabulary). Both grammar and vocabulary are taught and learnt through textual analysis involving translation from and into the target language. Linguistic understanding is demonstrated through displays of mastery in sophisticated grammar exercises.

However, this approach has proved to be increasingly unsatisfactory in producing competent MFL users. To return to my analogy of the car, it is clear that naming its various component parts will not be enough to teach you to drive. Even if you know how the brake and clutch system works, there is no guarantee you will be able to use them. Similarly, knowledge of vocabulary and grammar of a language is not enough to be able to use it properly 'on the road'. Many successful language learners are only too aware of this. Pushed to an extreme, learning the grammar and vocabulary becomes an end in itself, while the 'car' itself is left in the garage.

These thoughts can be explored further by looking at various models of language learning across the last century. By the 1930s, the human sciences were sufficiently advanced for psychologists to understand that language was more than a set of formal rules and contrasting lexis. For behaviourists, language was a skill; principally, an *oral* skill. Learning language, they concluded, entailed practising these skills until they had been mastered. The result of this thinking is seen in the proliferation of language laboratories in the 1960s. These learning sites presented students with a stock of phrases which were learnt by drilling, mostly in tape-based repetition exercises delivered over headphones. It was believed that error was the result of insufficient practice; hence, more drilling was prescribed. It was as if we learnt to drive by repeating gear changes and clutch movement in laboratory conditions. The assumption was that the mastered phrases would eventually link together to produce a fully operational linguistic system.

Such an approach to surviving on the road would be insufficient on its own since the situation is always changing and the driver has to adapt accordingly. Analogously, mastering stock phrases in language is not enough to deal with the complexity and sophistication of multiple linguistic situations. Psychologists began to write about this as early as the 1950s. Language does not work simply through the application of a series of stock phrases, but is prone to constant creation and variation. Its source is something other than memory.

Being competent

Early in the 1950s, the psycholinguist Noam Chomsky noticed that language was in fact quite a finite feature of the human brain. Most people had a limited vocabulary compared with that available, and most essential grammar could be summed up in quite a slim volume. And yet language was used in an infinite number of utterances. He concluded that what we know as language is in fact a surface phenomenon, and that its generation lies elsewhere, in the deep structures of the mind. He believed he had found evidence of this way of thinking about language by observing the acquisition of first languages. He observed that once a particular syntactical feature had been acquired by children, for example the position of adverbs, then this feature was more or less applied correctly in every case; whilst the behaviourist model would suggest each adverb was learnt separately. He concluded that there was an innate 'Language Acquisition Device' in the human mind that operated irrespective of the language.

This represented a major shift, so much so that we now refer to the Chomskyan *revolution*, and it is a model which has dominated how we think about language ever since.

Chomsky's own work is highly technical and he has little to say about second language learning let alone teaching. However, others have done so in his place and extrapolated these ideas to consider their implications for those attempting to gain competence in a language other than their first native tongue (see, for example, the work of Stephen Krashen 1981, 1982 and a summary in Lightbown and Spada 1993). *Competence*: what is it to be competent in a language? For Chomsky, competence is the language which may be available for use, which he contrasts with *performance*, that language used on any one particular occasion. For Chomsky, such competence is invariably defined in terms of grammar or syntax. However, others have noticed the relevance of this concept to other features of language.

For example, Hymes (1972) coined the phrase 'Communicative Competence', reasoning that to be an able language learner meant more than grammar mastery: 'there were rules of use' he writes, 'without which the rules of grammar would be useless'. Language had also to be appropriate, feasible, possible, coherent and cohesive. These notions were more formally expressed later as sub-categories of communicative competence: *Sociolinguistic* competence (what is appropriate); *Strategic* competence (how to solve problems and get by); *Discourse* competence (how to be coherent); and *Grammar* competence (how to make sense accurately) (see Canale and Swain 1980 and Bachman 1990). What does this model of language imply in terms of how we teach it?

From learning to teaching: communicative competence

As these ideas surfaced in the 1970s and 1980s, they exerted a strong influence on thoughts about practice in the second language classroom. Its main features were: first, that there was a natural 'Language Acquisition Device' in the human brain which needed to be activated if language learning was to take place; second, that competence included other aspects than simply grammatical mastery; and third, that the social and cultural context of language was its natural field of operation. These principles of learning coalesced in an approach to classroom pedagogy which directed how we set about teaching modern languages for most of the rest of the century: 'Communicative Language Teaching' (CLT). CLT teaches second language by analogy with first language processes (see Littlewood 1981). Hence, there is a high degree of oral speech directed at meaningful situations. The role of formal grammar learning is vastly reduced if not totally absent. The focus is on the individual as a social identity and the cultural context of his/her language use.

This approach to language learning and teaching is everywhere apparent in the General Certificate of Secondary Education (GCSE) and the National Curriculum (NC). GCSE set the trend in the mid-1980s with its model of foreign language as consisting of four skills – listening, speaking, reading and writing – and its focus on content in terms of pupil as host or tourist. Communication is all. Consequently, getting the gist of the message across is the prime objective in language use. Accuracy, though desirable, is of secondary importance. The NC takes its lead from this model; it has been subject to several working reports and revisions, but takes the four skills and the communicative emphasis as a given. The 1995 version (DfEE 1995) opens its Programme of Study with a section on *Learning and Using the Target Language*. The first part, *Communicating in the Target Language*, is in prime position and lists what pupils need in order to communicate. The four skills – or Attainment Targets in NC terms – chart the progress envisaged for pupils over nine levels as they move from simple one-word statements to sentences, longer passages and narratives. Open any coursebook aimed at GCSE or NC learners and the resultant materials and methodology are immediately apparent: colourful authentic materials, interactive activities, language to get things done. This style of language teaching is an inevitable result of thinking of language communicatively.

Certainly, much has been gained along the way of CLT, GCSE and NC. However, as we commence the new millennium, there are great concerns about modern foreign language learning in Britain. One of the bonuses of the new approach was the amount of target languages used in classrooms. Yet inspection evidence (Dobson 1998) reports how much of this is rote repetition initiated by the teacher. There is a concern that pupils cannot generate language independently outside of a series of set routines. Even more worrying is that a significant proportion of pupils seems to plateau out after their early years of language learning and thereafter make little progress. At the end of the last century, an inquiry was launched to ascertain 'where we are going in languages?' (Moys 1998). It was the biggest national survey ever conducted. Findings make sober reading: secondary pupils lack motivation or direction; nine out of ten stop learning languages at sixteen; university language departments are closing, leaving the sector in deep crisis (see *The Nuffield Languages Inquiry* 2000).

This is not the place to dwell on these issues, and there are many dimensions of policy and practice involved. Rather, I want to focus again on the way we think about language and the consequences of this thinking. GCSE and the NC are one consequence of thinking about language learning in CLT terms. But many issues remain unresolved. Do pupils acquire language by absorption (the justification for monolingual language teaching)? In practice, the aspiration to get pupils talking seems to be reduced to repetition and drilling more akin to the language laboratories of the 1960s than the interactive language use envisaged in the early days of CLT. Does grammar help or hinder foreign language learning? Common sense would suggest it must help, although research has not given unequivocal support to this notion (see Ellis 1990). Without a clear lead, the status of grammar in modern language teaching has ebbed and flowed. Take three or four coursebooks spanning the late 1980s to late 1990s, and track the way with which grammar is dealt. The first CLT modern foreign language coursebooks almost eschewed grammar altogether. The emphasis was on skills, notions and functions (see Wilkins 1976). Then, gradually, grammar returned, with the promise of an integrated approach, which became ever more explicit rule-teaching. This development hardly represents a return to the grammar–translation method. However, it is noticeable that grammar hardly gets a mention in the 1995 version of the National Curriculum (DfEE 1995). The nearest it comes to explicitly stating the need for grammar is way down, listed as number six in section three on *Language-Learning Skills and Knowledge of Language*, where it is stated that pupils should be taught to 'understand and apply patterns, rules, exceptions in language forms and structures' (p. 3). Yet, in the latest version of the National Curriculum (DfEE 1999), grammar features in second place of the Programme of Study: 'pupils should be taught ... the grammar of the target language and how to apply it' (p. 16). Clearly, teaching grammar allows a teacher to plan how to instruct a whole class on a particular linguistic item, but it can also mitigate against offering opportunities to use language personally or creatively.

This to-ing and fro-ing with grammar is a case in point of how uncertainties about language, how it is learnt, and therefore how it should be taught, go very deep. It is as if there is no escape from being caught in a cycle of recurrence, where the same issues of policy and practice return by seasonal variation.

The rest of this chapter deals with learning strategies and the part they might play in second language learning and teaching. I am not wishing to add to the methodological confusion (see Grenfell 2000 for a more detailed discussion of the present state of modern foreign language teaching) by introducing yet another element to the picture. Rather, I want to suggest that strategic thinking about second language learning and teaching is one way, a different way, of approaching classroom practice and enhancing pedagogic effectiveness. I want to approach consideration of learning strategies by looking at what learners do to learn.

The good, the bad and the unable language learner

Of course, language teaching methodology is always stated in general terms. Broad principles are sought that can be applied in a range of contexts. But language learning *per se* is always an individual concern, with individual variation (see Skehan 1989). If you are reading this book, by definition you must be a successful language learner. But how did you do it? You might not be able to tell us. Or you might believe you know how, but this belief might be mistaken. Chances are you used a whole set of techniques, approaches and skills, some more or less successfully, to gain competence. Can we help others attempting to follow in our footsteps? Can I tell another how to drive a car based on my experience? How far will it take us? What will be missing?

How do 'bad' or poor language learners characterize themselves? Take time to draw up your own list before reading on. My poor language learner is someone who cannot involve themselves in the language. They cannot memorize words, or understand grammar. When they do, they cannot adapt it from one context to another. They easily get confused and this puts them off, so they withdraw from engaging with the language. They are forever looking up words and seeing language as a puzzle which has to be solved rather than something they can use, that gets things done and in which they can express themselves.

This is a personal picture of a 'poor' language learner, and it is one in which I am sure we all, even as 'good' learners, recognize something of ourselves. Perhaps the message, therefore, is that there are no 'good' or 'bad' language learners, but potentially 'able' and 'unable' learners, and this ableness is determined by a whole set of personal and contextual factors interacting with each other (see Naiman *et al.* 1978/96).

This line of thinking led one second language researcher to draw up a list of what is needed to be a 'good language learner' (Stern 1975). He defines good language learning in terms of a series of strategies:

- planning strategy
- active strategy
- empathetic strategy
- formal strategy
- experimental strategy
- semantic strategy
- practice strategy
- communication
- monitoring strategy
- internalization strategy

It is not necessary to go into the detail of each of these; they speak for themselves! For example, a semantic strategy is clearly an intent to go for meaning over grammatical analysis in language use. Moreover, we recognize them from our own language learning, the extent to which we did or did not use them, and teaching experience, contrasting the good, the bad and the unable. In them, it is possible to see the strands of learning discussed earlier. So, there are the active, empathetic, semantic, experimental and communication-focused strategies which might characterize CLT. But, there are also the formal and monitoring strategies which we might expect to find in a grammar–translation approach. Practice strategies may well follow the repetition and drilling of audio-lingualism. And it is necessary that language is 'internalized' in order to be useful in making sense and meaning in language input and output.

Stern deliberately chose to express his good language learner in terms of a series of 'strategies', but his use of this word raises an interesting question. Commonly, a strategy is understood as a deliberate plan to bring about a desired aim or objective. 'Planning' features in pole position in Stern's list. It is possible to imagine someone setting out to be more communicative, experimental, or to practise more. However, if anyone is taken and thrust into a 'foreign' language context, we also know that, as if by natural process, the vast majority of individuals will acquire the language in due course. Much of this learning will occur almost involuntarily, merely as the result of efforts to survive or get by in the new environment. There is then an issue as to whether such good language learning strategies are conscious and deliberate, or automatic and unconscious.

There are clearly many features of language to be dealt with. We have already considered the formal aspects of grammar and meaning in language use in discussing CLT. But even grammar has other elements: morphology, phonology. And we saw in considering communicative competence that meaning is also dependent on dimensions such as coherence and cohesion, and a whole range of sociolinguistic features. Strategies might apply to any of these in different ways, at the level of manipulation and consumption of language. Yet, at the same time, a large part of language learning is about study, about the deliberate act of committing oneself to memorize or understand language, or planning to place oneself in a situation which it is felt will aid the process. These acts too might best be understood as 'strategic'. But the outcome of this thinking about the good language learner and strategies still seems to be quite a fragmented view of what language is. It is itemized in terms of component parts, features, and the use to which it is put. Unhappily, this view returns us to our opening analogy of a car and language: that by describing each item and teaching it, that by explaining each system function, the result is the fully competent driver. We may have moved on from straight grammar description and explanation, but the approach in GCSE and NC language learning remains pretty much the same. The assumption is that by itemizing we can render aspects of language discrete and impart them to our learners. Look at any coursebook, scheme of work or syllabus and you will see the outcome of this assumption, as their writers struggle to capture language, set it down on paper and then teach according to it. I am not arguing that such efforts are a waste of time or unnecessary. Of course, such detail is important. The problems begin when relative weightings between these aspects of language have to be worked out and methodologies designed to deal with them. Invariably, teachers operate as best they can, visiting each area in turn and making connections. It is then up to the 'black boxes' of the learners' minds to learn. Again, I am arguing that this way of thinking about language leads to a certain way of working with language, and it is my belief that it is not enough – on its own. Something else is needed to make the connections – for the learners *and* teachers. The next section begins to address what the 'something else' is.

Strategically thinking

Language as grammar? Language as communication? Language as function and notion? Language as meaning? Language as sound? Language as structure? Which is it to be? Of course, we are not in an either/or situation and the best response might be yes to all of these. In the last section, I raised the notion of strategy use in language learning, but to which model of language does this belong? A strategy is a planned approach to or a way of dealing with language which enhances learning; for example a deliberate aim for fluency rather than accuracy in social interactions or a selected means to memorize a list of vocabulary (see Brumfit 1984). A strategy involves thinking *about* language and thinking *in* language (see Wenden and Rubin 1987, O'Malley and Chamot 1990, Oxford 1990 and Oxford, 1993 for a range of definitions of 'strategy').

In a cognitive view of knowing, language is not itemized but forms part of one knowledge system. Cognition really refers to the processing of information in the mind. All systems are forms of information to be processed. But there is a fundamental distinction in cognition between knowing *that* and knowing *how*. For example, we might know that Paris is the capital of France but do we know how to get there? In Cognitive theory, the two sides of this distinction are respectively known as 'declarative' and 'procedural' knowledge. However, it would be wrong to see them as separate entities. Rather, it might be best to view them as a continuum between knowing something and the uses or procedures it can be put. It is helpful to think of language in these terms. For example, it is perfectly possible to see how grammar rules and vocabulary are forms of knowing *that*, and therefore form part of declarative knowledge. Similarly, in speaking a language, whether first or second, clearly, a whole set of *how to* systems have been proceduralized. Indeed, it is also possible to see how grammar–translation teaching methodology proceeds on the assumption that grammar rules taught become proceduralized. However, we know that this is not necessarily so and it is perfectly possible for someone to know a whole lot of grammar declarative knowledge without being able to use it. Audio-visual language teaching approached the problem from the opposite direction: with the assumption that exposure to the processes of language use and its procedures in the form of stock phrases was enough to instil the necessary declarative knowledge. It is possible to be able to use something – for example a particular functional phrase like asking for a cup of coffee – without knowing why it works. CLT in its strong form also makes this assumption: that communication is the end *and* the means of language teaching, and therefore exposure to the processes of language in use was sufficient.

We know that, with prolonged exposure to language, automatic processes in the brain take over and linguistic competence is gained. This is a necessary survival strategy for individuals and forms part of the need for self-control in one's surroundings, to get things done, to express oneself and interact with others. This sort of social adaptation to the environment, both physical and mental, is cognition in operation. Declarative and procedural knowledge are very close in this situation. Something is known as it is put into use. However, this natural state is not the situation in most modern language classrooms. Eric Hawkins (1987) once referred to modern language teaching in schools as 'gardening in a gale'. This analogy conjures up a brutal image of what happens to the tender young linguistic shoots, so carefully cultivated by the teacher for an hour or so, once they go out and are hit by the cold, stormy blasts of English everywhere else in pupils' lives. In this situation, relying on cognition is not enough: pupils will know things but not be able to use them, or use them but not know why. This situation is perhaps why experiences with CLT as enshrined in the English NC and GCSE over the past decade or so have yielded disappointing results.

We understand that elements of language – for example, pronunciation or a grammar rule – have to be known and used to be useful, but what of other dimensions of language? Above, I listed various strategies that might be used by the good language learner, but only one of these referred explicitly to grammar. What about all the others: for example, active strategy, experimental strategy, memorization strategy, and monitoring strategy? These strategies can also be *declared*; that is, stated explicitly and deliberately operated. Yet, such aspects of language learning are often overlooked. Or it is assumed that they go on automatically and therefore need not be explicitly taught. We know that good language learners do these things, but then assume this is a natural aptitude which individuals may or may not possess. It is possible to think of these strategies more systematically and teach them to learners for use as an integral part of language learning.

Cognitive theory has another category for such information processing: 'metacognition'. The prefix *meta-* signifies 'beyond'. So, metacognition is beyond cognition; in other words, beyond the direct processing of information to involve knowledge of the process itself. It is one thing to learn a word or grammar (cognition), another to know the best way of going about this learning (metacognition). This distinction opens the door to the possibility of introducing planning and monitoring approaches into language teaching. It also offers the option of explicitly selecting mental attitudes or approaches to various language tasks.

O'Malley and Chamot (1989) list a whole lot of these metacognitive strategies. Here are some of them:

- *Advanced preparation* Rehearsing the language needed for an oral or written task.
- *Self-evaluation* Judging how well one has accomplished a learning task.
- *Selective attention* Attending to or scanning key words, phrases, linguistic markers, sentences, or type of information.

All of these deal with knowledge about the learning process which may be available to the learner as part of their language learning. It *may* be available – some learners do these things, some learners do not. These metacognitive strategies are therefore distinct from the direct cognitive processes of actually working on the language itself in efforts to learn it. O'Malley and Chamot list these too as 'cognitive' strategies:

- *Note-taking* Writing down key words and concepts in abbreviated verbal, graphic or numerical form.
- *Resourcing* Using reference materials such as dictionaries, encyclopaedias, or textbooks.
- *Inferencing* Using information in the text to guess meanings of new items, predict outcomes or complete missing parts.

Clearly, there is a big difference between 'metacognitive' and 'cognitive' strategies. Having various strategies for planning and monitoring learning is qualitatively different from grappling with the language itself. In the above latter case, knowing how a dictionary is constructed, and therefore how to use it, is of a different order of knowledge to making inferences and guessing meaning from language. Some strategies also seem easier to use than others; some are quite mechanical, others involve sophisticated thinking and the linking of a wide range of types of knowledge. This easy/hard dichotomy is everywhere apparent in strategy work. Degrees of difficulty might also imply stages of learning, with easier strategies being used in early language learning, and the more difficult ones in advanced learners. To these distinctions we might add individual differences. For example, there are differences of gender, age and learning styles which may determine which strategies are employed by individual learners. Moreover, we might identify which strategies we think are most helpful for each stage of the learning process. Can we do this on the basis of our own successful language learning experience?

The point is to suggest that there is another way of thinking about language learning than established dichotomies between grammar and communication. Thinking strategically opens up ways of going about the language learning and teaching process which are not always apparent in established curriculums and syllabuses. This way of thinking does itself have a theoretical base. However, it also has very practical implications in terms of how we go about teaching languages. It is to this pedagogic concern that I now wish to turn.

Teaching strategically

Every language teacher has a strategy to teach, based on past experience and knowledge of present circumstances. Some of this strategic pedagogic knowledge comes from his/her own formative training as a 'language person' (see Evans 1988). Other aspects of teaching come from following a specific methodological approach. For anyone setting out to teach something, it is logical to isolate items and then design a way of imparting them to their learners. Following a grammar–translation method means listing grammar and vocabulary and devising explanations for them. Audio-lingual approaches draw up banks of structures for repetition. Even in the communicative approach, notions, functions and phrases are selected for a range of transactional contexts. In all these methods, what is taught *is* language. The strategic approach to teaching takes a radically different tack: what is taught is not what needs to be learnt but *how* to learn. What this means in effect is that lessons and schemes of work are planned not only in terms of language content – grammar, vocabulary, notions, functions, etc. – but the best means of learning all these. In short, strategic teaching is concerned with *learning to learn*.

Above, I noted a few strategies identified by research and made the point that some were clearly more sophisticated than others. So, looking up words in dictionaries, though extremely important, is rather restricted when compared with the multi-dimensional aspects involved in inferencing. We know that strategy used is highly individual-dependent, and that there are possibly large differences between gender, learning style, age, and stage of learning. We also know that, when faced with a foreign language, many learners grasp at the details of what they see or hear. They naturally want to dissect it, to itemize vocabulary, look up words in the dictionary, and analyse syntax. These 'bottom-up' processes are an important part of learning a language. However, we also know that *good* language learners very quickly develop a more holistic 'top-down' approach to language. They do not become so preoccupied with detail that they cannot see the wood for the trees. Rather, they aim for gist and the aspects of language which buy them most in terms of comprehension and making sense. They then manage the gaps by employing a range of social, cognitive and metacognitive strategies. The point is that in the normal language learning classroom, these approaches and strategies remain implicit, unstated and mostly unacknowledged. They are present but individual learners are left to develop them, or not, according to their personal dispositions, attitudes and aptitudes as part of some natural process that cannot, and should not, be interfered with. This approach to strategies creates the situation of 'good' and 'bad' language learners, as if it were a preordained inevitability. Strategic teaching, on the other hand, is about making the strategies available to all in a much more systematic way. But how to do this?

We must recognize the different orders of strategies. Some are quite broad with a wide usage: for example, 'elaboration' – relating new information to prior knowledge, relating different parts of new information to each other, or making meaningful personal associations with the new information. Others are quite specific and skill-dependent: for example, skimming and scanning in reading texts. Skimming requires gist comprehension; scanning refers to the search for specific information. In any of these strategies, there seem to be two basic approaches to teaching them. Either exercises are devised where, in order to complete them, the learner has to develop a certain kind of strategic position or approach to the task. Of course, these sorts of exercises occur by the way in language classrooms. Teaching strategically means being far more explicit and intentional in devising pedagogic activities with the goal in mind. A second approach to 'teaching strategies' is to teach them explicitly. In other words, they are listed for learners, explained, and opportunities provided to use them. This approach is known as 'Strategy Instruction' (SI).

Each approach has its pros and cons. The implicit approach will work quite deeply on learners' cognitive processes and broaden their use of language. However, what happens if the strategies do not stick? There is also the question of transferability from one language context to another. The explicit approach makes sure that there is no room for doubt and confusion as each strategy is openly explained and exemplified. However, we know from teaching grammar that explanation is not enough. We can get pupils successfully completing exercises, but there is no guarantee that these structures now enter actively into their competence and can be used in a range of contexts. Similarly, we might suspect that listing strategies and explaining them is no guarantee of their adoption on the part of learners. If this adoption does not occur it is probably because of the sorts of individual differences we have mentioned; either learners do not learn that way or are not yet at that stage of learning to be able to operate cognitively with language at this level. In order to understand what is to be done, there is one final ingredient which needs to be added to our discussion – 'Autonomy'.

From a teacher's point of view, it is for them to select and teach, and for learners to learn. The teacher has a larger view of what is needed to be known and where the learners are in the ladder of progression. However, in language learning, we also know that there is a 'Language Acquisition Device', that learners do broadly follow natural sequences of acquisition in the various levels and dimensions of language and that, consequently, pitching the content and process of learning out of line with these stages simply results in the learner crashing. What is needed is scope for the learner to work *at his/her level* and then for opportunities to move beyond it. This requirement necessitates some degree of autonomy on the part of the learner in the learning process. This autonomy may apply to the content of language learning, its process, and/or its assessment. It is not possible to be a successful language learner and not, to some degree, be an autonomous language learner. This statement explains the reality behind national findings that a lot of modern foreign language is being used in classrooms but not much of it is pupil-initiated. It is as if the product of language learning is being mimicked in the absence of its processes. Competence starts where autonomy begins: where learners take on board the language as an independent generating system. As we have seen, this requires the nuts and bolts of language, grammar and vocabulary, but it also requires processing skills. Strategic teaching and learning is one route to these skills. But how do we develop them within an autonomous framework?

Practical examples of Strategy Instruction (SI) in use are supplied elsewhere in this reader series (Harris 2001). Here, I shall briefly mention its grounding principles. SI is based on a sequence of activities which takes the learner from awareness, to exemplification, to application. This sequence of stages can be listed:

1   Preparation/consciousness raising.
2   Modelling.
3   Practice.
4   Action-planning/goal-setting and monitoring.
5   Focused practice and fading reminders.
6   Evaluation of strategy acquisition and recommencing the cycle.

In stage 1, learners reflect on the learning process and the notion of strategy use is introduced. In stage 2, certain strategies are presented, explained and demonstrated. Very often these strategies can be elicited from the learners themselves as examples of 'what you do' in this situation, how to learn, or how to deal with this problem. The focus for strategies can be selected by the teacher. This selection is made in due consideration of where the learner is at in their stage of learning, so attention needs to be given as to whether top-down or bottom-up, or a mixture of the two, strategies form the core of SI.

In stage 3, opportunities are created for the strategies selected to be practised in classroom contexts (see Grenfell and Harris 1998: especially chapters 4 and 5). In stage 4, the learners themselves plan their personal work programme and set targets for themselves. This plan entails them selecting strategies for their own use – what suits them best – and working on setting goals in applying them. Here, both cognitive and metacognitive process are developed as learners use various strategies and reflect on their usage.

In stage 5, there is further practice but explicit reminders, both personal and teacher-driven are removed. Slowly, it is hoped, the strategy is proceduralized as it becomes part of the learners' way of doing things. Finally, in stage 6, there is a process of reflection on the cycle and an evaluation of what has been achieved. This evaluation includes a self-assessment and a decision on what to do next as the cycle starts again from the top.

There are many questions about the cycle. For example, how long should it last? What proportion of class time should it take? How can it be integrated with 'normal' class work? To what extent can the sort of reflections and goal-setting be carried out in the target language and to what extent is English permissible? How do we move learners away from the more restricted strategies to start developing the more sophisticated ones? The accounts (ibid. 109–46) of teachers attempting SI with their classes suggest that a flexible approach to the above sequence needs to be adopted, at least in the first instance. Moreover, it may take collective work within school departments over two or three years before an explicit list can be drawn up detailing what strategies, when and how. However, teaching strategically opens up opportunities for autonomy and learning to learn which are not present in the traditional language classroom, albeit communicative.

Being a language learner

We all know that once we embark on learning a language, we never stop. This is as true for second languages as it is for our native languages. We also know that language is how we express ourselves – in one sense it *is* who we are. In recent years, there has been a recognition of the social cultural aspects of language. This recognition is enshrined in the Communicative Approach, but we have seen that its operation in practice can lead to language teaching which is every bit as one-dimensional as the methods of the past. The thrust of the social imperatives of languages has been fresh impetus recently by support from the European Union in its goal to found linguistic principles of European Citizenship. The Common European Framework (1996) represents language in terms of *savoir faire*, *savoir apprendre* and *savoir être*. The first of these relates to the know-how of language. But, strategically thinking, we know that the third of these, the *savoir apprendre*, is needed for this know-how to occur. In other words, learners need to learn but they also need to know how to learn. Only then can the third of these occur and learners learn 'to be' (*savoir être*) in *their* language – not that of someone else.

Further reading

Bachman, L.F. (1990) 'Communicative language ability', in *Fundamental Considerations in Language Testing*, Oxford: Oxford University Press.

Brumfit, C.J. (1984) *Communicative Methodology in Language Teaching: The Roles of Fluency and Accuracy*, Cambridge: Cambridge University Press.

Canale, M. and Swain, M. (1980) 'Theoretical bases of communicative approaches to second language teaching and testing', *Applied Linguistics*, 1(1): 1–47.

Department for Education (1995) *Modern Foreign Languages in the National Curriculum*, London: HMSO.

Department for Education and Employment (1999) *Modern Foreign Languages: The National Curriculum for England*, London: HMSO.

Dobson, A. (1998) *MFL Inspected: Reflections on Inspection Findings 1996/97*, London: CILT.

Ellis, R. (1990) *Instructed Second Language Acquisition*, Oxford: Blackwell.

Evans, C. (1988) *Language People*, Milton Keynes: Open University Press.

Grenfell, M. (2000) 'Modern languages – beyond Nuffield and into the twenty-first century', *Language Learning Journal* (In Press).

Grenfell, M. and Harris, V. (1998) *Modern Languages and Learning Strategies: in Theory and Practice*, London: Routledge.

Harris, V. (2001) 'Learning to learn: strategy instruction in the modern classroom', in A. Swarbrick (ed.) *Aspects of Teaching MFL: Perspectives on Practice*, London: RoutledgeFalmer.

Hawkins, E. (1987) *Modern Languages in the Curriculum* (rev. edn) Cambridge: Cambridge University Press.

Hymes, D. (1972) 'On communicative competence', in J.B. Pride and J. Holmes (eds) *Sociolinguistics*, Harmondsworth: Penguin.

Krashen, S. (1981) *Second Language Acquisition and Second Language Learning*, Oxford: Pergamon Press.

—— (1982) *Principles and Practice in Second Language Acquisition*, Oxford: Pergamon Press.

Lightbown, P. and Spada, N. (1993) *How Languages are Learned*, Oxford: Oxford University Press.

Littlewood, W. (1981) *Communicative Language Teaching*, Cambridge: Cambridge University Press.

McDonough, S.H. (1999) 'Learner strategies', *Language Teaching*, 32: 1–18.

Moys, A. (1998) *Where are We Going with Languages?* London: Nuffield Foundation.

Naiman, N., Fröhlich, M., Stern, H.H. and Todesco, A. (1978/1996) *The Good Language Learner*, Clevedon: Multilingual Matters.

The Nuffield Languages Inquiry (2000) *Languages: The Next Generation*, London: The Nuffield Foundation.

O'Malley, J.M. and Chamot, A.U. (1990) *Language Learning Strategies in Second Language Acquisition.*, Cambridge: Cambridge University Press.

Oxford, R. (1990) *Language Learning Strategies: What Every Teacher Should Know*, Boston: Heinle and Heinle.

—— (1993) 'Research on second language learning strategies', *Annual Review of Applied Linguistics*, 13: 175–87.

Richards, J.C. and Rodgers, T.S. (1986) *Approaches and Methods in Language Teaching: A Description and Analysis*, Cambridge: Cambridge University Press.

Skehan, P. (1989) *Individual Differences in Second Language Learning*, London: Edward Arnold.

Stern, H.H. (1975) 'What can we learn from the good language learner?', *Canadian Modern Language Review*, 31.

Wenden, A. and Rubin, J. (1987) *Learning Strategies in Language Learning*, Englewood Cliffs, NJ: Prentice Hall.

Wilkins, D.A. (1976) *Notional Syllabuses*, Oxford: Oxford University Press.

12 Treading a tightrope

Supporting boys to achieve in MFL[1]

Vee Harris

Introduction

Despite the concern expressed about boys' underachievement over the last five years, little seems to have changed: 'Boys achieve far less well than girls. The gender gap – a matter of concern across the curriculum – is greater in languages than in most other subjects' (Nuffield Languages Inquiry, 2000: 46). Debate as to the causes underlying boys' general underachievement has continued to flourish (Smithers 1996; Marshall 1996; Weiner, Arnot and David 1997; Mahony 1998). Within Modern Languages, there have been a number of useful studies (Clark 1998, Barton in this volume) using questionnaires and interviews to identify boys' likes, dislikes and preferences and an investigation along similar lines, commissioned by the Qualifications and Curriculum Authority (QCA), is currently taking place. This chapter does not attempt to provide a comprehensive discussion of what is a vast, highly complex and controversial issue. Rather, it seeks to draw together the findings of recent studies both in the teaching of English and also across a number of different research areas in Modern Languages. The aim is to identify what 'clues for good practice' already exist and to offer some tentative suggestions as to some immediate practical steps that could be taken within the Modern Languages classroom.

Whilst recognizing the obvious differences between the teaching of English and the foreign language, the fact that boys appear to underachieve in both areas seems to warrant serious consideration. Brumfit (1995: 5) indicates some of the common ground between the two subjects in his introduction to Language Education in the National Curriculum, where the authors cover a range of language-related areas including Drama, English Literature teaching and Bilingualism as well as Foreign Languages. He explains that 'all of us have been concerned with languages as expressions of individual and social wishes and needs, and all of us see "language" as inevitably embracing literary and creative needs, mass communication, social confidence and personal identity'. The fact that English is a core curriculum subject has meant that investigations to explore boys' attitudes and difficulties are 'one step ahead' of Modern Languages and there may well be lessons to be learned. At the same time, however, there is always the danger that attempts to draw comparisons across subject areas or to bring together research findings from a number of separate fields of study run the risk of treating complex arguments superficially.

The social and educational context

Before considering any implications for the classroom, there are a number of general points I would like to make to avoid misinterpretation. First, some boys continue to make excellent progress, particularly later in their educational career and we should be wary of stereotyping all boys as 'failing'. The Ofsted report (1998) *Recent Research on Gender and Educational Performance* noted that boys made somewhat greater educational progress than girls between GCSE and A level. According to the Chief Inspector of Schools, it is the failure of 'white working-class boys' in particular which is a cause for concern (Pyke 1996: 2). Clark (op. cit.) also observes that pupils from lower socio-economic backgrounds may be more likely to be ethnocentric and express disinterest in language learning, a suggestion that raises further issues in relation to opportunity and access. Yet, whilst we should seek to identify underlying patterns, it goes without saying that we must also avoid automatically labelling whole groups of pupils in our classrooms.

Second, in focusing on boys, I would not want to give the impression that in the past we have somehow overcompensated in favour of girls and that there is no further need to build on the initiatives that have been developed over the last ten years to promote their confidence and their learning. As Mahony and Hextall (2000) point out, girls still experience discrimination at school and the 'glass ceiling' continues to prevent women from reaching the higher posts at senior management level.

The final point is also related to the wider social and political context: namely that education alone cannot resolve the problems that some boys experience. The TV Panorama documentary, *Men aren't Working* (1995), indicated a range of possible social and economic factors that may be affecting some boys' current lack of motivation and academic success, including changes in patterns of employment. Indeed Mahony (1997: 7) questions the origin of the current anxiety about the underachievement of boys from Australia to the Caribbean, suggesting that it cannot be separated from developments in the global market economy:

> the displacement of the 'masculine' manufacturing base by the 'feminine' service sector requires high levels of communication skills and within this, the increasing proportion of casualized work is being carried out by white and black working class women (Walby 1990) … it is the world that has changed not the boys and one problem is that there is no longer a fit between many of them and it.

So boys may still be clinging to the 'macho identity' associated with manual labour, when there are few such jobs available. The Ofsted report on gender and educational performance (op. cit.) notes that some economic commentators are predicting that as many as 70 per cent of the new jobs that will be created over the next decade will be in areas traditionally occupied by women. So, whilst taking into account boys' likes and dislikes, it may be important to support these boys in challenging traditional notions of masculinity and in acquiring the new skills they need.

Even directly within the educational context itself, the situation is highly complex. There is a range of questions which are beginning to be examined, from the relationship between this group of underachieving boys and issues of race (Sewell 1997) to the effects of single-sex and mixed schooling and of single-sex groupings (Loulidi 1990; Clark and Trafford 1996). Clark (op. cit.) examines the impact of setting within Modern Languages and offers a range of different options for tackling the all too familiar problem of the preponderance of girls in top sets while bottom sets are full of demotivated boys. The take-up of the 'GCSE short course' may also need investigating if we are to have a clear picture of the current situation in school. A comprehensive survey similar to Powell's published in 1986 may be necessary to understand significant patterns and their underlying causes over a decade later.

The Modern Languages classroom

Motivation

Most Modern Languages teachers are only too familiar with the difficulties some boys seem to experience. At the risk of stereotyping, the broad picture that emerges is of these boys producing untidy, inaccurate written work, having poor organizational skills and lacking motivation (Clark and Trafford, op. cit.). Although only a small-scale project, the findings of a group of student teachers at Goldsmiths College appear typical, so I will draw on their observations throughout this chapter. The students conducted interviews in two schools with a number of groups of boys from Year 7 to Year 10 to ask them why they thought girls did better at Modern Languages than boys. Predictably, poor motivation emerged as a key factor: 'Us boys don't take it seriously. Some days, I just think oh it's French today and I ain't going to try very hard if I don't want.'

It is not possible in this short chapter to review the many studies of motivation since the seminal work of Gardner and Lambert (1972). We will see, however, that Dörnyei's (1998) Ten Commandments for Motivating Language Learners are recurrent themes, in particular:

- make the language classes interesting;
- personalize the learning process;
- promote learner autonomy;
- increase the learners' goal-orientedness;
- familiarize learners with the target language culture.

Cultural awareness

Let us start with the last point. One of the boys interviewed by the student teachers stated: 'The second biggest language is English – why don't all the French people learn our language?', reflecting the ethnocentricity noted earlier by Clark (op. cit.). Similarly, Taylor (2000), commenting on the fact that fewer boys than girls go on home-to-home exchanges, suggests that teenage boys may be less open to people of other cultures. Yet Barton (op. cit.) found that underachieving boys are in fact curious about cultural background information. So, it may be important to consider how it is presented. Whilst cultural awareness is an aspect of the National Curriculum Programme of Study, it is one that is often marginalized or trivialized in textbooks, reduced to a few photos of public buildings or regional landscapes, for example. Jones (1995: 1) offers a wealth of more meaningful activities that allow: 'learners to experience, learn about and explore "otherness", to seek more knowledge and more evidence and to be open to the possibility of changes of mind without being unsettled by the experience'. We will see in a later section how this learning to empathize, implicit in cultural awareness, may also be important in widening the range of reading material that boys tackle. Finally, both Jones's and Brown and Brown's work (1996) show how discovering about other cultures, whether of France, the francophone countries of Africa, or indeed any different culture may contribute to Dörnyei's commandment to 'make the language classes interesting'. As Clark points out (op. cit.: 8), many pupils find the subject matter involved in transactional tourist-type topics 'dull, superficial and irrelevant'.

Learner autonomy

We turn now to another aspect of motivation – autonomy. The boys' comments to the student teachers appeared to reflect a general concern about the lack of independence offered in modern languages lessons:

> Maths, Physics and that focus on you having to work things out for yourselves … in French, there's nothing you have to work out, the only thing you have to work out is to put words together to make a phrase. [And] like in IT, he tells us what to do and we can get on with it.

Barton (op. cit.) also notes that: 'Boys frequently chose as their favourites those school subjects which are less tightly structured by the teacher and allow pupils to work at their own pace.' Such comments appear to relate to research by Graham and Rees (1995) which suggests that boys need to have a sense of control by learning what they feel they need to know and in a way that they feel is appropriate to them.

They also found that boys attribute their lack of progress to the fact that, if the work seems irrelevant to them and fails to meet their 'personal agenda', they feel justified to 'muck about'. Girls on the other hand were more likely to respond to lack of success by a feeling of anxiety and of working harder, often settling down to rote-learning of vocabulary or grammar. This gender divide in response to 'failure' may in turn relate to attribution theory, summarized by Dickinson (1995) in an article linking motivation to learner autonomy. It appears that where learners attribute their lack of success to 'fixed' causes such as the nature of the task or their own inability, they abandon any attempt to make progress. In contrast, learners who believe that success or failure is not inevitable but depends on their own efforts tend to persist. So it may be that whereas the girls feel in control of their learning, recognizing what needs to be done in order to make progress, some boys feel it is out of their hands, readily attributing their lack of success to the task ('It's boring, a waste of time') or their ability ('I'm no good at French').

Graham and Rees advocate offering boys greater independence, so that they have some sense of control over what they learn. Towards the end of the article, they suggest the importance of raising pupils' awareness of the specific problems they experience and how to tackle them. And it is this area that, in my view, may be particularly significant in raising boys' achievement. There is, after all, nothing new in the call for greater learner autonomy and the last decade has seen a wealth of publications discussing the underlying rationale (Dickinson 1987; Holec 1988; Little 1989) and exploring practical implications for the secondary school class-room (Gathercole 1990; Page 1992). Yet when the Ofsted report (1995) *Modern Languages: A Review of Inspection Findings 1993/4* is considered, it appears that the process of enabling pupils to take charge of their learning is problematic. It notes the conspicuous absence, even in Years 10 and 11, of those aspects of the Programme of Study concerned with increasing pupils' independence. It may be possible to identify at least some of the reasons underlying the problem by exploring another area of research in Modern Languages, namely Learning Strategies.

Learning strategies and strategy instruction

In two articles (Grenfell and Harris 1993; 1994), we have charted some of the difficulties experienced when teachers try to shift from a teacher-centred approach to one that encourages greater pupil autonomy. In group work, for example, pupils often panicked simply because they did not know how to make sensible guesses about the meaning of the text they were reading or even how to use a dictionary. It seems that it is not enough to offer pupils greater independence in their learning; they need the tools or strategies that will enable them to understand how to go about it.

The general background to research into learning strategies and its place within current debates on communicative language teaching is outlined by Grenfell in the previous chapter. In essence, this research started off by trying to identify what it is that good language learners do: the strategies that they use, whether consciously or unconsciously, to make sense of and in an unfamiliar language. For example, when they read something, they first skim the text to spot familiar words and cognates (words that are like English words), and then use the context and their 'common sense' to guess the meaning of words that they do not know. Less successful language learners seem to both have a narrower range of strategies and to use them less frequently (O'Malley and Chamot 1990). More recent studies have started to explore the potential benefits of explicit 'Strategy Instruction' (SI), with promising results (McDonough 1999).

In relation to boys, the research is not conclusive but there is some evidence

(Oxford 1993) to suggest that female learners use more strategies than males. Macaro (1997) found that although boys in secondary schools used fewer strategies than girls before SI, when asked afterwards to comment on its effectiveness, a significant proportion of them felt that it had 'made a big difference' or 'some difference'. In both cases, numbers were greater for the boys than for the girls. Systematic and explicit SI could then provide one means of offering boys more control over their own learning. Rather than feeling that there is nothing they can do about their lack of success other than give up, it makes explicit what can be done to improve and locates the responsibility firmly on them. Instruction in memorization strategies may be particularly relevant since, according to the boys interviewed by the student teachers: 'Girls like have a better memory and Modern Languages is a subject where you have to remember a lot of things and it's hard to remember all of them words.'

In Grenfell and Harris (1999) we illustrate in detail how the strategies involved in the various skill areas can be taught. The sequence of steps in the proposed 'cycle of SI' moves from 'awareness raising' (for example, of how pupils already go about memorizing new vocabulary) to 'modelling' new strategies for them to try out, to the 'action planning' stage, where they identify the strategies that will help them tackle their own specific needs. If their problem is remembering the gender of a new word, they will need a different memorization strategy than if they cannot recall how to pronounce it. This stage can perhaps contribute to the 'goal-orientedness' to which Dörnyei refers.

However attractive SI might seem as an 'instant solution' to some of the problems underachieving boys experience, Little (1997: 2) warns us of the dangers of considering it as a bolt-on addition to a traditional teacher-centred pedagogy: 'If the pursuit of learner autonomy requires that we focus explicitly on the strategic component of language learning and language use, the reverse should also be the case: focus on strategies should lead us to learner autonomy.' Collaborative project-based work is essential to offer pupils opportunities to direct, monitor and reflect on their own learning, to develop the strategies they personally need and to 'borrow' each other's approach to the particular language learning task in hand. There is little point, for example, in encouraging pupils to pinpoint their own particular problems, if they are then not offered the space and the means to address them, or to identify areas of personal interest, if they are not allowed to plan how best to pursue them. Thus autonomy and strategy development are two mutually dependent processes. We meet here a dilemma, however. Even though boys report enjoying working independently, the socialization process is likely to have developed their competitive rather than collaborative skills. Barton (op. cit.) reports that one boy stated: 'If we're in groups everyone just tends to just cheat', and she notes that girls appeared more confident that they were able to work effectively in groups. A number of recent studies suggest that we should capitalize on boys' enjoyment of competitive games. Whilst this might prove effective in the short term, if the culture of 'Boys Don't Cry' (Askew and Ross 1988) is to be challenged and boys enabled to work collaboratively, then we may need to devote more time to making explicit exactly what is involved here too. In Harris (1992), I have tried to suggest ways in which pupils can be encouraged to draw up their own 'ground rules' for working in groups and teachers can recognize and validate pupils' collaborative skills.

In seeking to identify 'clues for good practice', it appears then that a careful balance has to be struck between offering boys greater choices in what they learn and providing them with explicit guidelines as to how to go about it: the strategies that will make their learning more effective. In the next section, we will explore what these principles might mean for each of the four skills. Alongside the two strands of independence and strategies, a third will emerge. If pupils are to be given greater choices in what they read, write or talk about, how can we make what is 'on offer' more meaningful? Unsurprisingly, given the importance of enabling boys to meet their 'personal agenda', we will find that many of the suggestions relate to a further set of principles: those of Communicative Language Teaching. Its focus on purposeful and personally relevant language use appears to be particularly important for underachieving boys, whether they are studying a foreign language or English.

From principles to practice: the four skills

Reading

According to the Ofsted report on Boys and English (1993), boys read less than girls, prefer to scan for relevant information rather than to read from beginning to end and to read factual information rather than stories. If the 'reading for personal interest and enjoyment' required by the National Curriculum is to be encouraged, an increase in the choice of reading resources available in the Modern Languages classroom will be essential, to take account of boys' preferences. This is not only in order to increase their motivation but also because a number of studies, summarized in Bugel and Buunk's article (1996), indicate the importance of the existing knowledge of the topic that readers bring to the text, in terms of facilitating its comprehension. There are few surprises in the male topic preferences identified in the article, which include cars, technology, and sports.

The nature of the reading tasks we set is also worth considering. Asking pupils to cut out one page of interest to them in a foreign language magazine and to devise five questions on it for another pupil may provide them with some sense of choice and a 'real audience', whilst saving us considerable time! Alternative tasks might include passing on the three most useful new pieces of information they discovered. As Clark and Hamilton indicate (1984: 13), a communicative approach involves 'using language for a purpose beyond that of merely practising forms'. Simply answering a set of routine comprehension questions fails to provide the context for 'personalizing the learning process' that Dörnyei advocates.

In seeking to cater for boys' preferences by widening the choice of reading materials and tasks, however, we need to be aware of the danger of reinforcing stereotypes and of reproducing the problems our science colleagues experienced some years ago when they sought to motivate girls through 'kitchen chemistry', where, for example, chemical formulas were linked to cosmetic components. There is a delicate balance to be struck if, in the longterm, we want to extend pupils' horizons, rather than limit them. Whilst it would be foolish to ignore such opportunities as the World Cup, we should be aware of their limitations. The Ofsted report on gender and educational performance (op. cit.: 29) notes that: 'Boys perceive the literacy experience as female, because, from an early age, reading and writing are associated with feminine forms of expression, especially the exploration of personal experience and feelings in stories and poetry.' It seems that boys find it harder than girls to empathize with the central characters. Yet, the ability to empathize is not only important in terms of combating ethnocentricity; it is also an increasingly essential 'life skill' in an age where employers are looking for good communication, rather than manual, skills. One way forward may be to capitalize on boys' appreciation of ICT to encourage them to use the internet to access the wealth of materials, not just factual but also fictional, from all over the world. Considerable care will be needed, however, to structure the task so that they are obliged to explore feelings and personal experiences and not just 'hard data'.

Whatever they choose to read, some boys rapidly abandon the task, finding the text too daunting or simply making wild guesses as to the meaning, reflecting the 'bare minimum' approach they adopt to much of their work in general (Clark and Trafford op. cit.). Alongside offering them greater choices in what they read, we may also need to provide structured guidelines as to how to read. Such strategies have become for us part and parcel of how we read an unfamiliar language, yet we cannot assume that pupils realize the value of spotting cognates, for example, or using pictures and the title for clues. One pupil I worked with failed to find any meaning in the sentence: '*Un homme américain arrive à la lune*', even though it appeared as a caption to a picture of an astronaut planting an American flag on the moon's surface! As Rubin (1990: 271) suggests, it seems that they 'assume that none of their prior knowledge can or should be applied to the learning task'. Providing boys with the systematic and structured 'way in' to reading longer texts may help make the task seem less daunting, encourage more sensible guesswork and improve their confidence and 'staying power'.

Listening

The relevance of communicative language principles and of SI emerges in relation to listening as well as reading activities. Barton (op. cit.) observes that 'boys are demotivated by listening tasks with no clear purpose'. Tasks where pupils simply have to note prices can be rendered more challenging and relevant by at least asking them to reach conclusions about the cheapest place to buy petrol. At the same time, we might also need to ask ourselves whether we teach pupils how to listen as opposed to testing them on what they have understood. When, for example, do we teach them to use background noises and tones of voice for clues or to predict, on the basis of the questions and the topic area, the words they will be likely to hear? Turner (1995) suggests that we tend to assume that listening in a foreign language will take care of itself and suggests ways of explicitly teaching the strategies involved.

Writing

Negotiating a choice of topics for their written work may improve boys' motivation initially but, without a clear and explicit framework, some of them may well feel insecure and rapidly lose enthusiasm. Others may write more extensively but without any real sense of direction. If the findings of the Ofsted report on Boys and English (op. cit.: 3) apply to Modern Languages, there may also be a danger that:

> Male bias in the topics boys wrote about (for example, a preference for violent subjects) emerged most frequently when unguided choice of subject was allowed. When a clear purpose was suggested for the work, or a particular type of reader designated, the results were less stereotyped.

The emphasis on 'purpose' and 'audience' echoes the communicative approach and one cannot help but wonder if the inevitable letter to an imaginary pen-pal about where they live meets the criteria. Alternative and more interesting tasks, such as describing a ghost house, are outlined in Adams (1998).

It may be helpful to offer not only more specific and meaningful guidelines as to the content of any writing undertaken but also as to the form it could take. It is worth considering the extent to which the following extract from *Boys and English. So what's the problem?* (Reynolds 1995: 17) applies to boys' performance in Modern Languages:

> Their standards of writing are poor. … Their ability to organize and structure complex and extensive texts is much less developed than girls. They dislike the drafting process and write much less extensively. … There are often extensive and systematic failures to spell following any discernible conventions. … Their handwriting can be poor to the point of indecipherability.

Reynolds goes on to stress the need for careful preparation of written tasks with clear guidance on everything from the mundane question of how much to write to the more complex area of how to structure their writing. For writing other than in narrative form, Reynolds cites the work of the Exeter Extended Literacy project (EXCEL), which has developed 'frames' as supports for writing in different genres, Explanation or Persuasion for example, or Discussion, as in the extract below:

> Some people think that … because … On the other hand, another group disagree with the idea that … They claim that … My opinion is …

Whilst some of the frames may be too complex for Key Stage 3 pupils, nevertheless making explicit how to structure particular types of writing may be essential, particularly if boys are to achieve in GCSE written coursework. It appears (Harris, Nixon and Ruddock 1993) that they pay less attention to coursework than to revision for traditional types of examination.

The reluctance some boys show to draft and redraft their writing raises the issue of whether they know how to go about checking their work and whether SI could help to remedy the problem. As experienced writers in another language, we realize that we will need to read through our work several times with different questions in mind each time:

- Does it make sense?
- Does it look right?
- Does it sound right?
- Is the style appropriate?
- Have I avoided my most usual mistakes?
- Are the tenses/adjectival agreements correct?

There may be a case for making each of these strategies explicit to pupils and 'modelling' how to go about it. In order to provide the extensive practice needed, they can be encouraged to check each other's work or, when they hand in their homework, to indicate at least one error they spotted on each re-reading, the words/rules they looked up, and the points they are still unsure of.

Encouraging and guiding such self-assessment appears to be important not only because it is part and parcel of assuming responsibility, of the 'goal-orientedness' Dörnyei refers to, but also because it can lead to a fruitful dialogue between pupil and teacher. The Ofsted report on English (op. cit.: 13) quotes a boy who wrote: 'I thought my last draft was much better because it was more concise and to the point', to which the teacher replied: 'You have made a lot of changes and you are right to say that it is more precise. However, much of what you have cut out is descriptive detail and you have lost most of the atmosphere'. Although the nature of the tasks we set and the difficulties of providing high-quality feedback in the target language pose particular problems for modern languages teachers, there may be lessons here not only about offering specific guidelines on how to make progress but also about responding to the content of pupils' writing as well as its grammatical features. The use of the mother tongue for this kind of feedback, as well as in the 'action planning' stage of the cycle of SI, may be justifiable, if it helps underachieving boys understand exactly what they need to do in order to make progress. The Ofsted report *Boys and English* (op. cit.: 3) concluded that: 'Boys' performance improved when they had a clear understanding of the progress they needed in order to achieve well.'

Speaking

The evidence of gender differences in the area of speaking is far from clear. Some argue (Clark and Trafford op. cit.) that boys welcome the opportunity to 'hold the floor'. Others (Powell and Littlewood 1982) suggest that boys are reluctant to speak out in public. In the 1998 article, I suggested that it might be worth exploring whether boys' attitudes to speaking change as they get older; if, as they approach adolescence, they become less and less willing to 'make fools of themselves' in public. Barton's study (op. cit.) appears to support this. Whatever their age, however, it seems that once again there may be a need to balance the opportunities for personal choice and creativity with a structured framework for any tasks undertaken and explicit guidelines as to the assessment criteria.

As early as 1986, Powell was reminding us of the fact that 'no child relishes the thought of spending hours just listening, repeating and being called upon to answer questions to which the answer is already known' (p. 62). He argued that boys may be less willing than girls to accept such tasks and that there was a need to ensure that 'rehearsal' leads to 'performance', that pre-communicative activities lead onto real communicative tasks. Boys particularly enjoy the creative and imaginative element of such tasks and again the independence from the teacher. Shyer pupils of either gender may also appreciate the opportunity to work in pairs or small groups. At the same time, however, without clear guidelines, some boys may tend to adopt a minimalist approach so that role-plays are performed perfunctorily or degenerate into the acting out of violent conflicts. As Reynolds (op. cit.: 16) points out in relation to boys' responses within the teaching of English: 'The use of drama techniques such as role-play is another extremely effective procedure, if it is used properly (by which I mean, in essence, specific rather than vague).'

Within Modern Languages, a more structured and at the same time more meaningful framework might include providing cue cards indicating a specific context for the role-play. If the topic is 'Personal Information', then they can ask and answer the usual questions but in the style of a particular type of film, or in line with the personality of two well-known characters (drawn from soap operas, the Royal Family), or in the context of a particular situation (doctor and patient, police officer and lost child, etc.). Other pupils then have to guess from the performance what was written on their class-mates' cue cards. The focus on 'purpose' and 'audience' is reminiscent of the earlier discussion of written tasks.

It is also important to make explicit the criteria for assessing the role-play, whether fluency, accuracy, length of dialogue, conviction of performance or a combination of all four, and to invite the class to apply them. As in the written tasks, peer- and self-assessment help pupils to understand the goals and allow them to take responsibility for measuring their own progress and establishing clear action plans for the future.

Vandergrift (1998) illustrates these principles in a checklist to guide pupils in preparing a presentation. Overleaf, I have adapted his original suggestions for a presentation on favourite pop stars.

Clearly-stated assessment criteria and meaningful outcomes may be particularly important if boys are to take oral work seriously and not view it, as one boy interviewed by the student teachers did: 'there's more opportunities to muck about in modern languages 'cos we have to get up and walk around and interview people'!

In principle, information gap activities should also provide well-structured opportunities for purposeful language use. In reality, however, pupils often tend to just look at each other's cards and ask, 'Wot you got?'! In Harris *et al.* (2001), we

Preparing my presentation

Name   Date

Communication • I have said the name of the pop star at the beginning of the presentation; • I have given 3 reasons why I like them; • I have described 2 things about them; • I have chosen a good phrase to finish off; • I have used some interesting pictures; • I have practised my presentation so I don't have to read from my notes.	
Language • I have checked that I have used the right tenses; • I have used different ways of giving my opinion; • I have used linking words like 'because' and 'although'.	
Strategies • I have used this grid to make sure my presentation is clear, interesting and accurate; • I have used reference books to help me. Dictionary Grammar book Other	

After my partner listened to me, this is what I have done to make my presentation better:

explore alternative approaches to meaningful oral work including tasks which, in Dörnyei's words, 'personalise the learning process' and group problem-solving activities. We suggest that such tasks do not necessarily imply abandoning familiar topic areas; it is more a matter of adding a slightly different slant to them. For example, instead of telling your partner, who lives in the same town as you, information of which they are already well aware (such as how many cinemas there are), you might describe the places that are personally significant for you ('where I buy my fish and chips; my granddad is buried here'). A typical problem-solving task might involve allocating families to flats in a new council building according to the families' size, daily routines, disabilities, etc.

Finally, let us briefly consider in what ways SI might facilitate underachieving boys' oral competence. They may feel particularly frustrated at appearing 'tongue-tied' as they approach adolescence, when 'image' is all-important. As one thirteen-year-old boy commented: 'I've been like learning it for two years and I'm still like speaking a two-year-old's language.' Whereas memorization strategies may be useful in 'fixing' new vocabulary in advance, pupils also need a range of tactics for dealing 'on the spot' with the inevitable problems that occur when their linguistic repertoire is not sufficient for their communicative needs and they struggle to keep the conversation going. Politzer (1983) reported that females used social communication strategies significantly more often than males, and it is possible that these boys in particular may benefit from learning to use 'filler phrases' ('bof, eh bien') that give them time to think, and all-purpose words ('le truc') that help maintain the flow of conversation. Harris (2001) suggests some activities for teaching 'fillers'.

Teacher attitude

A final area that not only relates to oral work (here in the context of whole-class teaching) but also returns us to the starting point of the issue of motivation is the nature of the teacher's response to boys. Whilst research (Spender 1982) suggests that boys receive approximately two-thirds of the teacher's attention in class (asking them questions is a useful tactic to prevent their attention from wandering), it is also clear that much of this attention is negative since it arises from discipline problems. Boys appear to receive less overt praise, even for written work. The Ofsted report on English (op. cit.: 3) found that: 'Boys received more open and direct criticism for weaknesses in written work than girls'. Insensitive feedback may foster the 'macho' image that boys are tough and that no consideration need be given to the potential for hurting their feelings. Given the nature of peer-group pressure amongst boys, however, as Barton (op. cit.) observes, it may not always be 'cool' to be praised in front of the class. Nevertheless, encouragement can always be provided on an individual basis, whether after the lesson or by positive comments on homework. Without it, there is a danger of perpetuating the downward spiral, whereby the unmotivated boys behave badly and produce poor-quality work, are harshly criticized, become even more convinced that they 'can't do languages' and feel justified in making even less effort.

Conclusion

This chapter has tried to suggest some ways of enabling underachieving boys to make progress. It has been argued that offering boys greater independence in what they learn and more meaningful tasks may be one means of improving their motivation. This may not be sufficient, however, unless, at the same time, they are shown how to tackle their learning. Barton (op. cit.) concludes from her research that the answers to boys' underachievement are not to be found in one single model; that although boys may appreciate some aspects of Communicative Language Teaching, in other respects a more formal, didactic model or at least a balance of approaches is required. Within those approaches, I would want to argue for a place for explicit instruction in strategies and their associated study skills.

I have also tried to suggest that, however tempting it may be simply to cater for boys' stated preferences, in the long term it may not help them cope with the demands of the new millennium and the requirements of a future labour market. Preliminary findings from the QCA research project (Cassidy 2000: 6) indicate that boys find topics such as friends, family life, shopping and so on 'alien'. Finding the balance between making the content of Modern Languages more appealing to them whilst not trapping them into stereotypically male identities will not be easy.

It seems that we may have to tread a very fine tightrope between giving boys greater independence and providing explicit SI so that they can fully exploit it; between offering them a choice of creative activities and making it clear what is expected of them; between acknowledging their preferences and extending their horizons.

Acknowledgements

I am very grateful to the students on the Goldsmiths' PGCE Modern Languages course 1995–6 for their willingness to reflect on and share with me the results of their discussions with the boys they interviewed.

Note

1   This chapter extends the arguments in my article 'Making boys make progress' that appeared in the Language Learning Journal in 1998.

References

Adams, J. (1998) *On Course for GCSE Coursework*, London: CILT.

Askew, S. and Ross, C. (1988) *Boys Don't Cry: Boys and Sexism in Education*, Milton Keynes: Open University Press.

Barton, A. (2002) 'Learning style: the gender effect', in A. Swarbrick (ed.) *Teaching Modern Foreign Languages in Secondary Schools: A Reader*, London: RoutledgeFalmer.

Brown, K. and Brown, M. (1996) *New Contexts for Modern Language Learning; Cross-curricular Approaches*, London: CILT.

Brumfit, C. (ed.) (1995) *Language Education in the National Curriculum*, Oxford: Basil Blackwell.

Bugel, K. and Buunk, B.P. (1996) 'Sex differences in foreign language text comprehension: the role of interests and prior knowledge', *Modern Language Journal*, 80(i): 15–28.

Cassidy, S. (2000) 'Girl talk puts off male linguists', *Times Educational Supplement*, 15 September.

Clark, A. (1998) *Gender on the Agenda. Factors Motivating Boys and Girls in MFLs*, London: CILT.

Clark, A. and Trafford, J. (1996) 'Return to gender; boys' and girls' attitudes and achievements', *Language Learning Journal*, 14: 40–9.

Clark, J. and Hamilton, J. (1984) *Syllabus Guidelines for a Graded Communicative Approach towards School Foreign Language Learning*, London: CILT.

Dickinson, L. (1987) *Self-instruction in Language Learning*, Cambridge: Cambridge University Press.

—— (1995) 'Autonomy and motivation; a literature review', *System*, 23(2): 165–74.

Dörnyei, Z. (1998) 'Ten commandments for motivating language learners: results of an empirical study', *Language Teaching Research*, 2(3): 203–29.

Gardner, R.C. and Lambert, W.E. (1972) *Attitudes and Motivation in Second Language Learning*, Rowley, MA: Newbury House.

Gathercole, I. (ed.) (1990) *Autonomy in Language Learning*, London: CILT.

Graham, S. and Rees, F. (1995) 'Gender differences in language learning: the question of control', *Language Learning Journal*, 11: 18–19.

Grenfell, M. (2002) 'Developing learning strategies', in A. Swarbrick (ed.) *Teaching Modern Foreign Languages in Secondary Schools: A Reader*, London: RoutledgeFalmer.

Grenfell, M. and Harris, V. (1993) 'How do pupils learn? Part 1', *Language Learning Journal*, 8: 22–5.

—— (1994) 'How do pupils learn? Part 2', *Language Learning Journal*, 9: 7–11.

—— (1999) *Modern Languages and Learning Strategies in Theory and in Practice*, London: Routledge.

Harris, S., Nixon, J. and Rudduck, J. (1993) 'School work, homework and gender', *Gender and Education*, 5(1).

Harris, V. (1992) *Fair Enough? Equal Opportunities and Modern Languages*, London: CILT.

—— (1998) 'Making boys make progress', *Language Learning Journal*, 18: 56–62.

—— (2002) 'Learning to learn: strategy instruction in the modern languages classroom', in A. Swarbrick (ed.) *Aspects of Teaching Modern Foreign Languages: Perspectives on Practice*, London: RoutledgeFalmer.

Harris, V., Burch, J., Darcy, J. and Jones, B. (2001) *Something to Say? Promoting Spontaneous Classroom Talk*, London: CILT.

Holec, H. (ed.) (1988) *Autonomy and Self-directed Learning: Present Fields of Application*, Strasbourg: Council of Europe.

Jones, B. (1995) *Exploring Otherness; An Approach to Cultural Awareness*, London: CILT.

—— (ed.) (1989) *Self-Access Systems for Language Learning*, Dublin: Authentik, CILT.

Little, D. (1997) 'Strategies in language learning and teaching: some introductory reflections', paper given at the CILT Research Forum *Strategies in Language Learning*, 22 February.

Loulidi, R. (1990) 'Is language learning really a female business?', *Language Learning Journal*, March: 40–3.

Macaro, E. (1997) 'Gender differences in strategy use', paper given at the CILT Research Forum *Strategies in Language Learning*, 22 February.

Mahony, P. (1997) 'The underachievement of boys in the UK', *Social Alternatives* 16(3) 44–50.

—— (1998) 'Girls will be girls and boys will be first', in J. Elwood, D. Epstein, V. Hey, and J. Maw (eds) *Failing Boys? Issues in Gender and Achievement*, Buckingham: Open University Press.

Mahony, P. and Hextall, I. (2000) *The Reconstruction of Teaching: Standards, Performance and Accountability*, London: RoutledgeFalmer.

Marshall, B. (1996) 'Attitudes set for a gender bender', *Times Educational Supplement*, 19 April.

McDonough, S.H. (1999) 'Learner strategies: state of the art article', *Language Teaching*, 32: 1–18.

Nuffield Languages Inquiry (2000) *Languages: The Next Generation*, London: The Nuffield Foundation.

Ofsted (1993) *Boys and English*, London: HMSO.

—— (1995) *Modern Foreign Languages: A Review of Inspection Findings, 1993/4*, London: HMSO.

—— (1998) *Recent Research on Gender and Educational Performance*, London: HMSO.

O'Malley, J.M. and Chamot, A.U. (1990) *Learning Strategies in Second Language Acquisition*, Cambridge: Cambridge University Press.

Oxford, R. (1993) 'Second language research on individual differences', *Annual Review of Applied Linguistics*, 13: 188–205.

Page, B. (ed.) (1992) *Letting Go – Taking Hold*, London: CILT.

Politzer, R.L. (1983) 'An exploratory study of self-reported language learning behaviors and their relation to achievement', *Studies in Second Language Acquisition*, 6: 54–68.

Powell, B. and Littlewood, P. (1982) 'Foreign languages. The avoidable options', *British Journal of Language Teaching*, 20(3): 153–9.

—— (1986) *Boys, Girls and Languages in School*, London: CILT.

Pyke, N. (1996) 'Boys read less than girls', *Times Educational Supplement*, 15 March.

Reynolds, R. (1995) 'Boys and English. So what's the problem?' *The English and Media Magazine*, 33: 15–18.

Rubin, J. (1990) 'How learner strategies can inform language teaching', in V. Bickley (ed.) *Language Use, Language Teaching and the Curriculum*, Institute of Language in Education, Hong Kong.

Sewell, T. (1997) *Black Masculinities and Schooling: How Black Boys Survive Modern Schooling*, Trentham Books.

Smithers, A. (1996) 'New myths of the gender gap', *Times Educational Supplement*, 3 May.

Spender, D. (1982) *Invisible Women: The Schooling Scandal*, London: Writers and Readers.

Taylor, A. (2000) 'Boy-free zone', *Language Learning Journal*, 21: 3–7.

Turner, K. (1995) *Listening in a Foreign Language. A skill we take for granted?*, London: CILT.

Vandergrift, L. (1998) 'The National Core French Assessment Project: design and field test of formative evaluation instruments at the intermediate level', *Canadian Modern Language Review*, 54(4): 553–78.

Walby, S. (1990) *Theorising Patriarchy*, Oxford: Basil Blackwell.

Weiner, G., Arnot, M. and David, M. (1997) 'Is the future female? Female success, male disadvantage and changing gender patterns in education' in A.H. Halsey, P. Brown and H. Lauder (eds) *Education, Economy, Culture and Society*, Oxford: Oxford University Press.

13 The potential impact of the National Literacy Strategy on MFL learning

Beate Poole

Introduction

In most subjects within the school curriculum, the efficiency and effectiveness with which children learn very much depends on their first language literacy skills and on the speed with which they take in and process information. In this respect, the learning of a foreign language is no exception. Within the artificial and limiting context of the classroom, as opposed to natural acquisition contexts, good foundations in first language skills are deemed important in learning a foreign language efficiently and successfully. Where these skills are weak or absent, underachievement, loss of motivation and challenging behaviour are often the result.

More than thirty years ago Pimsleur, Sundland and McIntyre (1966) claimed that 20–30 per cent of children underachieved in a foreign language because of poor auditory ability. Donaldson (1978) found that the division of speech into sounds and words was an achievement that not all children mastered with equal ease in their first language. She found that, on arrival at primary school, a considerable number of children had very little phonological awareness. They were unable to discriminate between individual words in a sentence and perceived speech simply as a continuous stream of sounds. Other children, however, already knew that speech could be broken down into its component parts and that there were sounds, words and sentences. Professor Eric Hawkins suggested that 'the trick of switching off internally is learned early and habits of defensive non-listening need to be unlearned' (Hawkins 1981: 229).

Studies in child development show that children of the same age differ very much in their ability to analyse language (Donaldson 1978, Wells 1981, 1985). Wells' seminal *Bristol Study* provided evidence that the degree of meta-linguistic awareness individual children developed depended very much on their linguistic environment and that language awareness was something that had to be learned. Particularly important was the quality of the dialogue between child and adult and the extent to which language awareness was explicitly encouraged through play, rhymes, games and stories. Wells found that, at the start of formal schooling, language 'awareness' or 'knowledge of literacy' was the most important predictor of educational attainment. Those children who started school with positive pre-school experiences, with an idea of what language was about and what books looked like, with an awareness that what was heard at a phonological level related to symbols on paper, were clearly ahead in their language development and, to a large extent, stayed ahead during their primary school years. In the context of foreign language learning, Eric Hawkins argued twenty years ago that a lack of preparation in awareness of language and insight into pattern on which depends the ability to process incoming messages rapidly, might explain why some children fail to learn foreign languages successfully. He suggested that up to one-half of those children starting to learn a foreign language simply lacked the necessary 'tools' (Hawkins 1981: 227).

This chapter aims to explore the potential impact of the primary school National Literacy Strategy (NLS) on 'levelling the playing field' for all children starting to learn a foreign language. It is not within the scope of this chapter to enter into a debate on the numerous definitions of the concept of literacy or 'multiple literacies'. Kenneth Levine's (1986) definition of literacy as the 'exercised capacity to acquire and exchange information via the written word' will be adopted, although the importance of speaking and listening skills in the development of reading and writing skills will not be ignored. At the time of writing this chapter in November 2000, the NLS had only been in schools for two years and many of the points made must be seen as 'impressions' or 'trends' based on acceptable theoretical positions. There is still much speculation and what is needed is sound empirical evidence of its cross-curricular effects and in particular its pay-off in the Foreign Languages classroom.

Literacy skills and foreign language learning

When children begin to learn a foreign language formally in a school environment, they inevitably move from what has so far been a largely unconscious approach in the acquisition of their first language, to a largely conscious approach in the learning of another. In such a context, children who are able to read and write and who have a degree of language awareness would seem to be at an advantage.

Cummins' 'interdependence hypothesis' (1979) postulated that the extent of children's command of their first languagecombined with a sound basis in conceptual and cognitive development, would affect their progress in the learning of another language. He went on to suggest (1980) that 'Cognitive Academic Language Proficiency (CALP) – those aspects of language which are closely related to the development of literacy skills in a first language (L1) and second language (L2), such as vocabulary development meta-linguistic awareness, the ability to deal with de-contextualized language and conceptual knowledge – was important in formal learning situations. Together with Swain (1986) he argued that children should be given the opportunity to develop a sound basis in their first language skills to provide them with the 'social-emotional environment in which the basic conditions for learning can occur and in which linguistic and cognitive development in the first language will support the same in the second language'.

There is little debate about the important role of the written word in first language and conceptual development and in the development of more abstract and sophisticated forms of memory. The transition from spoken to written language, learning to read and write, is an important step in enabling the child to dis-embed language from its immediate context. It involves learning a new code and brings consciousness to a process which so far has been largely unconscious. As Donaldson argued, being able to read provides the child with much more favourable opportunities 'for becoming aware of language in its own right than his earlier encounters with the spoken word are likely to have done' (Donaldson 1978: 91).

Through its permanent nature, written language inevitably draws the child's attention to form and provides insights into how language works. It enables the child to notice and focus on the structural properties of language and to form and test out hypotheses in his/her own time. The permanent nature of language allows the child to conceptualize, categorize and organize language. Written language thus encourages awareness of language that in turn encourages awareness of one's own thinking. The ability to distance oneself from language and to comment on language is an important component of the ability to deal with de-contextualized language (Torrance and Olson 1985). The skills and capacities needed to deal with de-contextualized language are very different from those involved when language simply arises from concrete experiences and situations. Some children find the transition from spoken 'communicative' competence to what Bruner (1967) called 'analytic' competence difficult as they are unable to dis-embed their thinking from the context of immediate activity. Being able to distinguish the word as an arbitrary label from the object it denotes, for example, is regarded as very important in dealing with language as a formal system (Tunmer, Pratt and Herriman 1984). This ability is crucial when learning a foreign language in the classroom where the child has to recognize that the label cannot be equated with the object itself and accept that *chien* or *Hund*, for example, are alternative ways of denoting the same thing.

When learning a foreign language, being able to read is important for a number of reasons. Not only does the written word provide an additional means of input and support for memory, it also allows learners to break down language chunks into their component parts, in disassembling language in order to reassemble and generate language of one's own choice and meaning. Snow and Hoefnagel-Höhle (1978), for example, provided evidence that first language literacy skills were crucial in syntactical development in a second language and argued that the ability to read and write was the reason why both adults and adolescents outperformed young children in learning a second language. Krashen and Terrell (1988) suggested that it takes three to four times longer to teach a set of language material without the aid of orthography.

Those children who are the better readers are likely to make the better language learners as both reading and foreign language learning require children to infer meaning in de-contexualized situations. Pre-literate children, for whom language is very much context-embedded and who function mainly in the 'here and now', are unlikely to be very efficient learners in the classroom where much language learning is 'de-contextualized' in the sense that it is not often easily supported by immediate contextual clues. (They have to express 'hunger' when they are not hungry or claim to feel pain when they feel perfectly alright.) During the pilot project *French from Eight* in the 1960s and 1970s, Burstall highlighted the introduction of written language as a 'critical period' in the learning process:

> To judge both from the test results and from the pupils' own comments, the introduction of reading constitutes a critical period in the language learning process. For some pupils, it provides a welcome return to a familiar medium of achievement; for others, it presents an almost insuperable obstacle to further progress.
>
> (Burstall 1970: 27)

While the introduction of reading was a major stumbling block for some children, others, the so-called 'more able', were dissatisfied with endless repetition and imitation, asked for explanations of structures and vocabulary and generally wanted to know what they were learning and why they were learning it. The child who has not achieved at least a basic level of competence in first language literacy skills might readily cope with imitation and repetition but s/he is likely to find the more formal and advanced aspects of foreign language learning more difficult, very burdensome, frustrating and eventually demotivating.

The National Literacy Strategy

Concerns over standards in literacy are nothing new. In 1975, the so-called Bullock Report, *A Language for Life*, made important proposals for the raising of standards in children's literacy skills. More than ten years later the Kingman Report proposed that the explicit and systematic study of language should be part of the curriculum:

> It is just as important to teach about our language environment as about our physical environment, or about the structure of English as about the structure of the atom.
>
> (The Kingman Report 1988: 4, par. 12)

However, it was not until September 1998 that the National Literacy Strategy (NLS) was introduced into the primary school curriculum with the intention of bringing about improvements in national standards of literacy and educational standards in general. The Secretary of State for Education, David Blunkett, envisaged that 80 per cent of 11-year-old children should reach the standard expected for their age, a National Curriculum level 4 or above, by 2002 (NLS 1998).

The daily Literacy Hour is intended for the explicit teaching of reading and writing and for the study of language at three levels: word, sentence and text, including phonics, spelling, vocabulary and grammar. The NLS suggests that teaching strategies should include direction, demonstration, modelling, scaffolding, explanation, questioning, initiating and guiding, exploration, investigating ideas, discussing and arguing, listening to and responding (NLS 1998: 8), and that teachers should combine whole-class, group, pair and individual work. It is also suggested that teachers should vary set times within the hour and adapt essential elements to meet pupils' needs.

The NLS encourages children to reflect on language and study grammatical features in their own right. It encourages the teaching of grammatical terminology and of a 'meta-language', a language for talking about language. However, as previously in the Kingman Report, a return to traditional grammar drills is not recommended. Instead, whole-class shared reading and writing is to provide the context for developing pupils' grammatical awareness and understanding of language as a system. The NLS for the school year 2000–1 focuses on the teaching of writing and includes strategies on whole-class exploration of texts, grammar and punctuation as well as shared writing. From September 2001 the NLS will also be introduced into the Key Stage 3 curriculum.

The teaching and learning content

Burgess and Hardcastle state that there has been much debate about what children should be taught in their English lessons: 'What should be taught about language, and more specifically about grammar, has been a controversial issue in English teaching throughout the century' (Burgess and Hardcastle 2000: 18).

It is not within the scope of this chapter to enter into a debate about the content of the NLS, its quality and quantity or timing and sequencing. Nor is it within the scope of this chapter to give a detailed description of this content. However, in order to contextualize the points discussed in this chapter, a range of examples will be given. The NLS Framework suggests, for example, that during the Reception year focus should be on phonological awareness, the alphabet and the linking of sound and speech patterns. It also suggests that children should use their experience of stories, poems and simple recounts as a basis for writing.

In Year 1 children should:

- segment words into phonemes and spell common irregular verbs;
- read a variety of texts with appropriate expectation, intonation and expression;
- draw on grammatical awareness to recognize the wrong word order;
- predict and group words;
- begin to use full stops and capitals properly;
- answer questions on a text;
- write stories using simple sentences.

In Year 2 children should:

- recognize the need for grammatical agreement;
- use standard forms of verbs in speaking and writing and use the past tense consistently;

- skim and scan texts;
- in writing use appropriate language to present, sequence and organize ideas;
- evaluate the usefulness of a text for its purpose;
- use synonyms;
- turn statements into questions.

In Year 3 children should:

- recognize a prefix;
- explore homonyms;
- use the term 'adjective' appropriately;
- investigate context and purposes of pronouns;
- read examples of letters;
- ensure grammatical agreement in speech and writing of pronouns and verbs;
- use a wider range of conjunctions;
- write an account of a story;
- use a dictionary.

In Year 4 children should:

- distinguish between and use accurately 'it's' and 'its';
- recognize and spell suffixes;
- understand the grammar of a sentence, word order, verb tense;
- understand use of connectives, adverbial phrases and conjunctives;
- review their own reading habits;
- write critically about an issue in a story.

In Year 5 children should:

- study the use of verbs, future tense and auxiliary verbs;
- investigate clauses and sentences;
- investigate prepositions;
- read and evaluate a range of texts;
- understand how writing can be adapted to audience and purpose;
- construct an argument in writing;
- build words from other known words and transform words;
- use a range of dictionaries effectively.

In Year 6 children should:

- secure their control of complex sentences;
- understand how clauses can be manipulated to achieve different effects;
- experiment with language, create new words;

- revise grammatical features of different text types;
- write an extended story;
- secure skills of skimming and scanning;
- appraise a text quickly.

The NLS Framework thus envisages that when leaving primary school the literate 11-year-old child should:

- read and write with confidence, fluency and understanding;
- be able to orchestrate a full range of reading cues (phonic, graphic, syntactic, contextual) to monitor their reading and correct their own mistakes;
- understand the sound and spelling system and use this to read and spell accurately;
- have fluent and legible handwriting;
- have an interest in words and their meanings and a growing vocabulary;
- know, understand and be able to write in a range of genres in fiction and poetry, and understand and be familiar with some of the ways in which narratives are structured through basic literacy ideas of setting, character and plot;
- understand, use and be able to write a range of non-fiction texts;
- plan, draft, revise and edit their own writing;
- have a suitable technical vocabulary through which to understand and discuss their reading and writing;
- be interested in books, read with enjoyment and evaluate and justify their preferences;
- through reading and writing, develop their powers of imagination, inventiveness and critical awareness.

(NLS Framework 1998: 3)

The following pages will explore the potential impact of the above knowledge, skills, understanding and abilities on the learning of a foreign language.

The Literacy Hour – voices from the classroom

The NLS Framework states that on leaving primary school children should read and write with confidence, fluency and understanding. A group of twenty children in Year 7 at secondary school were interviewed about their experiences of the Literacy Hour. These children had attended nine different primary schools but they almost all claimed to remember very similar activities and learning experiences. Only one child claimed that he remembered 'nothing'. The following were some of the typical comments made:

- We did loads of poems.
- We did a play about literacy.

- We did a scripted play and a comic strip.
- We read stories and then answered questions on the stories.
- Every time we had to read in four groups, best, second best and so on. The better the group the harder the story.
- We had to do planning sheets and fill in the plan of a story, the characters, plot, the beginning and end.
- We had a piece of paper and we had to write down the theme and the title and the story line, the plot and the scene and the area.
- We had to put all the full-stops and all the punctuation in a text.
- We had a story on a sheet and a story on the overhead projector and we had to spot the differences.

According to the Ofsted, 75 per cent of children reached level 4 or above in reading at the end of KS2 (Ofsted 2000). In the experience of one of the teachers interviewed, Beth, who assists with the Literacy Hour and who also teaches French, there is noticeable improvement in children's reading and writing skills in French as a result of the NLS. She commented on a number of aspects:

- a greater degree of attention to spelling, punctuation and the use of accents;
- increased ability to draft, redraft, edit and improve written work;
- greater awareness of sentence structures: for example, how to build more complex sentences from simple sentences through the use of connectives such as *puis, après, mais, aussi*
- recognition of cognates such as restaurant, café and sport;
- greater awareness of the importance of word order and appreciation that a change in word order can entail a change in meaning.

It would seem reasonable to suggest that if children are now familiar with reading a wide range of text types and understand the conventions of different text types, foreign language texts should be more accessible. Children who have mastered a range of reading strategies, such as how to look for key words, hypothesize, infer, deduce, predict and who do not give up as soon as they meet the unknown or the unexpected but persevere, take risks and guess intelligently, should be better prepared for dealing with a text. However, a cautionary note would seem appropriate. One cannot assume that children will automatically transfer their first language reading skills to reading in a foreign language. While the mechanisms, cognitive processes and strategies involved might be very similar (at least with languages of the same script), one cannot ignore other variables. The quality and quantity of the reading materials play a crucial role as does the 'systemic' knowledge (the knowledge of the language) and the 'schematic' knowledge (the knowledge of the world) required to access a text (Widdowson 1990). The last, 'knowledge of the world', is, of course, in itself a variable dependent on children's reading ability. Children will normally be able to access more challenging texts than they will be able to produce. However, it also seems to be the case that if learners are faced with a text that is too difficult, they tend to short-circuit the reading process, thus causing good first language reading habits to break down (Clarke 1980).

If, as a result of the NLS, children are familiar with the concepts of audience, context and purpose and, if they now know how to plan, draft, edit and proofread their work, producing a text should be less problematic. During the interviews, two children had also talked about rewriting stories from somebody else's point of view, of having to put themselves 'into the shoes of other people'. The capacity to 'empathize' should, in principle, help children with the affective demands of learning a foreign language.

Other spin-offs reported by teachers were neater handwriting, improved ability to copy and generally improved presentation of written work. However, according to Ofsted, 'improving standards of writing has proved to be much more of a challenge, both for the NLS and for teachers' (Ofsted 2000: 9, par. 49). While 75 per cent of children reached level 4 or above in reading, only 55 per cent reached this level in writing. Children's attainment in writing thus remains too low and lags far behind their attainment in reading. The gap between the performance of boys and girls, especially, remains a concern with boys doing less well than girls in all aspects of English, particularly so in writing. Over half the boys leave primary school without having attained the expected level 4: 'At present, far too many pupils leave their primary school ill-equipped for the writing demands of the secondary curriculum' (Ofsted 2000: 31, par. 136).

It is nothing new to state that good writing skills are more difficult to teach and harder to accomplish than good reading skills. With the start of the 2000–2001 school year much additional support for writing in the form of training and resource packs as well as a *Grammar for Writing* is put into schools. However, as Roger Beard wrote in the *Times Educational Supplement*:

> Writing is a complex business, involving the integration of several skills and abilities. It is similar to many games and sports: better performance does not just come from playing in more matches, but from developing discrete skills.
> (Roger Beard, 'Clarion call for another century',
> *TES Curriculum Special, English*, October 6, 2000: 7)

Reading and writing skills are both important in learning a foreign language successfully in the classroom; whether they are equally important from the start would very much depend on the aims and objectives of a programme, the age of the learners and not least the language pairs involved. It is unlikely that children in the early stages of learning a foreign language will produce extensive pieces of writing, let alone imaginative and creative pieces of writing. It is likely, however, that as a result of the NLS they can be given more challenging tasks than has hitherto been the case.

Dictionary skills

The NLS Framework suggests that in Year 3 children should have a secure understanding of the purpose and organization of a dictionary. In Year 5 they should be taught to use a range of dictionaries and understand their purposes and they should use dictionaries efficiently to explore spellings, meanings and deviations. Skills in using a dictionary are not only important life skills in their own right but must also be regarded as a valuable and indispensable aid to the learning and mastering of a foreign language. In the past, for many children their first encounter with a dictionary might well have been during the foreign language lesson. Beth reports that as a result of the NLS the children in her charge are able to use a dictionary or thesaurus effectively, that they are able to order words alphabetically and understand grammatical abbreviations such as n/v/adj/m/f/pl. One hopes that the comment made by one Year 7 child is atypical: 'Sometimes in the Literacy Hour the teacher would throw a dictionary in front of us and we had to copy from the dictionary into our books.'

Affective variables

Potential affective impacts of the NLS are just as important as cognitive ones. After all, children need to want to read. The NLS states that 'children should be interested in books, read with enjoyment and evaluate and justify their preferences'. However, it is unlikely that all children will leave primary school with a love for books. Most children interviewed claimed that they liked and enjoyed reading however, a couple of children also thought differently:

- We had to read and read and read, it was boring, the stories were boring.
- Out of the blue the teacher said, make up a poem book, I don't care, any poem, short or long.
- Reading is sissy. I don't need to read, I don't need a job, I'll be a footballer.

One child commented that his teacher gave them 'double credit points in the Literacy Hour and for ten we got a certificate', whereas another one commented, 'We had a scary teacher'. Potential unintended consequences of the NLS need to be guarded against. Overkill and a lack of modesty in designating what can be achieved could lead to counter-productive outcomes.

The explicit study of language

The 'L1 = L2 hypothesis' (Dulay and Burt) exerted much influence on foreign language teaching in the classroom. This hypothesis postulated that both first and second language acquisition development were subject to similar creative construction processes which would allow children to

> gradually reconstruct rules for the speech that they hear, guided by innate mechanisms which cause them to use certain strategies to organize that linguistic input, until the mismatch between the language system they are exposed to and what they produce is resolved.
>
> (Dulay and Burt 1976: 75)

Such beliefs in innate mechanisms lead to the conclusion that, in learning a second language, formal instruction was not necessary and that one should 'leave the learning to the children'. However, already in 1963, Belyayev stressed the need for a 'conscious analysis of various linguistic facts' in the learning of a foreign language. He argued that, if learners are to learn from language examples rather than the examples themselves, they have to notice language patterns, regularities and irregularities. They have to recognize grammatical functions and the relationships in syntax and semantics and how grammar can be manipulated to carry meaning – a crucial step in mastering the grammar of a foreign language. Schmidt (1990) suggested that conscious noticing, and attention to form in all aspects of language was important if language input was to be converted into intake. Van Lier (1996) argued that both language comprehension and language production required attention to form and that consciousness and language awareness were essential ingredients in successful language learning in educational settings as they enabled the learner to compensate for and cope with contextually restrictive variables. In the context of teaching English at primary school before the official introduction of the NLS, Bunting stated that:

> Learning about language gives children the analytical tools with which to test, judge, critique and question the language they encounter, so that they can understand how it is used, its meanings and intentions. To do this, children will need some terminology for talking about, describing and explaining aspects of language.

> (Bunting 1997: v/vi)

As was stated earlier, the NLS encourages the explicit study of language at word, sentence and text level and the teaching of grammatical terminology and technical vocabulary through which children understand and discuss their reading and writing. It is expected that the explicit and systematic study of language helps children to master the move from spoken language to written language and from dialect to standard variety and that it helps children to be more aware of the structural properties of language and of language as a system. Beth reported a number of effects of the explicit study of language on children's French:

- a greater awareness and understanding of language patterns, structures and rules generally, such as *ma/ta/sa* and *mon/ton/son* and increased ability to identify regularities and irregularities;
- increased awareness of the first, second and third person usage and of polite forms of address such as *vous/tu*;
- increased awareness of tense patterns;
- recognition of prefixes and suffixes such as *sur* and *par*;
- increased awareness of the structure of French compound nouns such as *chou-fleur, timbre-poste* or *belle-mère*;
- understanding of the concept of 'silent letters', for example in *sept* and *huit*;

- increased readiness to question exceptions to the rule;
- increased readiness amongst children to notice mistakes and correct each other.

Another teacher interviewed, Terry, who is co-ordinator of French at his present school and was the literacy co-ordinator at his previous school, agrees with most of these points and the comments made by the Year 7 children seem to corroborate the teachers' views:

- The Literacy Hour helps me learning French. I can recognize similar words.
- I think we have a better imagination from reading stories, what might happen when we read strange French words.
- Some words are similar and this makes it easier.
- It's almost the same alphabet just pronounced differently.
- French and English are sort of the same. Like silent letters, in the alphabet: when you say something in French like *deux sœurs* you don't say the 's'.
- We learned how to spell in English. In French you have to be high on spelling to get through to a French person. You have to get the apostrophe right to make sense. Their words are made up from Latin and English words are.
- It helps because both are languages. It helps with reading. Practising pronunciation in English helps you in French, the words get easier to pronounce. It helps with handwriting. It helps with learning vocabulary. The Literacy Hour extends your mind, we are used to answering questions and you can answer like an adult.

Not all children, however, could make connections. It is, of course, possible that those who commented that the Literacy Hour did not help, that learning French was a totally new experience, or who thought that grammar will help but were not sure how, might simply be unaware of any potential benefits or be unable to verbalize their thoughts. In Terry's experience, issues surrounding the application and understanding of grammatical concepts and terminology seem especially problematic. The NLS Framework suggests, for example, that in Year 1 children should use the term 'sentence' appropriately and be able to identify sentences in a text. In Year 2 they should secure their understanding of the terms 'vowel' and 'consonant'. In Year 3 they should use the terms 'prefix', 'synonym' and 'suffix'. They should also use the terms 'singular', 'plural' and 'adjective' appropriately and they should understand the term 'collective noun'. In Year 4 they should understand the term 'tense' in relation to verbs and use it appropriately. In Year 6 they should secure the use of the terms 'active' and 'passive'. Terry states that the NLS does indeed make it easier for teachers to talk about nouns, verbs, sentences and adjectives, for example, but he also states that in his Year 7 classes he often receives 'a lot of blank looks as if I was teaching this for the first time'. The following are some of the comments made by the Year 7 children with regards to grammar and grammatical terminology:

- We had to write a story with nothing but verbs.
- A noun describes a doing word.

- A noun describes a place.
- A noun describes a name.
- Cool as a cucumber is an alliteration.
- Suffix and prefix refer to the beginning and end of words.
- A verb is a doing word.

In answer to the question, 'What is an adjective?' children gave the following responses:

- I don't know.
- I don't know an adjective.
- I'm not sure.
- I heard it before.
- I can't remember.
- I'm no good at it.
- I get mixed up between verb and adjective.
- In a sentence I wouldn't be able to pick it out.
- An adjective is a describing word.
- An adjective describes a verb.

One girl also referred to 'innis' and 'outis' for speech marks and brackets while one boy made the following comments:

> An adjective is a describing word, a verb is a doing word, a noun can refer to a name, a place or an object. Grammar is very important. If you learn grammar you go to a level of posh speaking or politically correct. For example 'ain't', that's not grammar. You have to use 'have' or 'haven't'.

While some children thus seem to have a clear understanding of both concept and terminology, the comments made by others display a considerable degree of confusion. This suggests that much grammar teaching might simply have by-passed them. It is of course possible that some children understand the concept but do not remember the terminology. Perhaps they recognize the label but do not understand the underlying concept. In any case, much of children's understanding of grammatical concepts and terminology would seem a question of how teachers deal with grammar in the first place. Terry gave a vivid description of how he approaches the teaching of grammar and grammatical terminology:

> We look at the richness of language first. Then the nuts and bolts. Take the poem *The Highway Man* by Alfred Noyes. Such a rich poem with so many levels of meaning. And rich language ideal for looking at metaphors and so on. Once you've got the juice out of the body you're left with a skeleton. Then look at how the skeleton is built up. The details of language, use of pronouns, who do they refer to, ambiguity, apostrophes and so on, without ever losing the meaning of the poem. But you have to capture the audience first.

Such an approach is more likely to result in children who understand the concept of an adjective, for example, who can apply the terminology and who know how to use adjectives effectively in their writing. Contrast this with the experience of some of the other children:

- We had to fill in gaps in a booklet [grammar] and that was a bit boring.
- We didn't get enough practice.
- We didn't do much of that stuff.
- We had a nice teacher but we had to do grammar as a punishment when we talked too much. She'd say, that's it, we're doing grammar work in silence.

For some children formal language study might hold both interest and challenge while for others attending to formal aspects of language might appear a fruitless exercise. Within this debate, it is difficult to ignore the concept of aptitude in foreign language learning. It is known from language aptitude research (Caroll and Sapon 1959, Carroll 1981) and from research into learning strategies that the 'good' or 'able' language learner pays conscious attention to form, that s/he makes associations between sound and symbol and retains these easily, that s/he is able to recognize grammatical functions of linguistic entities and that s/he is able to infer or induce the rules governing a set of language materials (Naiman, Froehlich, Stern and Todesco 1978, O'Malley and Chamot, 1990). Whether these abilities suggest a special foreign language aptitude or whether they are merely a question of general intelligence and cognitive ability is beyond the scope of this chapter. However, in follow-up research to Wells' Bristol Study, Skehan reported a possible correlation between children's first language development and language aptitude at secondary school:

> … children who make more rapid development learning their own language seem, according to conventional tests, to do better learning foreign languages in schools.
>
> (Skehan 1988: 29)

The clearest relationship between first language development and foreign language learning aptitude seemed to be a child's rate in syntactical development and his/her use of auxiliary verbs. Torrance and Olson (1985) suggested that differences in children's ability to deal with de-contextualized language in their first language was related to their ability to use 'psychological' verbs such as 'think' and 'know'. There is much scope for further research into these important issues.

Listening skills

There is much anecdotal evidence that a growing number of children start primary school with a 'language delay' and without the speaking and listening skills generally taken for granted. Extensive classroom observations at primary school (Poole 1999) revealed that a considerable number of children were unable to follow formal instructions and simply lacked the necessary listening skills and associated attention and concentration spans to benefit from foreign language learning. The NLS Framework recognizes the importance of listening in the development of reading and writing skills and the interconnection of all four skills in successful literacy development. It thus states that:

> Literacy unites the important skills of reading and writing. It also involves speaking and listening which, although they are not separately identified in the Framework, are an essential part of it.
>
> (NLS 1998: 3)

A few implicit references to listening can be found in the objectives for each term such as 'identify and discriminate sounds and phonemes, play with rhyming patterns', 'notice difference between spoken and written story forms', (Reception year), 'identify and discuss patterns of rhythm and rhyme and other features of sound in different poems', 'comment on and recognize when the reading aloud of a poem makes sense and is effective', 'split familiar spoken compounds into their component parts, discriminate syllables' (Year 2), 'be aware of the different voices in stories, notice pronouns in speech' (Year 3), 'recognize the regularity of skipping songs and chorus in songs (Year 4), 'be aware of the difference between spoken and written language conventions', 'explore similarities between spoken and written stories' (Year 5), 'contribute constructively to shared discussion about literature, respond to and build on the views of others' and 'conduct detailed language investigation through interview' (Year 6).

Yet, only one explicit reference to 'listen' could be found throughout the Framework (in Year 5, term 3) and only one of the Year 7 children interviewed reported listening to tapes during the Literacy Hour. This one-off comment cannot be taken as representative; however, as listening skills are not explicitly assessed, it would come as no surprise if these were not systematically addressed. Beth suggested that the children in her charge had improved listening skills as a result of the Literacy Hour, reflecting themselves in better attention spans and better collaborative learning skills. However, improved listening skills amongst some children might well be an accidental by-product of the NLS rather than the result of systematic development. Much more focused and systematic teaching would need to take place to equip all children with the skills necessary for successful foreign language learning in the classroom.

The NLS and foreign language learning at primary school

There is at present no National Curriculum for foreign language learning at primary school. However, the Qualifications and Curriculum Authority (QCA) has published a scheme of work for French for KS2 (with German and Spanish schemes to follow) for those schools who wish to offer a foreign language. In this scheme of work it is stated that:

In key stages 1 and 2 children will have followed the National Literacy Strategy and will have knowledge of English, including grammatical awareness and knowledge of some grammatical terms. The scheme of work takes account of this and consolidates and builds on this work where appropriate. Children are encouraged to increase their knowledge of how language works and to explore differences and similarities between the new language and English or another language.

(QCA 2000: 7)

It is further stated that foreign language learning presents opportunities for the reinforcement of knowledge, skills and understanding gained in other areas of the curriculum such as English through

development of speaking and listening skills, knowledge and understanding of grammar and sentence construction. Opportunities to compare the foreign language with English or another language can be exploited through use of the alphabet, phonemes, rhyming patterns, sound/spelling links, dictionary work, formation of structures (such as singular/plural, gender, negatives, question forms, position of adjectives, imperatives), intonation, dialogues, poetry, different text types, formation of complex sentences.

(QCA 2000: 11)

A number of 'activities' are then suggested within each of the four attainment targets: listening, speaking, reading and writing. Under reading and responding, for example, it is stated that teachers should encourage the use of techniques used and developed during children's work in literacy and English by:

- replacing visual cues gradually with text cues;
- reading new words by sounding out and blending their separate parts;
- sounding out syllables in words to help memory;
- grouping similar sounds together;
- playing word games, e.g word and picture dominoes, matching pairs;
- sorting and dictionary work;
- shared reading of 'Big Books'.

(QCA 2000: 13)

Setting aside that the suggested 'activities' include exercises and tasks as well as teaching methodologies and learning strategies, they would seem to be stating the obvious in any context of language learning. The cover pages for each unit or topic include further self-evident comments such as 'teachers can build on aspects of children's work in literacy and English (Unit 1)', 'some suggested activities reinforce aspects of English and Literacy (Unit 2)', 'sound and spelling work reinforces aspects of the curriculum for English (Unit 3)', 'activities in this unit can be used to consolidate learning in literacy (Unit 6)' and 'activities in this unit could be used to complement learning in English and literacy (Unit 8)'. After Unit 8 any links to literacy in the section on 'links with other subjects' are conspicuous through their absence.

A closer perusal of the content of the scheme of work reveals a number of sporadic and random references to the Literacy Hour with little apparent underlying principle, structure or coherence. Although these references do include some useful suggestions, much of what is proposed is either self-evident or simply meaningless. It is sound to suggest, for example, that teachers should compare intonation patterns in English and French, that they should compare similarities in number patterns, compare how positive statements are changed into negative ones in French and English, compare the position of adjectives, or cross-reference and explore roots of words. However, it would seem to be stating the self-evident that 'children make use of their knowledge of English or another language in learning another language', that they 'could apply listening skills developed in English', that they 'could apply their knowledge of descriptive writing in English' or that 'there is the opportunity to make comparisons with English and other languages known by the children'. That teachers should 'remind children of their work with sounds and rhythms of poetry and of reading poetry aloud in English' or that they should 'remind children of their work in English and drama' would seem rather meaningless. What exactly does it mean to 'remind' children in the context of learning a foreign language? And what exactly does it mean to 'look at a text', especially to the teacher who is not a language specialist?

References to the NLS also include a number of unfounded assumptions such as 'children will be familiar with structuring dialogue in English (from writing dialogue in narrative and from play scripts in Years 4 and 5)' and 'children build on their knowledge of different text types'. As the comments made by the children and the findings by Ofsted showed, the fact that English teachers have dealt with these issues does not mean that foreign language teachers can assume these skills to be in place. Nor can they be assumed as automatically transferable. Besides, what exactly does it mean 'to be familiar' with something?

A much more principled and structured approach is required if foreign language teachers are to build systematically on what has been achieved during the Literacy Hour. The Nuffield Inquiry into the teaching of foreign languages recommended that, as a short-term measure prior to the full-scale introduction of foreign languages into the primary school, language awareness modules should be introduced into the NLS, 'the content of which would be designed to bridge the gap between English, literacy and foreign languages' (Nuffield Report 2000: 89, par. 6.6). In the light of the discussions in this chapter and the lack of empirical evidence in support of the 'younger' is necessarily 'better' theory for the learning of a foreign language in the classroom (for a detailed analysis see Poole 1999), it is likely that children will have a more coherent and beneficial language learning experience at primary school if aspects of a foreign language (or foreign languages) are integrated into the NLS rather than the other way around. Calls for a specific starting age to foreign language learning seem ill-conceived. The fundamental question is whether a child's first language foundations are stable enough to carry the building blocks for meaningful foreign language learning.

Concluding thoughts

There is much scope for large-scale, longitudinal research which crosses educational stages and which examines the progress and achievements of individual children to the age of 16 and perhaps beyond. A range of questions would need to be addressed such as: when and under what circumstances do individual children apply the knowledge, understanding and skills gained during the Literacy Hour? Are there differences between boys and girls and, if so, what exactly are these? Which aspects of the NLS have the greatest impact on foreign language learning? Is there a difference between different language pairs, e.g. English and French, English and German or any other pair? The effects of the NLS on the foreign language achievements of children whose first language is not English could also be investigated. Any piece of research would need to take into account the potential results of maturational factors and separate these from the likely effects of the interventionist NLS. Matched control groups are not feasible any more as all children follow the Literacy Hour. From September 2001 the NLS is extended to KS3 at secondary school and this will also have an effect on children's achievement.

While it is reasonable to assume that all children will benefit from the NLS, regardless of background and ability, one cannot assume that it will of necessity lead to better outcomes in foreign language learning if a number of theoretical issues are not understood and respected. First of all, what individual teachers do both at primary and secondary school is crucial. In the words of Professor Robin Alexander, 'one has to look at what is going on behind the label'. There is a need to look closely at the transition from primary to secondary school and investigate how secondary teachers build on and develop what has been achieved at primary school. It is unlikely that children will automatically transfer what they have learned during the Literacy Hour without any encouragement from their foreign language teachers. This means more text-based work and a move away from mindless repetition, imitation and extensive memorization of pre-fabricated language chunks to a conscious focus on language as a system, to a sharing of information and knowledge around the classroom: not a return to 'grammar-grind' but 'focus on language as a structure in meaningful situations' (Hornsey 2000: 139). In doing so, teachers should not hesitate to use grammatical concepts and terminology explicitly. After all, colleagues in Mathematics and Sciences do not apologize for using subject-specific terminology. It also means encouraging children to give their opinions and giving them credit for experimentation and for taking risks. This means re-establishing the mother tongue in its rightful place in the foreign language classroom. It goes without saying that collaboration between teachers of English and Foreign Language teachers is essential.

It would be unreasonable to assume that as a result of the NLS all children will become good language learners. A host of factors, cognitive and affective, are at play in successful foreign language learning. Affective factors are just as important as cognitive ones. If more children enjoy reading as a result of the National Literacy Strategy much will have been gained already. More will have been gained if children arrive at secondary school with improved attitudes towards language learning and regard the study of language as interesting, relevant and fun. Perhaps improved thinking skills and a questioning mind are some of the most valuable outcomes foreign language teachers can wish for. More learners who are not happy with endless repetition and imitation, who ask for explanations of structures and vocabulary, who want to know what they are learning and why they are learning it, can only make foreign language teaching and learning a more challenging and rewarding experience for all concerned.

Acknowledgements

I would like to express a sincere thank you to Beth Schluter, Terry Barker, Denis Slade, Sue Tippler and all the children who so generously gave their time to make this chapter possible.

Further reading

Belyayev, B. (1963) *The Psychology of Teaching Foreign Languages*, Oxford: Pergamon Press.
Bruner, J.S. (1967) *Studies in Cognitive Growth*, USA: John Wiley & Sons.
Bunting, R. (1997) *Teaching about Language in the Primary Years*, London: David Fulton.
Burgess, T. and Hardcastle, J. (2000) 'Englishes and English: schooling and the making of the school subject', in A. Kent (ed.) *School Subject Teaching, the History and Future of the Curriculum*, London: Kogan Page: 1–28.
Burstall, C. (1970) *French in the Primary School: Attitudes and Achievement*, Slough: NFER.
Carroll, J.B. (1981) 'Twenty-five years of research on foreign language aptitude', in K.C. Diller (ed.) *Individual Differences and Universals in Language Learning Aptitude*, Rowley, MA: Newbury House, 83–118.
Carroll, J.B. and Sapon, S. (1959) *Modern Language Aptitude Test MLAT*, New York: Psychological Co-operation.
Clarke, M.A. (1980) 'The short-circuit hypothesis of ESL reading – or when language comprehension interferes with reading performance', *The Modern Languages Journal*, 64(2): 203–9.
Cummins, J. (1979) 'Cognitive/academic language proficiency, linguistic interdependence, the optimal age question and some other matters', *Working Papers on Bilingualism* 19: 107–205.
—— (1980) 'The cross-lingual dimensions of language proficiency: implications for bilingual education and the optimal age issue', *TESOL Quarterly* 14: 175–88.
Cummins, J. and Swain, M. (1986) *Bilingualism in Education: Aspects of Theory, Research and Practice*, New York: Longman.
DES (1975) *A Language for Life*, (The Bullock Report) London: HMSO.
—— (1988) *Report of the Committee of Inquiry into the Teaching of English Language* (The Kingman Report), London: HMSO.
DfEE (1998) *The National Literacy Strategy – Framework for Teaching*, London: DfEE.
Donaldson, M. (1978) *Children's Minds*, Fontana.
Dulay, H. and Burt, M. (1976) 'Creative construction in second language learning and teaching', in H.D. Brown (ed.) *Papers in Second Language Acquisition*, 65–79.
Hawkins, E.W. (1981) *Modern Languages in the Curriculum*, Cambridge: Cambridge University Press.

Hornsey, A. (2000), 'Modern languages: searching for success', in A. Kent (ed.) *School Subject Teaching, the History and Future of the Curriculum,* London: Kogan Page, 133–55.

Krashen, S. and Terrell, T. (1988) *The Natural Approach: Language Acquisition in the Classroom,* UK: Prentice Hall International.

Levine, K. (1986) *The Social Context of Literacy,* London: Routledge and Kegan Paul.

Naiman, N., Froehlich, M., Stern, H.H. and Todesco, A. (1978) *The Good Language Learner: Research in Education, Series 7,* Toronto: Ontario Institute for Studies in Education.

Nuffield Languages Inquiry (2000) *Languages: The Next Generation,* The Nuffield Foundation.

Ofsted (2000) *The National Literacy Strategy: The Second Year,* Ofsted.

O'Malley, M. and Chamot, A. (1990) *Language Strategies in Second Language Acquisition,* Cambridge: Cambridge University Press.

Pimsleur, P., Sundland, D.M. and McIntyre, R.D. (1966) *Underachievement in Foreign Language Learning,* New York: MLA Materials Centre.

Poole, B. (1999) 'Is younger better? – A critical examination of the beliefs about learning a foreign language at primary school', unpublished PhD thesis, Institute of Education, University of London.

QCA (2000) 'A Scheme of Work for Key Stage 2', *Modern Foreign Languages Teachers' Guide,* QCA.

Schmidt, R. (1990) 'The role of consciousness in second language acquisition', *Applied Linguistics,* 11(2) 129–58.

Skehan, P. (1988) 'A comparison of first and foreign language learning ability' – a follow-up to 'The Bristol Language Project', *TESOL Working Document 8,* Institute of Education, University of London.

Snow, C. and Hoefnagel-Höhle, M. (1978) 'The critical period for language acquisition: evidence from second language acquisition', *Child Development* 49: 1114–28.

Torrance, N. and Olson, D.R. (1985) 'Oral and literate competencies in the early school years', in D.R. Olson, N. Torrance and A. Hildyard (eds) *Literacy, Language and Learning: The Nature and Consequences of Reading and Writing,* 256–84.

Tunmer, W.E., Pratt, C. and Herriman, M.L. (eds) (1984) 'Metalinguistic awareness in children, theory, research and implications', *Springer Series in Language and Communication* 15, Berlin: Springer Verlag.

Van Lier, L. (1996) 'Language awareness and learning to learn', in L. Van Lier (ed.) *Interaction in the Language Curriculum,* 69–97.

Wells, C.G. (1981) *Learning Through Interaction, The Study of Language Development,* Cambridge: Cambridge University Press.

—— (1985) *Language Development in the Pre-school Years,* Cambridge: Cambridge University Press.

Widdowson, H. (1990) *Aspects of Language Teaching,* Oxford: Oxford University Press.

14 Learning about effective teaching

Observations from a teacher educator

Kim Brown

Introduction

This chapter is about interactions between teachers and pupils in the Modern Languages classroom. It is about the inter-relationship between teaching and learning, learning and teaching based on lesson observations of student teachers. In the same way as we all learn from our pupils about effective teaching, so I have learned a tremendous amount from the student teachers I have met. Trying to understand why a particular activity or approach has been unexpectedly successful, or entirely unsuccessful with one group and fine with another, is all part of the fun and the challenge of learning to teach well.

The aim and objectives of this chapter are to help you develop your own individual style as a teacher, with a clear rationale for your practice, by:

- encouraging you to bring an inquiring and exploratory approach to your own teaching and that of others;
- encouraging you to focus on the quality of interactions in the languages classroom;
- encouraging you to listen to feedback from pupils in language lessons;
- helping you to think clearly about the complexities of effective classroom practice;
- extending your understanding of what is understood by 'good practice' in modern languages;
- helping you identify and develop the pedagogical skills that you will need to teach languages effectively;
- encouraging you to think for yourself about what is possible in the languages classroom.

Setting the scene

The current concerns with raising standards in schools focus particularly on the quality of teaching that pupils experience and the factors that influence their progress. As part of its school effectiveness programme, the government has recently commissioned a large-scale research project, the Hay McBer report (DfEE 2000), to try to identify characteristics of effective teaching. Eventually, it is planned that teachers will be assessed against this model as part of the ongoing assessment of their performance throughout their careers. The report proposes a model of effective teaching based on a combination of factors which influence pupils' progress: the teaching skills of individual teachers, the professional characteristics they bring to their job and the ways in which they help to build a positive climate in their classrooms. Some of these factors are to be found in the examples in this chapter. There have also been a number of other recent studies of effective teaching and learning which you will find very useful as you begin to consider your own development as a teacher (see for example, Leach and Moon 1999; Mortimer 1999).

This chapter is written with the findings of these publications in mind. Where these previous studies are generic in focus, and do not make distinctions between effective teaching in, say, History or English classrooms, we are concerned with factors which are specific to teachers of MFL.

The Hay McBer report was concerned to come up with a generalized picture of effective teaching and used quantifiable measures to support the development of their model. For example, they used data on the progress pupils made with their teachers over the course of a school year to help define effective teaching. In this chapter, the aim is to retain the complexities of learning to teach well by focusing on individual teachers and on different contexts in secondary schools. Instead of trying to come up with measures of effective teaching based on pupils' test results, I am suggesting that we can also learn a great deal about what works well in classrooms through studying the way in which teachers and pupils engage with each other in lessons.

You will have discovered as a pupil yourself that teachers all have their individual styles. Can you remember back to the kind of teacher you preferred? Can you say why their style suited you so well? Do you know yet what kind of teacher you wish to be? In your observations of lessons you will encounter many teachers with very different ways of going about teaching. This can be both very useful for you as you try out different approaches and potentially quite confusing. Particularly in modern languages, as we shall see in the next section, there is a certain tension about the best way to teach languages and you will need to be very clear of the reasons why you are doing the things that you do in your classroom if you are to become a good teacher.

You are training to teach in a rapidly changing world. There are global changes affecting us all, such as advances in technology or in the understanding of science and medicine. The new understandings of the way in which the brain works, for example, are beginning to change the way in which we think about teaching and learning. There are changes in the workplace, in people's attitudes to work and leisure, and in levels of poverty and wealth. The pupils we teach are growing up in this new world and they are different from my generation and yours. They have different interests and different expectations of life. If we are really to engage them in our lessons, we need to listen to them, learn from them and work with them.

Language teachers need to think carefully about ways of engaging pupils successfully because of growing concern about disaffection in language classrooms. The Languages for All policy has meant that we do now meet pupils in lessons who would not necessarily have chosen to study languages and who are less confident and often less co-operative language learners. You may already have seen classes of pupils who do not really want to be there. And yet these pupils keep turning up for lessons. Perhaps they are not as disaffected as we think they are. I want to suggest, somewhat controversially, that the problem of disaffection may lie as much with us as with them.

In the last few years, in response to the challenges presented by some pupils, there has been an increasing focus on *motivation* in languages, particularly at Key Stage 4 where the highest levels of disaffection are felt to be (see, for example, Chambers 2000). Teachers have quite understandably turned to games, fun activities, football and sweets to encourage and reward pupils' participation in lessons. And in response to pupils' perceived difficulties with language learning, there has been less emphasis on language structure and more on topic areas, vocabulary and transactional activities in an attempt to make language learning accessible to all pupils. In many lessons, pupils are asked to repeat and learn long lists of vocabulary when it is precisely the skills of listening and memorizing that they find the most difficult. The effort takes so long that often they do not get as far as discovering why they are learning these words or how to use them.

Perhaps it is just too ambitious for us to expect our pupils to be *motivated* by learning languages any more than they might be motivated by studying History or Science or Maths. By shifting the emphasis from *motivation* to *engagement* we might begin to challenge the climate of negativity currently discernible in some language departments in the UK (McPake *et al.* 2000). There is plenty of evidence in the lesson observations I draw on in this chapter to suggest that teachers *can* find ways of engaging pupils, of gaining their attention, keeping them occupied and on task. These include playing with sounds and words, looking at the origins of words, talking about cultural aspects of the language and its links with English, talking about language in English – all aspects of language learning that give our subject its sense of identity, its discipline (Lodge 2000) and which have been steadily lost in recent years: all aspects of language learning which actually help pupils to make sense of the language they are learning and which have tended to be denied to them through a confusion about effective language teaching. This is not a plea for a return to 'traditional methods' as we shall see in the next section, but I am suggesting that we have perhaps made a mistake in taking motivation as a starting point: that motivation might be, on the contrary, the outcome of engaging pupils for a sustained period of time in the serious discipline of learning a language.

An important part of the debate about raising standards is the need for fresh insights and new understandings to advance our thinking. In particular, we need to challenge pupils in their perceptions of themselves as failing language learners. There is always a tendency for people who work together to use jargon in their discussions. For example, we may all think we mean the same thing when we talk about 'good practice', 'progression' or 'disaffected bottom sets'. But what do people really mean by these terms? A recent research project in Norwich (NASC 1999) has shown how difficult it is for teachers to come to any consensus at all in their search for a definition of a disaffected pupil. The shorthand of jargon is useful in any area of shared professional activity but it is important to remember the complexity of the issues that can be masked by the label. You will need to challenge over-generalized issues in language teaching and stereotypes of pupils both during your training and on into your teaching career if you are to ensure that you help all those you teach to reach their full potential.

It is also important to be clear about the distinction between methodology and pedagogy. Language teachers tend to talk in terms of methodology: communicative methodology, for example. There is a sense that we all know what this means. There is a canon of activities that we all recognize as part of a communicative methodology: information gaps or three-stage question techniques, or the use of flashcards to present new language. And there are ways in which Language teachers generally organize their lessons which reflect the methodology as it has been interpreted: whole-class presentation, practice in pairs or groups, individual writing. But the methodology does not tell us very much about what individual teachers bring to the teaching of their subject; about the ways in which teachers interpret the exercises in the textbooks; about the strategies they use to help pupils understand a new language; or about the ways in which their teaching changes to cater for the different learning needs of their pupils. It is the difference that an individual teacher can make in helping pupils to learn or understand their subject more effectively through explanation or example, through their engagement with each other, that distinguishes pedagogy from methodology (Brown 2000) and that forms the focus of this chapter. The aims are:

1   to help you to identify the particular experiences, understandings and insights that you bring to the languages you will be teaching and to help you develop the pedagogical skills that you will need in order to teach these effectively;
2   to help you develop your own rationale for your practice, a strong sense of your pedagogical role in the languages classroom.

It is now time to consider these in more practical detail.

In the following section we shall begin with an example from lesson observations which illustrates the need for clear thinking about language teaching. The first looks at the conceptual question of the teaching of grammar within a communicative methodology. Questions like this are central to our understanding of good practice and effective teaching within our subject area. The second example is much more generally applicable to teachers across the curriculum and is concerned with a teacher's movement around the classroom during a lesson. The intention is to begin to understand some of the complexities of trying to establish what good practice is for different teachers working in different contexts with different groups of pupils and to see how far we can go in exploring the implications of an apparently simple generic classroom management strategy for teachers of modern foreign languages.

The final section focuses on the engagement of teachers and pupils in the languages classroom. The organizing principle is that of collaboration between you and your pupils in learning about language teaching and learning.

Clear thinking about language teaching

Teaching grammar

In this first example, a student teacher has just finished a lesson on the past tense in French. I was interested to know why she had chosen to use the mnemonic Mr Van de Tramps (sometimes also known as TV Mans Red Pram) when she introduced the verbs which took *être*. Her answer was that this was what the department did and so she had done the same. There are a number of points here which will help you to link into the argument. First, the mnemonic was used in schools at a time when language teaching started from the rules and worked towards application of them. Second, the teaching of grammar was usually in English and separate from any task of practical communication. Third, in my own professional experience, the mnemonic often caused more confusion than it solved, in that pupils could usually tell you which verbs belonged to the group but were much less sure of why they were there. More importantly, knowing the rule did not prevent them saying *j'ai venu/j'ai allé*. In other words, the concern here is that this new teacher was using a strategy for teaching grammar that came from an entirely different methodology from the communicative one in which she was being trained. What do I mean? To answer this we need to summarize some of the changes in language teaching in the last twenty to thirty years.

Try to find some old language textbooks and look at the contents pages. These will tell you a great deal about the way in which language used to be organized for the purposes of learning. You generally started with the definite and indefinite article, moved on to nouns, adjectives, pronouns and the present tense, and after one or two years you might have encountered some of the more complex tenses and moods. There was a perception that progression through the course took you from simple to more complex structures. In French, teaching the past tense with *être* came after *avoir*, presumably because it presented more difficulties in the written form with the agreements. But the difficulty with this approach is that it is not always the most simple structures that are the most useful and relevant.

This was what teachers of EFL discovered in the early seventies. They realized that the first questions they wanted to ask their students were – 'How long have you been here?', 'Have you ever been to England before?', 'Have you met your host family yet?' Was it possible to teach the present perfect tense, such a complex structure, in lesson one? This is precisely what English textbooks began to do, and Modern Language textbooks followed soon after. If you look at the teaching of language in terms of the relevance and usefulness to the learners, in terms of their practical needs for communication, a very different way of organizing language emerges. The starting point is the context and the communicative purpose; emphasis falls first on listening; reading and speaking, writing is a record of language that learners are already using, and the rules of the language emerge and are made explicit by teachers at the consolidation stages of the lesson. Contrary to the belief of many language teachers, the communicative approach never ruled out grammar; it simply moved it to a different place in the sequence of learning activities.

If we now go back to our example, we can understand the contradictions more clearly. Most of this lesson was taught in French. The pupils worked through a range of activities such as chorusing new language and guessing games with flash-cards, which would be recognized in schools as part of a communicative approach and yet the serious business of teaching grammar was taught out of context, before the pupils had practised using it and in English. In other words, the mnemonic disrupted the communicative flow of the lesson and tended to obscure pupils' understanding of the way the language worked. For example, the teacher tended to refer to the mnemonic as a point of reference rather than to their knowledge about language in any broader sense by asking questions such as, 'Why does this sentence take *a/est* ...?' and explaining that this was because 'it is not/it is in Mr Van de Tramp's list'. The difficulty with this is that it deprives pupils of the chance to learn and talk about the formation of the tense with an auxiliary verb and a past participle, knowledge about language that is transferable and which helps to extend their understanding of language in general.

If you ask most pupils what they did at the weekend, the first thing they tend to want to say is, 'I went ...' Why do we begin with *avoir* and not *être*? Which structure is more complex *orally*? Why don't we teach them together? This can give much more scope for creative story-telling: *Je suis allée en ville ... et j'ai acheté ..., je suis allé au restaurant ... et j'ai mangé ....*

The way in which teachers organize their lessons tells us a great deal about their understanding of language teaching methodology. You need to keep asking teachers why they do the things that they do so that you can begin to develop an understanding of issues such as this one and develop your own consistent, reasoned approach to your teaching. These observations were not a criticism of this teacher, but I wanted to know what evidence she had that this was an effective way of teaching grammar. The aim was to encourage her to develop a questioning approach to her teaching.

Getting your sleeves rolled up

This section focuses on teachers and pupils learning to work together. It considers three aspects:

- there is detailed analysis of the collaboration that is needed to ensure that teaching in target language is successful;
- the enhancement that light touches of English can bring to language learning;
- setting clear contexts for new language being presented.

The section ends with an exploration of the balance between support and chal-lenge that you will need to ensure for your pupils. Above all, it is your own assess-ment of pupils' strengths and needs that will help you plan and teach your lessons successfully.

We are in this together

Let's begin by thinking about the climate in your classroom. To what extent are you and your pupils really working together, listening and talking to each other? I have observed that where teachers create a sense of collaboration with their pupils, the atmosphere in the room tends to be good-humoured, warm and encouraging. There is a sense of shared endeavour in the way that these teachers talk to their pupils: 'Shall we try that again? Shall we do the first one together? Let's practise this together, shall we? Let's correct it all together, shall we?'

A very important part of getting the pupils on your side, to work with you, is to listen carefully to them. They often come up with good ideas and suggestions for lessons which reflect their own interests and needs. For example, in one lesson on birthdays, pupils added their own ideas for birthday celebrations to those planned by their teacher. These included trips to local theme parks and fairs, as well as more modest activities such as going to watch a video with friends and inviting friends for a sleep-over. Their ideas can give lessons a more personal touch and a greater sense of involvement in the language they are learning. Try to look for opportunities to plan new topics *with* your pupils, for example surveys on likes and dislikes (food or music) or on pocket money; planning a journey; shops they go to in a town; or what they like doing in their spare time. You may find it useful to evaluate the difference this makes to the feel of the lessons and the extent of the pupils' involvement in them.

Perhaps the most important aspect of collaboration in the language classroom is the use of the target language itself. Where teachers use French or German or Spanish as the main means of communication in their classrooms, there is plenty of evidence in my observation notes to show that this, in turn, enables pupils to do the same. Where teachers greet pupils individually as they come into the classroom, pupils take the initiative and ask their teacher the same question. Many teachers feel that the target language gets in the way of personal relationships in the classroom. But I have observed that it can actually help to build these. For example, in one lesson, which was taught wholly in German, there were many examples of spontaneous jokes between the teacher and her pupils. On one occasion, the teacher was trying to encourage pupils to speak more confidently – *Lauter bitte!* – in response to her questions. At a later stage in the lesson, when the class had become slightly restless, the teacher had to raise her voice to get their attention. A pupil shouted out good-humouredly, *Lauter butte!* The teacher replied accordingly with a powerful bellow and a smile – *Ist das laut genug?*

If we listen to pupils in our lessons, we begin to learn about aspects of language learning that they enjoy. Many of the pupils I have observed in lessons clearly enjoy the sounds of the language they are learning; they whisper new words to themselves and practise the correct pronunciation. In one lesson, I heard pupils near me saying, '*On se rencontre où? I love saying that, it sounds so good … on se rencontre où? on se rencontre où?*'. They were repeating it for the sheer pleasure of the sound. You can nurture pupils' fascination with language and support their learning through your own use of target language. By teaching in English, you are depriving them of many opportunities to hear the language, to learn new words in appropriate contexts, to improve their intonation and pronunciation: in short, to make progress in all aspects of language learning.

Going with the flow

It might be helpful, when it comes to teaching successfully in target language, to think of the flow of the lesson. If you want to carry pupils along with you, you will need to think about the pitch of your voice and the ways in which you modulate your voice to punctuate the lesson and guide pupils through the different activities. Try whispering or raising your voice to signal changes of activity, clapping your hands on occasion, or counting down – *cinq, quatre, trois, deux, un* or *zéro!* – until you get everyone's attention.

Activities such as chorus work can support the flow of language in the classroom. The pace and atmosphere in a lesson can liven up and there can be a real sense of teamwork in a well-organized chorusing activity. Pupils feel safe to experiment with the sounds of the language they are learning, protected amidst the voices of their classmates.

Even where pupils are co-operative, we need to be careful that their minds are engaged as well as their vocal chords. I have often watched pupils mindlessly mouthing words and sounds, as they stare out of the window or into space. In these cases, the chorusing had either gone on for too long or the pupils were not being asked to think as they were repeating the new language. They were simply going through the motions, hiding behind the chorusing rather than being engaged by it. So to keep pupils involved and to make it a useful and challenging activity, try moving words and captions around; for example, make deliberate mistakes or jump around unexpectedly as you indicate words or phrases to be practised so that you keep pupils on their toes.

So far, we have considered the flow of the lesson in terms of the sounds of the language around us, of keeping up a supportive amount of noise in the classroom. I now want to suggest, somewhat paradoxically, that one of the most effective ways of helping pupils to engage with the flow of the lesson may be for you or your pupils to stop talking. There are two reasons for this. First, if you speak less, you can look for ways to encourage your pupils to speak more. Some very effective language teachers make excellent use of body language and silences to encourage their pupils to be more vocal. I noted in one lesson a number of different ways in which a teacher did this: she turned off the overhead projector and simply waited for quiet without saying anything; she raised her own arm in silence to indicate hands up for answers; she gave pupils thumbs-up signals to encourage them to answer and barely whispered to a very timid pupil so that she felt safe to answer in a whisper. Any one or all of these strategies can help to keep pupils engaged and you to focus on your teaching. Second, if there is quiet in the classroom, pupils have a chance to think about the language they are learning. In one lesson, pupils began to shout out answers when a classmate hesitated in response to a question: '*Jonathan denkt,*' said the teacher firmly and made the class wait quietly until he had worked out the correct answer.

These teachers are helping their pupils to learn about learning by insisting on this thinking time. They had an intuitive sense of the importance of slowing the lesson down in this way. But it takes confidence and many new teachers need time to move towards a more reflective approach in their lessons. There is often a tendency to give the pupils a lot to do, but not perhaps enough time to do things carefully and thoroughly. If a task is worth setting in the first place, then it is important to give pupils time to do this well.

These examples are intended to help you to think about the classroom climate in terms of the flow of the target language, the way in which you use your voice and the need for quiet and time to think.

Making links with English

There are many examples in my observation notes of *light touches* of English in lessons full of French or German or Spanish. One exciting teacher I observed moved from Spanish to English effortlessly throughout the lesson, but for the most part kept the lesson in clear, accessible Spanish. She explained why the word for a pair of tights is *medias* (i.e. they cover half the body) by explaining and miming this and reminding pupils where they might have met this word before, i.e. telling the time (half-past); she had grouped the colours according to the rules governing agreements and explained that the four colours derived from fruit (*marrón, naranja*) and flowers (*rosa, violeta*) were invariable; she drew the pupils' attention to the different pronunciation of Spanish that they might hear from people who had learned Spanish in Madrid or in Latin America and explained the Arab influence on the *j* sounds in the language. She also drew effectively on her own experiences of living in South America, explaining to the pupils that her sons had had exercises and tongue-twisters to perfect their *r* sounds. In these ways, she helped pupils to learn new vocabulary by offering them mental hooks to hang the meaning on, explanations and a clear understanding of the way the language worked. The examples made the lesson interesting and gave pupils a rich experience of language learning.

There was an evident rationale in the way this teacher taught her lesson: she wanted to help her pupils understand some of the broader cultural and linguistic dimensions of the language they were learning as well as the meanings of the new words, and she moved between Spanish and English to do this.

Many teachers feel that teaching in the target language gets in the way of personal relationships with pupils; that it is not possible to teach grammar in English; that, for pupils who are less confident in themselves as language learners, the challenge is too great and reinforces their low self-esteem; and that it is just too tiring for teachers and pupils to keep up a whole lesson in German or Spanish or French. You need to make up your own mind about this. Until you have tried to teach a whole lesson, many lessons, in the target language, to a range of pupils of different aptitudes and with different attitudes to languages, you will not have the evidence you need to come to a reasoned position on it. It is a question of trying to identify the benefits and the constraints of teaching in the target language, of developing strategies where you can, to make it work, to understand why this might be important for your pupils and to know why you go into English when you do in lessons.

We have looked in some detail at strategies which help to maintain the flow of the lesson in the target language. Where these break down, it is often because the context is not clear. How can you avoid pupils guessing wildly at words you are trying to teach and disrupting the flow of the lesson? This is where we start the next section.

Setting a clear context

In two lessons I observed, student teachers hit problems trying to explain to pupils the meaning of *warum* and *pourquoi*. In both cases, they asked pupils to work out the meaning, but did not give them enough clues to go on. The result was that there was a lot of shouting out and silly, wild guesses. The teacher lost control of the lesson and it was much harder to proceed in German or French. The point about both of these words is that they are central to a question/answer exchange: *Why? Because ....* I suggested that a simple dialogue would make the meaning quite clear. For example, in the context of talking about school subjects, *Je déteste l'histoire ... Pourquoi? ... C'est difficile*, it is evident that the question elicits an explanation. By offering two or three examples on the same model pupils will be helped to understand both the function and the meaning of the words.

Try to think of your teaching points in terms of the stories they might generate, and situate them within a short dialogue at the presentation stages of the lesson. The examples which follow take as their focus the topic of daily routine and the teaching of a grammar point, in this case possessives. In each example, there are ways in which the language to be learned can be a prompt for story-telling. In the first lesson, the aim was to extend the pupils' understanding of daily routine by introducing the adverbs of time – sometimes, often, always – and the rule which governed their position in a sentence. There was a sequencing activity and a written exercise from their textbooks. What seemed to be missing was a context which might have made the use of these adverbs meaningful and engaging. As soon as someone tells you that they usually get up at three in the morning there is an implied story, an element of interest – three in the morning, that's unusual/interesting/why do you get up so early? The context generates the need to communicate and can give pupils a chance to use new expressions in a role-play or pair-work activity; in this case, twenty questions about the jobs people do might have been appropriate.

In the second example, the focus was on teaching the possessive form. This takes us back to the tensions we identified between a grammar-based approach and communicative teaching of language. In this lesson there was a lot of discussion about language structure but it tended to be in English and did not equip the pupils to *use* the structure confidently. For example, one boy asked how *sonnez* would be different if he was speaking about a girl. It was a good question and a role-play or a series of question/answer activities around the class would have helped to make the rule clear. In other words, pupils would learn about language structure through using the language in a meaningful context. Here is an example of a role-play I suggested might have supported this teaching point well:

Pupil A (fille):	Maman … tu as vu mes baskets …?
Pupil B (maman):	Tes chaussettes … oui! Tes baskets … non!
Pupil C (papa):	Qu'est-ce qu'il y a?
Pupil B (maman):	Elle a perdu ses baskets!

In addition to setting a context, a role-play like this can provide opportunities for chorus work, for rhymes (*tes chaussettes/baskets*) and for group work as well as creative opportunities for pupils to invent their own conversations following the same structure. Structured role-plays or dialogues can offer pupils a degree of support in the early stages of their encounter with the new language and the possibilities of challenge once their confidence grows – who can make up the longest/funniest/silliest conversation using this model? This takes us onto the theme of the final section.

Offering cognitive challenge

There is one final aspect of effective teaching which I should like to consider more fully and that is the level of cognitive challenge we offer pupils in the tasks we set. In one lesson I observed, pupils were asked to group expressions for the weather according to the seasons. This led to disagreement amongst them (in English) and I heard comments such as, 'Well, it sometimes rains in summer too' and 'No, it can be foggy in summer too'. They were clearly unhappy with the rather simple nature of the task. There were two things that struck me here. First, language teachers are often asked to teach topic areas which feature elsewhere in the curriculum. We need to ensure that we offer them activities with the same level of cognitive challenge as they meet in these curriculum areas if we want them to take our subject seriously. Second, in their resistance to the task, the pupils gave us a good idea for a better way of structuring this lesson. Why not plan the lesson in such a way that they are encouraged to agree and disagree with each other in response to generalizations or stereotypical statements made about the weather: 'It is always foggy in England', 'No, it's not, it is often very bright and sunny … '; 'It never rains in Spain', 'Oh yes, it does, it often rains in the north …'? The nature of this task generates a real need or wish in the pupils to talk to each other. As it turned out, this would have been particularly appropriate as a speaking activity in this lesson as the teacher had prepared a worksheet which dealt with the stereotyped view that it is always hot in Spain.

Once again, it was feedback from pupils that helped us to see how this lesson could have been planned and taught in a different and more appropriate way. Try to observe as many teachers as you can in different curriculum areas so that you have a good idea of the level of cognitive challenge that is expected of pupils in, say, Geography, Science or History. Look too at the different types of homework other teachers set. When a Geography project takes a Year 9 pupil four or five hours of research and writing up, and a series of German homework tasks of matching questions and answers, filling in blanks or learning ten words take a total of thirty minutes, we can begin to understand why some pupils do not take our subject very seriously. They want to get stuck in and we need to find ways of helping them to do this.

Conclusion

You begin to see how your planning and classroom management depend upon your understanding of pupils' needs which, in turn, comes from feedback from pupils and your previous assessment of their progress and their difficulties. The extent to which you see yourself as a learner about teaching and develop a real curiosity about pupils' language learning will determine the development of your pedagogical skills. We need to find ways to support pupils effectively on the one hand, so they do not give up out of frustration and a sense of failure and drop out of our lessons because they do not understand. And on the other, we need to find ways of challenging pupils by allowing them to encounter some of the complexities of the language they are learning and by helping them to experience a sense of independence as their confidence grows. In a way that a textbook cannot, you can build up a dialogue with your pupils about their learning, helping them to learn on the basis of your assessment of their needs and on your understanding of the possibilities of teaching your subject.

We have seen how important it will be for you to make up your own mind about ways of teaching based on your own evidence and exploration. Different strategies work for different teachers in different teaching situations. In my experience, there are few pupils who do not respond to their teacher's faith in them to have a go. With concern about disaffection amongst pupils and some teachers in schools, it is particularly important that we challenge this climate of negativity by focusing on effective ways of getting pupils involved in the serious business of learning languages.

Further reading

Brown, K. (2000) 'Creative thinking about a new modern languages pedagogy', in S. Green, (ed.) *New Perspectives on Teaching and Learning Modern Languages*, London: CILT.

Chambers, G. (ed.) (2000) *Reflections on Motivation*, London: CILT.

DfEE (2000) 'Research into teacher effectiveness, a model of teacher effectiveness', Hay McBer, London.

Leach J. and Moon, B. (eds) (1999) *Learners and Pedagogy*, London: Paul Chapman.

Lodge, A. (2000) 'Higher Education', in S. Green (ed.) *New Perspectives on Teaching and Learning Modern Languages*, London: CILT.

McPake, J., Johnstone, R., Low, L. and Lyall, L. (1999) *Foreign Languages in the Upper Secondary School: A Study of the Causes of Decline*, Edinburgh: SCRE.

Mortimer, P. (ed.) (1999) *Understanding Pedagogy and its Impact on Learning*, London: Paul Chapman.

Norwich Area Schools Consortium (1999) 'The curricular dimensions of disaffection' is a teacher-based research project funded by the Teacher Training Agency.

Part 4

Research and the MFL teacher

15 The impact of languages research on classroom practice

Joanna McPake

This chapter reviews recent literature on the impact of educational research on classroom practice in general and, specifically, in relation to languages learning and teaching. It focuses on the role which policy development has played in the Scottish context in mediating between research and practice, and argues that the potential for research to bring about change in classroom practice has not been fully exploited in recent years. To exemplify these issues, the chapter considers what has been learned from research relating to language learners' motivation, the messages this research has for classroom practitioners and the difficulties of conveying these messages to teachers. In conclusion, it is argued that the absence of reference to independent research in policy documents has obscured the origin of new ideas, and has made it difficult for teachers to understand or judge research findings. Moreover, the dominance of policy-led change over the past decade in Scotland has prevented teachers from seeing themselves as change agents, and has encouraged them to see the causes of problems in their classroom practice as largely beyond their control.

Introduction

Most educational researchers conduct their work in the belief that it will, or should, make a difference to the ways in which learners learn and teachers teach. Some research is intended to have a direct effect on classroom practice. Other types of research envisage indirect influence – through changes to school management practice, for example, or to the development of educational policy at local or national level. Some researchers see their work as primarily concerned with the building of theory, but even in this type of work there is usually an underlying expectation that new or refined theories will have some impact on teacher education at some stage.

Relatively few teachers take an active interest in educational research. Perhaps the most obvious reason for this is that teachers are busy people with little time or energy to read academic papers after several hours in the classroom followed by lesson planning, marking, attending meetings and all the other tasks which make up a teacher's working day. Even if teachers had more free time, however, it is arguable that they would become avid readers of research papers. Research reports and academic papers are rarely written with teacher audiences specifically in mind. Consequently, much of this material can seem highly technical or abstract, sometimes concerned with the minutiae of a particular aspect of learning, with justifications for particular research methodologies, or else with the working out of complex theoretical positions. It is easy to dismiss much research output as irrelevant to the 'real world' of teachers and students.

Over the last decade, the relationship between educational research and practice has been widely debated. This chapter summarizes the key issues emerging from the general debate in the UK, and relates these to similar discussions amongst researchers and practitioners in the field of language learning and teaching. The critique, both from researchers themselves and from research users – in particular those concerned with the development of policy – has focused principally on the failure of researchers to address issues relevant to the classroom and on dissemination methods which are frequently inaccessible to practitioners. In addition, however, in this chapter, it is argued that recent trends in the development of policy, both generally and specifically in relation to languages education, have focused on the 'bigger picture' (i.e. the nature of the curriculum, the structure of provision, etc.) and have also largely ignored what happens within the classroom. By implication, these developments have minimized the role teachers can play in bringing about change. The one major exception is the development of the Literacy Hour policy for English schools. However, the highly prescriptive approach similarly positions teachers as 'karaoke singers' (cf. Powney 1996). This view of teachers as implementers of policy determined by others rather than as change agents is likely to have reduced their interest in applying research findings to their own classrooms.

The impact of educational research on classroom practice

An extensive literature on the impact of educational research generally on classroom practice indicates that the relationship between research and practice is complex and often difficult to trace.

Researchers typically work within an academic environment and conduct research according to well-established 'rules' designed to safeguard the validity of the methods adopted and therefore the rigour of the findings. These 'rules' have little or nothing to say about practical applications of the findings, and indeed some researchers would argue that the implementation of research findings is the job of others.

Traditionally, within British education, research findings have reached classrooms via other agencies which might be termed 'research mediators'. These include local and national policy-making bodies, educational advisers and resource centres, the providers of initial and in-service education, teacher unions, and the publishers of textbooks and other educational resources. In different ways, staff in these bodies have in the past read and assessed research outputs and incorporated into their own dissemination activities findings which seemed relevant to the needs of students and teachers.

Thus the route of research-led innovation into classroom practice has been an indirect one and one which, to a certain extent, has been dependent on chance interactions. Even at national level, the lasting impact of new ideas depends on a particular political regime being in force long enough both to introduce new ideas and to support their implementation consistently. At local level, the adoption of new ideas is likely to vary considerably from one authority to another, depending on the academic, political and practical experience and inclinations of policy makers and advisers. Teacher Education Institutes (TEIs) are perhaps more likely to develop and maintain particular educational 'cultures' (though these may differ markedly from one TEI to another) but teachers' most sustained contact with TEIs will be during their initial teacher education. Subsequent contact with TEIs and other providers of in-service education is likely to be sporadic and their influence on experienced teachers is therefore limited.

The existence of such a plethora of organizations reading, interpreting and planning for the implementation of research findings, as part of their overall development role, can be regarded as a strength – providing that research genuinely underpins development. Given the absence of 'definitive answers' to most of the issues which researchers explore, variety in practice can be seen both to reflect this situation and to ensure sufficient flexibility in the development of classroom practice to allow local and individual needs and aspirations to be taken into account. Moreover, consensus which develops through multiple approaches to interpretation and implementation is likely to be fairly robust. In recent years, however, the balance of power among these various 'research mediators' has shifted towards national policy-makers, and one of the effects has been the development of a more critical perspective on the work of researchers and on the lack of direct connection between research findings and classroom practice.

Perspectives of researchers and users

Commentators on this issue include researchers themselves and research 'users'. The term 'users' includes those we referred to as 'research mediators' in the previous section, but also, by implication, teachers themselves, although, in fact, the voice of classroom practitioners is rarely heard in this debate.

The critique of research has developed in two directions. Some have challenged the quality of educational research generally, arguing that much of the work is unusable either by research mediators or by classroom practitioners because of fundamental flaws in conception and methodology (e.g. Hargreaves 1996; Tooley and Darby 1998). Defenders of current practices within educational research have responded by arguing that educational research cannot be compared with medical research (the principal paradigm against which detractors compared it), because of fundamental differences in the nature of the inquiry (Hodkinson 1998). Educational research is concerned principally with a social phenomenon which requires consideration both of the individual learner and of the social context in which learning takes place. Medical research is principally concerned with physical phenomena which (at least in conventional medical research) can be understood as following scientific laws and also primarily as quantifiable data.

Although the principal protagonists on both sides of this debate have been educational researchers, there have been interventions from policy-makers, notably Ofsted in England and a former minister for education in Scotland. These have raised suspicions among some educational researchers that the debate has been politically orchestrated in order to discredit educational research and leave the way open for policy-makers to act on their own initiative, without the need to take into account research findings which do not 'fit' with political concerns. These issues and others are explored in more detail in an edited collection of researchers' responses to a sustained period of criticism in the mid-1990s (Rudduck and McIntryre 1998).

The second element of the critique has been to focus on topics chosen for research and on the presentation of research findings (e.g. Hillage *et al.* 1998; Cordingley 2000). Some commentators have described researchers and classroom practitioners as talking 'different languages'. Thus researchers may fail to understand (and therefore to investigate) what teachers see as the most pressing dilemmas for their practice. They may also fail to understand (or to remember, as many educational researchers were once teachers themselves) the complexity of the classroom context, the need to act simultaneously on multiple levels and the pressure of achieving results in limited time. Researchers' training tends to lead them to isolate particular phenomena and to remove 'confounding variables' – other aspects of the context which make it difficult to see whether change is due to the effects of the particular practice under scrutiny or of something unrelated. It can therefore be difficult for them to see how what they have found can be reintegrated into classroom practice.

Teachers, on the other hand, are bombarded with vast quantities of information from different sources and do not necessarily have the time or the skills to identify the most valuable or the most relevant developments relating to their own work. They are likely to be looking for ideas which they can easily adapt to their classrooms, rather than theories which challenge current practice but appear to have few practical implications.

Following these sometimes heated disagreements concerning the nature, quality, relevance and accessibility of educational research, some signs of a developing shared understanding of how research can have an impact on the classroom are beginning to appear. Many researchers are keen for their work to have practical implications. Some key research mediators, particularly in England, have investigated in some detail ways of enhancing the impact of research (e.g. TTA undated; Hillage *et al.* 1998).

Three key recommendations have emerged for researchers:

- where possible, teachers should be involved in the research process;
- research findings should be disseminated in formats which are accessible to teachers;
- research funding should include a dissemination budget.

The Rowntree Foundation *Findings* series, which summarizes research funded by the Foundation on a wide range of social topics, is widely commended as a model of clarity in dissemination. The Teacher Training Agency's own *TTA Research Findings* series is modelled on this. Other government agencies, such as the Scottish Executive Education Department's *Interchange* series, also publish research summaries designed to be accessible to practitioners.

A complementary set of recommendations for policy-makers and classroom practitioners has also emerged:

- they should become more 'research literate';
- they should understand that the application of research findings can enhance practice;
- additional funding is needed for policy-makers and classroom practitioners to have the time and the support needed for them to access research.

In England, the TTA has set up the National Educational Research Forum as a way of actively promoting teachers' engagement with research. In Scotland, an annual conference, also known as *Forum,* has had a similar role for a number of years (see Brown and Harlen 1998).

Research into languages learning and teaching and its impact on practice

The general literature on the relationship between educational research and classroom practice rarely mentions languages learning and teaching. However, researchers in the field of languages education have addressed this question and identified a number of barriers to the uptake of research findings by teachers. Though the majority of these commentators are American, the issues they identify are similar to those debated in the context of educational research in England.

Commentators have noted:

- the difficulty for language teachers of processing research information, determining genuine and relevant advances in the field and interpreting research findings for classroom use, given the pressure of time, limited resources and support (Van Patten 1997);
- the small number of research studies based in language classrooms and the consequent lack of awareness among researchers about ways in which their research might best be shaped or presented for teachers' benefit (Van Patten op. cit.);
- the limited control teachers have over what they do in their classrooms, given the power of policy-makers and administrators to determine content, e.g. through the prescribing of textbooks and outcomes, e.g. through externally designed assessment (Crookes 1997);
- the need for researchers to ensure that they address issues which practitioners see as relevant to their work and to draw on what is known about the ways in

which teachers incorporate new ideas into their own thinking about practice (Ellis 1997);

- the importance of exploring different types of relationship between researchers and practitioners, and of understanding the implications of different models: e.g. are the purposes for which a relationship seems desirable to develop shared ways of thinking, to explore common concerns, to bring about change within classrooms or on a wider scale? (Pica 1997);

- the need, at least in a UK context, to understand that the relationship between research and practice can rarely be direct, given the powerful mediating role of forces such as national curriculums or guidelines, the inspectorate and other centralized bodies in determining what happens in the classroom (Johnstone 1999).

The policy factor

If we review the history of developments relating to language teaching in schools over the last decade, the force of this last point becomes very clear. Over the last decade, sweeping changes have been made throughout education, affecting language learning and teaching directly or indirectly. For example, major changes to language teaching and learning have been effected through:

- curriculum reform (e.g. through the National Curriculums in England, Wales and Northern Ireland and national guidelines in Scotland);
- changes to the structure of provision (e.g. the introduction of compulsory language learning or of provision for language teaching in primary schools);
- changes to the examination system (e.g. the introduction of Higher Still in Scotland and changes to the A level system in England);
- implementation of a national teacher education curriculum in England.

Through these kinds of developments, the position of policy-makers in education is becoming increasingly powerful, supported by current trends towards centralization of policy in relation to education and the concomitant decline in the role of local authority policy-makers and advisers. We have seen earlier that many policy-makers have, in the course of the 1990s, adopted a relatively sceptical attitude towards research. It may therefore be no coincidence that the potential for research to support innovation in classrooms has been downplayed. Firstly, the kinds of policies that have been the focus of attention in the last decade have made only very limited reference to what happens in classrooms. Policy-makers have been concerned, as we have seen, with the 'bigger picture', reforming curriculums and provision structures. The assumption may be that classroom practice changes automatically to fit the changing context. From this, teachers may infer that they do not themselves have a role in bringing about change, other than to follow the guidelines or prescriptions produced by policy-makers. In such a context, there would be little point in teachers considering how best to implement research findings in their classrooms. The credibility of educational research has been challenged and its role in development appears to be minimal.

Policy to promote language learning in Scottish schools

To illustrate this point, I am going to review action taken in Scotland in response to evidence that the number of students taking Highers in Modern Languages is in steep decline. Between 1976 and 1996, numbers fell by almost 50 per cent (McPake *et al.* 1999). The trend was becoming evident by the end of the 1980s, coincidentally a period in which it was widely held that monolingual, anglophone Britons would need markedly to enhance their language skills in order to meet the challenges of the single European market (introduced in 1992). Initial policy responses included:

- the introduction of the *Languages for All* policy, which recommended that all Scottish students in secondary education should study a language up to the age of 16;
- the phasing in of *Modern Languages in the Primary School*, which, over the 1990s, has ensured that virtually all Scottish students now study a modern language in the last two years of their primary education;
- the revision of Higher examinations in Modern Languages to enhance the communicative element and downplay the earlier emphasis on grammar and comprehension;
- the introduction of *5 to14 Guidelines* for the teaching of Modern Languages in the first two years of secondary school.

It is likely that all of these changes were, ultimately, underpinned by research: for example, the prevalent focus on communicative language teaching in the 1970s and 1980s; or international comparison studies suggesting that British students' language skills are weak compared with their European counterparts because they start language learning later and spend less class-time on this subject. However, there is little overt reference to this research in the documentation accompanying these initiatives, and little discussion of the changes to classroom practice which might accompany these, despite the likelihood that substantial changes would be required.

If we look simply at the impact of *Languages for All*, it is evident that teachers who have been accustomed to working only with students thought to be 'linguistically competent' (however defined by schools) are likely to need to change their teaching approaches when required to teach all students, regardless of ability. Those responsible for devising the policy doubtless argued that identifying *how* this policy was to be implemented was the responsibility of local authorities, advisers, school managers and teachers themselves. Indeed, a range of materials, and in-service courses aimed at supporting 'the full range of ability' in the language classroom, has ensued. It is also the case, however, that relatively little of this work has a basis in research. No national research into effective approaches for teaching the full range of ability in lower secondary classrooms has been commissioned in

Scotland. It can be argued that the absence of acknowledgement of these issues at national policy level led to consternation among teachers, and indeed resistance to the initiative in some quarters, because the concept that all children can benefit from learning another language (however laudable in theory and however well-established in practice in other parts of the world) was not common currency in Scotland at the time, and is still contested by some.

The effect of these initiatives was to increase very significantly the number of students entered for Standard Grade examinations in Modern Languages. This is not surprising, given that languages were now all but compulsory up to the age of 16, the age at which students sit Standard Grade. It might have been expected that the numbers of students taking Highers in Modern Languages would begin to rise again, partly because of the larger number of students qualified to do so (given the near universality of Standard Grade passes in Modern Languages for all students), and partly because the revisions to the Higher examination were intended to make it more relevant and more accessible. However, the number of students taking Highers in Modern Languages continues to decline. At the point at which students can choose whether or not to study a language, they are, in increasing numbers, rejecting this option.

It is arguable whether or not the continuing decline represents policy failure. Policy initiatives, as we have seen, did not set out to tackle this issue directly. The explicit aims of the policies listed above have been met: most primary students now study a language and virtually all secondary students continue their language studies to the age of 16. There was, however, clearly an expectation among policy-makers that these initiatives would enhance uptake in the upper secondary school. It was for this reason that a study of the causes of decline (generally referred to as FLUSS after the title of the report, *Foreign Languages in the Upper Secondary School*) was commissioned by the then Scottish Office Education and Industry Department (SOEID) and conducted by a team of researchers from the Scottish Centre for Information on Language Teaching and Research (Scottish CILT) and the Scottish Council for Research in Education (SCRE). The findings from this study, which are summarized in the next section, are set out in detail in the report by McPake *et al.* 1999.

Research perspectives on student motivation

Before looking at the outcomes of the FLUSS study, it is worth considering what several decades of research into language learner motivation might have to say about the reasons why people choose to learn languages or not. Within the field of languages education, there have been a number of influential studies, dating back at least to the 1970s. A first 'wave' of research is associated with psychologist Robert Gardner and colleagues (see in particular Gardner 1985). This research is concerned with the impact – positive or negative – of the social context in which language learners study and use languages. Its primary focus has been French–English bilingualism in Canada.

Key concepts in Gardner's work include the notions of *integrative* and *instrumental* motivation. *Integrative motivation* refers to a positive disposition in the learner towards native speakers of the language studied, including the desire to communicate with them, to understand the culture and, in a sense, to become 'more like' the native speaker community (i.e. to integrate with the community, or at least to be able to do so on occasions). *Instrumental motivation* concerns the personal gains the learner hopes to make by learning another language. These can range from passing examinations or gaining entry to a higher level of education to improving job-prospects or getting a pay-rise.

Gardner's work has been highly influential on subsequent research which has identified a wide range of sub-components of motivation. Researchers have also explored the effects of interactions among the different components. For example, integrative and instrumental motives are likely to interact with each other. Learners may be keen to communicate with native speakers of the language learned but, at the same time, they may also wish to pass exams. This particular combination is likely to lead to positive results, we may assume. However, it is also possible to be simultaneously positively and negatively motivated, and there are interesting discussions in the literature about the likelihood of different types of motivation negating each other. For example, are those with no interest in communicating with native speakers but keen to pass exams likely to be successful learners? And vice versa?

A second 'wave' of research has developed around the work of Zoltán Dörnyei (and others, e.g. Oxford and Shearin 1994). Dörnyei, as a teacher of English to Hungarian students, has been concerned to focus more specifically on learners' motivation in the language classroom. The model he developed (Dörnyei 1994) identifies three 'levels' of motivation: the *language level* (which embraces the integrative and the instrumental constructs), the *learner level* and the *learning situation level*. This last refers to conditions in the classroom likely to affect motivation, such as the nature of the course, the approach adopted by the teacher and the influence of the other students' attitudes, expectations, ways of working, aspirations, etc.

According to Dörnyei, those seeking to enhance learner motivation should attend to all three levels. Attention to one risks failure through uncontrolled influences elsewhere. Given the discussion earlier in this chapter, it is worth noting that Dörnyei sets out quite specific recommendations for teachers on how to address the different levels of motivation in their work. For example, in relation to promoting learners' self-efficacy, he writes:

> [teach] students learning and communication strategies, as well as strategies for information processing and problem-solving, helping them to develop realistic expectations of what can be achieved in a given period, and telling them about your own difficulties in language learning.
>
> (Dörnyei 1994: 281)

Similar suggestions are made in relation to all the components identified in the model.

Many researchers have conducted detailed studies of learner motivation which seek to explore the implications of the theoretical models developed by Gardner and Dörnyei. While these cannot be reviewed here in detail, for the purposes of understanding the Scottish dilemma, it is worth noting that those which have focused on younger learners' experiences and perspectives have argued that the learning situation level is more influential than traditional integrative or instrumental factors (which Dörnyei locates at the language level in his model). For example, Nikolov, who conducted a longitudinal study of her own students in Hungary, from the ages of six to fourteen, concludes:

> the most important motivating factors for children between 6 and 14 years of age included positive attitudes towards the language learning context and the teacher; intrinsically motivating activities, tasks and materials; and they were more motivated by classroom practice than by integrative or instrumental reasons … Instrumental motives emerged around the age of 11 or 12 but they remained vague and general. No trace of attitude towards speakers of the target language was identified in the answers to open questions.
>
> (Nikolov 1999: 53)

The notion of *intrinsic* motivation which Nikolov alludes to here has also been explored in more detail, in the Canadian context, by Noels *et al.* (1999). In their view, many of the features attributed by Dörnyei to the learner situation level can be regarded as aspects of intrinsic motivation, and they urge that more research into this aspect of motivation for language learning should be undertaken.

A study of the views of 'average' Year 9 students (i.e. 13-year-olds who were neither outstanding linguists nor among those experiencing high levels of difficulty with language learning) was conducted by researchers in Barking and Dagenham LEA (Lee *et al.* 1998). Their findings suggest that while the students were aware of instrumental goals for learning languages, such as facilitating travel or employment, their experiences of learning languages in school were what determined the choices they were about to make, either to continue or to abandon language study.

Chambers (1999) studied the motivation of learners of German between Year 7 (i.e. the first year of secondary education in England) and Year 9, in four comprehensive schools in Leeds. The stimulus to the study is a similar issue to that raised by the introduction of Languages for All in Scotland: i.e. that a number of students who would not previously have been expected to study languages are now present in lower secondary language classrooms (given the introduction of similar policies in England). He compared these students with counterparts learning English in Germany. He found a number of differences in contextual factors for the two groups (e.g. that German students were more likely to have parents who spoke English, to have heard English used or to have encountered opportunities where it would be useful to be able to speak and understand English) which were likely to have a bearing on motivation. However, he concluded that the most influential factor was the teacher and the relationship which s/he established with the students. Again, in view of the reported lack of interest among researchers in the application of their research findings, it seems relevant to note that Chambers includes a chapter describing a range of teaching activities which might be used to make students' experiences in the language classroom more enjoyable.

Lastly, let us return to the FLUSS study on the decline in uptake of Modern Languages post-16 in Scotland, mentioned at the end of the previous section. Student motivation was one of the issues investigated as a possible influence on decline. Students who participated in the study were 16- and 17-year-olds with the potential to continue studying languages at Higher level. All had been entered for Standard Grade examinations in Modern Languages at Credit level – i.e. the most challenging version of the examination, which best prepares students for studies at Higher level. The FLUSS students were therefore older than those involved in the studies by Nikolov, Lee *et al.* and Chambers discussed above. At this stage in their educational careers, they seemed more conscious of the instrumental rationale for subject choices than their younger counterparts.

However, many of the FLUSS students saw subjects other than languages as more immediately relevant to the kinds of goals they had set themselves: principally entry into further or higher education or into the careers of their choice. Their reluctance to continue to study a language to Higher was therefore markedly influenced by the view that other subjects were more likely to help them enter university or to be relevant to the careers they wished to pursue. This would appear to suggest that instrumental motivation to learn languages is unlikely to be strong for Scottish students, even when they reach the age when they become aware of these kinds of concerns.

If we cannot convince 16- and 17-year-olds that languages will be of value to them in their future studies or careers, can we instead build on their integrative motivation? (In passing, it is noted that this shift in focus begs the question as to whether there is any point to students learning language if it is really the case that language will not be useful to them in future. This is a challenging issue for those seeking to promote language learning in anglophone countries, but one which there is no scope to explore in this chapter.) The evidence from the FLUSS study suggests that this may be a more fruitful approach to take. Students indicated that they did not agree with the view that there was no need to learn other languages because of the dominance of English as an international medium of communication. Many expressed an active interest in learning more about the cultures of the countries whose languages they were studying, in travelling and in meeting and getting to know native speakers of theses languages. These views are consistent with the fact that those selected for participation in this study were Credit level students. Chambers, in his research (op. cit.) noted a correlation between positive dispositions towards foreigners and foreign cultures and success in language learning.

However, it also emerged from the students' responses that, in their view, the content of language lessons in Scottish schools rarely explored the cultural issues in which they professed an interest. In fact, students were critical of an approach which seemed to foreground the students themselves as the principal source of content; many students objected to such staple topics of conversation in the modern languages classroom as their own families, their pets, their hobbies, their school day, etc. As the data collected for FLUSS did not include classroom observation, we cannot say whether students' accounts of the content of language lessons are accurate. We have, however, raised, in our conclusions to this study and elsewhere (McPake, forthcoming) the question of the messages which the content of school language lessons gives about the purposes for learning other languages. If lessons focus mainly on developing the ability to discuss personal matters, the message seems to be that the main reason for learning a language is to facilitate social relationships (possibly one-sided) with native speakers of the language. If the focus is on transactions (shopping, asking for directions, buying train tickets), it is that it is useful to know other language when travelling or on holiday abroad. If there is no indication in the content that languages can help students to fulfil purposes such as acquiring or disseminating information in an educational or work environment, or developing critical perspectives on their own and others' cultures and societies, then it is not surprising that students fail to see the subject as relevant when asked to make subject choices which will have a major impact on their future education, their careers and on their social and cultural development as adults.

The following key points emerge from this brief review of motivation research:

- learner motivation is a complex phenomenon comprising many components relating both to the classroom and to external factors;
- those wishing to increase participation in language learning need to address all levels of motivation (as described in Dörnyei's model), as these factors interact with each other;
- it seems to be the case that the dominant influence on younger learners' motivation is the learning situation, rather than, for example, attitudes towards the language and the people who speak it, or views on the value of language in furthering educational or career goals;
- the difficulty of promoting instrumental motivation among anglophone students is widely recognized, but the content of school language lessons may (according to students' accounts) do little to enhance either instrumental or integrative motivation.

The impact of research on language learner motivation in Scotland

What influence has research into language learner motivation had on recent developments in Scotland? In view of the concerns about declining uptake at Higher noted above, moves to raise student motivation could be expected to be a key feature of both policy and practice. We saw that the FLUSS research project was commissioned, in 1996, to investigate the causes of decline in uptake, and that student motivation was one of a number of factors explored. The impact of this study will be addressed shortly.

Over the same period during which the FLUSS research was conducted, Her Majesty's Inspectorate in Scotland also compiled evidence from school inspections on language learning and teaching in the upper primary and in secondary schools. Their report on these inspections was published just before FLUSS in the autumn of 1998. In contrast to FLUSS, where the findings are based on questionnaire responses from students and principal teachers of Modern Languages, the focus of the HMI report was classroom practice. It is in this report, therefore, that we might expect to find direct evidence of the relationship between what happens in the classroom and students' motivation to learn languages.

Inspection is not conducted in the same way as research. The purpose of inspection is to make judgements concerning learning and teaching, rather than to investigate, to describe or to experiment. The remit for this HMI report was to pass judgement on the standard and quality of modern languages teaching in the upper primary and in secondary schools, drawing on inspection evidence collected over five years. Judgements were based on performance indicators published in earlier documents and on 'traditional analyses based on collective professional expertise' (HMI 1998: 7).

From the performance indicators cited in the report, student 'motivation and engagement' are listed as components of the quality of learning, along with 'pace of work, progress in learning, independent thought, and collaboration with other pupils' (HMI op. cit.: 21). Unexpectedly, perhaps, the inspectors' view of student motivation appears to have been largely positive. Comments on the quality of learning in S1 and S2 are typical of those made for each double year group. (The report covers P6/ P7, S1/ S2, S3/ S4 and S5/ S6.)

> The quality of pupils' learning [in S1/S2] was good or very good in just over 65 per cent of departments. In no cases was it unsatisfactory. Pupils were generally well motivated. Most were willing to take on some responsibility for their own learning, where that was encouraged by teachers. Weaknesses included instances where paired or group work was unstructured or too predominant. Expectations of pupils' learning were often too low. In some cases only a majority of pupils were making good progress in their learning.
>
> (HMI op. cit.: 21)

These are quite categorical judgements, though it is not necessarily easy to know how to make use of them. We can see that the judgement on quality of learning is reasonably encouraging overall (good or very good in 65 per cent of departments and unsatisfactory in none). Factors which appear to contribute to this outcome are high motivation and pupils taking some responsibility for their own learning. If teachers are seeking to improve the quality of learning in their classroom, they are more likely to focus on progression and on the role of pair and group work than on motivation or the promotion of independent learning, from this account. However, there are few clues to indicate what the inspectors mean by the terms they use, how they come to these judgements, or how schools can make use of the findings.

Some details emerge from other sections of the report, such as those which list the features of very good primary schools or secondary departments. For example, in the section on quality of teaching and learning (section 2.3), a sidebar describes practices in use in classrooms where teachers have high expectations of pupils' learning: these include asking children to 'memorize words, songs, chunks of text, facts about the language; undertake independent reading; complete projects' and so on (HMI op. cit.: 21). However, there is no explicit linking of these features with motivation or any of the other components making up the quality of pupils' learning. There is little help in the text for the reader who wants to know how these high levels of motivation are achieved or how teachers of S3 and S4, where there is some evidence of a dip, might enhance motivation.

There is no reference in the report to any research on motivation among language learners, or indeed to research in relation to any of the other aspects of language education, although teachers are criticized for 'an inadequate understanding of the principles on which their general approach to language teaching, and the methodology which they chose, were based' (HMI op. cit.: 17). Despite the inspectors' grounding in classroom practice, the report provides no opportunity for research-based findings to have any impact.

Although the detailed commentary in the report presents many positive findings, including those on motivation, the report as a whole was set in within a negative critical frame. The foreword to the report states:

> The report is not reassuring. It demonstrates quite clearly that, while there is some good learning and teaching in modern languages, the situation overall is far from satisfactory despite the extensive effort that has been put into transforming the teaching of modern languages in recent years and encouraging uptake by pupils.
>
> (HMI op. cit.: 3)

This section received a high level of media coverage when the report was first published – at a point at which teachers and local authorities had not yet received their own copies of the report. Influenced by press accounts, both policy-makers and professionals generally understood the report to be highly critical of language teaching. Pressure for action, in view both of the HMI report and of the FLUSS findings (published shortly afterwards), began to mount.

The response generated further policy activity, rather than action which would have a direct impact on classroom practice. Helen Liddell, the Minister for Education in Scotland at the time, set up an Action Group for Languages, the first time such a body had been created in Scotland for the purposes of exploring issues relating to the teaching of a school subject. The group met for eighteen months, hearing evidence from a variety of professional and academic bodies, as well as parents' organizations and other representatives of the wider Scottish public. The broad remit of the group was to secure the place of Modern Languages in the curriculum; to improve the quality of Modern Languages at Standard Grade; and to ensure a greater degree of continuity in language learning in schools. At the time of writing, the report is about to be published (Scottish Executive Education Department forthcoming), and so it is not possible to comment at this stage on its findings or recommendations.

These developments would seem to confirm the ascendancy of the policy-making process as the primary recipient of research findings. Researchers were represented on the Action Group and were also asked to present evidence to the group. In contrast to the somewhat bruising experiences of English educational researchers discussed earlier in this chapter, there was no sense in the proceedings of the Action Group that research findings were to be challenged on the basis either of the validity of the research approaches adopted or of the relevance of the research to the classroom. But it also seems likely that the research findings on which the Action Group report will draw will be included in 'pre-digested' form. Unless the report is very different from policy documents of the past decade, it will be difficult to distinguish research findings from other kinds of opinion gathered in the course of the group's work, and therefore hard for practitioners to identify or to judge the sources of information underlying policy decisions.

Why does this matter? It is not my intention to imply that research should, of right, have special status in the development of policy. Policy-makers need to be responsive to the voices of the profession and there is clearly a strong case for engaging in direct dialogue with teachers, advisers, teacher educators, employers, parents and students themselves. But it seems to me to be important that teachers should have direct access to research findings for two reasons.

Firstly, there is a danger that policy-led innovation accords little weight to teachers' own judgements about what is right for their own classrooms, but rather seeks to persuade teachers that policy-makers know better. This has perhaps been clearest when policy has been prescriptive, as with the National Curriculum in England. In general, however, policy documents tend to adopt a style in which the only evidence presented is that which supports the recommendations to be made. The existence of different perspectives is concealed and the possibility of debate and of reaching different conclusions from those drawn by the policy-makers is therefore minimized.

Second, evidence from policy activity over the past decade suggests that it has little impact on the classroom. This seems partly to stem from a belief among policy-makers that what needs to change are the 'big things' – curriculums, structures, examinations, etc. In relation to many of the issues policy-makers have tackled, perhaps they are right. But, as we have seen in relation to our review of motivation research, the evidence, at least in this case, suggests that change is most needed in the classroom. None of the proposed innovations to date address classroom practice directly. It may be, as was suggested earlier, that policy-makers believe that classroom change inevitably follows from the bigger changes. Again, they may be right in many cases, but the FLUSS research shows some worrying trends in teacher perspectives in relation to their own responsibilities which belie this view.

The principal teachers who participated in the FLUSS study saw the causes of decline in uptake at Higher as largely beyond their control, identifying two key influences: first, the perceived lack of relevance, among students, their communities and employers, of modern languages for career purposes; and second, a range of obstacles to effective provision, including insufficient time for language teaching, large classes, timetabling difficulties, and various other problems related to the nature of Standard Grade and Higher examinations. Principal teachers felt they could do very little to change these factors. They did not expect to be able to persuade students that languages were relevant to their careers, particularly as it emerged that some of these teachers agreed with these students that they were not relevant; nor did they feel that they had opportunities to change the nature of the examinations whose requirements are the principal influences on secondary school syllabuses. They did not even feel able to alter aspects of provision within their own schools, such as timetabling clashes with competing subjects (usually perceived to be sciences). One could argue that the rhetoric of policy-makers – that the changes to structures they were advocating would have positive effects on uptake and performance – turned against them. Teachers took the view that if performance suffered and uptake declined, this must be the fault of the larger structures.

Moreover, teachers felt that aspects of language provision which they could control had little impact on student motivation to continue studying a language after it ceased to be recommended for all students. For example, although principal teachers said that students in their schools had opportunities to spend time with the foreign language assistant, to go on visits or exchanges to a country where the language they were studying was spoken, to use new technologies as a way of enhancing their foreign language experience, and so on, most of those who commented felt that these kinds of activities had no discernible influence on students' decision to take Highers in Modern Languages. Again this might be seen as the reverse of the policy coin. At a time when many of these resources were being cut, the implication was that they were not central to the success of the subject. Thus even where these resources were available, teachers appeared now to see them as peripheral.

Conclusions

This chapter has explored the potential for research to have an impact on class-room practice from two perspectives. Firstly, it has reviewed the debate, largely in England, over the relationship between research and practice, in which educational research has been criticized in terms of quality, relevance and accessibility. Despite the heated nature of this debate, it appears to have had some positive outcomes, in which the importance of teachers understanding research findings and drawing on these in their practice has been reaffirmed, and action taken to make research more accessible. Second, it has explored the role of policy as an intermediary between research and classroom practice, through a 'case study' of the impact of research into language learner motivation on policy and practice in Scottish schools.

In this latter part of the chapter, it is argued that the dominance of policy as the principal promoter of change undermines teachers' ability to act as change agents on the basis of their own judgements and therefore does little to promote teachers' interest in research or ability to make use of it. Moreover, though policy-making often makes use of research, it is also argued here that the style in which policy documents are written tends to obscure research-based recommendations, blending the research findings with those from other sources. While this may be a valid approach to policy-making, it makes it difficult for teachers to identify the origins of ideas, or to apply their own judgement in relation to their value or relevance. Finally, it is argued that policy-makers' concerns have largely been with educational issues beyond the classroom and it therefore seems unlikely that changes promoted by policy, whether based on research findings or not, have had much impact on classroom practice.

This is conjecture, as, despite the very great changes in provision for languages in schools over the last decade, there have been few studies which have investigated the impact on classrooms. The available data, such as that from the teachers who took part in the FLUSS study, suggest that teachers are unconvinced – with good reason, given the continuing decline – that these changes have had positive effects on performance or motivation. What is worrying is the suggestion in these data that teachers do not see themselves or the work that they do as making any difference. Neither research nor policy recommendations will have an impact on the classroom if teachers continue to feel devalued in this way.

Further reading

Brown, S. and Harlen, W. (1998) 'A forum for researchers and users of research – Scottish style', in J. Rudduck and D. McIntyre (eds) (1998), *Educational Research: The Challenge Facing Us*, London: Paul Chapman.

Chambers, G. (1999) *Motivating Language Learners*, Clevedon: Multilingual Matters.

Cordingley, P. (2000) 'Teacher perspectives on the accessibility and usability of research outputs', paper presented at the *British Educational Research Association Conference*.

Crookes, G. (1997) 'What influences what and how second and foreign language teachers teach?', *The Modern Language Journal*, 81(1): 67–79.

Dörnyei, Z. (1994) 'Motivation and motivating in the foreign language classroom', *The Modern Language Journal*, 78(iii): 273–84.

Ellis, R. (1997) 'SLA and language pedagogy: an educational perspective', *Studies in Second Language Acquisition*, 19: 69–92.

Gardner, R.C. (1985) *Social Psychology and Second Language Learning: The Role of Attitudes and Motivation*, London: Edward Arnold.

Hargreaves, D.H. (1996) *Teaching as a Research-based Profession: Possibilities and Prospects*, Teacher Training Agency Annual Lecture.

Hillage, J., Pearson, R., Anderson, A. and Tamkin, P. (1998) *Excellence in Research on Schools*, London: DfEE.

HM Inspectors (1998) *Standards and Quality in Primary and Secondary Schools 1994 – 1998: Modern Languages*, Edinburgh: The Stationery Office.

Hodkinson, P. (1998) 'Naivete and bias in educational research: the Tooley Report', *BERA Research Intelligence*, 65(August).

Johnstone, R. (1999) 'Research on language learning and teaching 1997–1998', *Language Teaching*, 32.

Lee, J., Buckland, D. and Shaw, G. (1998) *The Invisible Child: The Responses and Attitudes to the Learning of Modern Foreign Languages shown by Year 9 Pupils of Average Ability*, London: CILT.

McPake, J. (forthcoming) *Parents' Perspectives On School Provision For Modern Languages,* Stirling: Scottish CILT.

McPake, J., Johnstone, R., Low, L. and Lyall, L. (1999) *Foreign Languages in the Upper Secondary School,* Edinburgh: Scottish Council for Research in Education.

Nikolov, M. (1999) 'Why do you learn English? Because the teacher is short', a study of Hungarian children's foreign language learning motivation, *Language Teaching Research,* 3(1): 33–56.

Noels, K., Clément, R. and Pelletier, L. (1999) 'Perceptions of teachers' communicative style and students' intrinsic and extrinsic motivation', *The Modern Language Journal,* 83(1): 23–34.

Oxford, R. and Shearin, J. (1994) 'Language learning motivation: expanding the theoretical framework', *Modern Language Journal,* 78(1): 12–28.

Pica, T. (1997) 'Second language teaching and research relationships: a North American view', *Language Teaching Research,* 1(1): 48–72.

Powney, J. (1996) 'Deprofessionalisation or teaching as karaoke', in B. Jeans and K. Rebel (eds) *Issues in Teacher Education.,* Felicitas Academic Press: Victoria, Australia.

Rudduck, J. and McIntyre, D.(eds) (1998) *Educational Research: The Challenge Facing Us,* London: Paul Chapman.

Scottish Executive Education Department (forthcoming) *Citizens of a Multilingual World,* Edinburgh: SEED.

Teacher Training Agency (undated) *TTA Research Findings: Drafting Research Summaries for TTA Publication,* London: TTA. (Available via the internet at http://www.canteach.gov.uk/info/library/tta00_04.pdf)

Tooley, J. and Darby, D. (1998) *Educational Research: An Ofsted Critique,* London. Ofsted.

Van Patten, B. (1997) 'How is language teaching constructed? Introduction to the Special Issue', *The Modern Language Journal,* 81(1): 1–5.

16 The invisible child

An MFL improvement and development programme in the London Borough of Barking and Dagenham[1]

Jeff Lee

Context and rationale

This chapter describes work done from 1997 onwards to improve standards of teaching and pupil attainment in Modern Foreign Languages (MFL) in the secondary schools of Barking and Dagenham LEA. This area of north-east London has a predominantly white working-class population. Socio-economic conditions have been stable for many years. Few pupils move to secondary schools in other authorities, and there is virtually no movement to independent schools.

In 1990 standards in MFL in the Borough's schools were well below national figures. Few pupils were entered for GCSE, and of these only a small proportion achieved an A–C grade. Over the next six years results improved rapidly and significantly as the pressure on schools to raise standards increased, accompanied by guidance from the LEA inspection and advisory service specifically aimed at improving GCSE results. This enabled the type of pupil who should have been reaching higher grades all along actually to do so. However, the number of pupils achieving the lower- and middle-order grades remained stubbornly high.

Over the last decade a central principle of the Borough's education service has been to reduce what has become known nationally as the long tail of under- and low-achievement: in other words, to achieve higher overall standards by raising the attainment of all pupils, rather than merely by boosting the performance of the most able. A key factor here has been the development of interactive whole-class teaching, the purpose of which is to move the whole class forward together. In this approach, developed in primary Mathematics and English teaching, high priority is given to collaboration and co-operation: pupils' contributions are valued and form a part of the teaching, so pupils know such contributions must be audible, articulate and listened to. The classroom layout, using a horseshoe desk arrangement, is important here, and the overhead projector (OHP) a vital tool. All this would play a crucial role in our later development work.

It emerged that improvement across the ability range in MFL would require development work focused on fundamental issues. The early stages of MFL teaching would need to change radically if pupils were to receive a solid foundation on which to build their learning, rather than depending on repair work in Key Stage 4.

The development work which followed differed from that usually undertaken in that it was long-term and sought to get at these fundamental issues of teaching and learning. It did not rely, for example, on providing in-service training on discrete aspects of MFL teaching such as 'Improving writing in Year 8' or 'Role-plays with less able pupils in Key Stage 3'. Such topics have their place, but on their own they are unlikely to bring about lasting improvements unless based on a clear and consistently applied pedagogy.

It became clear that this very issue of MFL pedagogy needed some radical rethinking. Although some surface features of MFL teaching were recognizable and commonly found, they were not in themselves enough to secure sound and sustained learning. Therefore they were not enough to constitute effective teaching, if it is accepted – as must surely be the case – that teaching must promote learning. Examples of surface features are: focus on learning language for communicative purposes – though actually these purposes are commonly reduced to a list of topics and situations; use of target language – though not always consistent; use of authentic or quasi-authentic materials; all four skills involved; activity-based lessons. It is not argued that these features do not matter or are somehow wrong or inappropriate, simply that they do not in themselves guarantee success for all pupils.

We began to hypothesize that some teachers develop a pedagogy and a range of teaching approaches which work for them. These may well be based on the principles of communicative language teaching, though these have perhaps become eroded over time. Other teachers, however, tend to rely on the surface features, perhaps thinking, with some justification, that they are doing what is needed. *What was it that made some lessons and teaching so much more effective than others?* The answers to this key question emerged only gradually.

Extending the hypothesis, some pupils – mainly the faster learners or those willing to put more effort and time into their learning – were perhaps managing to decode the teaching they received better than most and make progress on the basis of it. Many others, however, failed to do so, and ended up perceiving language learning – as did their teachers – as a set of surface features: they worked through a long series of topics, collecting from each some set phrases or chunks, and taking part in activities involving the four skills. Any larger-scale factors, such as grammatical insights or indeed any real linguistic progression, seemed to pass them by. Small wonder that many such pupils – notably the average pupils mentioned above – ended up with limited capabilities in the foreign language. The most problematic context involved teachers with limited pedagogical understanding and skills (and in some cases insecure grasp of the language) working with pupils with little capacity to make sense of the teaching. Another factor affecting pupils' performance in MFL was the then low level of general literacy among pupils in the LEA's schools; there has recently been massive improvement here, however.

None of this is intended to be critical of the efforts of MFL teachers. The vast majority work immensely hard in the classroom to set up a range of what they hope will be stimulating and successful activities. The problems relate to the fact that languages are in fact very difficult to teach, requiring not only a thorough grasp of the language being taught but also an ability to teach learners to operate in the language in all four skills, all this while not only presenting the foreign language as the matter to be taught but also using it as the main vehicle for teaching it, and while working in a national context which is, to say the least, somewhat ambivalent about the value of learning foreign languages. But the absence of a clearly defined and agreed pedagogy is the biggest problem.

The research work

All these issues were beginning to emerge by around 1995 as a result of the LEA's monitoring work in schools, so by 1996 we had some thoughts about how things might move forward. Also in 1996, the LEA MFL team was invited by CILT to take part in a joint research project: an extremely valuable intervention. It was agreed that the focus should be pupil motivation in MFL, with special reference to average ability pupils in Year 9. Such pupils often seem to lose their interest in language learning as they approach Key Stage 4, and this obviously affects the effort they put into language learning and the standards they achieve. If the key could be found to increasing motivation for these pupils, their standards of achievement – and hence overall standards – would rise.

It was decided to concentrate on a group of Year 9 pupils who are often given less than their fair share of attention precisely because they do not demonstrate any particular needs or aptitude: they behave well, generally do as required, and do not perform either especially well or especially badly. Hence the title for the research report: 'The Invisible Child'. Sixty-two such pupils from all Barking and Dagenham secondary schools were interviewed, using a standard set of twenty-five questions.

The questions were designed to show the extent to which pupils were motivated in two respects:

- through *extrinsic motivation*: deriving from rewards, incentives, future job prospects, a sense of the importance of the subject;
- through *intrinsic motivation*: deriving from a personal interest in the subject, enjoyment in the pursuit of it, a learner's inbuilt drive to succeed.

Pupils were asked whether they liked MFL (i.e. felt intrinsically motivated to work at them) and whether they thought languages were important (extrinsic motivation). But more importantly, the questions were designed to identify factors which affect intrinsic motivation by exploring their perceptions and experiences of various aspects of language learning: the progress they thought they were making, the purpose of activities in class, the difficulties they experienced, and whether/how they managed to overcome them.

The questions were in five groups. The first four dealt with pupils' responses to their experiences of language learning and aspects of pupils' intrinsic motivation. The last group deals more with pupils' views of the importance of language learning, i.e. with extrinsic motivation. The examples quoted are indicative of the type of questions asked:

1   *Subject preference*
    Put these subjects in order of preference/Why do you prefer your first choice?
2   *Modern language lessons*
    What kind of things do you do in your modern language lessons?/Were you clear what you were supposed to learn from your last lesson?
3   *Language learning*
    What do you need in order to learn a language well?/What sort of problems do you come across when you are trying to learn?
4   *Progress*
    Do you think the standard of your work is getting higher? If so, in what ways?
5   *Attitudes*
    Is it important to learn a foreign language?/Do you feel differently about language learning now compared to when you started in Year 7?

The questions were designed to enable pupils to talk about routine classroom experiences in everyday terms, rather than special events such as visits abroad, valuable though they might be. The project needed to focus on standard teaching and learning operations, the representative day-to-day provision which most pupils receive; nothing will compensate if pupils have problems with, or are demotivated by, the things that occupy most of their MFL learning time.

How pupils responded

Subject preference

MFL ranked six out of a group of seven subjects. There was little gender difference. Pupils explained their choice on the basis of classroom experience, not on the actual or perceived importance of the subject.

Modern language lessons

Most said they thought they were doing fairly well, usually in terms of getting better at speaking, reading and writing and/or getting better marks. They did not refer, even in simple terms, to aspects of progression such as using more complex language or having a wider range of vocabulary. They had little to say about the value or enjoyment of various classroom activities; they said spoken repetition was helpful, as was listening to tapes, but otherwise they were largely indifferent despite the efforts of teachers to include a range of stimulating activities. Copying and drawing were disliked and judged unhelpful. Crucially, they found it very hard to say what had been the learning objectives in their most recent lesson: they referred to topic areas or said what they did, but could not define any linguistic focus. Many claimed to have achieved the objectives (even though they could not define them), on the grounds that they had completed a task or carried out an activity according to instructions.

Language learning

When asked to say what made a good language learner, pupils mentioned a range of general skills and linguistic aptitude. Many thought of these as things that one either had or lacked: pronunciation, for example, was not seen as something that could be worked at and improved. (This is evidence for learned helplessness, the state of mind which assumes that one's own efforts cannot bring about improvement – hence there is no point in trying: a major demotivator.) When asked to identify things they found hard when learning a language, they mentioned fundamental linguistic points such as pronunciation, remembering meanings, spellings, accents/diacritics, and making sentences (i.e. grammar). In other words, by Year 9, many pupils had made little progress on these crucial areas – and they knew it. They received much help from teachers, but this was usually designed to help them with the task in hand, or to get past the immediate obstacle, rather than giving them longer-term strategies. As an example, help might be given with the pronunciation of an individual word, but not on developing the ability to recognize common letter groups and pronounce them in a range of words. Pupils did not find their textbook useful as a source of help on these and other issues: its chief value was as a source of word lists.

Progress

When asked to describe their progress over the last three years, most said their standard had risen, but there was little consistency in how this was justified. Examples were knowing some more words, having longer conversations, getting better marks in tests. The work had become more demanding and teachers were encouraging. They did not speak of being taught techniques or strategies to help with their basic problems.

Attitudes

Almost all said they thought languages are important, though not necessarily for them personally. Parents apparently shared these views. Most thought girls did better in languages than boys simply because they concentrated more. 35 per cent said they felt more positive towards languages now that in Year 7; 37 per cent had not changed; and about 28 per cent felt less positive, largely because they lacked any intrinsic motivation.

What the responses indicate

An overall picture emerged of the pupils' experiences, their responses to them, and the progress they felt they were making. They talked about their modern language learning in mainly positive or neutral terms; very little came through as explicitly negative. Pupils thought their teachers worked hard on their behalf and were doing much to help them learn. Teachers had generally convinced them of the importance of learning a foreign language. Pupils relied heavily on their teachers and in most cases placed great trust in them.

However, the pupils had a limited view of the nature and process of learning a foreign language. They could not talk, in anything other than vague terms, about what they were intended to learn, what had been learnt, and the extent to which they were successful in their learning. They could talk about what they did in lessons, but not about what they had learnt and could do as a result. They described in Year 9 a similar experience to that in Year 7, but without some of the novelty value. Textbooks, video and IT were making little impact. Pupils described lessons in terms of activities and topics. A few mentioned producing longer sentences, but most made no reference to real linguistic progression in terms of, for example, tackling longer texts, producing more complex language, or being able to talk about the past.

These pupils, for all their 'invisibility', were interested in their education. They had plenty to say, and what they said was often illuminating, but they were not well-equipped readily to articulate it. They derived some enjoyment and a sense of progress from their work, but the value of much of what they did escaped them. Some were aware of things going on behind their work which they could not grasp. They were not criticizing their teachers in all this, but they may unwittingly have been describing the effect on them of representative approaches to modern language teaching, with its emphasis on chunks of language met in the context of a topic, and lessons containing mainly sequences of activities from textbooks.

Most or all of these pupils were, in their own eyes, failing to crack the code of language learning. They saw their teachers doing things in and with the language that seemed destined to remain beyond their grasp. On this basis they would certainly not be well prepared for Key Stage 4 and beyond, and their ability to work independently would be very limited. Possibly the reasons why so many pupils become more demotivated as they grow older are lurking here. A worst-case scenario would be something like this: they do not feel they do very well in languages, but they are not clear what 'doing well' means; they cannot articulate their problems so do not receive enough of the right support; they do not learn the language by osmosis, simply by doing endless rounds of activities; and the answer provided in much of KS4 – to do similar things all over again – is no more successful. Thus negative attitudes develop or are reinforced, born of repeated work and repeated failure.

Of course not all pupils will respond in this way, and many teachers provide very good teaching for many or all of their pupils; but perhaps the seeds of discontent among many learners of MFL lie within the picture described above.

Improving motivation

The central question then was how to improve the motivation of all pupils, but especially those such as were involved in the research. It could be considered as a set of linked sub-questions:

- Can pupils be helped to a higher level of motivation, and if so how?
- What can and should be done to promote positive beliefs and attitudes on the part of pupils?
- What kind of curriculum and teaching will promote this?

Some answers can be offered in the form of a set of principles for maximizing motivation levels. There are things to be brought about, and things to be avoided. The focus is on actual classroom practice, the day-to-day work with which teachers and pupils are regularly involved. The emphasis is also on enhancing intrinsic rather than extrinsic motivation, by looking for those factors which engage the learners most directly and personally with the learning.

Pupils need to have or to experience:

- a sense of achievement and a belief that they can improve;
- a realization that this stems from their own efforts rather than from random external factors;
- a sense of curiosity about the language they are learning;
- a clear understanding of what learning a language is about, including the terminology involved;
- the ability to know when they are making real progress in it;
- the realization that they are developing skills of language use and language learning and acquiring techniques of mastering new language and applying it in new situations;
- goals set for them which are challenging but achievable;
- helpful learning activities which are clearly not assessment tasks;
- feedback which shows them how to improve as well as indicating their standard;
- active involvement in the work of the lesson;
- a sense, in an appropriate way, of control over their work and progress.

They should not develop or receive:

- a belief that their personal efforts will have no effect on their standard and progress;
- a belief that aptitude for learning a language is something fixed and owned by others, rather than largely an issue of time needed for learning;
- a high level of test anxiety born of a fear that they are always being assessed;
- confusion over the nature and purpose of what they are doing;
- praise for doing an easy task with little effort;
- an excessive emphasis on extrinsic sources of motivation;
- lessons which involve them in long periods of passive working.

The curriculum and teaching

The research findings indicated that there could and should be extensive changes made to the development of modern language teaching and provision. The following sets out some proposals to underpin such work (which will enable teachers to meet the main requirements of the revised National Curriculum (NC) Programme of Study):

- The Modern Languages curriculum and its teaching need to be made much more transparent, so that pupils can see the purposes behind what they are doing, both in lessons and over time.
- A much clearer view of what constitutes appropriate *linguistic* progression is needed.
- The teaching should include clear and precisely specified learning intentions.
- A clearer view of pedagogical issues and an appropriate methodology for MFL teaching are needed, linked to an agreed terminology for the various aspects of MFL teaching.
- Pupils need time to master the various aspects of language learning, and more focused help to enable them to apply and manipulate the language they meet.
- The skills of language learning must be fixed in learners early if they are to develop independence later. This includes the understanding of principles which will help them in long-term learning, not simply the immediate problem with a word.
- Pupils must be taught effective and efficient ways of memorizing new language items.
- More importantly, however, pupils need to be taught the smaller words and features of a language which do not naturally arise in or belong to any topic (what could be termed the 'core' language): essential if pupils are to work beyond the level of the word list or their basic pre-learnt 'chunks'.
- Pupils need to be shown what constitutes a quality response at any level, and how to emulate it.
- Pupils need to be taught the precise techniques which they need in order to incorporate, for example, a new language item into known language, and then be given enough time to practise them.
- Pupils sometimes need help with and demonstration of basic routines such as how to set out their work, note new language items, etc.
- Curriculum, teaching and course materials need to take all the above into account. Teachers need to know in *precise terms* how a given set of materials is to be used, what they are for, and what learning is supposed to accrue from their use.

Where next?

All this emerged from the 'Invisible Child' research programme. The findings were set against the views which we had begun to develop earlier (see 'Context and rationale'). We found those views supported, amplified and to some extent explained by the research findings. To make sure that we were not unique and that Barking and Dagenham pupils were no different from any others, the findings have been presented to audiences of teachers and others in different parts of the country, often where different socio-economic conditions apply; we established that our findings were immediately recognized and accepted as likely to apply generally.

We also needed to help teachers to move forward, to address the problems rather than simply live with them or trust in short-term repairs (which usually do not work). What were the approaches to teaching which any MFL teacher could use and which would ensure pupils would not end up in Year 9 unclear about what learning a language involved, uncertain of so many basic points about the language they were learning, and frustrated because so much still seemed beyond them?

To take the work forward, we used the following categorization of teacher knowledge and skills:

- subject knowledge: their personal grasp and knowledge of the language;
- pedagogical knowledge: their ability to make the language learning process accessible to learners;
- craft knowledge: the ability to manage the classroom, organize the learning, establish good classroom control.

Our work would focus on pedagogical knowledge, the art of transmitting the language to the learners. A teacher with insufficient grasp of the language will always struggle, as will one who cannot relate to young people and get them to do what is needed in the classroom. But we were not looking for superstars, for teachers with massive charisma who rely on it for most of their teaching. An inspirational teacher is obviously a great asset to schools and learners, but we wanted to help *all* teachers to be and feel more successful in their teaching, by identifying things that any teacher with the necessary subject and craft knowledge would be able to do. We also argued that if pupils are clear on what they are doing and are better motivated as a result, classroom management is likely to be easier.

Key features of effective teaching

We were not in the business of telling teachers exactly what to do and how, but we needed to:

- help schools to provide teaching which matched our recommendations (see 'The curriculum and teaching');
- move teachers forward from mere adherence to the surface features (see 'Context and rationale');
- help to make the job of teaching languages more manageable and rewarding for all teachers and pupils alike.

Above all we needed to describe and exemplify what makes for effective teaching in MFL. The principal features which make MFL teaching effective (so that all pupils *learn* a foreign language as opposed to merely *doing* it) can be summarized as follows:

1   *MFL teachers in a school (and more widely) need a clear and consistent view of the language learning process* and give due attention in their teaching to:

   - knowledge of vocabulary, sounds and spellings and their relationships, and principles/patterns of structure and grammar;
   - skills of language use and language learning;
   - understanding of how language functions and its components work together;
   - techniques for, among other things, manipulating and combining items of language.

2   *Lessons need to have clear, detailed and precise linguistic learning objectives,* shared with and made clear to pupils and 'fixed' or reviewed at the end of the lesson.

3   *Explicit teaching of 'core language':* defined as those items and aspects of language which are not topic-specific: it includes (a) language essential to building sentences (points of grammar, key verbs, inflexions, patterns, etc.) and (b) the small but essential language items of general use (e.g. words for 'but', 'if', pronouns, gender markers, and everyday adjectives and adverbs). NB: in the guidance materials provided, topic-related items are called 'peripheral language'.

4   *Checking for learning throughout the lesson* to make sure all pupils have grasped a point or can do a specific thing.

5   *Frequent opportunities for pupils to practise and use* new vocabulary, techniques and concepts intensively and *to a high standard.*

6   *Modelling:* giving pupils a clear picture of what constitutes a *good* response to a task, at any level; and more importantly, of the process of producing it by emulating the expert, namely the teacher. This is a teaching stage, most helpfully used with writing and speaking, from one minute's pair work to the production of an extended piece of writing. Modelling involves working through something with pupils, pointing out how it is being done, what is needed to do it well and what the teacher will look for in any assessment, e.g. number of words, presence of adjectives, some complex multi-clause sentences.

7   *Demonstrating and teaching specific techniques,* e.g. how to pronounce the written word, how to learn vocabulary, efficient use of resources, reading for meaning. The teacher as expert in the craft of language learning, sharing that expertise with learners.

8   *Distinguishing between 'activities' and 'tasks':* the two words are often used interchangeably in text books and elsewhere. Hence the suggested distinction: an *activity,* for example practising the new language met last week, with access to help if need be (book, teacher, etc.); a *task* for which pupils will have to rely on

their own resources and learning and on which they will be assessed. Pupils need to know which they are doing.

9 *Discriminating feedback*: keeping the balance between valuing the *fact* of a pupil's contribution or response and its *quality. Not* automatically or indiscriminately praising pupils for work done; making it clear when responses or pieces of work are good and why, and actively helping others to produce them too.

Into the classroom

Teachers needed to be helped to put all this into practice, without re-learning their craft from scratch. The findings of the research and the principles for effective teaching have been presented to all our schools and teachers, along with written guidance on basic routines for the classroom to ensure that day-to-day practice is efficient and focused. Some pilot schools and teachers were identified and helped to develop their practice by building on what they already did and the materials they already used. The concept of a 'materials overlay' emerged: guidance showing among other things how to set learning objectives for a unit of work, covering knowledge, skills, understanding and techniques; how to identify the core language that pupils would need to master; how to check for learning; how and what to model. Two examples follow.

Examples of teaching guidance

These examples are based on two sub-units in *Équipe* Book 1. They consist of step-by-step guidance for teachers and accompanying OHP transparencies and worksheets. The aim was to ensure teachers do all the teaching needed to make sure *all* pupils can progress with the units and learn specific points of language. Some older courses did not lend themselves readily to this approach, and indeed the work has shown the need for much more carefully designed and structured teaching materials.

The materials are descriptive, rather than prescriptive: they show how a given unit or sub-unit can be taught effectively by incorporating the features that matter. They set out approaches to teaching which teachers can increasingly take over for themselves, adapting and modifying in the light of experience and circumstances.

The first is an early example; the second is more recent, with some changes to headings to reflect the revised NC terminology. In the first example, headings such as Ua and Wa refer to the relevant learning intentions: Ua = 'Understanding, item (a)'; Wa = 'Writing, item (a)'.

ÉQUIPE 1 – UNIT 1 – BIENVENUE!

Frères, soeurs et animaux

STEP 17 *(30 minutes)*

LEARNING INTENTIONS

Skills

Writing

All pupils will
a   be able to copy accurately a simple written account
b   be able to personalize the account by substituting peripheral vocabulary

Understanding

All pupils will
a   understand what a grave accent is, and learn the terminology
b   understand the purpose of, and how to use, the '*Expressions clés*' feature of the text book

PRESENTATION

Present transparency UN1E8, which is a simplified version of Nathalie's letter on page 18.

Ua

Draw attention to the grave accents (introduce the terminology *accent grave*) and the apostrophes.

PRACTICE

Wa

1   Pupils copy the text into their exercise books. Allow approx. 5 minutes. All pupils must begin promptly.
2   Insist that a great effort is made to write accurately and check work when complete.

Towards Wb, Ua

1   Work with the class to identify words/phrases which may need to be removed/replaced to create a personal account.
2   Pupils come to the front and underline these words on the OHT, as follows:
     Je m'appelle *Nathalie Delacroix*.
     J'ai *douze* ans et j'habite à *Dieppe*.
     J'ai *un frère et une soeur*.
     J'ai *un chien et deux chats*.

3   Ask pupils to underline them in their books.

4   Now ask four pupils to give their own personalized accounts (orally) by making substitutions. Begin with a more able pupil. End with a less able one. Insist on clear speech audible to the whole class.

CHECK FOR LEARNING

Ub, Wb

1   Check with the class that they can all write their own version and spell the words they need correctly. This could require reference to 'Expressions clés' on page 19, which provides negative statements (e.g. *je n'ai pas d'animal*) as well as positive ones.

2   Explain to pupils the use of the 'Expressions clés' feature as a revision aid.

3   Pupils write their own account. This should take place in class. It should be marked for communication and accuracy.

OHP TRANSPARENCY UN1E8

Je m'appelle Nathalie Delacroix.
J'ai douze ans et j'habite à Dieppe.
J'ai un frère, Sébastien, et une soeur, Isabelle.

ÉQUIPE 1 – UNIT 3 – J'AIME ÇA!

Les passe-temps

STEP 4 *(Estimated time 70 minutes)*

PUPILS SHOULD LEARN

Pupils work with a 'toolkit' and models to express preferences and opinions about leisure activities in writing.

LEARNING OUTCOMES

Pupils produce written sentences and/or paragraphs of up to 30 words expressing preferences and giving opinions.

POSSIBLE TEACHING ACTIVITIES

1   Display the '*boîte d'outils*' at the top of transparency WRTOOL.
    Point out the different types of language that can be used to create a written paragraph explaining preferences and opinions, i.e.
    (a) les expressions de préférence (*j'aime* … etc.)
    (b) les passe-temps (*la natation* etc.)
    (c) les adjectifs (*marrant* etc.)

(d) les expressions avec les adjectifs (*c'est* ... etc.)

(e) les petits mots importants (*mais* etc.)

2   Now reveal the three model passages from the OHP.

Ask pupils to explain what is good about each model, e.g. all models contain at least one expression from each box.

The final model contains *all* the expressions from

(a) les expressions de préférence (*j'aime* ... etc.) to

(b) les expressions avec les adjectifs (*c'est* ... etc.) to

(c) les petits mots importants (*mais* etc.).

3   Pupils write their own sentences and paragraphs. Allow 5 minutes. Before they start, give 2 minutes' thinking time – looking at the transparency – to prepare mentally. They may use reference materials if they wish to check on the spellings of different pastimes, etc.

4   Following marking, pupils could later memorize their accounts and reproduce them in class (5–10 minutes?) to inform National Curriculum assessment (AT4).

5   Worksheet GAPSSHT features gapped texts (supported and unsupported) with an emphasis on core vocabulary. This could be used for homework to prepare for and/or consolidate written competence. Quick oral preparation in class will ensure that all pupils can succeed.

POINT TO NOTE

Pupils should see that Exercise B provides a further example of recycling known language (i.e. the days of the week) with new language (i.e. expressions of liking and disliking.)

OHP TRANSPARENCY WRTOOL

j'aime ... *j'adore* ... *je n'aime pas* ... *je déteste* ...	*(la natation)* *(le skate)* *(l'ordinateur)* *(les animaux)*	*et* *aussi* *mais*
c'est ... *ce n'est pas* ...	*(marrant)* *(intéressant)* *(fatigant)*	

J'adore le skate et le tennis. Je n'aime pas la danse. C'est nul.

J'aime l'équitation. C'est génial! J'aime aussi les animaux et les jeux-vidéo. Je déteste le football et la pêche.

J'adore l'ordinateur. C'est intéressant. J'aime aussi les animaux, le cinéma et la peinture, mais je n'aime pas le vélo et je déteste la natation. Ce n'est pas marrant et c'est fatigant.

UNITÉ 3: J'AIME ÇA!

Les passe-temps, pages 36, 37

WORKSHEET GAPSSHT

Choisis le bon mot

Oui	pas	la
Cathy	et	C'est
intéressant	Tu	

EXERCICE A

Patrick: J'aime (1) natation. (2) aimes la natation aussi, (3)?
Cathy: (4), j'adore ça. (5) super! J'aime aussi la musique (6) la télévision.
Patrick: Moi, je n'aime (7) la télévision. Ce n'est pas (8).

Exemple

1   la

EXERCICE B

Nicole: J'aime les jeux (1). Et toi?
David: Non, je n'aime (2) ça. C'est nul! Tu (3) le cinéma?
Nicole: Oui, c'est super. J'aime aussi l'ordinateur (4) la peinture. Tu aimes (5) animaux?
David: Oui, j'adore les (6) et les chats, (7) je déteste les souris.
Nicole: Moi, j'aime les souris, mais (8) n'aime pas les serpents. (9) aimes le lundi, David?
David: Non, mais j'adore le vendredi et (10) samedi.

Exemple

1   vidéo

Conclusion

Developments locally have been in the right direction. The revised National Curriculum, together with its supporting schemes of work, makes the requirement to teach grammar and sound–spelling relationships much more explicit and should encourage teachers to rely less on the topic base, though it will take some time for new teaching materials to emerge and prove themselves.

Teachers and pupils involved in our local development work have responded positively so far: when asked questions similar to those put to the 'invisible' Year 9 pupils of two years ago, a large number of Year 7 and 8 pupils of all abilities could now readily identify the points of language they had been learning and language-learning skills such as the use of cognates to establish meaning. They are clear on the purpose of what they do. One school has decided not to set pupils as rigorously and so early as formerly, because all pupils are progressing satisfactorily in Year 7. Teachers involved with the pilot work have gained a consistent view of MFL teaching which enables them to share ideas more easily and gives them a reference grid against which to judge, for example, the quality of teaching materials, their own professional development, and even the quality of applicants for teaching posts. Teachers in the project, when taking on new pupils/groups in Year 8, know what has been taught and in what depth: expectations can thus be consistent year on year. Lessons now include a strongly reflective and cognitive strand, giving pupils time to master – not just meet – new language. Incidentally, the methods used (involving OHPs and many visual and written prompts) enable the target language to be used much more easily and consistently: it is, so to speak, no big deal.

Although the direction is in our view correct, some issues remain to be resolved. The need for new and more appropriate materials has been mentioned. The need for Year 7 to provide learners with a much firmer foundation for language learning has become self-evident, but the result has been that many of the standard topics have not been covered in the usual way. They could not be if pupils were to make the right start, but this means that the rate of learning and progress will need to accelerate in Year 8 and beyond. If the foundations are in place, however, pupils should be able to collect language more efficiently as time goes on, so that independent working becomes a reality for them. The National Literacy Strategy also promises to have a positive effect here.

Finally, the work in our pilot classrooms can look slow and rather flat to an observer used to the hectic non-stop round of activities often found in Year 7 classes. At times there is silence, but it is usually the silence of reflection, of mental processing, of concentration. It is also the silence born of the classroom conventions associated with interactive whole-class teaching (see 'Context and rationale'), where pupils are required to listen to each other and to speak to the whole class when giving a response: the teacher does not always repeat a response which is correct, nor praise it unnecessarily. Silence brings its own discomfort for teachers used to constant sound.

However, we will need to ensure that pupils have opportunities to use and learn language outside the central core work, and to be creative in its use. For this reason some project teachers are also involved in the TALK Project, run by Janeen Leith, which helps teachers to promote spontaneous talk in the classroom by pupils. The combination of a strongly cognitive and focused approach for core work, with time and space for pupils really to learn how to say the things they want to say, seems to us the right balance. Time will tell.

Note

1   The research work on which this chapter is based was carried out in the London Borough of Barking and Dagenham in 1997 as a study of the attitudes to the learning of modern foreign languages shown by Year 9 pupils of average ability. The full report is published by CILT as *The Invisible Child* (1998), by Jeff Lee, David Buckland (Advisory Teacher MFL, Barking and Dagenham LEA) and Glenis Shaw (Language Teaching Adviser, CILT).

    The term 'we' in this chapter refers to the MFL inspection and advisory team in Barking and Dagenham LEA, namely Jeff Lee and David Buckland.

17 Learning styles

The gender effect

Amanda Barton

Introduction

This chapter discusses the effect of gender on pupils' learning styles. While it is now well documented that learners approach foreign languages with a range of preferred learning styles – often grouped together under the generic headings of visual, auditory and kinaesthetic – relatively little has been written on the impact of gender on learning styles. Recent GCSE examination statistics suggest that gender is a significant variable in determining pupils' achievement: in 1999, 47 per cent of girls obtained an A*–C grade compared with 31 per cent of boys (DfEE Statistical Bulletin 1999). This gap seems to have increased over the last few years, rendering MFL the subject area in which the disparity between girls' and boys' performance is at its greatest.

Reasons for the gender imbalance

This chapter sets out from the premise that pupils' attitudes and approaches to language learning are shaped by numerous external influences which inform their socialization. The role played by parents, teachers, the media and the child's peers may place boys in a disadvantageous position with regard to language study.

From birth, boys and girls receive differential treatment according to their sex; parents may dress them differently, play with them differently and use different kinds of language in interaction with them. One study has revealed that while teachers tend to join in with boys' play, their interactions with girls are more verbal (Wilkinson and Marrett 1985). The kinds of toys given to boys and girls are often determined by the child's sex, and these may encourage differential learning styles. Boys' toys – for instance, cars, building kits and puzzles – foster manual dexterity, creativity and spatial ability. Girls' toys, by contrast, largely resemble human or animal life – dolls, ponies, soft toys, hairdressing models – and may promote human contact and communication. It has been suggested that the dearth of male primary school teachers is responsible for boys' devaluation of reading and writing, skills which they associate with female primary teachers (Millard 1997; Bleach 1998).

Some attempts have been made to explain the gender imbalance in MFL by referring to 'biological' arguments which focus on the physiological, hormonal and neurological differences between males and females (see, for instance Marrin 1997; Moir 1998). This chapter is not concerned with theories such as these. There are three reasons for this: first, media coverage of this kind of biological research is often misleading since it endeavours to engage human interest by glossing over significant, complex details, in order to create 'black and white' articles and programmes which appeal to large audiences by being both simplistic and sometimes sensationalist. Second, it would appear that scientists have yet to reach a consensus on their findings regarding linguistic aptitude; this field of research is characterized by considerable inconsistencies and contradictions. Third, and perhaps most importantly, the media dissemination of such theories often seems to confuse learning styles with abilities. Ability describes the individual's potential for success within a particular field, and it is of necessity restricted. Learning styles 'describe the ways individuals prefer to work' (Head 1996: 61). They are not strictly prescribed, in that individuals may select from a range of styles depending on the circumstances and may also adapt and develop their learning style to achieve the desired learning outcome (ibid.). To accept the argument that boys are not biologically predisposed to learning languages would be both defeatist and destructive, since it would involve imposing restrictive boundaries on boys' potential for developing their interactional and communicative skills.

Current texts on male and female learning styles stress that while patterns common to males and females respectively have been observed, the number of similarities found between the sexes may be equal to, or greater than, the number of differences (see, for instance, Murphy and Gipps 1996). While any study of boys' and girls' learning styles needs to bear this caveat in mind, common trends amongst adolescent males may be made more evident by peer pressure, to which boys are more susceptible than girls (Maccoby and Jacklin 1975), that forces them to conform to accepted norms of behaviour.

Background

The chapter relates some of the findings of research which set out to explore the reasons why so many boys fail to achieve their full potential in MFL. The research involved working with five UK secondary comprehensive schools who were endeavouring to raise pupils' achievement in the subject through piloting single-sex initiatives. The data was collected over a two-year period, from 1996–8, by means of interviews and informal discussion with pupils and staff, workshops with teachers, a range of questionnaires and classroom observation of pupils in Years 8, 9 and 10 (aged 13 to 15 years).

Boys' preferred learning styles

The following list summarizes traits perceived as common to boys who underachieve in languages and which were identified by teachers involved in workshops. They are not ranked according to their perceived importance:

- disorganized
- attention-seeking
- tendency to produce limited language
- mobile
- need variety, otherwise limited concentration
- show little responsibility for their own learning, blame others
- enjoy hi-tech work
- enjoy games
- poor at forward planning, looking at anything long-term
- enjoy creative, imaginative work
- curious about cultural background information
- appreciate a clear structure to work, clear sense of direction and progress
- appreciate rewards, reassurance, encouragement
- appreciate immediate feedback about performance and progress
- need to know that the subject has some vocational value
- enjoy competition

While many of these characteristics may be common to male adolescents regardless of which subject they are learning, they may be thrown into relief by a subject which, in many respects, does not conform to the adolescent male's expectations of work, and which may be invested with a feminine image. These traits are examined in greater depth below, with reference to the four Attainment Targets.

Listening

The difficulty of listening to a foreign language, particularly on audio cassette, is often commented upon by pupils of both sexes. Chambers' survey of 191 Year 9 pupils revealed that listening was the least popular of the four skills (Chambers 1993). It is generally recognized by researchers and teachers that boys' aural skills at this stage are inferior to girls' and that boys, especially, struggle with MFL as a subject which makes more demands on these skills than any other. Pupils in interviews frequently identified the speed of listening texts as the main problem and recognized that it is much easier to understand the familiar voice of the teacher who makes concessions with regard to pace. Boys and girls often commented that individual control over the speed at which the tape was played would facilitate listening and boost their confidence.

Responses to specific listening tasks

Boys often dismiss listening as a passive activity. Where the listening task has a 'hands-on' application, such as filling in a grid, or where it involves creativity, games or the use of visuals, boys' responses are commonly more positive than girls', as the results in the table show:

	Percentage of boys (n = 60)	Percentage of girls (n = 72)
Following directions from a tape to find a building on a map	28	12
Listening to a tape and filling in a grid	30	15
Listening to a description of someone wanted by the police and drawing that person	48	25
Watching videos	72	58

Classroom observation of a lower-ability boys' group provided a good example of the way in which boys are demotivated by listening tasks which have no clear purpose and involve listening for its own sake, and motivated by those which involve them filling in an information gap. The class quickly became restless when asked by the teacher to listen to one of the boys describing himself but became quiet and attentive when the task was modified so that they had to guess who in the class was being described.

Speaking

There is considerable research evidence to suggest that speaking is perceived by many boys as enjoyable, and in some cases as the most or only enjoyable aspect of the foreign language lesson. Almost a third of the boys in the 1983 sample for the HMI study *Boys and Modern Languages* mentioned oral work as their favourite activity and similar findings were described by Batters (1988) and Aplin (1991). The responses to a questionnaire, administered to 288 Year 8 pupils, seem to corroborate this theory: 'speaking' gained more of the boys' 'enjoy a lot' and 'enjoy' votes than any of the other three core skills.

It should not be assumed, however, that boys' enjoyment of speaking is automatic and unconditional. Speaking is not always taken seriously by boys who perceive that 'real' work involves writing and has a tangible outcome. There is also some evidence to suggest that boys' willingness to contribute in class may be dependent on their age; out of a sample of 799 pupils, 41 per cent of boys in Year 7 claimed to enjoy speaking, compared with 28 per cent in Year 8, 30 per cent in Year 9 and 18 per cent in Year 11. To some extent this was observed in classes in pupils' interactions with the teacher in the foreign language; while the Year 8 boys generally responded promptly to the teachers' questions in French, the Year 9 boys appeared to become increasingly reluctant to volunteer answers. In the Year 10 boys' group, hands were rarely raised and the teacher was forced to elicit answers by selecting respondents. It should be recognized, however, that these differences could also be attributed to other variables such as the teaching style and the relationship between the class and the teacher.

Older boys' reluctance to speak publicly in a foreign language may be attributed to peer pressures operating on male adolescents which cause them to interpret demonstrations of co-operation with the teacher, or academic diligence, as a threat to their image and status in the group. On a number of occasions, boys who seemed to enjoy a high profile in their respective groups in Years 9 and 10 by virtue of their non-co-operative, trend-setting male images, were observed to declare loudly their ignorance in response to the teacher's questions, when other evidence suggested that this was a sham.

Speaking was identified as a popular activity by both boys and girls in interviews, although more girls than boys expressed their dislike. The majority of boys and girls seemed to appreciate the comparatively greater practical value of learning how to speak a language rather than how to write it. Of 799 pupils who responded to the questionnaire statement, 'It is better to learn how to speak French/German rather than how to write it', 61 per cent of boys and 59 per cent of girls agreed.

In interviews a number of boys explained their choice of speaking as the most enjoyable activity by referring to the difficulties they experienced in writing, particularly with spelling:

(Year 10):   [I enjoy speaking.] I'm not so keen on the writing because I'm not very good at spelling it, but I can speak it better than I can write it ....

(Year 10):   If you're speaking you can say what you think and it might come out better than if you write it on paper.

Responses to specific speaking activities

Boys, it seems, respond very positively to speaking activities which involve drama and role-play, while girls are less enthusiastic. Enjoyment of this activity may be attributed to boys' general liking of drama; numerous boys in interviews cited drama as their favourite school subject, in contrast with only a handful of more assertive girls. A number of teachers attributed this preference to boys feeling more confident in a definite imaginary role as opposed to the uncertain role imposed on them in class.

'Moving around the class, interviewing others' proved to be almost equally popular with boys and girls. While mobility is often cited as an important variable in enhancing boys' learning, this suggests that girls may also respond positively to an active learning style. Boys are, however, often aware that their own lack of self-discipline may prevent them from participating sensibly in such an activity, as the following interview extract illustrates:

AB: How about this one, 'moving around the classroom ...'?
G: We ain't done that.

AB: But if you were to do it?
G: Chaos.
M: It would be funny, 'cos we'd all be messing about.
S: Everybody would be running around.

Reading

There would seem to be a significant disparity in boys' and girls' attitudes to reading in a foreign language, with girls responding far more enthusiastically than boys. Several reasons have been cited by academics to explain boys' lack of interest and inferior aptitude in reading across the curriculum: the feminine, passive image of reading; the unappealing content of reading material; and the necessary alienation of the reader from others, an isolation which boys, who crave the security of company, resent (Shaw 1995). In interviews, however, the large number of boys across the age-range who identified reading in a foreign language as unenjoyable generally gave the following reason for their dislike:

Boy (Year 9):   … the books don't know what level you're at, and there are words I've never seen before, and it confuses me.
Boy (Year 7):   I don't really like reading because I don't understand what they're saying. Miss has to tell you.

The 'they' mentioned in this second quotation refers to cartoon-strip characters in a textbook; this statement would seem to suggest that the frustration engendered by non-comprehension overrides the potential appeal of comic-style texts usually enjoyed by boys. It can also be inferred from the pupils' dependence on the teacher, often referred to in interviews, that pupils lack the knowledge or incentive to access unknown vocabulary in dictionaries or glossaries.

Girls sometimes associated their occasional dislike of reading with anxiety:

(Year 9):   If you don't understand you don't feel like asking the teacher in front of other people who can, who know the word.

Such anxiety is, however, more commonly a major reason for girls' liking of reading. One Year 10 girl, for instance, clarified her preference for reading and writing by adding that she was not confident enough to appreciate speaking French. More reserved boys were also more likely to express a more positive attitude to reading in preference to activities which demanded public participation.

Responses to specific reading tasks

Reading activities are generally more popular with boys if they involve physical activity, visuals or IT, as the findings in the table show:

	Percentage of boys (n = 60)		Percentage of girls (n = 72)	
	Enjoy	Dislike	Enjoy	Dislike
Reading cartoons/comics	67	5	39	7
Moving around the classroom, matching up signs on the walls with English signs on a list	47	8	39	18
Reading about the different way of life in France	22	25	29	19

The boys' enthusiasm for comics clearly contrasts with the girls' less positive response, and while the prospect of moving and reading text in a different medium appeals to large numbers of both sexes, dislike is registered by a greater number of girls. Both sexes demonstrate negative attitudes to reading for cultural background information, a task which has no practical outcome.

Writing

Boys' generally negative attitudes to writing, and the difficulty they experience in writing, is now well documented. The HMI study of boys and languages (1985) found that written work was one of the least popular activities with boys learning MFL, while Aplin more recently concluded that both sexes disliked writing more than anything else (1991), a conclusion confirmed by this study. Of 799 pupils who responded to a questionnaire, 50 per cent of boys registered a negative view, compared with 38 per cent of girls.

Most boys cited the difficulty they experience with spelling as their main reason for disliking writing. Writing was also sometimes criticized on the grounds that it was less useful than speaking and served no practical purpose. This point was more often made by boys, but also sometimes by girls:

Girl (Year 9):   If you go to France you're not going to write everything down, are you? It's not really important, writing.

Boy (Year 10):   [I enjoy it] when we do practical stuff like plays and someone has to read out their things and that. I don't like it when we're just, like, writing things out.

A handful of boys and girls also made the point that writing was difficult because they were unable to manipulate the language. One girl, observed in class, left the writing section on a test paper blank because, she said, she was unable to write sentences, and one boy commented:

(Year 8):   I don't like the writing because you don't know how to put things together, 'cos there's little things like 'is' that we'd say and you don't know the things like that.

Many pupils equated writing with copying from the board, an activity to which boys, particularly, do not respond well.

Responses to specific writing tasks

Formal, reading comprehension-style tasks are, it seems, disliked by both boys and girls, while there is a clear difference in responses to letter-writing tasks; such tasks are of considerably greater appeal to girls, even if the letter is to be sent to a real recipient. This suggests that when writing is given a practical outcome, in the form of a recipient who may respond, its appeal to boys is not automatically increased. Combining writing with visuals, in posters or cartoons, or writing a piece of drama which will be performed, seem to be more effective means of boosting both boys' and girls' motivation, as the following analysis of question-naire responses shows:

	Percentage of boys (n = 60)		Percentage of girls (n = 72)	
	Enjoy	Dislike	Enjoy	Dislike
Designing your own cartoon in French	65	8	47	10
Writing a role-play with a partner	35	18	35	8

Writing a letter can also be made much more appealing to boys if it is word-processed; IT is, it seems, a means of transforming the most mundane writing task into one of interest for boys and, to a slightly lesser extent, girls.

Activities most enjoyed by pupils in language lessons

Boys most often selected the following features as the most enjoyable aspects of learning a language: games; IT; activities which are regarded as practical or active, such as moving around the classroom to conduct a survey and making videos; and role-plays. Lower-ability pupils in particular often regarded games as the only redeeming feature of the subject:

AB: Where is French on a scale of subjects if your favourite is at the top and your worst at the bottom?

Lower-ability boy (Year 7): It's nearly at the bottom for me, just far from the bottom. That little bit at the bottom is just for the games.

Boys were particularly motivated by games and resented their disappearance from lessons; one boy nearing the end of Year 8 related how the teacher no longer played games with the class, a tendency also observed by HMI in older classes (1985). Boys of all abilities generally equated progress with fun:

High-ability boy (Year 9):   I feel I haven't learned nothing this year. I learned a lot
                        more last year. It was more fun last year.

Using IT was usually regarded as highly enjoyable; many of the boys in Year 10 in
one school selected a module based on a French software package as the most
enjoyable activity, and numerous boys claimed to enjoy playing computer games in
the target language.

    While girls also often picked out games as particularly enjoyable, they were more
likely than the boys to select passive activities which did not draw attention to
themselves, such as reading, writing postcards, doing projects and producing wall
displays. More self-confident girls, however, tended to select activities similar to
those chosen by the boys.

The importance of other variables

Both boys and girls seemed to favour working in pairs or groups rather than on their
own.

    Girls, however, appeared more confident that they were able to work effec-
tively in groups, pointing out that they preferred to be quietly corrected by a
partner than by the teacher in front of the class. In contrast, boys sometimes
demonstrated an awareness of not working well in groups, as a group of Year 8
boys admitted:

AB: Do you prefer speaking to the teacher or speaking in pairs or groups?
M: Speaking to the teacher.
S: Yeh, 'cos if we're in groups everyone tends to just cheat and …. [some
        laughter, general agreement]
D: The teacher knows what you're saying and people in your class only know
        as much French as you do, so they just ….
S: They can't really correct you.

While boys often seem to be heavily dependent on the teacher, they also value
being allowed to work independently. It is of interest that boys in interviews
frequently chose as their favourites those school subjects which are less tightly-
structured by the teacher and allow pupils to work at their own pace and enjoy
some freedom of movement: subjects such as such as Art, Technology, Music,
Drama and PE. The higher-ability Year 9 boys were observed to be working most
conscientiously and sensibly on tasks which were not strictly teacher-directed,
such as writing and producing display work. One Year 7 boy qualified his claim to
have enjoyed working in the computer room by adding:

    But it would help if she didn't walk around saying, 'You've done that wrong!'
    It'd be better if she'd just sit down and let us get on with it.

Homework and tests

Homework and tests were both rated highly by the boys who were asked about their importance in questionnaires. This point was often borne out in interviews with boys' reluctant admission of the necessity of tests:

(Year 8):   I don't like them but they make you remember.
(Year 9):   Having regular tests [is important]. I don't like them but it would make you learn better.

In contrast with girls, however, many boys were unaware of how to revise for tests, often lacking any knowledge of the range of strategies which could be used.

Competing

Boys are generally regarded as thriving on competition. Observation suggested that the younger the boys, the keener they were to compete with each other. A considerable number of the teachers of all-boys groups described capitalizing on the boys' interest in the progress of the parallel all-girls groups; competitions in singing, grammar and vocabulary knowledge were organized and perceived by teachers to be highly motivating, particularly for the boys. Boys in interviews often mentioned their interest in knowing how the girls were progressing and were keen not to fall behind. Such interest was rarely expressed by the girls.

Image awareness

An awareness of image, and the desire to maintain a 'cool' image in front of their peers, appear of much greater importance to boys than to girls. While boys often denied this in interviews, observation frequently confirmed it. Boys' behaviours in class were often characterized by confused expressions of inconsistency; boys in Year 10 seemed particularly sensitive to the threat posed to their image by doing well in class. This often caused them to react unfavourably to the teacher's attempts to commend them publicly or draw attention to them. In one instance, the teacher's warm compliments on an excellent poster were met with a mixture of pleasure and embarrassed grunts. When the teacher suggested that the work be shown to the headteacher, the boy uncertainly articulated a half-objection and suggested that his friend's poster be submitted instead. He refused to allow the researcher to see his work, pointing out its poor quality, a claim which was clearly inaccurate.

On another occasion the teacher's attempts to make the most potentially disruptive boy in the group the centrepiece of the lesson, by describing his road accident, were received by the boy with apparent apathy, which the teacher found to be extremely frustrating. The boy, who usually enjoyed being the centre of attention, could not, it seemed, resolve being thrust into the limelight by legitimate means; centre-stage was usually achieved through his own disruptive behaviour. It appeared that he could not risk damaging his well-established 'tough' image in class through complying with the teacher, even though the teacher was attempting to gratify him.

There are obvious difficulties in attributing boys' behaviours to their image awareness, particularly as boys seem to have little understanding themselves of the phenomenon when it is directly addressed. Contradictory behaviours in class, such as the two described, seem to point towards the confusion felt by boys in reconciling their desire to do well in the subject with continuing to enjoy the esteem of their friends.

The role of the teacher

Pupils of both sexes frequently indicated that the effect of individual teaching styles on their learning was paramount. Questions about the pupils' reasons for their enjoyment of the subject and their claims to be working hard were answered, in the overwhelming majority of cases, with references to the teacher's perceived competence:

Boy (Year 10):   It's actually because of the teacher. Years 7, 8 and 9 I found a bit boring because you just had to sit down and shut up and listen. This year there's a bit of humour in it as well …. We've got a good teacher.

Boys (Year 8):

M: We've had more of a laugh [this year], he's funny. It's because of the teacher ….

G: He's a good teacher. Star teacher definitely. You have to have a good teacher.

When pupils in single-sex groups were asked why they felt differently about learning French, most referred first of all to the change of teacher and teaching style. Many negative views derived from pupils comparing their current teacher's style with a previous teacher who they had perceived to be better. 'Having a good relationship with the teacher' was identified as important by boys and girls, while boys attributed more importance than girls to the teacher having a sense of humour.

Several pupils, particularly boys, were critical of teachers who failed to provide adequate or appropriate revision opportunities:

Boy (Year 9):   They don't give us a chance to go over the work we've done. They expect us to do a lot of it at home, but you don't do it because you think that's too hard, forget about it. We need some lessons where you revise. You forget about the things you've done in Year 7, the easy stuff.

Girl (Year 9):   If we don't understand a word she won't go back and explain it. We have to carry on to the next subject, so we just leave it, not understanding. That's why I've found it so hard.

The girls in this group also commented on the teacher's failure to revise the mistakes they had made in tests, which they regarded as a lost learning opportunity. Boys, particularly, appreciated teachers outlining the aims of the lesson at the outset and reviewing them at the end, lending a clear structure to the lesson.

Teachers' ideas of revision work do not, it seems, necessarily tally with pupils'; boys' preference for active, whole-class revision was expressed through objections from Year 9 boys when the teacher handed out worksheets intended to be worked through as revision.

A similar lack of coherence and continuity was noticed by pupils who were taught by different teachers from one year to the next. Girls in Year 8 highlighted the disadvantages of being taught by several different supply teachers within one year, each of which 'just did what they wanted to do'. One Year 8 boy underlined both the importance of the teacher explaining new concepts to pupils and implied the problems encountered when a change of teacher results in new learning habits being forced onto pupils:

> We're not learning as we did last year. We're doing it in a totally different way. It's a bit harder ... Last year we'd write it down and the teacher would explain it but, like, we don't this year. We've just got it on paper and we put it in our books.

Boys' preference for active learning, it seems, is not accommodated in the distribution of pre-printed vocabulary lists.

In interviews, most pupils seemed, on the whole, quite satisfied with the amount of target language spoken by the teacher in class; like tests, its necessity was given priority over the difficulty and frustration it sometimes caused.

The sex of the teacher

The issue of whether the sex of the teacher was perceived by pupils to affect their learning was also raised in questionnaires and interviews. The pupils' responses should be seen against a learning background dominated by female teachers; 52 per cent of the 799 pupils who responded to one questionnaire had had no experience of being taught by a male teacher. Conversely, only 4 per cent had ever been taught by males. Pupils' limited contact with male teachers of Modern Languages should be borne in mind when considering their responses.

Most pupils, it seems, are not convinced of the benefits of being taught by a teacher of the same sex as themselves. In response to the questionnaire item 'It's better to be taught by a teacher of the same sex as yourself', 47 per cent of pupils disagreed, while 36 per cent were unsure. In interviews, a considerable number claimed to perceive no difference between being taught by male and female teachers, some insisting that there were greater differences between individual teachers regardless of their sex, and that it was the quality of their teaching that mattered:

Boy (Year 9):   It's different teachers, not just different sex teachers, it's just different teachers really.

Boy (Year 9):   I've been taught by two women in French and I would just accept a man to teach us. I'm not bothered. I don't think there'd be any change. It's if you're being teached (sic) good. ... Not just like make everyone sit and give you a big lecture. They actually teach, they do games and all that ....

Some pupils in interviews who initially denied any differences in the teaching approaches of males and females, however, subsequently went on to describe some. This could, perhaps, be seen as confirmation that many pupils' initial answers were determined by their reluctance to be seen as sexist. Pupils' awareness of the teacher's sex does, however, appear to be heightened in single-sex groups.

Conclusion

Where differences exist between boys' and girls' learning styles, they should always be regarded with caution. It should be remembered that any gender-focused study will tend to highlight differences between the sexes, rather than similarities, and runs the risk of promoting stereotypes in an effort to deconstruct them. Boys, and girls, are clearly not homogenous groups, and numerous factors other than gender, such as ethnicity, social class and personality, influence pupils' learning styles and their achievement.

Consideration of generic male learning patterns, and the increasing imbalance in examination performance, do seem, however, to raise serious reservations about the intrinsic appeal of Modern Languages to boys, particularly if the teaching is modelled on a more traditional approach. Communicative language teaching, which relegates strictly academic practices in favour of an emphasis on authentic, purposeful communication might be supposed to enhance boys' learning. However, as the data above suggests, the answer is not to be found in a single model; while boys may appreciate some aspects of communicative teaching, such as 'information gap' exercises which demonstrate that language is a means to an end, there is also a suggestion implicit, for instance, in the views of boys who commented on revision, that a more formal, didactic approach, or at least a combination of methods determined by the needs of the group, might be preferable. The key, it seems, lies in the teacher's ability to differentiate his/her teaching style to accommodate the needs of the individual whose learning style is inevitably informed, to some degree, by his/her gender.

Further reading

Aplin, R. (1991) 'Why do pupils opt out of foreign language courses? A pilot study', *Educational Studies*, 17(1) 3–13.

Batters, J. (1988) 'Pupil and teacher perceptions of foreign language learning and teaching', unpublished PhD thesis, University of Bath.

Bleach, K. (1998) (ed.) *Raising Boys' Achievement in Schools*, Stoke-on-Trent: Trentham.

Chambers, G. (1993) 'Taking the "de" out of demotivation', *Language Learning Journal*, 7: 13–16.

Head, J. (1996) 'Gender identity and cognitive style', in P. Murphy and C. Gipps (eds) *Equity in the Classroom*.

HMI (1985) *Boys and Modern Languages*, London: DES.

Maccoby, E. and Jacklin, C. (1975) *The Psychology of Sex Differences*, Stanford: Stanford University Press.

Marrin, M. (1997) 'Mr. Evans is right about women MPs', *Sunday Telegraph*, 9 March.

Millard, E. (1997) *Differently Literate*, London: Falmer Press.

Moir, A. and B. (1998) *Why Men Don't Iron*, London, HarperCollins

Murphy, P. and Gipps, C. (eds.) (1996) *Equity in the Classroom*, London: Falmer.

Shaw, J. (1995) *Education, Gender and Anxiety*, London: Taylor & Francis.

Wilkinson, C. and Marrett, C. (eds) (1985) *Gender Influences in Classroom Interaction*, London: Academic Press Inc.

18 Spanish and English

Two ways of writing, two ways of reading

Salvador Estebanez

Introduction

There is a vast literature on the Psychology of Reading for English and a relatively scarce one for Spanish. In both cases we are still very far away from being able to provide a comprehensive model of the psychological processes involved in reading. In fact, reading is one of the more complex functions executed by the human mind; it involves 'lower order' visual processing, 'higher order' cognitive processes and the interaction of the two. Most of the literature centres upon the English language, but there is an implicit assumption that the results are universally valid, and yet there are strong linguistic arguments to question this catholicism. In a study of English as a second language (ESL) reading, Clarke (1980) found that adult Spanish speakers who were actually competent readers in their first language (L1) tended to revert to poor or inefficient reading strategies when they were asked to read English texts that exceeded their knowledge of the language. Clarke contends that proficient readers transfer their reading skills for the new language up to a point. A limited proficiency in the second language (L2) can 'short-circuit' the reader's system, and cause even a good reader to revert to poor reading strategies in the new language.

The aim of our research is to try to establish whether Spanish and English subjects (Ss) have different processing strategies when they read Spanish and English words respectively. In addition, if we find that there are different processing strategies at work, we will explore the plausible sources of those differences. Furthermore, we will investigate whether bilingual Ss in both languages keep the plausible distinctive strategies of each language or whether they adopt a new compound one.

How do monolingual subjects recognize written words?

Reading is a complex and dynamic process characterized by the interaction and co-operation of many skills, which are theoretically isolable in component skills analysis models. Yet 'reading' may not have a universal meaning. As Coltheart *et al.* (1980) suggest: 'Brains may be similar from one culture to another but orthographies certainly are not.' While all orthographies serve to transcribe the words of spoken language, they differ in the nature of the units they transcribe: alphabets transcribe phonemes; syllabaries, such as the Japanese Kana, transcribe syllables; and logographies, such as Chinese and the Japanese Kanji, transcribe words. Thus, it is plausible to suggest that different orthographies may give rise to readers using different sensory and cognitive processes in order to achieve word recognition. For example, Mann (1986) suggests that Japanese learners have the option of following a visual or a mixed phonological/visual route in learning how to read Japanese. His research suggests that Japanese schoolchildren, when they are learning new symbols, use the mixed route if they are good readers, and use only the visual route if they are poor readers. Chinese is also frequently cited as an example of a writing system which allows readers to access the meaning of its symbols without having to pronounce them, although recent research (Tzeng and Hung 1992) suggests that the reading of Chinese also involves reliance on phonological information.

Our research is centred upon possible perceptual differences between Spanish and English, which share a common alphabet. Therefore, it would appear that both languages have 'Phoenician' readers. Unfortunately, it may not be as simple as that. English and Spanish differ in at least two fundamental reading skills which we need to consider for the purpose of this research:

1   The visual perception of graphemic features, and in particular, the use of graphotactic regularities, i.e. systematic variations in the patterning of letters.
2   The ability to apply orthographic rules in spelling-to-sound translation, i.e. phonological recoding.

A reader has to see the written word first; this requires an initial process of visual decoding. Once this process is ended, the reader may or may not activate the auditory abstract representation which corresponds to the already activated visual representation. The reader then activates the corresponding lexical entry in the mental lexicon, having followed the visual and/or the auditory route. Finally, word recognition is achieved by the reader retrieving into awareness the meaning of the activated lexical entry.

It appears that there are at least two fundamental processes involved in decoding orthographies, which involve following the visual and/or the auditory routes from the written stimuli to the mental lexicon. Baron and Strawson (1976) call 'Phoenicians' individuals who rely heavily on spelling–sound correspondence rules, and whose reading behaviour is characterized by a tendency to read regular words well, but to misread exceptional words. The individuals who rely on word-specific associations are called 'Chinese' readers. They read regular and irregular words well as long as they are familiar, but cope badly with any unfamiliar word. It is possible to suggest that even languages which share the same script but have different orthographic systems may be processed in different ways. In particular, it is plausible to suggest that English, although it has an alphabetical script, may be read in 'Chinese' fashion; otherwise, how can we arrive at the correct pronunciation of the words 'enough' and 'though'? Conversely, given the highly regular orthography of Spanish, most Spanish Ss might be 'Phoenicians' because they may not need to develop the 'direct route', that is, the 'visual route'.

How do bilingual subjects recognize written words?

Given the difficulty of establishing the processes involved in written word recognition by monolingual speakers, it may appear overambitious to research the processes followed by bilingual readers. Indeed, the comparison of reading acquisition in L1 and L2 is rather complex:

- the skills of L1 reading may interact with the acquisition of L2 reading skills: the similarities and differences between L1 and L2 may facilitate transference or may cause interference;
- Ss learn to read L1 after oral acquisition; in L2 they mostly acquire both skills simultaneously.

However, studying Ss acquiring an L2 offers at least one clear advantage: cognitive development and acquisition of the first language occur simultaneously; this means that it is often difficult to separate the two. In the case of a youngster or adult learning a second language, there is no further significant cognitive development. Thus, by looking at L2 acquisition, it can be inferred which processes are similar to L1 and therefore must have a linguistic origin, and which processes are different and can be attributed to cognitive development.

It is plausible to suggest that the variations between languages in the mapping relation between writing and speech may result in different literacy skills. Unfortunately, there are many possible sources of differences. Without intending to provide a comprehensive list, we can suggest the more obvious: the processing of individual graphemes; the rules that control the grouping of graphemes; the degree of regular correspondence between spoken language and orthography; the degree of phonemic and graphemic redundancy; and also reading habits.

If different languages have different visual strategies for word recognition, they may give rise to conflicting processing strategies in visual recognition in L1 and L2. In particular, emerging L2 literacy skills may suffer from interference from an L1 which has a different script. Alternatively, L2 literacy may be helped by a similar script in L1.

Are Spanish and English different? Linguistic differences as potential sources of specific word recognition strategies

English and Spanish are two relatively close languages in the context of world languages. In particular, they have in common the Roman script. There are, however, many linguistic differences – at the phonological, morphological, syntactical and lexical levels – between the two.

Phonemic/graphemic level

Spanish has a much higher regular correspondence between graphemes and phonemes than English. There are thirty-eight phonemes in English versus twenty-four in Spanish; i.e. English has 58 per cent more phonemes than Spanish. In particular, it has twelve vowel phonemes versus five in Spanish. However, Spanish and English have the same five vowel graphemes. Clearly, these vowel differences are at the root of the complexity of English orthography versus the simplicity of the Spanish one. Table 18.1 provides an account of the number of phonemes and graphemes for Spanish and English.

Table 18.1 Comparative phonemic/graphemic analysis

		English	*Spanish*
Consonant	Phonemes	24	19
	Graphemes	21	24 (ch,ll,ñ)
Vowel	Phonemes	12	5
	Graphemes	5	5

Hanna *et al.* (1966) identify the graphemic representations of all phonemes in English. For example, the phonemes /a/ and /k/ have sixteen and thirteen different representations each. Therefore, phonographically, English has many more representational units than the twenty-six alphabetic signs. Spanish, on the other hand, has twenty-nine alphabetic signs, including the ñ, and the digraphs *ch* and *ll*. After allowing for allophonic variation, Spanish has a fairly regular phonographic representation. The main source of spelling difficulties are: the use of *b/v* which are phonemically identical, the use of *g/j* followed by *e/i*, the mute *h*, and the *ll/y* whose phonemic difference is being lost. These spelling difficulties in Spanish can be greatly alleviated by simple explicit graphotactic rules.

There is a higher ratio of vowels to consonants in Spanish words. Besides, Spanish tends to follow a CVCV structure whereas English favours consonantal clusters. The clear syllabic structure of Spanish allows Spanish readers to segment words easily. It seems that there is no reliable segmenting procedure in English that would result in a correct translation of graphemes into sound. Venezky (1970) conducted the most comprehensive examination of the grapheme-to-phoneme translation in English. He concluded that graphemic patterns can only be classified according to the degree of predictability in terms of their translation into sounds. It seems, therefore, that Spanish has a higher phonographic regularity and analyticity than English.

Syllabic level

Spanish has a much simpler syllabic structure than English: there are a few hundred Spanish syllables versus many thousands in English. For example, after a vowel, in the same syllable, the Spanish speaker can choose either a single consonant or none at all; he cannot choose two or more consonants as the English speaker can. The English speaker can choose a single consonant phoneme, eg. *limb* /lim/; two: *limp* /limp/; three: *limps* /limps/; or even four: *glimpsed* /glimpst/. Another example of differences concerns word endings: Spanish only allows eight single consonantal phonemes as word endings, /s/ /T/ /m/ /n/ /l/ /r/ /y/ /w/, and no clusters.

Morphemic level

It has been claimed that English orthography represents morphology rather than phonetics. Frequently, phonetic information is sacrificed in favour of morphology; for example, the silent grapheme in *damn* is preserved and is sounded in *damnation*. The inflectional morphology for the plural is orthograhically represented as either *-s* or *-es*, whereas the phonemes include /z/ /iz/ /s/. The past tense is represented as *-ed* and yet the phonemes are /t/ /d/ /id/. Thus, the morphographic representation remains constant in spite of the phonetic variation. In derivational morphology the case is even more compelling; for example, we have *phóto-graph*, *photó-grapher*, *photo-gráph-ic*. In this example, in addition to phonemic changes, there is also a systematic change in the pattern of stress.

Most Spanish words contain overt morphological endings: number, tense, person and aspect in verbs; gender and number for nouns and adjectives. Morphology and phonology have equal status.

Visual lexical density: orthographic neighbourhoods

Spanish words, on the whole, tend to be rather longer than their English counterparts, or rather there is a complex interaction between length and frequency in these two languages. English has a higher proportion of short words among its most frequent items, whereas Spanish high frequency items tend to be longer than in English; this difference gets smaller with infrequent words. For example, there are a very large number of four-letter words in English. This means that it is often possible to produce a large number of other four-letter words which differ from an originally given word by just one letter.

If we compare Spanish words in the same way, there is some indication that the one-letter replacement sets tend to be rather smaller than is the case for English. Table 18.2 compares the sets of words derived from the word 'mire' in English and in Spanish.

We can see that the replacement sets of Spanish words are considerably smaller than those of English words. It seems, then, that there are fewer orthographic neighbours in Spanish than in English words, especially when short and frequent words are considered. This higher visual density of English words may give rise to specific attentional processes, for example English Ss having to choose between a larger number of activated lexical entries.

Table 18.2 Sets of words derived from 'mire'

English				Spanish			
dire	mare	mile	miry	gire	more	mine	mira
eire	mere	mime		tire		mime	miro
fire	more	mine		vire			miró
hire		mise					
pire		mite					
sire							
tire							
wire							

Asymmetry of correspondences in reading and spelling

Another linguistic characteristic which may have considerable implication for word recognition procedures is the much greater asymmetry of correspondences in reading and spelling in English than in Spanish. According to Hanna *et al.* (1966) there are fifty-two phonemes corresponding to 102 graphemic patterns in English. It is clear that the ambiguity of correspondence is much greater in spelling than in reading; for example, the word *thief* can be considered regular from the point of view of reading but irregular from the point of view of spelling. In Spanish the word *hacer* can only be read in one way; if we heard it we could spell it as *hacer* or *acer* since the *h* is mute. However, apart from the specific spelling difficulties previously mentioned, Spanish has a fairly symmetrical correspondence between reading and spelling.

Conclusion

It is plausible to suggest that the various linguistic differences between Spanish and English, previously analysed, may give rise to distinctive processing strategies used by Spanish and English Ss when recognizing written words. The next section explores which strategies might be affected.

Plausible specific word recognition strategies in Spanish and English based on linguistic differences

Holistic versus component procedures

Chinese and Japanese Kanji are logographic languages, i.e. each word is represented by a written symbol. English and Spanish are both Roman alphabetical languages. It could be suggested that the Chinese and Japanese read words holistically, whereas English and Spanish read words by identifying the individual component letters first. However, there are several linguistic factors that may make the process of recognizing English words closer to Chinese than to Spanish:

1   Spanish has simpler phono/graphotactics than English: Spanish phonotactics allow for a few hundred different syllables, whereas English has many thousands. In English, there are many graphs, digraphs and poligraphs which represent a consonantal phoneme. In order to pronounce them correctly the corresponding word must be visually perceived in its entirety, because only then can one be certain of how to pronounce it. An example is the pronunciation of *ough* in *tough, though, hiccough, cough*.

2   A consequence of the limited consonantal clustering range which is possible in Spanish is that Spanish words may be less appropriate for holistic perception. This is due to the fact that consonants provide all the ascenders and descenders in a word, which are essential for the design of whole-word envelopes. English Ss, on the other hand, may be able to perceive distinctive word contours, given the thousands of consonantal clusters available. This may result in English Ss relying more on holistic perception rather than on letter-level encoding.

3   The units of recognition in a word may be different for the two languages: the basic unit of oral Spanish is the syllable; in English, it is the stress group, which tends to coincide with the full word. How can English Ss decide the correct stress for *convict* – noun or verb – without first accessing the mental lexicon? Spanish, on the other hand, has the diacritic accent, *canto/cantó*, (song/sang). The English reader, besides relying on holistic word perception, has to infer from contextual meaning the difference between *insult/insult*. Spanish readers can rely on the diacritic accent to continue using syllabic processing towards word recognition: *hablo/habló*.

4   Spanish Ss do not need prior access to the mental lexicon in order to assign the phonemes to a written word whereas English Ss do for many words. Otherwise, how can an English reader assign the correct pronunciation to homographs? The words *row* or *tear* require not only perception of the whole word; contextual meaning must also be taken into account in order to assign them the correct pronunciation.

5   In English it is clear that the ambiguity of correspondence is much greater in spelling than in reading, whereas in Spanish there is hardly any ambiguity in either direction. This difference in asymmetry between reading and spelling in English and Spanish may mean that in English, Ss are much better readers than writers (spellers), whereas this may not apply to the same extent to Spanish Ss. A child already has an auditory mental lexicon developed when he/she encounters the written word. Thus, a written representation of that word-sound, however irregular, suffices to achieve recognition. However, when it comes to spelling, the child has no visual mental lexicon. In dictation, the English child probably has to rely more on memory, recalling the whole written representation of the word, whereas the Spanish child can rely more on the regular correspondence of phonemes to graphemes. In time, this may result in English Ss using holistic procedures in word recognition whereas Spanish Ss may depend more on bottom-up strategies.

The visual versus the auditory route to the mental lexicon

Chinese readers, having a logographic orthography without reference to sound, may read without activation of the pronunciation. On the other hand, English and Spanish readers, having the Roman alphabet and a direct relation between sound and orthography, may activate the pronunciation of the words, even if they are reading silently. However, Spanish words compared with English words are characterized by their regular orthography. English, being phonetically irregular, may encourage the use of the visual lexical route in reading – the reader picks up the word without it recurring or referring to the phonological processing unit; whereas Spanish, being phonetically regular, may also use the phonological route – involving the activation of phonemes in order to recognize the word. This difference is reflected in the popularity of the 'look and say' reading methods for English, and the use of syllabic reading methods for Spanish.

The difference in orthographic regularity is particularly significant in the case of vowels. Spanish with five phonemes to five graphemes seems to make the activation of the phonological route unavoidable, whereas English, with twelve phonemes to five graphemes, may discourage phonological activation.

Visual lexical density: orthographic neighbourhoods

Another linguistic factor which may give rise to a different processing strategy is the different visual lexical density of Spanish and English. Spanish words, on the whole, tend to be rather longer than their English counterparts, or, rather, there is a complex interaction between length and frequency in these two languages: English has a higher proportion of short words among its most frequent items, whereas Spanish high frequency items tend to be longer than in English.

The lesser visual density of Spanish words is due to the very limited range of consonantal variation in Spanish. These phonographic differences may give rise to a different processing strategy for consonants and vowels between English and Spanish.

The morphophonemic factor

The morphophonemic nature of English orthography, reflecting meaning more efficiently than sound, may reinforce the direct access to the visual mental lexicon without activation of the auditory equivalent. It may be that English Ss process written English logographically (Smith 1979; Massaro 1975c) whereas Spanish Ss process written Spanish phonographically, i.e. a direct translation between spelling and sound which does not involve the consultation of the mental lexicon. In other words, the English writing system seems to be constructed to convey meaning first, and to be read aloud second.

The converse seems to be true for Spanish orthography. Spanish verbs, nouns and adjectives are inflected by means of suffixes. Thus, Spanish speakers are deprived of the final clues in words; for example, citation forms of verbs in Spanish are marked with one of three endings in the infinitive case: *AR, ER, IR*. These endings undergo changes if the verb is used in context; while the stem of the verb usually, though not always, remains unaltered: the forms *mira, mire, miró* are part of the verb *mirar*. This raises the question of whether five-letter verbs such as *mirar*, *comer* and *vivir* are effectively handled as three-letter words with largely predictable inflections. A similar case can be made for nouns and adjectives to be treated as a stem plus an inflection.

Preliminary conclusion

We have described linguistic differences between English and Spanish orthographies which may influence the way in which Spanish and English Ss may process written words. We have argued that the evidence points towards English Ss using holistic procedures to recognize English words whereas Spanish Ss may rely more on bottom-up processing for the recognition of Spanish words. Furthermore, it is possible that Spanish Ss may rely more than English Ss on phonological activation for word recognition.

The linguistic differences between English and Spanish are real enough. However, no amount of descriptive linguistics and plausible hypotheses about psychological procedures are evidence of what subjects actually do. Thus, throughout the next experimental phase, there is a need to differentiate clearly between 'linguistic characteristics', such as English having a larger number of phonemes than Spanish, and 'psychological procedures' that may or may not be influenced by the former. The hypotheses have to be experimentally tested in order to prove their validity. The first stages of this research will try to prove that Spanish and English Ss do in fact use different recognition procedures. If the answer is positive, subsequent experiments will attempt to isolate the specific linguistic differences that may be responsible for the distinct recognition patterns detected in native speakers of each language.

Methodology

Experimental analysis centred on visual recognition has been present in Psychology since its beginning as an empirical science. In particular, perception of the written representations of 'linguistic units' – graphemes, morphemes, written words, clauses and sentences – has a well-established line of research. However, one of the most fundamental and persistent difficulties in visual recognition is separating the cognitive from sensory factors and the interaction between the two. In particular, visual word recognition represents the best example in which cognitive factors are clearly influencing the perception of the visual stimuli. Subjects are clearly affected by syntactic and semantic factors when dealing with the recognition of written words. But subjects are also likely to be affected even at a more basic level, at the graphemic level. The basic components of visual stimuli in words, the graphemes, are a special subset of the shapes category. This subset has the following characteristics: a finite set, nameable, very familiar, and they are the constituents of words. Thus, it is plausible to suggest that given these characteristics of the graphemes, Ss may process graphemes in a different way to arrays of shapes in general, even before morphological, syntactic or semantic factors are taken into account.

Our experimental technique

The experimental technique used in this study is based on Hammond and Green's (1982) which they themselves had adapted from Phillips (1971). Ss are required to look at a target on a screen and subsequently decide whether or not the target is present in a displayed array. The *time* it takes to make such a decision is the basic information on which the pattern of visual recognition is based. The subject registers his/her decision by pressing either the *YES* or the *NO* key. It is the simplicity of this task that makes it so appropriate for this research.

Procedure

All Ss receive oral instructions in their mother tongue. Essentially the instructions state that individuals look at a character presented on a screen (one of twenty-six capital letters of the alphabet), and then determine whether the shown character is present or not in a subsequent array of characters. They are required to press the key marked *YES* if it is present, and the key marked *NO* if it is not. In half of the trials, randomly selected, the pre-designated target is in the array; in the remaining half it is not. When the target does occur in the array, it is located equally, often at each character position. Targets and array elements are selected at random from the character set. Responses are to be made as accurately and as rapidly as possible. Half of the Ss in each group answer *YES* with their right hand and *NO* with their left; the other half do vice versa; in other words, the assignment of hands to keys is counterbalanced across Ss.

Results

The main analysis concerns the Reaction Times (RTs) for correct *YES/SI* responses. The mean latency for correct target detections – as a function of the position of the match within the screen – is calculated for each subject. The software also records the RTs for the *NO* responses, as well as the speed and number of errors in order to establish any trade-off between the two. A series of analyses of statistical variance (ANOVAs) is conducted to assess the statistical significance of the results.

Psycholinguistic interpretation: word recognition models

Unfortunately, there is not a consensus among researchers about a word recognition model. Basically, there are three types:

1   The letter-integration model: it predicts that word recognition is preceded by a letter-identification stage (Gough 1972).
2   The holistic model: it predicts that the cognitive encoding of words always occurs at the word level first, and that component-level encoding occurs only after word-level encoding is complete.
3   The race model: it predicts that the encoding process is viewed as occurring at feature, letter, and word levels simultaneously, with the ultimate level of representation being the one whose level of encoding is completed first (Healey and Drewnowski 1983).

There are enough reported data to support all three models. However, the letter-integration one is out of favour among researchers at present. Researchers are having an intensive debate in favour of either the race or the holistic model.

Application of the experimental technique to this research

In determining the scanning strategy for linguistic stimuli, the cognitive factors must themselves be influenced by the linguistic characteristics of the language of the subject. Different writing systems might encourage their readers to develop characteristic search procedures depending on how the writing system works. Learning a new writing system might involve not just the acquisition of a new set of symbols, but also the acquisition of a new set of procedures. If this is the case, the search functions of a non-native speaker of a language may be different from the search functions of a native speaker of the same language. Furthermore, the search functions of the non-native speaker may change over time with increased linguistic proficiency in L2 in general, and increased experience in the L2 script in particular.

Specifically, the aim of this research is to try to establish the existence of specific visual processing strategies in word recognition for Spanish and English. The individual visual units, the graphemes, are identical for both languages since they share the Roman alphabet. Thus, any differences that may be detected must be due to the language-specific patterns of clustering those graphemes into words, and their phonological translations.

First experimental stage: Experiments I to IV

In Experiments I to IV we used the described forced-choice visual recognition matching task: Ss were required to look at a target on the screen and subsequently decide whether or not it was present in an array. This technique was introduced to explore the role that letter position plays in word recognition. We conducted four experiments. In the first one we wanted to establish whether the universally-claimed U-shaped RT-function for non-alphanumeric stimuli was in fact produced by Spanish Ss, as well as by English Ss. The results of Experiment I established that Spanish and English Ss do produce a similar type of response, in terms of speed and position, when the stimuli consists of arrays of non-letters. This first finding eliminates the possibility that any differences that we could subsequently find in the processing of letters by English and Spanish Ss might have had an unspecified non-linguistic origin. In this experiment, both groups of Ss produced a similar U-shaped RT-function, which reflects a search procedure that begins at the centre and then maps the array in a sideways fashion.

The next step was to substitute the non-letter stimuli with letters. The following examples illustrate what the subject sees on the screen: the target and the array:

	Experiment II	*Experiment III*	*Experiment IV*	*Experiment IV*
Target	v	la	t	r
Array	varot	matelopasu	blast	colar

This was done for single letters in Experiment II, and for syllables in Experiment III. The array of letters was randomly generated by a computer. Each letter had an equal chance of being selected, with only one condition: that no letter could appear more than once in the array. We assumed that this generative procedure would result in arrays which would not look at all like any real Spanish or English words. Thus, we wanted to establish whether or not Spanish and English Ss would process non-language-specific arrays of letters in a similar fashion. The results clearly established two different processing strategies: English Ss produced the typical M-shaped RT-function (Hammond and Green 1982), whereas Spanish Ss were significantly slower and continued to produce the U-shaped RT-function typical of non-letters.

The word activation procedures followed by English Ss resulted in both ends of the array, and especially the left one being recognized significantly faster, as opposed to significantly slower in the case of non-letters. We interpreted these results according to the race models in word recognition: the RT advantage of the beginning and end of the array may be explained in terms of whole-word encoding strategies winning the race in the case of English Ss. On the other hand, the non-word strategies followed by the Spanish Ss resulted in the U-shape RT-function, which was similar to the one obtained for non-letters.

As in the experiments that prompted this research, Spanish Ss continued to produce significantly slower latencies. Why would English Ss identify individual letters in a randomized array faster than Spanish Ss? And perhaps more importantly, why does the RT-function differ so significantly for the initial and final positions of the array? Initially, we proposed that the slower latencies of the Spanish Ss might have been due to two factors:

1 the loss of any potential RT advantage which might have been due to the use of holistic procedures;
2 the likely phonological activation of the target letter, which in Spanish means that it is probably preceded by the article *la*; for example, when Ss see *o* on the screen, they would keep it in the short-term memory (STM) as /lao/.

Consequently, this longer phonological string might have slowed down the matching procedure.

We analysed the randomized letter array in terms of graphotactics and concluded that it had a closer resemblance to an English word than to a Spanish one. Consequently, we inferred that English Ss might be scanning the array as if it were an English word, whereas Spanish Ss were not scanning it as a Spanish word. We reasoned that English Ss, due to the irregularity of English orthography, automatically apply ordinary word recognition strategies. Specifically, they extract positional and sequential information of individual letters, the initial and final positions having particular perceptual salience. The application of these procedures results in English Ss achieving faster retrieval into awareness of the presence of a target letter in the array.

Since the randomized array in Experiment II was sufficient to trigger word recognition strategies in English Ss, we decided to have an array with a Spanish look in Experiment III. Ss had to identify a previously shown syllable (CV) in a meaningless syllabic array, made up of five CV syllables. Thus, the stimuli reflected the very regular syllabic structure of the Spanish language. The results, however, continued to be similar: English Ss produced the M-shaped function, and the Spanish the U-shaped one. Clearly, Spanish Ss dealing with the identification of target units in meaningless letter arrays do not activate real-word recognition procedures, whereas English Ss do.

By this stage we were convinced that English Ss were processing the various meaningless arrays as real words, and yet, so far, we had not used English words. Therefore, we used real words in Experiment IV to see if our previous conclusions were correct. In addition, we deduced that if latencies for Experiment IV were similar to those in previous experiments, we could conclude that the identification of individual letters is not facilitated by the letters being part of a word. In other words, there is no lexical facilitation effect. This would mean that letter identification takes place before lexical access to the mental lexicon. If that is the case, it would provide support for the letter-integrative models in word recognition. If, on the other hand, latencies were significantly smaller, the implication would be that there was a facilitating lexical effect in letter identification, and this would support holistic models: Ss perceive the whole array first and, subsequently, descend into sub-lexical analysis. As whole words are perceived faster than non-words, Ss should show smaller latencies in letter identification, reflecting the RT advantage in the holistic stage of perception.

The results from Experiment IV confirmed that English Ss were using word recognition strategies in randomized arrays, i.e. they produced similar RT-functions. They benefited from using real words by producing smaller latencies, but we could not conclude that there was a lexical facilitating effect, because the result was just outside the 5 per cent significance level. The bilingual E-group produced a remarkably similar function to the monolingual English group. This result strongly supports the hypothesis that bilingual Ss develop L2 specific word recognition strategies.

Contrary to expectations, Spanish Ss did not produce a different RT-function.

Thus, the introduction of real Spanish words did not alter their recognition procedures. This seems to provide evidence that Spanish Ss, when trying to identify the
presence of a letter in a word, scan the word in the same way as they would meaningless arrays: a rather flat RT-function without special attention paid to initial and
final positions. They continued to produce significantly longer latencies than
English Ss. Again, the bilingual S-group produced a remarkably similar function to
the monolingual Spanish group.

The introduction of *meaning* in the array in Experiment IV had not produced a
modification of the RT-function. It appears that the semantic component of the
word, and therefore the likely access to the semantic mental lexicon, does not seem
to affect the search procedures of the array when Ss are looking for a target letter.
As Blum and Johnson (1993) suggest, there does not seem to be a lexical facilitating effect when the task is to decide whether a target letter is present in a word.
Our results confirm Blum and Johnson's conclusion, and we had used very high
frequency words.

Thus far, the results from the experimental technique employed in Experiments
I to IV – target letter identification in an array – provided us with strong support for
our main hypothesis: the existence of different word recognition strategies for
Spanish and English. The differences between English and Spanish Ss seemed to
point towards English Ss benefiting from some holistic procedures – shorter latencies for beginnings and endings of the array – whereas the Spanish Ss did not. We
concluded that Spanish Ss were less dependent on positional and sequential information than English Ss. We reasoned that the higher visual density of English
orthography, with a higher number of orthographic neighbours, resulted in less
redundant positional and sequential information in English words than is the case
in Spanish words, for example, *tap, pat, apt* or *hat, hit, hot, hut*. As a result, English
readers need to develop, to a larger extent than Spanish readers, word recognition
strategies that take positional and sequential information.

At this point, we were beginning to make strong claims which were totally
dependent on one experimental technique. Therefore, another technique had to
be introduced in order to substantiate our claims and to enable us to continue our
research.

Second experimental stage: Experiments V and VI

In the first experimental stage, we had established that English Ss apply word
recognition strategies to the identification of letters in arrays whereas Spanish Ss
did not. Furthermore, the strategies applied by English Ss were not dependent on
pronounceability or lexical access. They were strategies applied at the feature
extraction and interpretation stages. Those strategies involved the extraction of
positional information of the individual letters in the array, with particular
salience given to initial and final positions. English Ss were applying a kind of
orthographic syntax that governs the assemblage of letters into words. Since the
source of the differences between English and Spanish Ss seems to be that English
Ss automatically apply unconscious knowledge of graphotactics when scanning

letter arrays, whereas Spanish Ss do not, we needed to conduct a further analysis of Spanish and English orthographies. In particular, it was necessary to identify an important graphotactic characteristic that differs significantly in the two languages. Then we could test through an experiment whether the isolated graphotactic variable had a psychological reality in terms of word recognition procedures. If the answer was positive, we could then be confident about our previous conclusions.

The regular/irregular orthographies of English and Spanish differ most when referring to vowels. There is already some evidence that English readability is affected differently by vowels and consonants. Gelb (1963) maintains that English is readable without vowels but provides no empirical evidence. Liberman *et al.* (1967) found that medial vowels caused most errors in children reading aloud. This is explained in terms of vowels having a more ambiguous letter–sound correspondence than consonants.

Consequently, we analysed the differences in vowel/consonant density and distribution in the two languages in the most frequent five-letter words in the two languages. We found a much higher density of vowels in Spanish and a very regular distribution; Spanish words tend to follow the CVCV structure, whereas English favours consonantal clusters. In other words, Spanish has a much higher level of information redundancy concerning position and sequence of vowel/consonant distribution. We were then in a position to see if the graphotactics procedures supposedly at work in English Ss in previous experiments were also used by Spanish Ss.

What we needed then was a new experimental technique. We decided to use a lexical decision task because it activates word recognition strategies without requiring any retrieval into awareness of individual letters within a word. Thus, in Experiment V, Ss had to decide whether or not a five-letter array was a word. In other words, in order to be able to answer, Ss had to access their mental lexicon and retrieve the lexical entry into awareness. The attentional analyticity of Experiments I to IV – retrieval into awareness the presence of a letter in an array – contrasts with the attentional wholism of the lexical decision task in Experiment V – retrieval into awareness of the lexical status of a whole array. When Ss had to make a decision whether a five-letter array, with only one spelling mistake, was a word or not, they scanned the array, matched it against their closest orthographic entries in their mental lexicon and then made a decision. This process did not require a conscious sub-lexical analysis.

Taking into account our orthographic analysis concerning vowels and consonants, we hypothesized that Spanish Ss would find it much harder than English Ss to make a lexical decision task where the decision depended on vowels as opposed to consonants. The results from Experiment V clearly corroborated our predictions: Spanish Ss took significantly longer and made more errors when they processed a vowel-misspelled word. As expected, Spanish Ss found the processing of vowels in Spanish words significantly more demanding than English Ss in English words. This result was consistent with the orthographic analysis: the higher vocalic density of Spanish results in the activation of a higher number of orthographic entries in the mental lexicon, and, therefore, it takes longer to make the lexical decision. Once again, the results of the bilingual Ss clearly follow the pattern of the monolingual Ss. The following examples illustrate the misspelled words the subjects saw on the screen:

	Experiment V	*Experiment V*
Target	custar (costar)	thurd (third)

The introduction of the second experimental technique led us to some conclusions which could not have been reached with the first experimental technique. Encouraged by it, we decided to introduce a third one in our research: Ss were presented with a word with either a vowel or a consonant missing. The Ss had to guess the correct word. We argued that this technique reflects better the word recognition procedures that take place in natural reading: Ss are only trying to read a one-letter-missing word, rather than consciously deciding the lexical status of a letter array. The following examples illustrate the misspelled words the subjects saw on the screen:

	Experiment V	*Experiment V*
Target	*nico (unico)	*horn (thorn)

The results were highly consistent with those found in Experiment V. In particular, English Ss were significantly faster and made fewer errors than Spanish Ss when dealing with vowel-missing words. English Ss made significantly more errors than Spanish Ss with consonant-missing words.

These results seem to confirm that the significantly different processing strategies followed by Spanish and English Ss are dependent on the specific graphotactics of each language. Admittedly, we have only looked in detail at the vowel/consonant variable, but, having confirmed that this linguistic factor has psychological consequences in word recognition, we believe that other orthographic characteristics may also play a part in the psychology of reading. We conclude, therefore, that readers of languages that share a common script, such as English and Spanish, develop language-specific word recognition strategies which are dependent on the orthographic characteristics of each language.

We are also confident that we have been able to confirm that bilingual Ss follow the word recognition strategies of monolingual Ss according to language.

Conclusion

Experiments II, III and IV showed that English Ss are significantly faster at detecting the presence of a target letter in an array. This is particularly true for the initial and final positions of the array. We have claimed that this is due to English

Ss having a greater reliance on positional and sequential information of individual letters for word recognition than Spanish Ss.

We based our hypothesis on the spreading activation models. We suggested that the English Ss' greater dependency on letter information has a linguistic origin: the irregular orthography of English and the much higher density of orthographic neighbourhoods. In other words, English has a much lower level of orthographic redundancy than Spanish. Our results from Experiments V and VI support our claim. Spanish Ss had more difficulty in deciding the lexical status of an array, or retrieving the correct lexical entry, when the decision depended on a vowel whereas English Ss had more difficulties with consonants. Our linguistic analysis of the stimuli shows a greater number of orthographic neighbours for Spanish when it affects vowels, and similarly for English when it concerns consonants.

Perhaps the most spectacular results of this research concern bilingual Ss. When the stimuli consisted of real words, they clearly followed the processing strategies of the monolingual Ss according to language. These results not only confirmed the distinctive processing strategies of English and Spanish Ss, but also that bilingual Ss keep the two strategies separate for each language.

Syntax used to be the fashionable area of linguistics. Di Sciullo and Williams (1987) described the mental lexicon as follows: 'the lexicon is like a prison – it contains only the lawless, and the only thing that its inmates have in common is their lawlessness'. But more recently, the lexicon is back in fashion. Steven Pinker (1994) illustrates this point: 'I want to show that the lexicon ... is deserving of respect and appreciation. What seems to a grammarian like an act of brute force incarceration ... is actually an inspiring feat.'

Arguably, during the last decade, there has been renewed interest in word recognition in L1 research but not in L2, particularly in word decoding (Koda 1996). Yet, despite high levels of oral proficiency, bilingual readers tend to suffer from low levels of recognition competence (Segalowitz et al. 1991). We hope that our work contributes to fill this gap. The knowledge about the varying levels of positional and sequential letter information required for word recognition in each language could be applied to facilitate the reading acquisition processes of both L1 and L2. For example, increasing the size of letters in specific positions in a word, controlling the order and frequency of word presentation according to graphotactic difficulty, and maybe showing the existing morphemes in one word in different colours, may be of significant pedagogical value. It can also provide the basis for a psycholinguistic analysis of orthographic errors, or reading difficulties in L2. Given the consistently slower latencies produced by bilingual Ss, a type of orthography which facilitates their word recognition processes may make a significant difference. Further research is required to establish these plausible pedagogical advantages. In the meantime, the work reported in this thesis has implemented some of the necessary groundwork for this future research, and suggested a number of promising routes which future researchers might want to take advantage of.

Further reading

Baron, J. and Strawson, C. (1976) 'Use of orthographic and word-specific knowledge in reading words aloud', *Journal of Experimental Psychology: Human Perception and Performance*, 2, 386–93.

Blum, T.L. and Johnston, N.F. (1993) 'The effect of semantic priming on the detection of letters within words', *Memory and Cognition*, 21(3): 389–96.

Clarke, M. (1980) 'The short-circuit hypothesis of ESL reading or when the language competence interferes with reading performance', *Modern Languages Journal*, 64(2): 203–9.

Coltheart *et al.* (1980) *Deep Dyslexia*, London: Routledge and Kegan Paul.

Cziko, G. (1980) 'Language competence and reading strategies: a comparison of first and second language oral reading errors', *Language Learning*, 30(1): 101–116.

Di Sciullo, A.M. and Williams, E. (1987) *On the Definition of Word*, Cambridge, MA: MIT Press.

Gelb, I.J. (1963) *A Study of Writing* (second edn) Chicago: University of Chicago Press.

Gough, P.B. (1972) 'One second of reading', in J.P. Kavanagh and I.G. Mattingly (eds) *Language by Eye and by Ear*, Cambridge, MA: M.I.T. Press.

Hammond, E.J. and Green, D.W. (1982) 'Detecting targets in letter and non-letter arrays', *Canadian Journal of Psychology*, 36(1): 67–82.

Hanna *et al.* (1966) *Phoneme-Grapheme Correspondences as Cues to Spelling Improvement*, Washington: US Dept of Health, Education and Welfare.

Healy and Drewnowski (1983) 'Investing the boundaries of reading units: letter detection in mispelled words', *Journal of Experimental Psychology*, Human Perception and Performance, 9: 413–26.

Koda, K. (1996) 'L2 word recognition research: a critical review', *The Modern Language Journal* 80: 450–60.

Liberman, A.M. *et al.* (1967) 'Perception of the speech code', *Psychological Review* 74, 431–61.

Mann, V.A. (1986) 'Temporary memory for linguistic and non-linguistic material in relation to the acquisition of Japanese Kana and Karji', in H.S.R. Kao and R. Hoosain (eds) *Linguistics, Psychology and the Chinese Language*, Centre for Asian Studies: University of Hong Kong.

Massaro, D.W. (1975) 'Visual features, preperceptual storage, and processing time in reading', in D.W. Massaro (ed.) *Understanding Language*, New York and London: Academic Press.

Phillips, W.A. (1971) 'Does familiarity affect transfer from an iconic store to a short-term memory?', *Perception and Psychophysics*, 10: 153–7.

Pinker, S. (1994) *The Language Instinct*, Harmondsworth: The Penguin Press.

Preston, M.S. and Lambert, W.E. (1969) 'Interlingual interference in a bilingual version of the Stroop Colour Word Task', *Journal of Verbal Learning and Verbal Behaviour*, 8, 295–301.

Segalowitz, N.S., Poulsen, C. and Komoda, M. (1991) *Lower Level Components of Reading Skill in Higher Level Bilinguals: Implications for Reading Instruction*, AILA Review, 8: 15–30.

Smith, M.C. (1979) 'Contextual facilitation in a letter search task depends on how the prime is processed', *Journal of Experimental Psychology: Human Perception and Performance*, 5: 239–51.

Tzeng, O.J.L. and Hung, L. (1992) 'Psycholinguistic issues in reading Chinese', in H.C. Chen, and O.J.L. Tzeng (eds) *Language Processing in Chinese*, Amsterdam: North Holland.

Venezky, R.L. (1970) *The Structure of English Orthography*, The Hague: Mouton.

Index